Hierarchy and Organisation

Most people take the conditions they work and live in as a given and think that it is normal that societies are stratified and that organisations are hierarchical. Many even think that this is the way it should be—and are neither willing nor able to think that it could be otherwise. This book raises the awareness of hierarchy, its complexity and longevity. It focuses on a single but fundamental problem of social systems such as dyads, groups, organisations, and whole societies: *Why and how does hierarchical social order persist over time?* In order to investigate the question, author Thomas Diefenbach develops a general theory of the persistence of hierarchical social order. This theory interrogates the problem of the persistence of hierarchical social order from very different angles, in multidimensional and interdisciplinary ways. Even more crucially, it traces the very causes of the phenomenon, the reasons and interests behind hierarchy as well as the various mechanisms which keep it going.

This is the first time such a theory has been attempted. With the help of the theory developed in this book, it is possible to interrogate systematically, comprehensively, and in detail how peoples' mindsets and behaviours as well as societal and organisational structures and processes enable the continuation of hierarchy.

Thomas Diefenbach is Professor of Business Ethics and Organisation Studies at Ritsumeikan Asia Pacific University (APU), Japan. His research focuses on sociophilosophical and critical analysis of organisations, individuals within organisations, the morality of human behaviour, and the ethical dimensions of social systems. In his latest monograph *Management and the Dominance of Managers* (2009) he developed a comprehensive and multidimensional model for critically investigating managers' power, interests, and ideology within an organisational context.

Routledge Studies in Management, Organizations, and Society

This series presents innovative work grounded in new realities, addressing issues crucial to an understanding of the contemporary world. This is the world of organised societies, where boundaries between formal and informal, public and private, local and global organizations have been displaced or have vanished, along with other nineteenth century dichotomies and oppositions. Management, apart from becoming a specialized profession for a growing number of people, is an everyday activity for most members of modern societies.

Similarly, at the level of enquiry, culture and technology, and literature and economics, can no longer be conceived as isolated intellectual fields; conventional canons and established mainstreams are contested. **Management, Organization and Society** addresses these contemporary dynamics of transformation in a manner that transcends disciplinary boundaries, with books that will appeal to researchers, student and practitioners alike.

Other titles in this series:

Hierarchy and Organisation

Toward a General Theory of Hierarchical
Social Systems

Thomas Diefenbach

LONDON AND NEW YORK

First published 2013
by Routledge
711 Third Avenue, New York, NY 10017

Simultaneously published in the UK
by Routledge
2 Park Square, Milton Park, Abingdon, Oxfordshire OX14 4RN

*Routledge is an imprint of the Taylor and Francis Group,
an informa business*

First issued in paperback 2015

Library of Congress Cataloging-in-Publication Data

Diefenbach, Thomas, 1965–
    Hierarchy and organisation : toward a general theory of hierarchical
social systems / by Thomas Diefenbach.
        pages cm. — (Routledge studies in management, organizations, and
society ; 24)
    Includes bibliographical references and index.
    1. Organizational sociology.   2. Organizational behavior.
3. Hierarchies.   4. Social structure.   I. Title.
    HM786.D54 2013
    302.3'5—dc23
    2013002594

ISBN 978-0-415-84392-8 (hbk)
ISBN 978-1-138-19506-6 (hbk)
ISBN 978-0-203-75293-7 (ebk)

Typeset in Sabon
By Apex CoVantage, LLC

Contents

Figures

Tables

Preface

Hierarchy has been one of the cornerstones of human society since chronicles began. There was and is stratification in almost all cultures and societies; groups and organisations are organised hierarchically; and even most dyads and personal relationships are based on the idea that some members are superiors and others are subordinates. That something has been around for such a long time could be sufficient reason to take a closer look at it. From an intellectual perspective, the widespread existence and continuation of hierarchical social order represents an intriguing puzzle: although hierarchy, by definition, privileges the few and disadvantages the many, most people do not openly object to it, even contribute *actively* to its continuation (members of the ruling elites and other superiors, of course, but also most common people and subordinates).

The reasons for this seem to be many rather than singular. Therefore, this book interrogates the problem of the emergence and persistence of hierarchical social order from a wide variety of angles, in multidimensional and interdisciplinary ways. It does not just look at (formal) hierarchy in organisations—although hierarchical organisations are perhaps the most obvious and commonly known forms in which hierarchy is realised and practised. Rather, it will examine hierarchical social relationships between superiors and subordinates *in general*—i.e., the way in which unequal social relationships develop into, and persist as, hierarchical social orders at individual and also group levels, as organisations or even (stratified) societies. Thus, this book is an attempt to put forward a general theory regarding the emergence and persistence of hierarchical social order: a 'general theory of hierarchical social systems.' It attempts to drill down to the very causes of the phenomenon, the reasons and interests behind hierarchy, and the various mechanisms that keep hierarchy going.

But intellectual curiosity was only part of the reason for writing this book. It was written more out of disappointment and ill feeling. Hierarchy is in direct opposition to some of the best ideas humanity has produced, for example: democracy, equality, fairness, and justice. Hierarchy directly and ferociously flies in the face of these values. It allocates privileges, prerogatives, resources, and opportunities in ways that are undemocratic, unequal, unfair, and unjust. It divides people into small groups of privileged leaders and members of various power elites on the one hand, and the masses (themselves divided into several strata) on the other. It defines many—too many—social situations as unequal relationships between superiors and subordinates. Probably the worst aspect of hierarchy is not that it empowers the few but rather that it oppresses, exploits, and infantilises the many. Highly intelligent and capable adult human beings are turned into, and treated like, toddlers.

That dyads, groups of people, organisations and institutions, whole societies, and our daily lives are governed to such a great extent on the basis of formal and informal hierarchical principles and mechanisms is neither a natural law nor a functional necessity. Why do we think that our social relationships should be organised and function hierarchically? That this is 'natural' or 'normal'? Is it just that we believe that this is 'the way things are'? And why do many think that we need leaders and followers, that people need leadership and guidance, that there 'should be'—even '*must* be'—superiors and subordinates? Although we live in 'modern times,' with information, knowledge, ideas, and opportunities available on a scale never seen before, many societal and organisational structures and processes have remained in the Middle Ages.

People deserve better. This book is about developing a general theory to help to explain and to *critically* analyse the persistence of hierarchical social order. If, as a society, we understand better why and how hierarchy has been around for so long, some people may begin to think about how to overcome it—and perhaps they will find a way. In this sense, this book is for everyone who does not want to accept our social realities as a given.

This book had been developed over quite a few years. During that time, some parts were presented at international academic conferences and afterwards published in academic journals. Specifically:

- Sections 2.1 ('An Extremely Brief History of no Change') and 2.2.2 ('The System of Hierarchy') were part of the introductory chapter of a special volume for the journal *Research in the Sociology of Organizations* on 'Reinventing bureaucracy and hierarchy: from the bureau to network organisations' (Diefenbach and By 2012).
- Section 4.4 ('Subordinates' Boundary Crossings') was published as a chapter in the same special volume under the title 'Boundary crossing—subordinates' challenges to organisational hierarchy' (Diefenbach and Sillince 2012).
- Section 4.5 ('Superiors' Boundary Crossings') formed the main part of a working paper titled 'When does superiors' deviance threaten organisational hierarchy?' and published within the working paper series of the German University in Cairo (Diefenbach 2011).
- Parts of Sections 3.4.1 ('Routine Behaviour and Boundary Crossing') and 4.3 ('Boundary Crossings and Their Operationalisation') were

used in the special volume chapter (Diefenbach and Sillince 2012) and the working paper (Diefenbach 2011) mentioned above.

- Section 4.6 ('Hierarchy in Different Types of Organisations') was published in *Organization Studies* under the title 'Formal and informal hierarchy in different types of organisations' (Diefenbach and Sillince 2011).

As one can imagine, such a large project has required time, effort, and dedication. But, first and foremost, it needs intellectual spark and imagination. Core ideas of this book (concerning how hierarchical relationships are based on people's mindsets and boundary crossings) were developed in conversations and collaboration with my colleague and friend, Professor John A.A. Sillince. Moreover, it was *his* intellectual rigour and knowledge that facilitated the formation of the ideas and, as a more or less direct consequence, enabled the book to come into being. John is not only one of the world's leading academics in the area of organisation studies (and particularly in the field of discourse analysis) but also a true scholar—something rarely found nowadays, especially not in business schools. With his words and deeds he is a great inspiration for many, and if we had more people like him this book would not be necessary.

Beside John's intellectual stimuli, I am grateful for the tremendous job Hazel Harris did as copy-editor. Special thanks also go to Laura Stearns, publisher, and Lauren Verity, editorial assistant (both Routledge / Taylor & Francis Group), who were very helpful throughout the publishing process.

I would also like to thank my colleagues at the Research Office of Ritsumeikan Asia Pacific University (APU) for all their help and support (with regard to all my research projects, not just this book) and for a smaller APU fund that helped with completing parts of the editorial work for this book.

Finally, I would like to acknowledge the huge impact of all the hierarchical organisations (and the people working there) with which I have worked over the past three decades. If I hadn't experienced at first hand what hierarchy can do to people (including myself), this book would not have been written.

Thomas Diefenbach
Beppu, Japan, January 2013

1 Introduction

> *'In our unhappy world it is impossible for men living in society not to be divided into two classes, the one the rich who command, the other the poor who serve; and these two classes are subdivided into a thousand, and these thousand still have different gradations.'*
>
> Voltaire, 1750 (cited in Kramnick 1995, p. 418)

There is an (almost) eternal beast that has reigned over humanity for the best part of its history. It is amongst us—between individuals and in groups, organisations, and whole societies. Kingdoms have been built on it, religions would have not come into existence and reached global dominance without this 'heavenly power,' and societies allegedly would descend into chaos without it. Modern organisations—the economic, political, social, and cultural institutions that govern our lives—exist in harmonious symbiosis with this beast. Its name is 'hierarchy'. It holds people ransom, makes or breaks them at will, and savages everyone who dares to look into its eyes and challenge it.

In fairytales, beasts seem to be invincible—until a fearless hero or heroine comes along and defeats them ('and then they lived happily ever after . . . '). Unfortunately, we don't live in a fairytale world. Hierarchical order survives (almost) all challenges and has persisted through time. And hierarchy is still alive, more than ever before.[1]

This claim that hierarchy is so persistent might be seen as an exaggeration. Apparently, we live in an ever-changing world. In change-management seminars all over the world, presenters regularly (try to) impress their audiences with the adage that change is the only thing that does not change in today's challenging world. Organisations are constantly turned upside down by restructuring, and change-management initiatives follow each other in ever faster cycles of latest management fads and fashions (Kieser 1997; Abrahamson 1996) (e.g., business process re-engineering, knowledge organisation, lean management, networks, new public management, total quality management, and virtual organisations). New organisational forms have emerged and have widened the spectrum, from very hierarchical and bureaucratic forms to hybrid and postmodern forms of organisations (Clegg et al. 2006; Courpasson and Dany 2003). Even whole societies have found themselves in a state of permanent makeover; globalisation and technological innovations have changed them way beyond what humans have ever imagined.

However, these epochal developments and the ubiquity of 'change for change's sake' may draw attention away from the fact that there are many things that remain stable and hardly change—if ever. For example, even in more open and dynamic societies with a high degree of social (upward) mobility, stratification, class-based opportunities and status, and social inequalities often remain fundamental features. Despite modern ideas, new trends and technologies, societal institutions and daily life continue to function according to fairly old-fashioned hierarchical rationales.

This becomes even more obvious when one looks at organisations. Despite the constant introduction of new business concepts and change rhetoric, key principles and mechanisms of management and organisations do *not* change; the hierarchical order of social relationships, the dominance of superiors and obedience of subordinates, the privileges and prerogatives of the former and the tight control of the latter—whatever the actual change initiative (seemingly) advocates (Diefenbach 2009a; Courpasson and Clegg 2006; Rowlinson et al. 2006). According to Laurent (1978, p. 225),

> Ample historical and empirical evidence suggests that—even though they may declare that they do not like it or do not value it—people do in fact obey authority to an incredible extent as soon as they become part of an organizational hierarchy.

On the basis of his comprehensive and detailed empirical research into failed attempts to design and maintain nonhierarchical types of organisations, in 1915 Michels formulated his famous and widely known 'iron law of oligarchy' (1966, p. 365): 'Who says organization, says oligarchy.' Countless historical examples support the assertion that even far-reaching attempts to change social order sooner or later merely produce yet another ruling elite and subservient followers, along with inequality and injustice, and exploitation and oppression.

Since hierarchy is so persistent, apologists for unequal societies and orthodox organisations might have a point when they claim that hierarchy is a general tendency when groups of humans organise themselves. For example, Zaleznik (1989, p. 150) stated that:

> In human groups hierarchy in the distribution of power is a general tendency that has been verified in many observations and experiments. In study after study of group formations in work and 'natural' groups, leaders and followers align themselves into a remarkably predictable relationship with few at the top and many at the bottom of the power pyramid.

Even critical researchers have made the same observation, and they have come to similar conclusions concerning rules and patterns of vertical social relationships (Courpasson and Clegg 2006, p. 327; Clegg et al. 2006, p. 330; Scott 1990, p. 61). According to social dominance theory (Sidanius et al. 2004; Sidanius and Pratto 1999), it seems that (almost) all human societies are structured as group-based hierarchies in which a few dominant groups 'possess a disproportionately large share of positive social value such as political authority, power, wealth, and social status, whereas the subordinate groups possess a disproportionately larger share of negative social values including low power, low social status, and poverty' (O'Brien and Crandall 2005, p. 1, paraphrasing Sidanius and Pratto 1999, p. 31). Almost all societies and other social systems represent a stratified cosmos of higher and lower social positions. Stratification and hierarchy—persistent patterns of ruling elites and disadvantaged groups—seem to be our common cultural heritage (Daloz 2007, p. 50; Mills 1956, pp. 147–8).

Thus, one way of reconstructing human history is to see it as a great (or not so great) procession and succession of power elites in which rulers and privileged minorities come and go but the institutions and structures remain in place. To put it differently: whereas the relationships among the various power elites, groups of superiors, and ruling classes are relatively dynamic, the societal structures and institutions in stratified societies are relatively static. Although societies and organisations change in many respects, most of the changes either happen on the surface or merely repeat, in a slightly different design, longstanding key social principles and mechanisms; we have change but no change.

The hierarchical system has always been there; it provides the 'one great scaffolding' that has existed throughout time. The various generations and classes are filtered through this scaffolding; they occupy, maintain, and shape little parts of the system for a while for the pursuit of their own interests until they are succeeded by the next group or class. People come and go, but the system remains. All we are witnessing is the eternal return of the always same (Nietzsche 1990).[2] Hierarchy persists throughout the centuries and throughout the endless comings and goings of social orders. It is one of the '(almost) eternal beasts' that has stalked humanity since chronicles began.

Therefore, the question is not so much which particular group rules a certain society. Ruling elites come and go, and their faceless members are fairly exchangeable without too much ado. The more intriguing thing is that there exists in almost every society a deeply embedded notion that it is 'normal,' 'good,' and desirable to have leaders and elites, superiors and subordinates, and hierarchical social relationships.

Why could, or even should, we see this as a problem? Hierarchy definitely has advantages. It provides and guarantees a certain kind of order and stability, along with protection and conservation (Prentice 2005; Zaleznik 1989). It offers opportunities for career and personal development as well as monetary and nonmonetary advantages, privileges, and prerogatives—especially for those who are higher up the social ladder. But even for people lower down the pecking order it at least provides orientation, a feeling of security, and perhaps some hope for a better future or at least justifications for suffering. It is claimed that hierarchy represents (one of) the best and most efficient solutions for the functional requirements of smaller and larger social systems (e.g., groups, organisations, and whole societies) as well as their management (Donaldson 2003; Jaques 1990). And, this state of equilibrium not only applies to functional structures and processes (Gersick 1991; Gouldner 1960) but also to the social relationships within the hierarchical system. There is a balance of power, reciprocity, and common and mutual interests between superiors and subordinates, leaders and followers (Mast et al. 2010, p. 461; Van Vugt 2006). Leaders provide the guidance their followers (allegedly) need, and followers execute what their leaders want to be realised.

However, hierarchy also has disadvantages—and they far outweigh the actual and alleged advantages. Hierarchy does not simply mean the various functions within a society, the official structures of an organisation, or the formal, task-oriented relationship between superiors and subordinates. It *primarily* means the creation and maintenance of unequal social relationships between people at dyadic, group, organisational, and societal levels. Hierarchy *systematically* enables and guarantees unequal distribution of and access to institutions and resources, power differentials and opportunities, privileges and prerogatives, and tasks and duties (Daloz 2007; Sidanius et al. 2004; Gould 2002; Sidanius and Pratto 1999; Gouldner 1960; Mills 1956). It represents institutionalised differences in power, resources and opportunities; some people are privileged and others are discriminated against. *Hierarchy is antidemocratic, unfair, and unjust.* It means advantages and enrichment for the few, and disadvantages and limitations for the many; *every* form of hierarchy, whether dictatorial or democratic, has such principles of social inequality, oppression, and exploitation incorporated into its blueprint. Hierarchy benefits superiors and disadvantages subordinates *systematically and with necessity* (Jermier 1998; Williams and Swartz 1998, p. 306; Gouldner 1960, p. 174). As a consequence, people are not only treated differently but also have different life chances, even life expectancies. Because of hierarchy, people have different pasts, presents, and futures.

Whether people reflect consciously on the advantages and disadvantages of hierarchy or not, most regard hierarchy as the natural and normal state of affairs. This is how they have been socialised in one institution after another ('from the cradle to the grave'), this is how the organisations they work for are designed and function, and this is how they organise and maintain even their private lives and social relationships; it is 'the way things are.' Many even think that this is the way things *should* be and are neither able nor willing (anymore) to think that things could be, even *should* be, otherwise (Fairtlough 2005, p. 9). Most people do not realise how hierarchical their personal lives and workplaces actually are: how much they have internalised the way of thinking along the lines of superiority and inferiority, how much they reconstruct hierarchical relationships on a daily basis that otherwise would not exist, and how much they live to the tune of the beast. They do not realise how much they contribute to the very conditions they silently criticise every day. One of the strongest ideologies imaginable is the steady force of daily routine shaping the unconscious functioning of the individual.

We take too many things for granted without really questioning them—but we can do better; according to Crozier (1964, p. 54):

> Social scientists are too often content to describe vicious circles, neat reinforcing feedbacks, without trying to go deeper. Description is indispensable, but it is not enough. Even if one can present only venturesome hypotheses, one should try to understand the origin and the possibilities of survival of these patterns of relationships whose unfavorable consequences have appeared, in the short run, to reinforce stability.

As people concerned with social affairs, and especially as academics and researchers, we must not take anything for granted. On the contrary, we must investigate *every* part of social reality as thoroughly as possible until we find the most fundamental underlying principles, mechanisms, causes, reasons, and consequences. And we must question and criticise *everything and everyone* (including ourselves) in order to provide a sound basis for analysing existing conditions as well as for developing and realising alternatives that are hopefully better.

Hence, this book will, at least, contribute to raising awareness of hierarchy and its complexity and longevity. It will focus on a single, but quite fundamental, problem of social systems such as dyads, groups, organisations, and whole societies: *why and how does hierarchical social order emerge and persist over time?*

In order to investigate this question, a 'general theory of hierarchical social systems' (or 'general theory of the emergence and persistence of hierarchical social order') will be developed. With the help of this theory, this book will reveal and discuss the main principles and mechanisms behind why and how hierarchy works and persists on a daily basis (between individuals and groups of people, and within organisations and at the societal level)—whatever the specific historical or cultural context.[3]

The book will systematically and comprehensively interrogate how exactly people's mindsets and behaviours, as well as institutions, structures, and processes, enable the continuation of hierarchy. It will analyse how superiors and subordinates reason and act within hierarchical settings, and how their actions, interests, identities, emotions, and moral characters shape their social relationships and (in most instances) contribute to a further strengthening of hierarchical social order. It will also show how hierarchical social relationships become abstract organisational order, and how hierarchy is institutionalised and, via several mechanisms of systemisation, turns into the long-lasting phenomenon—or beast—as we know it. The idea, or hope, is that this book will enable a better understanding of exactly why and how hierarchy works, why it hardly changes, and what specific factors could lead to changing it.

The problem of the emergence and persistence of hierarchical social order will be tackled largely in terms of how it affects people; with regard to social phenomena, people are seen as the decisive element. The main argument is that hierarchy is in people's heads (or in their hearts and minds) and that they therefore behave in ways that conform to hierarchical notions—even when they deviate from social expectations of dominance and obedience.

In order to analyse and explain people's reasoning and why they act within, and for, hierarchical social order, the concept of 'mindset' will be developed. Mindset comprises people's interests, identities, emotions, and moral characters. It is proposed that these four factors (or realms) together shape people's behaviour, or social actions, and hence contribute significantly to the emergence and continuation of social order, in this case hierarchical social order. The theory developed here suggests that the realisation and continuation of hierarchy depend mainly on how the people involved (i.e., superiors and subordinates, members of power elites, and the masses) perceive and interpret the social situation they are in, how they act and interact, and how this feeds back into the principles, institutions, and mechanisms of the hierarchical social system.

The idea of hierarchy is deeply ingrained in people's perceptions of their social environment, how they make sense of that environment, how they come to conclusions about what it means to function well within hierarchical structures and processes, and how they behave and act. But most people's ability—and willingness–to function well is not only dependent on lifelong socialisation, if not conditioning; it is also an outcome of their particular interest in supporting and maintaining the hierarchical system, in actively contributing to the very social system that to a great extent makes them who they are. Superiors *and* subordinates have vested interests in developing and stabilising their unequal relationship because it allows them to remain in the system, to enjoy the advantages the system offers, and to pursue their interests within the boundaries the hierarchical system provides. In so doing, *both* contribute routinely and indirectly, but also quite consciously and actively, to the functioning and continuation of the hierarchical social order. Superiors *and* subordinates keep the system of hierarchical social order going.

The argument put forward so far is based on, and starts with, the idea of *methodological individualism* (i.e., that social phenomena are the result of the behaviour of individual actors and that they can be explained accordingly). However, methodological individualism is used here only in its weak version— i.e., it is assumed that individual actors are only *one* aspect of the whole process and that their actions are only *one*, although a crucial, part of the explanation.

In this sense, *abstract organisational order* and *institutions* will also be part of the theory developed here, and it will be argued that such abstract entities play an important part in (further) stabilising and strengthening the hierarchical social system. Institutions not only provide principles and standards, norms and values, and structures and processes—they also provide causes and influence. For example, there is a whole range of actual advantages for those who behave and function smoothly within the boundaries of the hierarchical, unjust, and oppressive social system. The advantages and disadvantages, opportunities and threats a hierarchical system provides shape, to a considerable extent, people's mindsets and behaviours (i.e., their interests, identities, emotions, moral values, and actions).

What is crucial, though, is to identify the exact relationship and dynamic processes that exist between hierarchical social systems/institutions on the one hand and individuals on the other. In order to relate people and institutions, another concept will be introduced: *systemisation,* which comprises six mechanisms (socialisation, adaptation, synchronisation, institutionalisation, transformation, and navigation). Systemisation, along with its mechanisms, is a multidimensional and interactive process that links hierarchical institutions and individuals; it ensures that people function within any kind of hierarchical system and, in doing so, guarantees the persistence and continuation of hierarchical social order (Theorem 33, Section 3.7). With the model of systemisation, it is possible to explain the dynamic and dialectical relationships between individual actors and institutions.

Probably the main characteristic of the theory proposed here is that it links individual and institutional elements *within a single theoretical framework;* the theory stretches from the mindsets and social actions of individual actors via the dynamic relationships between different actors (superiors and subordinates) to the emergence of abstract organisational order and of organisational and societal institutions that then in turn influence individual actors.[4] To put it more generally, individual, interpersonal (micro), organisational (meso), and societal (macro) levels are linked by *one* theory.

On this basis, the theory put forward here attempts to explain why hierarchical social order functions and why it is so persistent over time. For this:

1) The theory starts with the core structure of all hierarchical social relationships: the *direct and unequal relationship between individual actors.* People are superior or subordinate depending on situation, circumstances and other relevant factors.

2) In the tradition of methodological individualism, the theory then focuses on *people's mindsets* (operationalised as interests, emotions, identities, and moral character) and *social actions* in order to explain how superiors and subordinates reason and act as individuals within a hierarchical context.

3) It then explains how superiors' and subordinates' mindsets and social actions develop into *routine behaviour* and *boundary crossing.* Unfolding as multiple dynamic processes, both lead to the institutionalisation of the direct superior–subordinate relationship as an *abstract organisational order.*

4) The theory then describes how, over time, differentiated *institutions* (e.g., sociocultural,, material/economic, legal, political, technological, and environmental) emerge out of these multiple dynamic processes and start to exist on their own. They favour or put at a disadvantage certain individuals or groups of people according to their social status and position.

5) It then shows how individual actors and institutions (or hierarchical social systems) are linked dynamically via several mechanisms of *systemisation* (socialisation, adaptation, synchronisation, institutionalisation, transformation, and navigation). These mechanisms happen within the logic of hierarchical social order and, thus, reiterate and strengthen it.

6) However, the theory also assumes that there is always *individual freedom* and that people use the space in hierarchical systems to navigate their way through institutions and social relationships. Since this also entails *individual responsibility,* moral development and ethics are an integral part of social reality as well as of any reasoning about it.

Altogether, the general theory describes and analyses hierarchy—*any* hierarchical social system—as a comprehensive and consistent, multidimensional and differentiated 'social cosmos' of various elements (superiors and subordinates, social roles and positions, mindsets and social actions, abstract organisational order, institutions and resources) interacting with each other via various mechanisms of systemisation (socialisation, adaptation, synchronisation, institutionalisation, transformation, and navigation). Persistent hierarchical social order is a complex framework of dominance and obedience, tangible privileges and prerogatives, and unequal and unjust allocation of resources, rights, and opportunities.

As one can imagine, the theory developed here has not emerged out of the blue. On the contrary, it makes use of and draws insights from a whole range of social theories,[5] such as:

- anthropology and cultural studies—for example, Scott's 1990 socioanthropological concept of 'public and hidden transcripts,' for analysing boundary crossing;

- psychology—for example, Sidanius and colleagues' sociopsychological 'social dominance theory', for explaining and analysing group-based social hierarchies (Sidanius et al. 2004; Sidanius and Pratto 1999);

- sociology—for example, Mousnier's 1973 sociological approach, for analysing 'social hierarchies' and stratification, and Granovetter's 1985 (sociological) institutionalism, for understanding institutions as conditions and outcomes of social phenomena;

- economics/political economy—for example, Beetham's 1991 'legitimation of power' theory and Braverman's 1974 'labour process theory', in order to reveal the ideological foundations of the capitalistic system;

- management and organisation studies—for example, Alvesson and Willmott's (1992a, 1992b) 'critical management studies', for describing and analysing management and orthodox organisations in critical terms;

- ethics—for example, Kohlberg's 1973 'stages of moral development,' in order to assess people's morality;

- critical theory—for example, Brookfield's 2005 comprehensive description of 'critical theory' and development of a critical perspective; and

- various interdisciplinary or multidisciplinary concepts such as power (Clegg et al. 2006; Courpasson 2000; Weber 1980; Lukes 1974); (self-)-interest (Force 2006; Hindess 1986); ideology (Abercrombie et al. 1980); social identity (Ashforth and Mael 1989; Tajfel and Turner 1979); and emotions (Lazarus 1991; Hochschild 1983; Kemper 1978a).

Despite their different perspectives, the aforementioned approaches have in common that they interrogate the status quo or certain aspects of social reality, as well as ideologies about it, more or less *critically* (Alvesson and Willmott 1992a, p. 13). This is perhaps the main aim of the theory developed here; it is about explicitly describing and explaining hierarchy as a comprehensive and multidimensional system of power and control; identifying and critically discussing the specific interests and identities, statuses and responsibilities, and privileges and prerogatives of certain individuals and groups of people within such a system (e.g., superiors and subordinates, and power elites and the masses); demonstrating that dyadic relationships, groups, organisations, and whole societies are anything but value-free, neutral, and functional endeavours, and revealing and criticising the (dominant) ideologies around hierarchical or otherwise oppressive regimes.

The book comprises six chapters. After this introductory chapter, Chapter 2 will interrogate why hierarchy has been around for so long and why people are relatively reluctant to change it. A brief historical account will be followed by some discussions of differing views concerning the origins of hierarchy and its moral justifications, the structures and processes of hierarchy, and the people who form hierarchical social relationships.

The aforementioned general theory of hierarchical social systems will be developed in Chapter 3. At its core it comprises a basic (and then differentiated) model that describes how actual differences between superiors and subordinates (in terms of positions, power and control, social actions, interests, social identities, emotions, and moral character) create systematic patterns of hierarchical ordering. The theory will then be developed further in order to address the dynamic aspects and main mechanisms of systemisation that enable the continuation of hierarchical social order. It will then be explained why ethics is a necessary part of any social theory. Finally, the theory will be compared with two other, widely known, theories that also deal with the relationship between individuals and systems: Giddens's structuration theory and Sidanius and colleagues' social dominance theory).

In Chapter 4, the general theory will be used to analyse some key problems concerning the persistence of hierarchy: 1) how the routine behaviours of superiors and subordinates work together towards the persistence of hierarchy, 2) how most deviance and boundary crossing by superiors and subordinates contributes to the further stabilisation and continuation of the hierarchical social order, and 3) how hierarchy persists in various types of organisations as an interactive combination of formal and informal hierarchy. The analysis will also show which specific behaviours and boundary crossings of superiors and subordinates might be system-threatening (i.e., might challenge the very foundations of any hierarchical system in such a way as to potentially lead to system change).

The theory will then be applied in Chapter 5. One of the most famous examples of deviant behaviour in the history of humanity will be used in order to investigate how boundary crossing challenged a stratified social system in various ways and at all levels. It will be shown how, in this example, boundary crossings in the areas of social action, interests, emotions, identity, and moral character led to mutually reinforcing processes and the escalation of conflict, with quite dramatic outcomes.

Finally, Chapter 6 will reflect on why things almost always don't change, in particular why even the best and most well-intended attempts to change the hierarchical social order so often do not really change things or even produce worse results than before. Based on the theory developed here, the chapter will provide explanations for the hierarchisation even of non-hierarchical systems and how people (and their moral development) and institutions relate to each other in such settings. This final chapter also indicates new directions for analysis and criticism of hierarchical social systems as well as ideas for the development of true alternatives.

2   The Longevity of Hierarchy

'Such was, or may well have been, the origin of society and law, which bound new fetters on the poor, and gave new powers to the rich; which irretrievably destroyed natural liberty, eternally fixed the law of property and inequality, converted clever usurpation into unalterable right, and, for the advantage of a few ambitious individuals, subjected all mankind to perpetual labor, slavery and wretchedness.'

J.-J. Rousseau, *Discourse on the Origin of Inequality*, 1755
(cited in Kramnick 1995, p. 428)

2.1   AN EXTREMELY BRIEF HISTORY OF NO CHANGE

As indicated in the Introduction, the prevailing understanding within human sciences is that most societies and other complex social systems, such as organisations, are structured as group-based social hierarchies—and that these structures are fairly persistent (Sidanius et al. 2004; Sidanius and Pratto 1999; Scott 1990; Zaleznik 1989; Mousnier 1973; Dahrendorf 1971; Davis and Moore 1971; Laumann et al. 1971; Moore 1971; Mosca 1971; Wrong 1971; Mills 1956).[1] One way or the other, social systems are stratified and based on hierarchical social relationships of superiors and subordinates. But has this *always* been the case—i.e., is this really 'typical' for humans and human society?

Some anthropologists stress that, throughout the Paleolithic Era (i.e., from about 2,500,000 BCE to 12,000 BCE), there were hunter-gatherer groups (so-called 'band societies') that were probably fairly egalitarian (Harman 2008). However, the position taken by the majority of people is that 'society' actually only began when humans became 'civilised,' and that 'civilisation' emerged sometime between 25,000 BCE and 12,000 BCE. During this period humans settled down, started to use advanced food-growing and food-storage techniques, and developed more complex social structures (N.N. 2010a).

Moreover, it is the dominant understanding, if not to say ideology, of 'civilisation' that it defines a sedentary society largely in terms of unequally distributed private property and ownership, division of labour mainly in vertical terms, and class structure. The idea of social differentiation is closely linked to social stratification. According to such an understanding, writers (and rewriters) of history as well as its leading actors and their followers converge to one overarching historical concept of 'civilisation' as a stratified, class-based society based on private property. Even more cynically, *only* stratified class-based societies with private property are 'civilised,' which means that all others are *not*—i.e., they are 'barbaric.' Thus, by mere definition, human society is reduced to 'civilisation,' 'civilisation' is described very narrowly as 'stratified societies' (where the many are ruled by the few based on private property), and all possible alternatives are either excluded from the historical accounts or defined as 'uncivilised.'

In the face of such an understanding of civilisation, it is quite logical that ancient history is largely reconstructed as individuals' struggles to achieve social dominance, and that archaic high cultures are largely portrayed as hierarchical societies, with the focus predominantly on the leaders, their lives, and their (assumed) concerns. As a consequence, historical accounts provide only very one-sided pictures of people's personalities, morality, words, and deeds; ancient rulers, despots, and the rich usually are portrayed in quite enhancing and flattering terms, and followers and common people are portrayed in more reductive rather than enhancing, and quite selective terms. The bottom line is that superiors are superiors because they are superior and subordinates are subordinates because they are inferior. These cartoon-like portraits of people who really existed, together with the surviving architecture, artefacts, and documents, enable us to conclude that those ancient societies were organised in a fairly hierarchical manner (Mousnier 1973, p. 9). In ancient societies, key social relationships were reduced to functional relations between rulers and ruled, masters and slaves, and superiors and subordinates. Such relationships were primarily based on power and control, and on the egocentric will of the former groups with little regard to the interests and well-being of the latter (Starbuck 2003, pp. 146–150; Kittrie 1995, p. 60).

The situation did not get much better in medieval societies, and in many respects it got worse. For example, Christian societies were highly stratified; they constitute an almost perfect example of how exploitation and ideological justification can go happily hand in hand. The Catholic Church especially had accumulated unprecedented political and administrative power and, as a result, unimaginable wealth and large regular incomes for its mostly unscrupulous members. It went to great lengths to make sure that both itself and society as a whole were organised into one comprehensive and consistent hierarchical order (Mousnier 1973, p. 103)—which allegedly was God's will. Even the angels in heaven were arranged hierarchically and 'in perfect harmony' with the eternal order (see Parker 2009). And, if people still had doubts that the holy trinity of hierarchy, control and (self-)punishment did not represent the best of all possible worlds, the Inquisition would 'help' them to find the right way. It, too, embodied a 'perfect', hierarchically organised system of surveillance and control, investigations and convictions, punishment and torture (Given 1997).

Autocratic and oppressive regimes based on and protected by an elaborate system of religious beliefs did not only emerge in the Western world; they have prospered in almost every culture, for example, Africa (Christianity, Islam, traditional African religions), the Americas (Christianity, Native American religions), Asia (Buddhism, Confucianism, Hinduism), and the Middle East (Islam, Judaism). Some religions may be more humane and some may be more horrific than Christian belief and the Christian church, but *all* explain and justify the universe, the world, the state, social relationships, and human affairs in hierarchical terms. Any theocratic society is hierarchical and oppressive by definition. Religion thus is not only 'opium for the people' (as expressed by Karl Marx) but also constitutes concrete spiritual and physical chains for the vast majority of people.

But then came the Age of Enlightenment and capitalism—and with them perhaps some optimism that scientific and technological progress would transform into social progress. Yet, any hopes that modernity would change at least some of the fundamental principles and most appalling features of stratified societies diminished very quickly, even in the early days of capitalism. What entered the historical scene was simply a new version of what one can term 'stratification via differentiation'; in the words of Abercrombie et al. (1980, p. 106):

> The bourgeoisie became gentrified, aping the lifestyles and social mannerisms of the old landed aristocracy, and buying themselves and their heirs into the ranks of the landed interest, so that the dominant class remained [. . .] the 'sociological' heirs of the pre-industrial aristocracy.

The capitalist society simply replaced old ruling elites with new ones, threw the masses into the slaughterhouses, and turned whole societies upside down—while leaving the logic of superiority and subordination, of oppression and exploitation, intact. The ends remained; all that had changed was the means. And the means became even more numerous, and increasingly comprehensive, efficient, and horrific. Capitalism offered a whole new range of methods for ruling, exploiting, and controlling the masses. In 1911, one of the most famous and infamous proponents of the industrial system of hierarchical order, oppression, and exploitation, F.W. Taylor, provided the blueprint for what would become the prevailing ideology of organisation through to the 21st century (1967, p. 26):

> Those in the management whose duty it is to develop this science [scientific management] should also guide and help the workman in working under it, and should assume a much larger share of the responsibility for results than under usual conditions is assumed by the management. [. . .] And each man should daily be taught by and receive the most friendly help

from those who are over him, instead of being, at the one extreme, driven
or coerced by his bosses, and at the other left to his own unaided devices.
This close, intimate, personal cooperation between the management and
the men is of the essence of modern scientific or task management.

Scientific management became the new *Pater noster* for rulers and ruled
alike. The late 19th and the whole of the 20th centuries saw not only the
spreading of bureaucratic/orthodox organisations all over the world (Clegg
2012; McKinlay 2012) but also the worldwide emergence of a new profession, if not class: the *managers* (Diefenbach 2009a; Burnham 1941).
Management is largely understood as line management; the managerial
organisation is designed along lines of 'command-and-control,' dominance
and obedience. Interpreted in such a way, management is now at the core of
almost every private- and public-sector organisation, whether in market or
command economies, or Western or Asian societies. Globalisation and new
communication technologies have only hastened this process of a manageri-
alisation (i.e., further hierarchisation) of already stratified societies.

And hierarchical structures and processes are more alive than ever. Most
modern, even most postmodern, organisations are very hierarchical—
though perhaps in more indirect, informal, and sublime ways in addition
to the more direct and relatively crude mechanisms of formal hierarchy.
Postmodern organisations come with vertical *and* horizontal power—and
control mechanisms more comprehensive and sophisticated than ever before
(Byrkjeflot and du Gay 2012; Lundholm et al. 2012; Brown et al. 2010;
Parker 2009; Clegg et al. 2006; Courpasson and Clegg 2006; Akella 2003;
Courpasson 2000). Despite the rhetoric of 'teamwork,' 'networks,' 'empowerment,' and even 'intrapreneurship,' the very logic of hierarchical order and
control continues to rule our organisations. These organisations continue
to function on the basis of an uneasy relationship between several levels of
managers and employees, and between superiors and subordinates.

It is not much different at the level of society. True, most contemporary societies are no longer divided into clearly identifiable classes sharply
demarcated from each other (e.g., as during the era of feudalism or early
capitalism, or in societies based on any sort of religiously defined differences). The societies of economically developed and democratic countries,
particularly, have become more like patchworks—more multifaceted and
multidimensional.[2] They offer a whole range of values, some of which go
against the traditional understanding of hierarchy as a formal and static system. For example, individualism, nonconformism, and even consumerism
seemingly lead individuals to find their own ways within—but also across
and against—existing hierarchical structures and processes. Various new
social groups (such as entrepreneurs), new lifestyles (such as 'Generation
X'), new patterns of behaviour (such as social networks), and new virtual
realities (such as the internet) can be seen as social phenomena that negate
the ideas and mechanisms of social stratification and class society.

They do, indeed—at least in some respects and to a certain extent. But there are also reasons to be cautious about attributing too much to these novelties. One is that these trends have not replaced older structures and processes of stratification and social dominance; they have *added* to them. Social and especially socioeconomic differences still put people into hierarchical relationships with each other. In addition, even the new structures and processes related to individualism and individualisation are not necessarily antihierarchical or nonhierarchial. Even amongst the individualists who embrace these new trends, one can easily identify patterns of behaviour that set people apart vertically. Most entrepreneurs are only innovative concerning technologies, products, or services; in contrast, their business models and the organisations they set up are fairly orthodox. Most members of 'Generation X' are highly competitive, constantly rank people and things, and are very status-oriented. Within social networks, one can find 'opinion leaders' and other active members who contribute considerably to the emergence of informal hierarchies. And virtual worlds on the internet are becoming more and more similar to the 'real world,' i.e., stratified and compartmentalised. Hence, although these structures and mechanisms are perhaps more differentiated and informal compared to the more traditional ones of formal hierarchies, modern and developed societies and social groups are still fairly stratified, unequal, and hierarchically organised.

Moreover, the new social phenomena represent telling evidence that hierarchical social structuring is increasingly seen in *positive* terms, as less oppressive. For example, hierarchical patterns are widely appreciated and admired since they seemingly stand for a 'merit-based' system—i.e., a 'performance-oriented' assessment and remuneration of people's efforts and a 'fair' handling of individual behaviour. Progressing upwards through the societal classes or organisational layers (and not changing the system)— evidenced by ideas such as 'aspiring to a middle-class lifestyle,' 'upward mobility,' and 'making a career'—has become a social ideal in many societies and countries, developed and developing alike.

Even in the face of several postmodern megatrends, hierarchy is still the leading principle. Even in the most 'modern,' technologically and economically advanced, dynamic, and patchwork-like societies, social differences and inequalities still translate into hierarchical patterns and differences. In some ways, hierarchy is now even *more* appreciated than ever before and people are keener to function and strive within hierarchical social relationships. Thinking (and acting) in hierarchical terms remains people's primary rationale in most social contexts, whether societal institutions, organisations, peer groups, or even their private relationships. In most societies, societal stratification, hierarchical structures, and mechanisms continue to dominate social reality. The social systems have just become more differentiated and colourful—wolves in sheep's clothing.

Thus, when one looks at human history, one indeed can conclude that hierarchy has been a more or less welcomed companion of humans from the very beginning. In almost every culture and epoch, the notions of stratification and hierarchical social relationships, of ruling elites and followers, and of superiors and subordinates can be identified. In archaic cultures the ruling elites were made up of druids, priests, prophets, royals, rich citizens, and the military; in medieval societies there were royals, clergy, knights, aristocrats, and merchants; in capitalism some royals and aristocrats remained, but in competition with as well as mingling with capitalists, the bourgeoisie, and the military; and in postmodern societies we have bureaucrats, technocrats, managers, politicians, and professionals (and, in a few antiquated countries, still royals). All these groups and classes are examples of the fundamental principle that seemingly rules humanity: social systems are structured hierarchically. As Laurent (1978, p. 223) has said, 'The pecking order seems to have pervasive effects across cultural, structural and political systems.' Whether societies consist of clearly demarcated classes or more of a patchwork of clusters and groups of people, whether they are more static or more fluid, or whether the boundaries between the groups are more closed or transparent—in most societies there still seems to be a deeply embedded tradition and understanding that stratification and hierarchical relationships between people are 'normal,' even desirable and worthwhile.

But is hierarchy *always* the case? In many societies there have been famous thinkers who developed alternative ideas. For example, during the Age of Enlightenment the English philosopher John Locke (in his 1689 'The Second Treatise of Civil Government', quoted in Kramnick 1995, p. 395) reasoned about a 'state also of equality, wherein all the power and jurisdiction is reciprocal, no one having more than another.' Similarly, the German philosopher Immanuel Kant's second version of his 'categorical imperative' (the fundamental principle that people should be treated as ends in themselves and not only as a means) can be seen as a claim for an egalitarian society (Parker 2002, p. 105). The Italian philosopher Antonio Gramsci's concept of emancipation, the German sociologist Jürgen Habermas's theory of a power-free discourse (Levy et al. 2001, p. 3), and the Brazilian educator Paolo Freire's 1970 work *Pedagogy of the Oppressed* and idea of humanisation (Freire 1996) also represent fascinating alternative models to a hierarchical society. And there have been many more Western and Asian philosophers who have reasoned about 'Utopia' (for example, Morus in 1516; see Morus 1987)—i.e., 'better' societies where people are free and enjoy equal status and opportunities, and where institutions are fair and just. Such ideas are vivid proof that hierarchy is not the only way of organising social systems (Fairtlough 2005); hierarchy-free, egalitarian, and nonoppressive organisations and whole societies are *theoretically* possible.

Moreover, there are countless empirical examples showing that hierarchy-free organisations and societies are *practically* possible. For example, when one has a closer look only at the epoch since early capitalism, one can easily identify various attempts to establish alternative, democratic, and even egalitarian organisations, communes, and whole societies. Participative democratic organisations have experimented with ideas such as employee participation in strategic and operational decision-making ('workplace democracy'), empowerment, autonomous work groups, joint consultative committees, profit-sharing, and share-ownership (even copartnership) and worker-owned firms (de Jong and van Witteloostuijin 2004; Wagner 2002; Rothschild and Ollilainen 1999; Wilson 1999; Wunderer 1999; Boehm 1993; Kelly and Kelly 1991; Rosen 1984). In addition to these democratic organisations, there has been a whole range of attempts to create 'hierarchy-free' organisations, such as heterarchies (Fairtlough 2005), collectivist organisations (Rothschild-Whitt 1979), and utopian communities (Kanter 1972). The most determined and far-reaching attempts to realise and practice nonhierarchical forms of work and collaboration can be found where people agree on 'egalitarian-democratic' criteria as the leading principles of their coexistence and cooperation (Rothschild and Ollilainen 1999, p. 598). The fundamental idea is that no member of a social system should be allowed to dominate others in any form (Fournier 2002, p. 206; Boehm 1993, p. 228).

This is not to say that all of these attempts overcame hierarchy successfully, especially not after the initial periods of their (over)enthusiastic foundation. According to Kanter (1972, p. viii), such 'communal orders represent major social experiments in which new or radical theories of human behaviour, motivation, and interpersonal relations are put to the test'. Sooner or later, many of even the most serious attempts to establish truly hierarchy-free organisations or communities either failed, were terminated, were changed into a combination of traditional and alternative structures and processes, or even turned into quite oppressive regimes, becoming a nightmare for most of those involved. Very often, attempts to establish Heaven on Earth end up as Hell on Earth—or as Heaven on Earth for *some* and Hell on Earth for *many*.

Nonetheless, and this is crucial, the fact that at least for *some* time there have been social systems (such as communes, organisations, or networks of organisations) without formal or even informal hierarchy is sufficient evidence to counter the argument that hierarchy is *always* the case.[3] Not *all* but *almost all* social systems have been structured as group-based social hierarchies. Hierarchy might be the prevailing mode of social ordering in *almost* every epoch and culture—but 'almost' does not mean 'always.' Thus, hierarchy is *not* a 'natural law'; social relationships do not necessarily need to be hierarchical. Hierarchy might be (or might have been so far) the unnormal normality of almost all societies, organisations, and groups—but not with necessity. There *can* be hierarchy—but *it could be otherwise!*

2.2   GOOD AND NOT SO GOOD REASONS WHY HIERARCHY HAS BEEN AROUND FOR SO LONG

Since social systems can be organised and maintained in various ways, their specific design and functioning need to be explained and justified—especially the latter: *every* social order needs to be justified. Especially the hierarchical construction of social reality (the notion that actors are not only different but allegedly unequal, and the conclusion that, therefore, there should be superiors and subordinates who are provided with different rights and duties in accordance with their social rank) is not immediately plausible and accepted. *Social dominance and inequality are not self-evident;* there must be 'good' reasons for the fact that hierarchy has been the prevailing and all-pervasive mode of organising since the chronicles of humanity began. In this section some of the main claims concerning why hierarchy has been around for so long will be discussed—and why it should not have been around for that long. The discussion will focus on four areas:

1) *The origins of hierarchy:* where does hierarchy come from and to which 'higher powers' can the roots of hierarchy be traced back?

2) *The system:* how does hierarchy work and what are the functional advantages of hierarchy?

3) *The people in hierarchies:* what does hierarchy mean for people and why do hierarchies place superiors and subordinates in their 'right' places?

4) *Moral justifications for hierarchy:* why is hierarchy 'the best of all worlds,' why do people deserve what they get from hierarchy, and why is hierarchy a fair and just system?

2.2.1   The Origins of Hierarchy

A crucial part of providing an overall justification for a given social system is to trace it back to its origins. There is a compelling reason for doing so; if these origins are acknowledged, or even admired, the system's existence is justified and people will accept the social order more easily and willingly. And, of course, the more 'superior' these origins, the more 'superior' the system.

Rulers and ruling elites are very aware of the logical necessity, emotional persuasiveness, and practical advantages of this idea. Thus, they usually claim that the system (and, hence, their reign, social positions, privileges, and prerogatives) is built on the 'highest,' 'strongest,' and 'most eternal' principles possible. However, the problem is that, from a logical point of view, such first principles cannot simply be deducted from other principles since then they would not be the first, highest, or strongest ones. They, therefore, need to be introduced 'somehow' by 'something' or 'someone' from 'somewhere.' Whatever this is, it is 'the ultimate source of authority' (Beetham 1991, p. 70). And, since it is the first and greatest source, it justifies and legitimises literally *everything:* the leading principles of a given social order, the structures and processes put in place, and people's roles, positions, opportunities, and destinies within the social system. By linking their reign to a 'higher' power, representatives and proponents of a certain social order can explain the origin of it (Mosca 1971, p. 264) as well as giving it the accolade of superiority and longevity, if not eternity.

In the case of hierarchy, there have been three main authoritative sources: 1) 'divine command' (e.g., God, gods, or some other eternal force); 2) 'natural law' (e.g., 'pecking order,' 'survival of the fittest'); and 3) 'sociopolitical doctrine' (e.g., private property, market inefficiency, bureaucracy). Arguments put forward by proponents of a hierarchical system in order to justify and defend it can overlap all these three sources. This book focuses particularly on the last two because, within an economic, social, or organisational context, they are how aspects are predominantly explained and justified, at least in secular societies.[4]

In the tradition of biologism or sociobiology (Wilson 1975), hierarchical social order is portrayed as the 'natural' state of affairs of all creatures (Van Vugt 2006, p. 354). According to biologism, 'nature' is the ultimate force—and what is 'natural' is 'good' and 'normal.' Approaches such as classical and neoclassical economics, conservative and neoliberal political theory, orthodox management, and organisation studies follow in their core such argumentation. For example, Zaleznik (1989, p. 149) stressed that 'Ranging from the animal kingdom to human groups, relationships form into a hierarchy.' According to this position, it is 'the nature' of social relationships that they are organised hierarchically. Whether people compete or collaborate, as soon as they come together, differences will play out 'naturally' and be enhanced by the dynamics of social interaction. These differences will manifest themselves in different social positions that reflect the superiority or inferiority of those involved—the famous (infamous) 'pecking order.' This is the 'natural order of things'—and what nature has as its plan is, of course, good and should not be changed.[5]

However, one can argue that hierarchical relationships are anything else but 'natural.' Societies and organisations can be seen to a large extent as the products of clashing values and beliefs and also of the ideological conflicts and social struggles of certain individuals and groups of people (Friedman 1977; Braverman 1974), *not* as abstract natural forces. For example, Fournier (2002, p. 200) argued that 'grassroots protest movements remind us that nothing is the product of autonomous, inevitable, faceless "forces", everything has to be decided.' The organisation and maintenance of social groups, organisations, and whole societies do *not* follow natural laws but are open to different accounts and developments. Everything that happens within the social realm is the intended or unintended outcome of *human creation* (Rueschemeyer 1986, p. 2). And everything that is done, made, and caused by humans can be so and so—*but it could also be otherwise.* Even whole social systems, or key parts and aspects of them, can be designed and maintained in different ways. With regard to the problem of hierarchy, this means that social differentiation (i.e., division of labour via specialised roles) *does not necessarily* have to lead to social stratification (i.e., a system of unequally privileged groups and individuals) (Ravlin and Thomas 2005, p. 976; Mousnier 1973, p. 10; Wrong 1971, pp. 132–3). Work and social relationships do not of necessity have to be organised hierarchically. Other designs are possible—theoretically and practically.

In this sense, references to 'nature' or so-called 'natural laws' for the purpose of justifying specific social arrangements and human affairs as inevitable and good (if not to say the best of all imaginable possibilities) are *ideology* (Abercrombie et al. 1980, p. 96). 'Ideology' can be understood as a value-based belief system that provides explanations and justifications (for a certain design of the world, for social systems, for stereotypes of people and their place in the world) that suggest inevitability and necessity (Diefenbach 2009a). The idea that groups of people, organisations, and even whole societies should be organised and maintained hierarchically is even the 'dominant ideology' (Abercrombie et al. 1980). Hierarchical systems do not endure because of certain 'natural laws,' 'the law of nature,' or even 'supernatural forces' but because of people who make such claims dominate the ideological and social struggles within the social system and are able to convince many others.

2.2.2   The System of Hierarchy

In order to explain the functional aspects of hierarchy (i.e., the functioning of hierarchy as a system), naturalistic interpretations and justifications of social phenomena are still used, but no longer as the primary ones. Since the early 20th century they have been replaced by functionalistic and technocratic arguments about (manmade) 'rational design'—as demonstrated by F.W. Taylor's 'scientific management' in 1911 (see Taylor 1967). Orthodox management and organisation theorists portray organisations and management primarily in functional terms (Donaldson 2003; Jaques 1990; Zaleznik 1989; Lawrence and Lorsch 1967; Taylor 1967; Blau 1964; Chandler 1962; Drucker 1954; Friedman 1953; Fayol 1949). Organisations are described as rationally designed enterprises, functioning smoothly because of thought-out plans, policies, and procedures. Management is said to be based on allegedly 'value-free' and functional concepts; 'management tools have no feelings and no emotions; tools take care of the general interest.' (Courpasson 2000, p. 156).

In this sense, managerial ideology ('managerialism') explains and legitimises hierarchy and power relations in functional terms (Chiapello and Fairclough 2002, p. 187; Jaques 1990, p. 127). Hierarchy is said to be the most efficient way of organising things—and people, of course. It goes without saying that any system that is functional and efficient (and fits into its environment—again, a functionalistic argument[6]) is made to last. Every now and then, the system might need a degree of adaptation to changing circumstances, but its fundamental principles, main structures, and processes will remain intact.

Indeed, one can admit that the functional aspects of hierarchy *can* represent and produce quite considerable advantages; if roles and responsibilities are clearly defined and demarcated from each other, people can focus on carrying out the required tasks. If nothing else intervenes, nontask-related issues might be quite reduced. Merton (1961, p. 50) argued that,

The chief merit of bureaucracy is its technical efficiency, with a premium placed on precision, speed, expert control, continuity, discretion, and optimal returns on input. The structure is one which approaches the complete elimination of personalized relationships and nonrational considerations (hostility, anxiety, affectual involvements, etc.).

Hierarchy can enable the smooth, regular, and in certain ways efficient functioning of organisational policies, structures, and processes. Moreover, because of clearly demarcated areas and levels, explicit rules and regulations, and formalised procedures and routines, hierarchical social order provides its members with some kind of stability, predictability, certainty, and security (Crozier 1964, p. 55). Every hierarchical social order stabilises the behaviour of people. Hierarchical order and control, and rules and regulations can be powerful tools to limit and reduce the power that some people would otherwise have over others (Courpasson 2000, p. 156). A fully developed rule-based hierarchy protects subordinates against arbitrariness and randomness and reduces *some* forms of organisational misbehaviour (while, at the same time, providing the conditions for other forms of mistreatment). In some respects, hierarchical order means protection from others by rules (Crozier 1964, p. 189). It, therefore, is understandable that 'the least empowered in an organization often support the very rules they might be expected to resist because, lacking other forms of power, they can use rules to limit what others can do to them' (Jacques 1996, p. 111). In addition, most subordinates even believe that, if hierarchy were no longer around to provide order and discipline, then disorder, chaos, and even anarchy would emerge (Zaleznik 1989, p. 151). Hence, because of 'good' functional reasons it is allegedly even in the interest of those lower down the hierarchical pyramid to keep it intact.

However, and this is crucial, all the functional advantages hierarchy may or may not provide can be achieved by other means—and without the downsides of hierarchy. For example, 'order' and 'restraint' do not only emerge out of hierarchical arrangements. Cooperative forms of organisation, together with robust policies and procedures of democratic governance and people's developed understanding of active citizenship, can also achieve social order, stability, and continuity—possibly more so, and in more efficient and convincing terms, than hierarchical order and top-down control. Ethical principles, if internalised by people and practised on a daily basis, can provide certainty and security even for the less powerful. Empathy and strong beliefs in equality and democratic decision-making, together with a high level of moral development, can shape people's perceptions and attitudes to an extent that hierarchy and hierarchy-conforming behaviour (almost) disappears.

Moreover, hierarchy does not eliminate social conflict between individuals or groups (e.g., over power, influence, and resources) but establishes 'the terms of engagement for such competition' (McKinlay and Wilson 2006, p. 659). Although hierarchy prevents *some* forms of nontask-related social conflict, at the same time it simply produces and enables *other* forms of nontask-related social conflict. It changes the rules and conditions of the game, *not* the game itself. One might even argue that hierarchy is *primarily* a functional tool for channelling and managing social conflict (Mintzberg 1985; Burns 1961; Thompson 1961). It, thus, is quite inappropriate, if not to say misleading, to portray hierarchy as mere 'technical' structures and processes. As in any social system, in a hierarchical system there are individual and group interests that strive for power and control, and there is political behaviour at work.

Hierarchy is not (only) about 'functional aspects' but a tool for the functional design and management of 'social affairs.' It therefore makes much more sense to regard organisations as 'political organisations' (Burns 1961, p. 258) or 'negotiated arenas' (Cohen et al. 1999, p. 475) in the tradition of organisational behaviour (Mintzberg 1979; Cyert and March 1963; March and Simon 1958). The political order of organisations (i.e., their governing principles, policies, and procedures), power relations (i.e., domination of particular individuals and groups over others), social inequalities (i.e., differences between individuals and social groups), and individual and group interests (i.e., people's different interests stemming from their social roles and positions) are the real functional imperatives that characterise and drive a social system like hierarchy.

In this sense, one could say that hierarchy is mainly a tool for gaining and securing privileges and prerogatives for *specific* individuals and groups of people. Social systems such as hierarchy are the functional instruments (and preconditions) for certain individuals' or groups of people's struggle for social dominance and exploitation. The primary function of hierarchical social order is to guarantee and to support the interests of leaders and ruling elites. For example, management is not about a 'value-free' conduct of office, but, as argued by Bachrach and Baratz (1970, pp. 43–4),

> A set of predominant values, beliefs, rituals, and institutional procedures ('rules of the game') that operate systematically and consistently to the benefit of certain persons and groups at the expense of others. Those who benefit are placed in a preferred position to defend and promote their vested interests. More often than not, the 'status quo defenders' are a minority or elite group within the population in question.

The ideology of hierarchy is basically an attempt to legitimise specific individual or group interests and unequal power relationships in order to secure the privileges of power elites and the continuing participation of subordinate groups and classes in exploitative social relations (Stoddart 2007, p. 196; Beetham 1991). This is what hierarchy does, and what it is really good at; it provides and protects a social order that is advantageous for *certain* groups of people and *their* interests, privileges, and prerogatives—for those who rule, and for those who obey and follow. In this sense, hierarchically achieved and maintained forms of order and control, hierarchical leadership, autocratic rules, and any other social dominance of little or uncontrolled power elites are incompatible with the notion of democracy *in principle*. Organisational hierarchy—hierarchy in general—is *antidemocratic* and alien to the idea of a liberal, fair, and just society (Rothschild and Ollilainen 1999).[7] *Hierarchy is a fundamentally antidemocratic and oppressive social order.* There cannot be much legitimacy of, and justification for, any hierarchical social system—at least not in societies that claim to be just and democratic.

However, at the same time, its antidemocratic and oppressive character is one of the main reasons why hierarchy has been around for so long. Hierarchy lasts not because it is functional as a rationally designed system but because it is functional (or instrumental) for *some* individuals and groups: for a few to rule the many, for those who seek social dominance, and for the power elites who exploit a social system for selfish purposes while claiming that they 'serve the whole' (their country or an organisation) unselfishly. That hierarchy primarily guarantees the privileges, prerogatives, interests, and positions of superiors is the very reason for its existence and continuation.[8]

2.2.3 The People in Hierarchies

Hierarchy is also said to be efficient because it puts people in their 'right' places; there are those who rule and those who follow—allegedly for good reasons.

For example, within orthodox leadership and management literature, managers and leaders are usually portrayed as skilful and competent superiors who can manage and lead organisations at will (Kark and Van Dijk 2007; Ilies et al. 2006; Van Vugt 2006; Gill 2003). The idea of leadership is closely accompanied by rhetoric about the (necessary) skills and competences of leaders; leaders seemingly have, or at least are capable of and willing to develop, all the positive leadership attributes and behaviours suggested by textbooks and proponents of orthodox leadership ideology and business ethics (Siebens 2005; Aronson 2001; Masi and Cooke 2000; Bass et al. 1987; Burns 1978). It is the leaders, and only the leaders, who see the wider picture, have the relevant knowledge and abilities, and therefore know what is best for the social system and the people (Gill 2003, p. 309; Samra-Fredericks 2000, p. 249; Ellis 1998, p. 231).

In contrast, common people are not able to fully understand what leaders and superiors do and what it takes to be a leader, so it is said. There are 'deeper mysteries' about leaders and leadership; the 'spiritual consciousness is awe and wonder' (Friedman et al. 2005, p. 26). Fournier and Grey (2000, p. 12), give some more hints:

> The manager has been depicted as a mythical figure requiring a rare blend of charismatic flair which cannot be routinized and codified in

rules transferred through scientific training. This aura of mystification and glory with which managers (of the right kind) have been sanctified by the popular literature has served to increase the potential power and status of management.

There is a conscious and unconscious mystification of people higher up organisational hierarchies or societal class systems simply because they are higher up the hierarchy. As Thompson (1961, p. 493) explained,

> Incumbents of high office are held in awe because they are in touch with the mysteries and magic of such office [. . .] Since one knows less and less about the activities of superordinates the farther away on the hierarchy they are, the more the awe in which he holds them and consequently the greater their prestige or status.

As one can imagine, the reality of superiors is quite different; 'flawed leaders are everywhere' (Kellerman 2005, p. 3). Ashforth (1994) found that the acquisition and use of power (particularly) tend to corrupt the power holder. Leaders often develop increased self-esteem, or even megalomania, but at the same time devalue the worth of others. Over time, this leads to distorted images of oneself and others and corresponding attitudes and behaviours by both the power holder and his or her subordinates. 'Organisational misbehaviour' of managers and leaders, i.e., 'acts which manifest disrespect for a subordinate's dignity or provide obstacles to a subordinate's performance or deserved rewards' (Vredenburgh and Brender 1998, p. 1339) is widespread (Vardi and Weitz 2004). In their empirical study, Diamond and Allcorn (2004, p. 24) found that

> Organizations are comprised of individuals in positions of authority with varying degrees of self-esteem and self-cohesion from 'good enough' to deficient and from healthy to excessive narcissism.

And they concluded that

> The presence of moral violence within the workplace is shaped by a combination of hierarchic structures of dominance and submission and narcissistic executives, who are supported by compliant and idealizing subordinates. These leaders compensate for intrapersonal deficiencies and inner emptiness (narcissistic deficits) by striving to occupy positions of inordinate power and authority and by demanding the admiration and loyalty of followers.

Such personality traits and behaviour raise moral questions. For example, in their study on managerial misbehaviour, Rayburn and Rayburn (1996) found a close relationship between personality traits and *ethical orientation;*

they called it 'Machiavellianism.' This term describes 'an individual that has an immoral reputation for dealing with others to accomplish his/her own objectives, and for manipulating others for his/her own purpose' (p. 1209). Rayburn and Rayburn also found empirical evidence that Machiavellians are more likely to be ambitious individuals and that individuals of higher intelligence tend to indicate that they would behave less ethically in given situations. Ambitious people, with their one-dimensional achievement orientation (i.e., focus only on what is in their personal interest), are not only more willing to engage with organisational politics but (on average) will also be more successful in pursuing their personal goals within an organisational context—i.e., they will make a career. Vickers and Kouzmin (2001, p. 105) provide quite a direct, but not unrealistic, description of this kind of person:

> The modern careerist epitomizes the 'damaged' organizational actor, who appears to say and to act as is required through a process of adaptation which is beneficial for career advancement but disastrous for emotional health. This is evidenced by the apparent promulgation of 'automatons' [. . .]—colourless, dull and unimaginative individuals characterizing the quintessential 'organization man' [. . .]—an essentially calculating animal pursuing the necessities of organizational life.

Boddy (2006) called people with such mindsets 'organisational psychopaths,' According to him, organisational psychopaths 'are employees with no conscience [. . .] who are willing to lie and are able to present an extrovert [. . .], charming façade in order to gain managerial promotion via a ruthlessly opportunistic and manipulative approach to career advancement' (p. 1462). He argues that organisational psychopaths are found more in larger organisations because these provide more sources and opportunities for political manoeuvring, power, prestige, and money (pp. 1462, 1466).

Overall, it might not be possible to finally decide whether it is people with already distorted personalities who make a career within hierarchical organisations and become superiors or leaders or whether it is the hierarchical structures and processes that damage people and change them into organisational psychopaths. The reality is probably a combination of the two. But, whatever the cause and the effect are, it remains a fact and serious problem 'that bad or at least unworthy people often occupy and successfully fill top leadership positions, . . .' (Kellerman 2005, p. 4).

Either way, since *any* hierarchical social order is the incorporation and extension of superiors' direct power and means the institutionalisation of their individual and group interests, superiors usually have little interest in fundamental change. For example, at the end of their empirical research into politicians' interests, norms, and values, Bowler et al. (2006, p. 434) concluded: 'once in power, politicians may develop a great deal of positive affect for current institutions and a resistance to change'. Parker (2002, p. 189) came to a similar conclusion with regard to managers:

Managers have too much invested in managerialism to make them likely to rebel en masse. They have identities, qualifications, salaries and status through being what they are, a full dinner-pail, so why should we assume that they will wish to disinvest and join movements for reform?

Ruling elites defend and justify the status quo—*any* status quo (Wrong 1971, p. 134)—because it made them superior and guarantees the continuation of their privileges, prerogatives, advantages, and opportunities, which stem from that particular system of unequal social relationships. All that superiors want is to keep the hierarchical social order intact—by (almost) any means, as long as it protects them and their interests. Even most members of aspiring new classes and ambitious careerists do not want system change. What they want is a larger share for themselves—and they can achieve this goal only as long as the system functions.

Although subordinates' positions in the hierarchical system are different from those of their superiors, there is a similar contrast between their public image and actual behaviour. The official 'ideology of subordinates' largely complements the dominant ideology of leaders and leadership. Since the focus is mainly on the system and its performance, the efficient functioning of subordinates is mainly portrayed in instrumental ways. The ideology is largely about subordinates' fit with the prevailing hierarchical structures and processes and their smooth functioning within institutions. At the same time, 'good' reasons are provided for why subordinates are lower down the hierarchical order, why they deserve to be there, and why this is the way it (always) should be. Hence, this ideology is largely about explaining and justifying 'the way things are,' why subordinates are followers and have to function accordingly, why this is good and right, why this will not change, and why this should not change (Jost and Hunyady 2005, p. 260).

As a consequence, besides their deeply internalised feelings of inferiority, subordinates also often have a strong sense of belonging—i.e., happiness at being part of the very hierarchically structured group, organisation, or nation that makes them subordinates. For developing such notions of belonging (and the corresponding behaviour), they are provided with specially designed moral ideas of obedience and serfdom so that they know not only how but also why they must function well, why this is good for them, and why they should feel proud of it (Scott 1990, p. 58); employees' work ethos, people's nationalism, and soldiers' pride are vivid, and at the same time sad, examples of how efficiently this cynical ideology works. Subordinates regularly function well not only because they *have to* but also because they *want to,* since they have been made to believe and to enact what constitutes 'the good subordinate.'

And most people *are* 'good' subordinates, indeed. They demonstrate 'a willingness to comply with authority, a preference for impersonal and formal relationships with others on the job, a desire for strict adherence to rules and procedures, and a need to identify with the organization and conform to norms' (Ashforth 1994, p. 759). Although most subordinates experience their lower, limited, and patronised status as constraining and often humiliating and would escape if they could (Beetham 1991, p. 3), they nonetheless try their best to function and to fit in on a daily basis. Most people, most of the time, comply with hierarchical systems. Even their occasionally deviating behaviour and boundary crossings do not really challenge the hierarchical social order. They happen, and remain, *within* the logic of the hierarchical system and simply reiterate the importance and legitimacy of superiors and the system.

That members of power elites regard their privileged positions as 'normal' and the continuation of their dominance as desirable is understandable. Mosca (1971, p. 270) explained this quite convincingly:

> Suppose now that a society gradually passes from its feverish state to calm. Since the human being's psychological tendencies are always the same, those who belong to the ruling class will begin to acquire a group spirit. They will become more and more exclusive and learn better and better the art of monopolizing to their advantage the qualities and capacities that are essential to acquiring power and holding it. Then, at last, the force that is essentially conservative appears—the force of habit. Many people become resigned to a lowly station, while the members of certain privileged families or classes grow convinced that they have almost an absolute right to high station and command.

However, it is puzzling that in almost all cultures and societies even most 'ordinary' people regard it as normal that some minorities are privileged whereas the majority of people are disadvantaged—whatever merits or criteria one applies. Actually, there is nothing normal about this—and there is nothing normal about the fact that most members of those societies do *not* see this as problematic. In the face of all the inequality, injustice, oppression, and exploitation that are systemic for hierarchical social systems, it does not seem rational that subordinates and members of other disadvantaged groups largely obey, function, and behave as expected by the system (Jost and Hunyady 2005, p. 260). The range and scope of subordinates' compliance with hierarchical systems is a well-established puzzle, and prompts questions that have already been asked a hundred times (Stoddart 2007, p. 191; Brookfield 2005, p. 160; De Schweinitz 1979, p. 838):[9] *Why do subordinates support, even actively contribute to the very system that oppresses and disadvantages them? Why are most subordinates keen to develop self-images and attitudes that are congruent with hierarchical social order and the expectations of their superiors?*

One possible explanation for people's tendency to function smoothly within oppressive structures is that it corresponds with psychological needs for order, structure, and security and to avoid uncertainty and ambiguity (Jost and Hunyady 2005, pp. 261–2).[10] There might be some truth in it.

However, the problem with such explanations is that they may suggest that such needs are 'natural'—but they are *not*. For example, toddlers do not show obedient behaviour automatically. They *learn* to obey, to behave, and to fear more powerful persons during the early stages of their primary social-isation (usually within the family). And only after countless interventions by various superiors (e.g., parents, nannies, or other guardians) do toddlers and young children slowly develop sociopsychological patterns of 'appropriate' behaviour which then manifest as personality traits. People are *made* to accept, even appreciate, hierarchical institutions and to fit into them via end-less processes of socialisation, indoctrination, and conditioning in all sorts of primary, secondary, and tertiary education institutions until they behave and act appropriately. As early as 1784, Immanuel Kant, the great German philosopher, wrote (cited in Kramnick 1995, p. 2):

> After the guardians have first made their domestic cattle dumb and have made sure that these placid creatures will not dare take a single step without the harness of the cart to which they are confined, the guardians then show them the danger which threatens if they try to go alone. Actu-ally, this danger is not so great, for by falling a few times they would finally learn to walk alone. But an example of this failure makes them timid and ordinarily frightens them away from all further trials.

Many contemporary employees are not much different from these late-18th-century 'domestic cattle'; 'bureaucratically-oriented individuals tend to be somewhat insecure, suspicious, authoritarian, dogmatic, and lower in ability, and tend to place a higher value on conformity and order' (Ashforth 1994, p. 759). Although most employees are already subordinates *before* they join a (new) organisation, they will still be subject to further social conditioning and professional socialisation. 'Identity regulation' (Alvesson and Willmott 2002, p. 621) of their existing and prospective members is a serious issue and of great concern for hierarchical systems. For example, the management of workers' 'insides'—their hopes, fears, and aspirations—is at the heart of modern management techniques (Alvesson and Willmott 2002, p. 620). External measures of identity regulation and the externally initiated and supported internalisation of dominant values and beliefs (via promises and threats, rewards and punishments) are accompanied by a whole range of self-controlling practices. Hence, *if* one includes 'psychological needs' for hierarchy in one's argumentation, it is important to stress that these needs also have a social dimension—i.e., that they are (also) created and nurtured *socially* and that they could be changed (the question then, of course, is how this can be achieved).

Hierarchical social order, thus, is to a great extent about the systematic degradation and infantilisation of subordinates (Diamond and Allcorn 2004, p. 26; Jacques 1996, p. 81). Subordinates are expected to develop 'patterns of behaviour that dehumanize, depersonalize, and infantilize' (Diamond and

Allcorn 2004, p. 26). Subordinates learn that their superiors *want them* to feel helpless (Bassman and London 1993, p. 22). And, indeed, over time most subordinates show the appropriate levels of 'learned helplessness' (Van Vugt 2006, p. 361). Throughout history, making subordinates fit into a hierarchical social order has meant trimming people's intellectual, psychological, and moral capabilities. It has resulted in the severe deformation of the human personality. But socialised, conditioned, and trimmed subordinates will not challenge the system—'To remain calm is the first civic duty!'[11]

2.2.4 Moral Justifications for Hierarchy

As argued above, it is the key principle of hierarchical social order that it provides superiors and subordinates with *different* opportunities, means, privileges, and prerogatives with which to pursue their interests, to develop their identities and personalities, and to enjoy all the advantages and material resources they can accumulate as a result of their roles and positions within the system (Braynion 2004, p. 449; Jacques 1996, p. 120; Beetham 1991, p. 50; Rueschemeyer 1986, p. 31; Thompson 1961, p. 486). If a social system (e.g., an organisation or society) is hierarchical, societal institutions and resources represent a comprehensive framework of *structural* social asymmetries. Opportunities, quality of life, and even life expectancy are either better or worse, depending on where people are on the hierarchical ladder—whether they are superior or subordinate.

Because of such far-reaching consequences, the specific design and mechanisms of a social system need to be explained and justified. Moreover, in the case of a hierarchically organised social system, it is also necessary to explain and justify why there are superiors and subordinates at all. One way or the other, there must be 'good reasons' why superiors inherit positions higher up the hierarchical order (and enjoy the privileges and prerogatives that come with them), why they deserve to be there, why they must be there—and, equally, why subordinates deserve to be where they are and get what they get, and why they are subordinates.

It is one of the primary problems of the proponents of any hierarchically organised social system to explain 'why one group is dominant and another dominated, why one person gives orders in a particular enterprise while another takes orders' (Chiapello and Fairclough 2002, p. 187). Stories or even theories about the system's origin, claims about its functional superiority, and comprehensive descriptions of the roles and positions of its different members provide some explanations and justifications. But the system must also be justified on *moral grounds*. Proponents and opponents alike know very well that hierarchical social order means social differences, that social differentiation leads to social stratification, and that social stratification produces social inequality. Where they differ is whether or not they consider this to be justified and fair. There needs to be a compelling reason or principle that justifies the social differences. According to Beetham (1991, p. 59),

The inequality of circumstance between dominant and subordinate is justified by a principle of differentiation, which reveals the dominant as specially qualified, suited or deserving to possess the resource, pursue the activity or hold the position which forms the basis of their power, and the subordinate as correspondingly unsuited or unfitted to do so, and hence rightly excluded from it.

Proponents usually try to justify hierarchical structures and processes, and inequalities and differences in life chances, as the result and as a reflection of people's different merits—whether these actually exist or are specifically constructed. 'Merits' can be anything: performance, capabilities, political success, skills, experience, age, social background, line of descent, divine will, or providence. 'Merits' are very adaptable; they are used as the principle of differentiation for *any* hierarchical system, be it a dictatorship, monarchy, oligarchy, communist regime, orthodox business organisation, or public-sector organisation. 'Merits' are an all-purpose arsenal of weaponry. With such rhetoric, proponents of hierarchy particular try to explain and justify (Diefenbach 2009; Beetham 1991):

1) superiors' and power elites' rule, and their elevated positions, privileges, and prerogatives;

2) subordinates' lower positions and duties;

3) why this constellation is the most efficient and just way to organise the society, organisations, and everyone's work and lives.

This is the very idea of hierarchical social order: certain people are *superiors* because they are (factually or allegedly) fitter, older, more knowledgeable, more experienced, or in possession of whatever merits and criteria are the most crucial or most appreciated in a given social system. And certain people are *subordinates* because they are (again, factually or allegedly) less fit, younger, less knowledgeable, less experienced, or otherwise less skillful or less capable. Superiors and subordinates are what they are, deserve to be where they are, do what they do, and get what they get for 'good reasons.'

However, the moral justification of hierarchy as a merit-based social system depends entirely on whether or not it is possible to allocate people to social positions exactly according to their merits—i.e., whether or not positions and merits correspond to each other perfectly. This would only be the case under *ideal conditions*—i.e., if, and only if, 1) merits can be identified and measured completely, 2) the absolute number of social positions and absolute merits are exactly the same, 3) relative numbers of social positions (i.e., positions at different hierarchical levels) and differences in merits are exactly the same, 4) there is complete information, and 5) allocation of people to social positions according to their merits is done by a rational decision-maker.

Obviously, such a model of 'perfect hierarchy' belongs to the same class of models like the 'perfect market' or 'homo oeconomicus'—and, hence, would face the same criticism of its unrealistic assumptions. It might be possible to imagine a perfect case when all ideal conditions are met. But such an ideal model does not help much to cope with the theoretical and practical problem of allocating candidates to social positions according to people's merits when there is *imperfect* correlation between positions and merits or *incomplete* information about merits.

The problem lies especially in the measurement, or measurability, and appreciation of 'merits'—i.e., those criteria that qualify a candidate for a certain position. Most merits are either qualitative and cannot be measured at all (e.g., 'personality' or 'quality of a leader') or are operationalised and measured in ways that do not perfectly match the measurement of social positions. Whereas merits can be measured on a range of possible intensities, social positions within a hierarchical social order can only be measured in positive natural numbers (i.e., a social position is either superior to another position or not). As a consequence, the differences between social positions and the differences between the merits of those people who occupy these positions are rarely identical. Thus, merits are appreciated differently— which contradicts the fundamental principle that a merit-based hierarchical system allocates social positions in a fair and just way.

One can easily construct hundreds of examples where qualitative or quantitative merits of people, on the one hand, and the social positions provided by the system, on the other, cannot be matched perfectly (either because of differences in the absolute number of people and positions or because of how social positions and people's merits are relative to each other). What all these theoretical models of imperfect hierarchy have in common is that there is a larger or smaller disparity between the appreciation of merits and the allocation of candidates to social positions. As a consequence, since merits are not appreciated according to their 'true' value, people do not achieve the social positions they deserve (either in absolute or relative terms). Thus, the system is not fair.

The systemic insufficiency of hierarchy as an allocation mechanism becomes even more of a problem when it is about real, existing hierarchical social systems. The reality of hierarchies is very different from the theoretical models of perfect or imperfect hierarchies. As everyone knows, even if the selection of candidates for social positions is *officially* solely or primarily merit-based, the *actual* selection process within hierarchical organisations happens very differently; information (about candidates) is not complete, the available information is interpreted in different ways, subjective factors play a role, and candidates are finally picked for a whole range of reasons other than their actual merits. Usually, the allocation of people to social positions is a combination of so-called 'rational' *and* subjective factors—whereby very often the former provide the official reasons and justifications and the latter represent the real (but unofficial) reasons behind a decision.

Moreover, in any hierarchical system, there are always more resources, privileges, and prerogatives higher up than further down the hierarchical ladder—systematically and with necessity, because higher positions are ascribed more responsibilities. The same cannot be said about merits. The higher a social position within a hierarchical system, the more merits are required (in order to cope with the greater responsibilities). But merits are allocated *un*systematically amongst people because they stem from many factors that are not (completely) part of the hierarchical system (e.g., people's personalities, social backgrounds, previous memberships or actions, continuous development).

This means that, the higher the social position is allocated within a hierarchical system, the less likely it is that the person who inherits that position will have the corresponding level of merits required for that position. As a result, people higher up the hierarchical social order have comparatively more responsibilities and enjoy more privileges and prerogatives than their actual merits warrant.[12] At the same time, many others receive not just comparatively less but too little in return for their merits, effort, and contributions. Hence, the unjust and unfair privileging of the few means not only marginalisation but also *exploitation* of the many (Burnham 1941, p. 123). In every hierarchical system there is a *structural asymmetry* with regard to the appreciation of people's merits; individuals or groups of people with higher social positions receive a relatively larger share of the overall outcomes in relation to their merits than people lower down the hierarchical ladder. As a consequence, *any* hierarchical social order privileges a few and disadvantages the many *systematically*. This is a fundamental and systemic flaw of hierarchy and is always the case, whatever the actual hierarchical system.

All in all, one can say that attempts to justify hierarchy as a merit-based system simply do not work, for the following main reasons:

1) The *model of perfect hierarchy* copes only with one highly unrealistic case (perfect match between social positions, candidates, and their merits with complete information and a rational decision-maker). It does not address the central problem of hierarchy—i.e., matching social positions and candidates in the face of incomplete information about merits and with human subjectivity kicking in.

2) *Models of imperfect hierarchy* struggle with the measurement or measurability of merits and, thus, cannot guarantee a fair allocation of candidates to social positions.

3) *Real, existing hierarchies* show that there is a fundamental structural asymmetry with regard to the appreciation of people's merits; people higher up the hierarchical ladder receive a relatively larger share of the overall outcomes in relation to their merits than people lower down.

In the face of such results it is difficult, if not to say impossible, to argue that hierarchy is based on merits as the main principle of differentiation and that people are allocated to social positions in accordance with their merits—whatever these are. When it is about hierarchical social systems the differentiation between superiors and subordinates might incorporate *also* the aspect of merit—but definitely not to the extent proponents of hierarchy claim and want people to believe. The selection and appointment of individuals for positions or functions higher up follows very different logics; the privileges and prerogatives superiors and members of power elites enjoy have little to do with their actual merits. Because of the systematic privileging of people higher up the hierarchical ladder and the systematic marginalisation and exploitation of the many lower down the hierarchical ladder, *any* hierarchical social order is unfair and unjust *in principle*—and it is done so deliberately; hierarchy is a social order *specifically* designed, institutionalised, and maintained for social dominance, discrimination, exploitation, and parasitism (Sidanius et al. 2004, p. 847; Beetham 1991, p. 58; Gouldner 1960, p. 165). For dominating minorities, hierarchical social order is one of the most suitable forms of a social system to extract labour, goods, services, or any other values from a majority (Scott 1990, p. 21).

2.3   WHY DOES HIERARCHY PERSIST?

As Section 2.2 showed, although hierarchy is the prevailing mode of structuring for many social systems, it is not undisputed.[13] There are fundamentally different views concerning hierarchy's origins, hierarchy's system, people's images and actual behaviour, and hierarchy's moral justification:

1) The *origins of hierarchy* are either explained by reference to 'divine command,' 'natural laws,' or 'sociopolitical doctrine,' or are seen as 'human creation' and traced back to social conflict about social positions and resources.

2) The *system of hierarchy* is either portrayed as 'rational design' (with functional and efficient structures and processes providing order and protection for everyone) or as an 'antidemocratic system' (providing unjustified privileges and prerogatives for a few, and inequality, injustice, discrimination, and exploitation for the many).

3) The *people in hierarchies* are either portrayed as skillful and capable superiors leading inferior and dependent subordinates or as conditioned and damaged personalities routinely showing organisational misbehaviour, obedience, infantilisation, submissiveness, and learned helplessness.

4) With respect to its *moral justification*, hierarchy is either portrayed as a 'merit-based system' where people inherit positions and enjoy privileges they deserve or as an 'unfair and unjust system' specifically designed and run in order to privilege the few at the expense of the many.

Hierarchical social order is contested on theoretical grounds as well as (sometimes) in reality. This is not surprising since it is one of the basic models for organising the work and lives of people. But Section 2.2 also showed that there are many 'good'—or not so good—reasons for its persistence. Every hierarchical system comprises elements and mechanisms that enable it to last over very long periods of time. Hierarchy lasts because it is a very powerful system, because it works, and because it has a lot to offer: it provides its members with a whole range of opportunities to pursue their own interests and to enjoy material advantages, psychological rewards, and privileges and prerogatives they could not find easily elsewhere.

But it does so *selectively*. It primarily supports, and guarantees, the interests of superiors, powerful rulers, and ruling elites—i.e., it protects the interests of a few against those of the many. *Hierarchy is antidemocratic, unfair, and unjust in principle.* Moreover, hierarchy can be criticised as one of the main reasons behind the pathetic and schizophrenic status quo of many of our institutions, organisations, and social relationships as well as the distorted personalities and behaviours most of us demonstrate. Hierarchy is *very* problematic because it does far more harm than good. Why it has nevertheless reached hegemonic status in so many cultures throughout the centuries and millennia requires explanations. Why and how exactly does hierarchy persist? And why don't people change it? Are any of the 'good reasons' offered above valid? If not, who or what is to blame? The system? The people? Both? Or perhaps no one, because this is just 'the way things are'? Hierarchy needs a comprehensive theory to explain its emergence and persistence. This theory will be developed in the next chapter.

3   A General Theory of Hierarchical Social Systems

'*Such was, or may well have been, the origin of society and law, which bound new fetters on the poor, and gave new powers to the rich; which irretrievably destroyed natural liberty, eternally fixed the law of property and inequality, converted clever usurpation into unalterable right, and, for the advantage of a few ambitious individuals, subjected all mankind to perpetual labor, slavery and wretchedness.*'

J.-J. Rousseau, *Discourse on the Origin of Inequality*, 1755
(cited in Kramnick 1995, p. 428)

3.1   INTRODUCTION

In the previous chapter it was shown that hierarchical order has been a welcomed as well as unwelcomed companion of humanity for the best part of its recorded history. Whether or not hierarchy actually should be the norm and (unnormal) normality of social systems must be determined via further scrutiny. But it is certain that it has been fairly persistent. Thus, the fundamental question is: how *exactly* can the emergence and persistence of hierarchical social order be explained? To this end, a general theory of hierarchical social systems will be developed step by step in this chapter (and then applied in Chapters 4 and 5). Following is a rough outline of how this will be done:

First, a model concerning the *core structure of hierarchical relationships* will be created that describes hierarchy as an unequal *social* relationship between superior(s) and subordinate(s) (Section 3.2). The model is grounded in the traditional understanding of hierarchy and power-based relations between individuals. However, its explicit inclusion of formal and informal hierarchy makes it slightly more nuanced.

In Section 3.3 the model will be further developed by incorporating people's actual behaviours, thoughts, and deeds. It will be argued that superiors' and subordinates' *mindsets* (i.e., their interests, identities, emotions, and moral character) as well as their *social actions* can be seen as direct consequences of their social roles and positions. This notwithstanding, the case against (causal) determinism will also be made—i.e., feedback loops, which lead to a more differentiated model, will be incorporated. It will be shown that *individual freedom, reflextivity,* and *responsibility* make a crucial difference with regard to how people see and do things within the specific situations or social contexts they are in.

With the introduction of the key elements and their relationships, the foundation is thus lain for developing the *basic dynamic processes* of hierarchy. Section 3.4 provides a framework for interrogating *routine behaviour,* but also, and more importantly, deviating behaviour of both subordinates and superiors—i.e., *boundary crossings* in the areas of social action, interests, identity, emotions, and moral character. It will be demonstrated that routine as well as deviating behaviour can trigger multiple processes that lead to the introduction of *abstract organisational order* and, hence, a further strengthening of hierarchical social order.

In Section 3.5 the focus shifts towards the context of hierarchical systems. For this, the *societal dimensions of hierarchical social order* will be discussed. Especially with regard to some key sociocultural and material/economic institutions and resources, it will be analysed how they contribute to the institutionalisation and continuation of hierarchical social order. It will be shown that, at the societal level, the preconditions for hierarchy are more numerous—and more comprehensive and favourable—than is often perceived.

After having developed all relevant aspects concerning individuals (Sections 3.2–3.4) and institutions (Section 3.5), it will be time to relate the two. Section 3.6 describes the *dynamic* links between individual reasoning and acting on the one hand and longer-lasting social systems and societal institutions on the other. For this, a new model, *'systemisation and its main mechanisms,'* will be developed that comprises processes of socialisation, adaptation, synchronisation, institutionalisation, transformation, and navigation. Systemisation represents a crucial part of the explanation of why hierarchical social order persists.

Section 3.7 then provides an overview of the complete general theory of hierarchical social systems and will summarise the main argument for why and how hierarchy persists. The argument will be based on all the *theorems* that have been formulated in the sections before (see Appendix 5 for a summary). The theorems provide specific definitions and descriptions of the theory's elements and their relations as well as propositions and explanations concerning the dynamic processes leading to the continuation of hierarchy.

In Section 3.8 it will be argued that *ethics* is an integral part of social reality as well as an integral part of the scientific reasoning about social reality. In particular, it will be demonstrated that within social sciences any investigation or research design (as well as any analysis of data or recommendations) will be interest-based and value-laden. Overall, it will be shown that *social science is applied ethics.*

Finally, Section 3.9 will provide a very brief comparison of the theory developed here with two prominent theories that also address system-people relationships and the persistence of social systems: Giddens's structuration theory and Sidanius' social dominance theory.

3.2   THE CORE STRUCTURE OF ALL HIERARCHICAL SOCIAL RELATIONSHIPS

In the social realm, 'hierarchy' is primarily *not* a functional or technical organisation of abstract elements; it relates *people* and it defines *social* relationships. Hierarchical social relationships can emerge in various ways. For example, there can be an initial event, a first encounter, when people who do not know each other consciously or unconsciously establish a hierarchical social relationship either via some crude physical action (e.g., fight, bodily intimidation) or via more sublime (socio-)psychological processes of signalling and perceiving dominance or obedience. Moreover, there may also be socioculturally defined aspects in play that contribute to people showing signs of superiority and inferiority. Such aspects can be *anything*: race, gender, age, physical appearance, symbols, attitudes, behaviour, intellect, ability and keenness to communicate—or whatever might be interpreted as 'higher' in a particular social context.

However, people often find themselves in situations where a hierarchical social order has already been established. Throughout their life, they encounter institutions and organisations that are structured quite hierarchically (e.g., family, nursery, school, army, university, and public- or private-sector organisations). Hence, they experience hierarchies as fully developed and elaborate systems into which they must fit. In Section 3.6 further analysis of mechanisms such as 'socialisation' and 'adaptation' will shed more light on such processes. But, again, it is *people* who represent the existing order (with the help of a whole range of means) and who show the newcomer where his or her place is, how to function, and how to behave.

Whether a hierarchical social relationship has just emerged or is predefined by some institutional context, this 'special relationship' is based first and foremost on the principle of *inequality*. It is a relationship of rights and duties allocated *deliberately unequally;* 'hierarchy' stands for dominating and obeying, giving and receiving orders (nowadays often called 'advice,' 'support,' 'help,' or 'guidance'), controlling and being controlled, telling and being told, guiding and being guided, leading and being led, having and not having, exploiting and being exploited. It is the fundamental idea and key characteristic of hierarchy that privileges and prerogatives are allocated unequally amongst members of the social system according to a system of social rank—whatever the specific criteria this is based on. Hierarchy means the systematic introduction, establishment, maintenance, and ideological justification of *social inequalities* between individuals or groups of people (Diefenbach 2009a, p. 126; Sidanius et al. 2004; Levy et al. 2001, p. 10; Sidanius and Pratto 1999; Pollitt 1990, p. 6; Shrivastava 1986, p. 365;

Abercrombie et al. 1980, p. 130; Mousnier 1973; Laumann et al. 1971). Thus, with regard to the model to be developed, it can be noted:

> Theorem 1: In the social realm, hierarchy represents social relationships based on the principle of inequality—i.e., rights and duties are allocated deliberately unequally.

A 'relationship' means that at least two elements are linked, or related to each other in certain ways. In the case of social relationships the elements are *specific or constructed actors* such as individuals, groups, or larger social aggregates (e.g., organisations, social classes, or even nation states) (Scott 1990, p. 61; Mosca 1971, p. 252).[1] Via hierarchy, actors inherit the social positions of either superiority or inferiority. Throughout this investigation, 'superior(s)' and 'subordinate(s)' will be used as general terms for the varying statuses and positions of the actors involved in any kind of unequal social relationship. 'Superiors' are those actors within the hierarchical relationship whose decisions and actions others have to take into account as a 'given.' 'Subordinates' are these others—i.e., actors whose decisions and actions are influenced by their 'superiors' and may change accordingly; usually, superiors and subordinates are intertwined in dynamic processes of actions and (anticipated) reactions. Within a hierarchical system, most situations are defined by such dynamic hierarchical relationships of superior(s) and subordinate(s).

People are seen as either superior or inferior solely because of the notion of hierarchical relationships. If there were a different understanding and a different social system, for example an egalitarian one, people's individual differences would *not* transform into (notions of) superiority and inferiority. But, in hierarchical social relationships—and *only* in hierarchical social relationships—they do.[2] It is social labelling based on the idea of inequality that makes one person (allegedly) more 'superior' than the other. The unequal relationship between at least one superior and one subordinate is the nucleus of any hierarchical social order. In this sense, one might say:

> Theorem 2: At its core, any hierarchical social order is defined by *dynamic hierarchical relationships between at least two specific or constructed actors*—'superior(s)' and 'subordinate(s)'—who inherit different social positions of superiority and inferiority.

Nonetheless, such a proposition is *not* meant to suggest that complex hierarchical social systems are dichotomic—i.e., that there are only two distinctive (groups of) actors (e.g., superiors and subordinates). This would only be the case in a truly dyadic hierarchical system (e.g., a relationship, marriage, or partnership of two based on the principle of inequality). In general—i.e., for any hierarchical system that comprises two *or more* actors—the superior-subordinate relationship is understood as a *relational* construct. 'Relational' means that actors are superior or subordinate with regard to others—which implies, first, that within any complex hierarchical social system there are many (layers of) individuals or groups of people who are superiors and subordinates to each other and, second, that every actor can be in one moment superior and in the next subordinate. People may dominate in one group but be followers in another. When people are 'superior' or 'subordinate' depends on the specific situation, the actual people involved, and other relevant criteria such as institutional context. For example, superiors very often become subordinates when they leave one office and enter another. In changing circumstances, people almost instantly change their behaviour, even switch their identities—which is part of the classic notion of authoritarianism: 'a tendency to be dominant toward one's inferiors and submissive toward one's superiors' (Adorno 1950, referred to in Ashforth 1994, p. 760). Laurent (1978, p. 221) described this (schizophrenic) system of relative superiority and subordination and the (schizophrenic) people within it quite poignantly:

> Every manager is a Janus head; depending upon the angle from which we look at him or her, we will see alternatively the autonomous leader or the dependent follower. The former can be seen as a unique totality, the latter as a subservient part. The organizational existence of the manager is contingent upon the coexistence of other Janus heads above and below.

With such a relational perspective it becomes clear(er) that the hierarchical construction and justification of social reality is primarily about creating and maintaining social differences between individuals and groups (Laumann et al. 1971). All in all, it might be proposed that:

> Theorem 3: The superior-subordinate relationship is a *relational* construct—i.e, within complex hierarchical systems all actors are either superior or subordinate to at least one other actor, depending on the actual situation.[3]

The specific characters of 'the' superior and 'the' subordinate depend on the actual situation as well as the historical context. For example, people can be superior or subordinate because of formal (and highly formalised) roles such as monarch and vassal, priest and believer, master and slave, aristocrat and peasant, landlord and tenant, capitalist and worker, manager and employee. But there can also be biological, physical, cultural, psychological, sociological, or material factors that make people either superior or subordinate, such as gender, physiognomy, nationality, personality traits, class, or income—or a hundred others. Whatever the factual or constructed specific factor that is used as the criterion of differentiation, the factor establishes a *power differential*—i.e., it makes one actor more powerful than the other actor. Hierarchy is closely related to *power and control*—with necessity (Brown et al. 2010; Clegg et al. 2006; Barker 1993). The inequality between superior and subordinate can only last because there is a power differential between the two. Power is a constitutive part of direct social relations between people, but especially a structural component of hierarchical social relationships, in order to institutionalise and legitimise this very hierarchical relation and the roles and positions of the parties involved as superiors or subordinates (Turner 2005, p. 2; Spierenburg 2004, p. 627; Finkelstein 1992, p. 508; Willmott 1987, p. 253; Zeitlin 1974, p. 1090).

Power, as is widely known, is a multidimensional phenomenon. For example, in his ground-breaking work, Lukes (1974, pp. 11–25) identified three different dimensions of power: the one-dimensional view (behavioural—i.e., when one person has power over another person); the two-dimensional view (institutional—i.e., when the values and beliefs of a person or group of people have become the prevailing ones of a social system); and the three-dimensional view (hegemonic—i.e., when even the subordinates think that the prevailing norms and values reflect their interests). Multidimensional concepts (based on Lukes's and others' work) have also been developed (Diefenbach et al. 2009; Clegg et al. 2006). We will come back to such multidimensional understandings later, when the model becomes more differentiated.

For the time being—i.e., with regard to the core model of hierarchical relationships—only the first dimension of power needs to be addressed. According to Max Weber's famous definition in 1921, power means 'any ability to impose one's own will in a social relationship, even against opposition, regardless of what this ability is based on' (1980, p. 28, my translation). The 'ability to impose one's own will' is largely interpreted as the ability to directly influence and control the actions and nonactions of others. This is where Robert A. Dahl's classic definition of power (1957, cited in Lukes 1974, pp. 11–2) is even clearer: 'A has powers over B to the extent that he can get B to do something that B would not otherwise do.' In this sense, it can be formulated:

Theorem 4: The superior-subordinate relationship is defined primarily by a *power differential* through which the former can impose his/her will on the latter directly or indirectly, even against opposition.

Within established hierarchical systems, the 'enforcement' of the special relationship between superiors and subordinates can happen via *formal* and/ or *informal* means. So far (e.g., in most parts of management and organisation studies), 'hierarchy' has been understood (and analysed) largely as *formal* hierarchy and has been used almost synonymously with organisation; formal organisation means hierarchy—and hierarchy means formal organisation. In the tradition of Weber and his description of bureaucracy (1980, p. 124), 'hierarchy' can be seen as vertical *formal* integration of official positions within one explicit organisational structure whereby each position or office is under the control and supervision of a higher one. In a formal hierarchy, the official roles and positions of all members of the system are clearly defined and demarcated from each other (Finkelstein 1992, p. 508; Willmott 1987, p. 253). Person-independent rules create a stratified system of social positions—i.e., people are put in unequal relations to each other via an anonymous or abstract order. Although it is a *social* order that defines social relationships, it exists partly on its own—and in it its own right. Hence:

Theorem 5: Hierarchy can be a *formal order* of unequal person-independent roles and positions that are related to each other via direct lines of top-down command-and-control within an explicitly defined organisational structure.

Nevertheless, people can be in vertical social relationships not only via anonymous or official rule systems but also via unofficial mechanisms. These mechanisms can be found particularly in the area of social interaction (e.g., norms and values, attitudes and behaviours, physical action and inter-action, verbal communication and discourses). Such processes are highly person-dependent (Zenger et al. 2001, p. 2), i.e., they are informal. According to such an understanding, *informal* hierarchy can be defined as follows:

Theorem 6: Hierarchy can be an *informal order* of unequal person-dependent social relationships of dominance and subordination that emerge from social interaction and may become persistent over time through repeated social processes (e.g., communication and routine behaviour).

Altogether, the core model describes hierarchy as *a system of formal and/ or informal social relationships that are based on the principle of inequality and a power differential between at least one superior and one subordinate.* Figure 3.1 displays the core model visually.

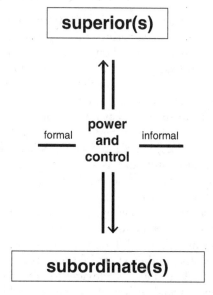

Figure 3.1 The core structure of any hierarchical social relationship.

Of course, social reality is complex—and always more complex than our theories or models suggest. Larger social systems, such as organisations and societies, comprise many layers and clusters of social groups—for example, different classes or levels of management and employees (Currie and Procter 2005; Floyd and Wooldridge 1994, 1992; Jaques 1990; Mousnier 1973). In addition, modern societies became more patchwork-like and fluid (while keeping traditional principles, structures, and processes of stratification and discrimination). Moreover, social groups or classes are usually not homogenous but rather quite differentiated in themselves, comprising subgroups, shifting constellations, and changing alliances. Clashes between and within ruling elites are as ubiquitous as division amongst the oppressed (Hambrick 2007; Diefenbach 2005; Mintzberg 1985; Hambrick and Mason 1984).

This means that in any complex hierarchical social system there are countless core structures representing hierarchical social relationships. They overlap, are connected to each other, and together form larger patterns and structures (while at the same time some social relationships might *not* show this superior-subordinate constellation). Complex social systems have many features and institutions—and we will come back to them when the core model is developed further. But what makes the core model so important is that it highlights the most typical characteristic of hierarchical social systems: the fundamental principle that makes them work.

3.3   PEOPLE'S MINDSETS AND SOCIAL ACTIONS

3.3.1   Identities, Emotions, Interests, and Moral Character

As one can easily imagine, because of their different positions and statuses within the hierarchical system, superiors and subordinates have quite different views on the world in general and on the social system in particular. This section will more closely examine why and how superiors' and subordinates' social actions, interests, identities, emotions, and moral characters are relevant to the constitution, continuation, and, hence, persistence of hierarchy.

In certain ways, social reality exists and is objective. It exists *as such* as concrete phenomena (e.g., the man-made material world and built environment, products and services, people and people's behaviour, language and communication, virtual reality) and as abstract entities (e.g., numbers and symbols, written or otherwise conserved language). Artefacts continue to represent social reality even when there are no people. At the same time, 'reality' (especially social 'reality') is also subjective, constructed, and reconstructed by people; phenomena and artefacts carry a meaning (or different meanings) or are meaningful to different people in different ways. People perceive, interpret, shape, and even create social reality according to their social and cultural backgrounds, worldviews, experiences, emotions, and thoughts. In this sense, social reality, including hierarchical and nonhierarchical social relationships, happens to a great extent in people's minds. As Laurent (1978, p. 221) concluded so poignantly concerning organisational hierarchy, 'The pyramid is well grounded in everybody's mind.'

This is the core of the problem of hierarchy's persistence: *hierarchy is in people's heads,* in the ways superiors and subordinates see themselves and others, make sense of the world, and, as a consequence, act in it. People *first* create and reproduce hierarchy in their minds *and then* behave and talk accordingly. All external use of power and force; all silly 'pomp and circumstance' and ridiculous symbols and ceremonies, all ideological 'explanations' and 'justifications' of hierarchy, all actual attitudes and behaviours, as strongly and routinely held as they might be—all of these are only secondary compared to people's minds. Most people are physically (and legally) free, but their minds are imprisoned. If one wants to understand why the core model of hierarchical social order works so 'well'—i.e., why the system of superiors and subordinates continues to function 'well' regardless of the actual situational and historical context—one needs to start with the view that hierarchy is first and foremost a sociopsychological issue:

Theorem 7: Hierarchy is first and foremost in people's *minds.*

What is going on in people's minds is crucial—because how people make sense of themselves and others as well as of the (social and natural) world in general influences how they act.[4]

In order to get a more differentiated picture, people's minds will be divided into four elements: 1) identity, 2) interests, 3) emotions, and 4) moral character. This division follows the three classical (Western) philosophical questions concerning the individual and his or her place and role in the world and complements them by adding 'emotions' as a fourth fundamental question of human existence: 1) 'Who am I?', 2) 'What do I want?', 3) 'How do I feel?', and 4) 'What shall I do?'. They mean in particular:

1) *Who am I?* How people see the world and act within it depends to some extent on how they see themselves (in isolation and amongst others)—i.e., it is linked to their 'identities' (Musson and Duberley 2007; Elstak and Van Riel 2005; Gabriel 1999; Ashforth and Mael 1989; Tajfel and Turner 1979). Since humans usually exist and develop amongst others (i.e., within social communities), human identity is largely a 'social identity' (or a pattern of different social identities). According to Tajfel (1978b, p. 63), social identity can be understood as that part of an individual's self-concept 'which derives from his knowledge of his membership of a social group (or groups) together with the value and emotional significance attached to that membership.' An individual's self-image stems from his/her social and cultural background, roles and positions, rights and duties, and privileges and prerogatives in a given social system. In this sense, a person's identity

is (also) relative to the social context and to other actors (Sluss and Ashforth 2007). Therefore, it comprises characteristics that are quite persistent and (almost) nonnegotiable self-image(s) of the individual as well as aspects that are relational and change according to the situational context people find themselves in (Tajfel and Turner 1979).

2) *What do I want?* Whatever their roles and positions are, people usually actively take part in a social system via their thoughts, words, and deeds. People think, talk, and act consciously and/or unconsciously. If they focus on something (or someone) consciously, they have an 'interest' in it (Darke and Chaiken 2005; Hendry 2005; Meglino and Korsgaard 2004; Moore and Loewenstein 2004; Miller 1999; Suttle 1987).[5] 'Having an interest' in something (or someone) means a person's or group of people's conscious attraction towards a certain object or objective. This can mean either a (noninstrumental) curiosity in something or an (instrumental) desire to achieve something whereby the understanding of the object or the realisation of the objective is deemed by the person or group of people as useful, advantageous or otherwise 'desirable' (after due consideration). Because of their interests (besides other relevant factors), people see things in certain ways and act accordingly (Meglino and Korsgaard 2004; Hindess 1986). In this sense, interests are one of the key elements of people's mindset.

3) *How do I feel?* Whereas interests may cover the more conscious and partly rational aspects of human reasoning and acting that take shape largely after due consideration, 'emotions' (Lazarus 1991; Hochschild 1983; Kemper 1978a) address mental states that arise more spontaneously and that are accompanied, perhaps even triggered, by physiological and/or neural changes.[6] However, Kemper (1991, 1978a, 1978b) proposed that, in addition to physiological and psychological aspects, emotions are also the outcome of sociological aspects, especially power and status (Stets and Asencio 2008). He therefore noted (1978b, p. 31) that there is also a '*social* context for emotions since it is mainly other actors who provide the positive and negative reinforcements in the course of interaction'. For example, Mignocac and Herrbach (2004, p. 221) explained that 'Work often has an affective dimension: anxiety due to the threat of redundancy, happiness after the successful completion of a project, anger or resentment towards one's supervisor, jealousy of a promoted coworker, pressure-related stress are but a few of the affective states that can be experienced at work.' 'Emotions' influence human reasoning, decision-making, and acting—and probably to a larger extent than many approaches consider; 'emotions are a powerful force in the structure and change of societies' (Scheff 2000, p. 84). In this sense, 'emotions' will be an explicit element of the model developed here and are regarded as an integral part of social relationships that covers all the phenomena that influence people's mental states.

4) *What shall I do?* Finally, it is acknowledged that people also make sense of everything (and everyone) in terms of 'right' and 'wrong.' How people think and act depends to a great extent on their values and convictions—i.e., their morality or 'moral character'. According to Pervin (1994, p. 108), moral character can be defined as an individual's disposition to demonstrate a consistent pattern of moral behaviour across a range of situations. In order to discuss differences in people's moral behaviour—or the morality or immorality of their thoughts and deeds—Kohlberg's 'stages of moral development' will sometimes be used (O'Fallon and Butterfield 2005; Rahim et el. 1999; Maclagan 1996; Crain 1985; Kohlberg and Wasserman 1980; Kohlberg and Hersh 1977; Kohlberg 1973).[7]

In order to differentiate aspects of people's minds analytically, and to indicate that the mind is not one (consistent) entity but a complex phenomenon comprising different elements, instead of 'mind' the term 'mindset' will be used throughout this book.

Altogether, the core model of hierarchical social order becomes more differentiated when superiors' and subordinates' mindsets are an explicit part. With the inclusion of people's identities, emotions, interests, and moral characters, one can get a better understanding of why and how hierarchy works—and continues to work because of these elements. They are a 'normal' part of our construction and sense-making of the world—of the social construction of reality (Berger and Luckmann 1966). With regard to the further development of the core model of persistence of hierarchical social order, it therefore can be concluded that:

Theorem 8: Superiors and subordinates have *specific mindsets* that can be differentiated analytically into identities, interests, emotions, and moral character.

Social roles and positions (besides other factors) change the way people see and interpret things. The same issue looks very different depending on whether it is seen from a superior's or from a subordinate's point of view. In this sense, people's mindsets are largely shaped by their social roles and positions. With regard to the model of the direct relationship between superiors and subordinates, it can be suggested:

Theorem 9: Superiors' and subordinates' identities, interests, emotions, and moral characters are shaped by their different roles and positions within the hierarchical social order.

At the same time, superiors' and subordinates' mindsets (besides other factors) shape their *social actions*. According to Max Weber (1980, p. 11), 'social actions' (or inaction or toleration) take into account the past, present, and even (assumed) future actions and attitudes of others—i.e., they happen in the social realm. Hence, 'social action' can be understood as people's conscious and unconscious, verbal and nonverbal attitudes, behaviours, actions, or interactions that have relevance or even consequences for others—whether intended or unintended. Social action can, but does not necessarily, take place in the immediate (physical) presence of others. Nowadays it can happen in very far-removed places or increasingly in the virtual presence of others (e.g., internet-based communication, and personal and mass media). Social action means one's being and acting (or not acting) in the world. Whatever the circumstances of the actual situation or the wider context, it is people's mindsets that drive their social actions. In this sense it can be proposed:

> Theorem 10: Superiors' and subordinates' mindsets shape their social actions.

From a *practical* point of view, one can say that people's identities, interests, emotions, and moral characters shape how they see and interpret the world; these form people's ideas, behaviour, decisions, and actions. From a *theoretical* point of view, one can say that the different elements of people's mindsets represent crucial explanatory links between context, people's reasoning, their decisions, and their actions.

Putting all this together, the simplified core of the model developed here so far proposes that people's social roles and positions shape their mindsets and their mindsets shape their social actions. Figure 3.2 shows these links.

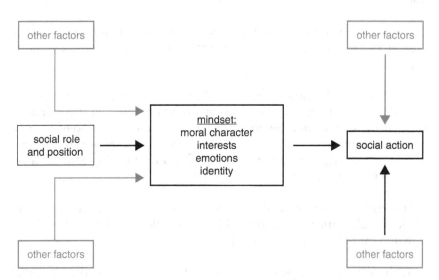

Figure 3.2   Direct relationships between people's social roles, mindsets, and social actions.

The links from social role/position via mindset to people's social actions definitely entail some cause-and-effect relationships. It should be noted, though, that these direct links are only *one* aspect of the complex relationship between social roles, people, and people's actions. Thus, the model developed so far should be regarded only as an intermediate or partial result. In the next sections, it will be differentiated further by adding more elements as well as more relations among them.

Nevertheless, it is an important aspect of social systems and social life that people's social roles and positions shape their identities, interests, emotions, and moral character, and, as a consequence, to a great extent their social actions. Figure 3.3 shows a slightly more differentiated model of the superior-subordinate relationship.

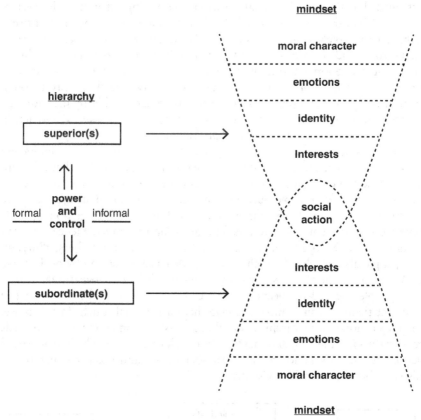

Figure 3.3 Differentiated superior–subordinate relationship.

3.3.2 Determinism, Individual Freedom, Reflexivity, and Responsibility

Social systems, and in particular hierarchical social systems, usually provide robust structures and processes that guide people's reasoning and actions (though perhaps in different ways and to varying intensities, depending on the type of system and actors in question). Hierarchical relationships represent comprehensive frameworks for how people think and act according to their roles and positions within the system (and what happens if they behave or don't behave as expected).

However, a theory based only on the assumption that people's social positions (almost) determine the way they think, feel and act (e.g., causal determinism) would be too simplistic and 'mechanistic.' It would be not very different from positivistic social theories or functionalistic managerial concepts that claim that politicians, managers, and employees (only) do what is officially portrayed as their functions—and that any deviance from these public images is an exception that proves the rule. In contrast, here it is assumed that the specific social positions people inherit in a social system such as a hierarchy shape their behaviour to some extent but not entirely. Whatever people's situation, there is *always* some leeway. Whether their social roles and positions are superior or subordinate, people have always room for discretion—and they make use of it consciously or unconsciously on a daily basis in order to do things and to navigate their way through institutions and social relationships. There is something highly individualistic about how people make sense of phenomena, make decisions, and act. In other words, there is always *individual freedom*.

Individual freedom means not only that people are aware of the limits *and* opportunities their social positions provide for them but also that they take into account (some) consequences of their reasoning and acting—i.e., they *reflect* on some actual or possible outcomes of their actions. Humans are 'reflective practitioners' (Schön 1983) within certain settings. Via their actions, people reflect on their identities, interests, emotions, and morality. Hence, one can assume *feedback loops* from people's social actions to their mindsets; while acting, people also develop (and change) as persons (this notion obviously refers to Argyris and Schön's 1978 theory of single- and double-loop learning). Moreover, people might also reflect on their social roles and positions—i.e., they (re) interpret them (within limits) and give them a personal touch. In this sense, the direct model of hierarchical social relationships can be extended towards *reflexivity*—i.e., the idea that there are feedback loops leading back from social actions to people's mindsets and their social roles and positions. Figure 3.4 displays these relationships visually.

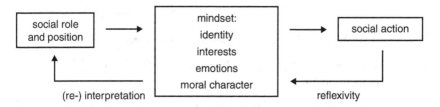

Figure 3.4   Feedback loops between people's social roles, mindsets and social actions.

Moreover, feedback loops suggest that individual freedom and individual reflexivity mean *individual responsibility,* since people are aware of the possibilities as well as the outcomes of their actions. Usually, (most) people can be held responsible for what they do:[8] people are responsible for (the pursuit of) their interests; how they interpret, shape, and develop their identities; their emotional behaviour; which norms and values they adhere to; and which decisions and social actions they do or do not take. Thus, the inclusion of feedback loops in the model of people's social roles and positions, mindsets, and social actions provides a crucial basis for: 1) addressing *individual freedom,* which can explain individual differences in people's thoughts and deeds within a social context; 2) stressing *individual reflexivity* as the foundation for individual behaviour and development; and 3) acknowledging and assessing *individual responsibility* with regard to how individual freedom is used. Accordingly, with regard to the model developed so far, it can be suggested that:

> Theorem 11: Within any social system, individuals always enjoy a certain degree of *individual freedom,* (are able to) reflect on their actions and the situation they are in *(reflexivity),* and, thus, carry *individual responsibility* for how they think and act.

3.4   BASIC DYNAMIC PROCESSES

3.4.1   Routine Behaviour and Boundary Crossing

As outlined above, people's mindsets (i.e., their identities, emotions, interests, and moral character) trigger and shape their social actions within a certain social context, in this case hierarchical social order. As reflective practitioners with grades of individual freedom, superiors and subordinates can demonstrate both *routine behaviour* ('routines') and *deviant behaviour* ('deviance' or 'boundary crossing').

Compared to the more complex issues of deviance and boundary crossing, routine behaviour does not represent much of a problem (at least not for the proponents of an existing order; for those who want system change it is a *big* problem, indeed). Most routines—i.e., any repetitive pattern of behaviour or events (Howard-Grenville 2005)—that are related to the roles and positions of people within a (hierarchical) social system might be called 'tasks.' Routine behaviour then means the fulfillment of those tasks: conscious or unconscious performing and functioning according to the requirements of a given system and within the parameters set by the system.

In this sense, routine behaviour represents not just *any* pattern of behaviour but the application of the prevailing logic and principles of the social system. In a hierarchical system, these are principles of domination and obedience; it is the task of the superior to dominate (and to carry out routinely all related tasks) and it is the task of the subordinate to obey (and to carry out routinely all related tasks). The fulfillment of these tasks makes sense for both of them because this is what their social roles and positions require (and what others expect). In this sense, there is no need to think in more fundamental terms about one's status or tasks or about the principles of the hierarchical social relationship. Superiors and subordinates function routinely and, in so doing, reinforce the very hierarchical social system that makes them function. Routine behaviour contributes considerably to the stability and continuation of hierarchy and to its structures and processes, since it happens largely without reflection on fundamental issues. It therefore can be said that:

> Theorem 12: Most of superiors' and subordinates' *routine behaviour* is about applying the prevailing principle of hierarchical systems—i.e., about carrying out their primary and related tasks to dominate and to obey, respectively.

But there is, of course, not only routine behaviour. One could say that routine behaviour happens within *boundaries*. Within the social realm, a 'boundary' is very similar to a 'norm'—i.e., 'a standard or rule, regulating behaviour in a social setting' (Jary and Jary 2005, p. 424). A boundary can be understood as a formal or informal social norm concerning what is (or is not) 'allowed,' 'appropriate,' and 'acceptable' (Andersson and Pearson 1999, p. 452). Nonetheless, in contrast to 'norms' (which are more accurately '*shared* beliefs' and, at least officially, *unite* people), 'boundaries' primarily *divide* people, their actions, and their worldviews.

Boundaries exist particularly in the context of hierarchical social systems. Here, boundaries represent 'social and cultural barriers between dominant elites and subordinates' (Scott 1990, p. 132). They define, confine, and demarcate not only the positions and statuses of superiors and subordinates but also their roles and responsibilities and their privileges and prerogatives. Most of people's ways of thinking and acting and their mindsets and social actions are defined and shaped by boundaries. Hierarchical social order, like any social system, functions mainly because boundaries are accepted, adhered to, and confirmed on a daily basis by all parties involved—at least officially. People act in circumscribed ways that uphold the specific expectations for social action that are attached to their positions (Biggart and Hamilton 1984, p. 543). It is much about what one can do and what one cannot—or must not—do in public (i.e., in the presence of 'the other').

At the same time, besides their public face, subordinates *and* superiors nurture beliefs and self-images and carry out activities that are hidden from others—especially 'the other side.' Besides their 'public transcripts,' people have comprehensively developed 'hidden transcripts' (Scott 1990). Scott defined the public transcript as 'the open interaction between subordinates and those who dominate' (p. 2) and the hidden transcript as 'discourse that takes place "offstage," beyond direct observation by powerholders' (p. 4). Boundaries, hence, are crucial for the relationship between superiors and subordinates. They play a key role in terms of the pursuit and conduct of their public *and* hidden transcripts—as well as in terms of keeping those two areas apart; hidden transcripts must be kept hidden since they otherwise could disturb or even upset the social order. A boundary is the line drawn into the sand that one must not cross.

But this is what people do in the social sphere: they (try or pretend to) comply with rules and expectations, *and* they cross boundaries. According to Scott (1990), boundary crossing means that hidden phenomena such as actions or beliefs ('transcripts') come into the public domain—i.e., become known to other parties. In this sense, when thoughts and deeds which are usually kept hidden become public, they go against what is otherwise regarded as 'normal' and are potentially upsetting. Consequently, 'boundary crossing' can be understood as *any noncompliance with prevailing norms, values, and/or expectations of others involved in a specific social situation.*

Boundary crossings can happen *in all areas*—i.e., social actions, interests, emotions, identities, and moral character:

- Perhaps the most obvious cases of boundary crossings can be found in the area of *social action.* For example, saying things that shouldn't be said in a particular situation, symbolic acts or gestures, and doing things that are not allowed all constitute acts of boundary crossing.

- In a similar way, people should show (or make claims regarding) the 'right' *interests,* especially those that correspond with their social roles and positions. Yet, their actual interests can be quite different and if they surface they may clash quite seriously with what is expected and accepted.

- This is equally true concerning people's *emotions.* Very often, the social context, the people involved, and the issues in question decide what are the 'right' emotions people should, or even must, show. If people do not show these emotions, or do not show them in the right way or at the right intensity, others will perceive this as inappropriate.

- Social *identities,* too, have to accord with what is expected; in every social system there are usually more or less developed repertoires concerning the identity of role-holders—i.e., what is, or should be, a 'good' superior and a 'good' subordinate. However, people's actual (self-) concepts and identities do not necessarily correspond with those images.

- This, finally, also suggests that there can be quite fundamental differences between the norms and values that are communicated and praised officially and superiors' and subordinates' actual *moral characters.*

Whether it is people's social actions, interests, emotions, identities, or moral character; boundary crossings are nothing unusual. On the contrary, whether in daily battles at an individual level, in groups of people trying to pursue their specific goals within a certain social context, or in class struggles on a historical scale, boundaries are being challenged, shifted, and crossed almost constantly (Passini and Morselli 2010, 2009). As Barrington Moore (cited in Scott 1990, p. 192) explained:

> In any stratified society there is a set of limits on what [. . .] dominant and subordinate groups can do. [. . .] What takes place, however, is a kind of continual probing to find out what they can get away with and discover the limits of obedience and disobedience.

Public transcripts complement each other and hidden transcripts are kept away from the public as much as possible, but *both* play important parts with regard to the functioning, stabilisation, and continuation of the social system. Thus, it can be said:

> Theorem 13: Superiors' and subordinates' *deviating* mindsets and social actions (*boundary crossings* between hidden and public transcripts) are a normal part of any hierarchical social order.

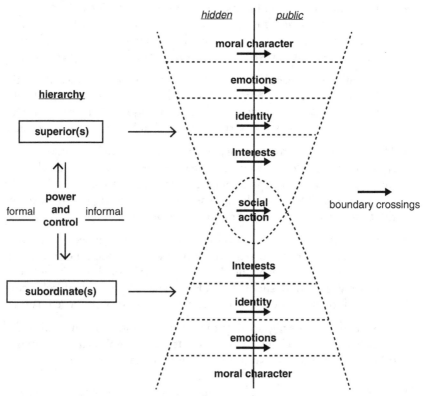

Figure 3.5   Boundary crossings between public and hidden transcripts.

However, *any* boundary crossing will bear more or less serious consequences for the parties involved as well as for the whole social system, though with different implications and intensities. Superiors' and subordinates' *deviations* from expected social actions, accepted interests, prescribed identities, or prevailing norms and values not only challenge but also often re-establish or even strengthen hierarchical social order.[9]

All in all, it can be concluded that the hierarchical relationship between superiors and subordinates is a multidimensional social system of different areas separated and held together by boundaries between public and hidden transcripts that can be crossed. Figure 3.5 displays the idea of boundary crossings visually and adds it to the model developed so far.

3.4.2 Multiple Processes

At face value, hierarchical social order seems to be a relatively static system of superiors' and subordinates' compatible, synchronised, and mutually supporting routine behaviours. Nevertheless, it can also been seen as a fairly dynamic system that is almost constantly challenged and confirmed via multiple processes of crossing and re-establishing boundaries. These dynamic processes unfold as shorter or longer sequences spanning several differing areas, such as sense-making and the actions of the actors involved. In complex social systems, there are usually quite a few of these sequences happening at any given time.

Such multiple dynamic processes of social interaction between superior(s) and subordinate(s) (or within those groups) can be positive or negative for the parties involved as well as the whole social system. According to social exchange theory (Blau 1964) and the concept of reciprocity (Gouldner 1960), positive action can trigger a similar response and can lead to a 'pattern of mutually contingent exchange of gratifications' (Gouldner 1960, p. 161). Yet, within a hierarchical system, most boundary crossings representing positive deviations do not last long. For example, overperformance by subordinates might initially prompt rewards but will probably raise the expected level of performance in the future. It then will cease to be deviant behaviour and will become routine. As another example, within a strictly hierarchical organisation, a superior's *laissez-faire* leadership style could be seen as positive deviance. Yet it could also be perceived by subordinates not as empowering but as a sign of weakness or lack of interest by the superior. This may simply be exploited by (some) subordinates; alternatively, subordinates might demonstrate a truly strong and independent identity, but then be either reduced again to 'good' (i.e., obedient) subordinates or forced to leave.

Generally speaking, *positive* deviance from norms or expectations does not automatically trigger (multiple processes of) positive actions and reactions, as the theory or common sense may suggest. On the contrary, it might even produce *negative* responses or neutralise the positive deviance by 'normalising' it. But, however the actual sequence unfolds, multiple processes of positive boundary crossings (including negative consequences for some of the actors involved) usually do not threaten the stability of the system.

In contrast, multiple processes of *negative* boundary crossings might represent more serious challenges not only for the people involved but also for the whole system. The widely known 'tit-for-tat' strategy is such an example of 'negative' norms of reciprocity—i.e. 'in sentiments of retaliation where the emphasis is placed not on the return of the benefits but on the return of injuries' (Gouldner 1960, p. 172). It is quite common that a boundary crossing that has either real or perceived negative implications or consequences for others may trigger (multiple) processes of 'retaliation' or 'revenge.' If, for example, subordinates publicly disobey an order, this likely not only triggers negative social actions from their superiors (i.e., immediate punishment) but also possibly lead to questioning of the leading norms and values of the system. Moreover, there is a high chance that (some or many) superiors would take such behaviour personally—i.e., they would see their status and identity as superiors as being challenged. As a consequence, superiors may fight back not only in practical terms but also on ideological and personal grounds. This, in return, may be perceived by their subordinates as patronising or intimidating, and may lead to further negative (even more severe and cunning) actions, with a high probability of further counteractions on the side of the superior(s).

As this example shows, the problem with multiple processes of negative boundary crossings is that they can increase in intensity. A negative boundary crossing might lead to longer-lasting processes during which reciprocal and mutually reinforcing behaviours become a vicious circle of increasingly stronger actions and counteractions with increasingly negative consequences for some or even all parties involved ('conflict escalation'—Zapf and Gross 2001, pp. 499–504; Andersson and Pearson 1999, p. 458; Wall and Callister 1995, p. 529; Ashforth 1994, pp. 770–1; Collinson 1994, p. 51; Kim and Smith 1993, p. 38).

This is exactly what superiors *do not* want; there should be only *one* conflict escalation *ever:* when the superior struggled to become superior. As soon as the superior succeeded in getting and establishing his or her role and position, there should be only two types of conflict: internal conflicts the superior chooses to create and to fight (e.g., with other superiors concerning available resources or with a subordinate who has been singled out as a black sheep) and conflicts with external forces (the 'evil-doers'), which can be quite convenient in order to draw attention away from internal problems. All other conflicts are not in the interest of the superior, since escalation of conflict constitutes a real danger for him/her (and other proponents of hierarchical social order); without further intervention, conflict escalation can easily get out of control. At the end of this escalatory path there can be only one result: the end of the system and, hence, the end of the superior's reign. It therefore shall be proposed:

Theorem 14: Negative boundary crossings can lead to *dynamic multiple processes* and an *escalation of conflict* that increasingly threatens the stability and continuation of the system of hierarchical social order and, more crucially, the role and position of the superior(s).

3.4.3 The Emergence and Continuation of Abstract Organisational Order

The brief discussion of routine behaviour and boundary crossing as well as of multiple processes in the sections above indicated another key characteristic of hierarchical social order. Besides the original power differential between superior(s) and subordinate(s), it is especially the dynamic aspects that unfold within that unequal relationship that contribute to the persistence of the hierarchical system. For example, routine behaviour is not only about the completion of current tasks. It is the nature of routines that they prompt expectations and anticipations that the same reasoning and actions will reoccur (under the same or similar circumstances), even if there are different people involved (a different superior or subordinate). This is crucial. At first, superiors and subordinates have a *direct* unequal relationship because of a power differential (as the core model of hierarchical social order shows). And *direct* power (and control) works quite well in many respects. But, with the possibility that routine behaviour will continue even in the face of a replacement of the actual superior and/or subordinate, the direct hierarchical social relationship between superior and subordinate changes into an *abstract organisational order:* what used to be specific interests of particular individuals now appears to be the interests of role-holders, what used to be individual identities is now portrayed as the identity of 'the' superior and 'the' subordinate, what used to be individual emotions is now 'emotional intelligence,' what used to be individual opinions and beliefs is now prevailing norms and values, and what used to be individual behaviour carried out by particular people becomes a faceless functioning within the parameters and requirements set by an abstract system. This is what abstract organisational order does to a hierarchical social relationship: superiors' and subordinates' ways of thinking and acting come to represent general patterns and characteristics of 'the' superior and 'the' subordinate—whomever those actual people are or might be.

Theorem 15: Because of expectations that routine behaviour will continue even when people are replaced, the direct hierarchical social relationship between superiors and subordinates changes into *abstract organisational order* and their ways of thinking and acting come to represent general and anonymous characteristics of 'the' superior and 'the' subordinate.

The transformation of direct hierarchical social relationships into abstract organisational order can take on many forms. 'Abstract organisational order' can mean 'organisation' as the term is often understood—i.e., private- or public-sector organisations. But it can also mean nongovernmental organisations, political parties, charities, social enterprises, temple communities, religious orders, and monasteries. Moreover, abstract organisational order is also exemplified by rules and regulations, rituals, or ceremonies. And it is represented by even larger institutions and megastructures, such as fiefdoms, monarchies, the modern nation state and its institutions, or supranational organisations.

These examples show that abstract organisational order is meant to do much more than manage superiors' and subordinates' routine behaviour. In Section 3.4.2 it was argued that deviance/boundary crossing can lead to dynamic multiple processes and an escalation of conflict that can threaten the stability and continuation of the whole system as well as superiors' positions within that system. With the emergence (or at least the possibility of) conflict escalation, superiors realise that multiple processes of boundary crossing can be quite unpredictable and threatening. They are not fully controllable with the existing *direct* power and control superiors have over their subordinates. Superiors, therefore, introduce additional systems and measures of *indirect* power and control—for example, a new layer of hierarchy comprising positions with the task of supervising, controlling, managing, and punishing (other) subordinates (e.g., foremen, lower managers); special units whose task it is to keep subordinates in line (e.g., educational institutions, law-enforcement units, personnel departments); or policies and procedures that guarantee subordinates' functioning and behaving well (e.g., especially data-gathering and surveillance systems, performance-measurement and management systems, and control and punishment systems).

In this sense, abstract organisational order not only stabilises routine behaviour and handles (particularly subordinates') deviant behaviour but also supports and further strengthens superiors' positions, concentrating even more power and resources in *their* hands and serving *their* interests (Lacey 2007, p. 133). It provides *massive* leverage in terms of superiors' power and capabilities of ruling and controlling their subordinates. Abstract organisational order not only means the transformation of the direct hierarchical relationship between specific superiors and subordinates into general and abstract patterns but also (and especially) the institutionalisation of superiors' direct power. It might therefore be said:

Theorem 16: Abstract organisational order is the extension and institutionalisation of superiors' direct power by other means.

Of course, abstract organisational order, however comprehensive and sophisticated its measures might be, does not, and cannot stop, (multiple processes of) deviance and boundary crossings. What abstract organisational order does is to define, organise, and handle deviance. This creates two paradoxes.

One is that, although by definition deviance goes against the established order, it has to fit into the prevailing framework of definitions, understandings, and ways of doing things in order to be identified as deviant behaviour. Every order creates its own opposition. Only when deviant behaviour/boundary crossing is recognised as such by the established order (and handled accordingly) does it 'exist.' For example, the actions of Robin Hood and his band of 'merry men' could only be identified as deviant behaviour because they lived within a certain area, probably Nottinghamshire, where laws explicitly defined the concept of the 'outlaw'. Moreover, the laws dictated that Robin Hood's approach of 'robbing from the rich and giving to the poor' was illegal whereas the Sheriff's approach of 'robbing from the poor and giving to himself and his entourage' was legal or legalised. In this sense, one might say that, via the introduction of abstract organisational order, not only the right routine behaviour but also deviant behaviour and boundary crossing become institutionalised.

The second paradox is that, although abstract organisational order is introduced to reduce (or at least to handle) deviance, it actually creates *more* deviant and opposing actions. It does so especially via its rules and regulations, which define not only what is or should be but also what should *not* be. And there are always more possibilities in the latter category. For example, in the medieval period and later, Christian belief came with comprehensive and minute catechisms and guidelines about how to conduct the 'right life.' But over time, the rules and regulations with regard to what were portrayed as 'non-Christian beliefs' or even heresy became even more comprehensive. Over several centuries the Inquisition went to great lengths to define, identify, and punish all sorts of deviance, opposition, and other unwelcomed behaviours. At the end, it could have been (almost) anything—and in large parts of medieval Europe the dungeons and torture chambers of the Inquisition were full of 'heretics.'

With regard to these two paradoxes it can be formulated:

Theorem 17: Via abstract organisational order, existing forms of deviant behaviour and multiple processes of boundary crossings are defined, organised, and managed—and new ones are created.

This shows that abstract organisational order is not a static system that, once designed at the drawing board, will remain unchanged. Hierarchical social order based on a direct power differential *and* abstract organisational order is quite a dynamic, self-reinforcing system. The additional organisational elements (such as rules and regulations or layers of formal organisational structures and processes) especially provide new opportunities for dynamic multiple processes to unfold *in addition to* the direct ones already happening. The abstract principles and measures themselves become part of those processes and might be changed and developed further. Moreover, new components might be added each time there is a perception that there is a need for them. Thus, the organisational elements of hierarchy become more numerous, and more comprehensive and detailed. *Expansion* is built into the blueprint of hierarchical social order. Whether expansion is intended or not, it *will* expand over time.

> Theorem 18: Any system of hierarchical social order *will expand over time*—i.e., will become more comprehensive and thorough because of the introduction of abstract organisational order and the processes it triggers.

But abstract organisational order does even more. Hierarchical social order is already problematic in and of itself because it is created primarily for the *specific* interests of *certain* people. Hierarchy is particularly designed to provide superiors and members of power elites with advanced positions and power as well as a whole range of opportunities, privileges, and prerogatives that come with their social positions. In contrast, subordinates do not have these advantages simply because they are subordinates.

This is the nature of hierarchy—and abstract organisational order shall represent this unequal social relationship. Abstract organisational structures and processes, rules and regulations, and policies and procedures are *especially* designed to mirror the direct hierarchical relationship and power differential between superiors and subordinates. Because of this, abstract organisational order very often cannot deliver what it could or even should do—for example, provide efficient, fair, and just rules and regulations and policies and procedures. As long as direct hierarchical relationships constitute the prevailing social order, any abstract organisational order will be designed and maintained largely according to superiors' individual and group interests (Dillard et al. 2004, p. 10), though it will not *appear* as such. Abstract organisational order *seems* to be merely functional and is deliberately portrayed and justified as such, when it is in fact an abstract *social* order that repeats, constitutes, and protects at a more general level what were originally direct, power-based, unequal, and unjust relationships between individuals. Hence, as soon as direct hierarchical social relationships are institutionalised as abstract organisational order, the realisation of individual and group interests happens largely in disguise. The institutionalisation of unequal and unjust direct hierarchical relationships as abstract organisational order (while at the same time the latter disguises this fact) is one of the key problems of humanity. In other words:

> Theorem 19: The institutionalisation of the direct, hierarchical, unequal, and unjust relationship between superiors and subordinates as abstract organisational order means the disguised institutionalisation of superiors' individual and group interests.

This differentiated model of hierarchical social order is displayed visually in Figure 3.6.

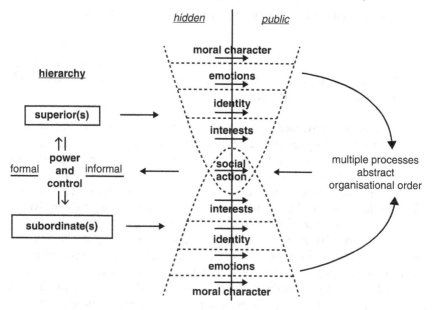

Figure 3.6 Emergence of abstract organisational order.

3.4.4 Individual Freedom, Responsibility, and Accountability

One could assume that the emergence of abstract organisational order means a reduction of individual freedom and responsibility on the one hand and an increase in individual accountability on the other. In this way of thinking, while rules and regulations limit people's elbow room, explicit and detailed policies and procedures free them from individual responsibilities but more sophisticated performance-measurement and control systems hold them more accountable. Thus, people are reduced merely to functioning elements. However, the picture is more differentiated.

Since abstract organisational order is designed primarily according to *superiors'* interests and maintained in order to continue direct hierarchical relationships of power and control with other means, individual freedom is *reduced* on the side of the subordinates. Rules and regulations become more numerous and more detailed the further one looks down the hierarchical ladder. It is subordinates' primary task to comply with whatever they have to comply with, and in this sense their individual freedom and responsibility are reduced indeed. The situation is different, though, when it comes to subordinates' individual accountability. Organisational principles of achieving, functioning, and efficiency put the burden of demonstrating performance and producing data about it especially on the shoulders of the subordinate. Within a hierarchical framework, performance-measurement and management systems never hold superiors accountable, always subordinates, because it is in principle the former who ask for results and the latter who have to deliver them. Thus, individual accountability is *increased* for subordinates.

> Theorem 20: With the introduction of abstract organisational order, subordinates' individual freedom and responsibility *decrease* but their individual accountability *increases*.

For superiors, however, it is a very different story. For them, abstract organisational order provides *additional* opportunities because it is they who formulate the principles and details of the systems, they who supervise the systems' realisation and they who are provided with more tools of control and sanctioning. Hence, their individual freedom and individual responsibility are *increased* rather than reduced. At the same time, their individual accountability is *reduced*. Officially, they are, of course, still responsible—in theoretical terms as well as according to their own rhetoric. They, therefore, do not refuse the idea of being held accountable. In practical terms, however, it is a different story; if something goes wrong, superiors usually have little difficulty in finding a scapegoat. And the more comprehensive structures and processes, policies and procedures are in place, the more opportunities superiors have, if necessary, to minimise the role they played and to point the finger at others. As a consequence, the larger the abstract organisational order, the less superiors are held accountable—while at the same time they are provided with even more opportunities, individual freedom, and responsibilities. But this is exactly what has been intended from the very beginning; abstract organisational order is the logical extension of the direct hierarchical relationship between superiors and subordinates. Abstract organisational order is tailor-made for superiors' and ruling elites' individual and group interests.

> Theorem 21: With the introduction of abstract organisational order, superiors' individual freedom and responsibility *increase* whereas their individual accountability *decreases*.

3.5   SOCIETAL DIMENSIONS OF HIERARCHICAL SOCIAL ORDER: INSTITUTIONS AND RESOURCES

3.5.1   Societal Institutions and Resources

Altogether, 1) the direct power differential between superiors and subordinates, 2) the dynamic processes of routine and deviant behaviour that exist between them, and 3) the abstract organisational order that institutionalises their direct unequal relationship represent an *autopoietic and self-sufficient system*—a system famously exemplified in Daniel Defoe's depiction of Robinson Crusoe and his companion, 'Friday,' on a remote tropical island. Nonetheless, in contrast to this fictional case, most (hierarchical) social systems and their members are usually part of larger social entities, for example a society. This means that superiors' social dominance and the direct hierarchical social relationship between superiors and subordinates are also based on a whole range of *societal institutions and resources*.[10] The most relevant institutions and resources might be grouped and listed as follows (Diefenbach 2009a, p. 126; Sidanius et al. 2004; Levy et al. 2001, p. 10; Sidanius and Pratto 1999; Beetham 1991, pp. 48–50; Pollitt 1990, p. 6; Shrivastava 1986, p. 365; Willmott 1984, p. 361; Abercrombie et al. 1980, p. 130):

1) *Material, economic:* land, property, goods; money, financial assets; income allocation, modes of production; dissemination and consumption.

2) *Legal:* rights, duties, ownership, entitlements.

3) *Sociocultural::* norms and values, ideology, tradition; positions, status, tasks, functions; artefacts, symbols, rites, rituals; information, knowledge; social background, upbringing, memberships; social infrastructure (e.g., education, health care), public life.

4) *Political:* constitution, political actors, and agendas.

5) *Technological:* access to and knowledge of technologies.

6) *Environmental:* physical and virtual entities, locations and spaces.

7) *Organisational:* institutions as 'organisations' that deal with all the issues stated in 1)–6)—i.e., government and governmental institutions, nongovernmental organisations, private organisations (e.g., companies), public-sector organisations (e.g., schools, prisons, hospitals, higher-education institutions), courts and other legal institutions, political parties.

There is not enough space to discuss all of them. However, it will be shown that at least some material, economic, legal, and sociocultural institutions and resources contribute quite considerably to the differentiation between superiors and subordinates and between ruling elites and common people. It will be demonstrated that especially the proponents of a hierarchical social order can usually tap into a whole range of quite different institutions and resources in order to secure the long-term existence of the system—as well as their positions within it.

3.5.2 Some Material, Economic, and Legal Institutions and Resources

Land has always been important for humans since territory meant access to hunting grounds, food and water, and other physical and even spiritual resources; territory made the difference between survival and disappearance. It was therefore often disputed. In this sense, it meant not only material but also social dominance. And, with the first signs proclaiming 'This is our land!' (e.g., paintings on mountain rocks indicating a spiritual site, artefacts signalling boundaries, a fence made of branches protecting a certain area, or traces of human activities), land became an *institution*. Power over territory was often achieved via physical force, but it was increasingly accompanied by the concept of ownership—and ownership became the new superiority.

Moreover, with the emergence of farming and settlements, land also increasingly became economically important. Traditionally, land has been named as the first economic resource (or 'factor of production'), probably because (classical) economics began during a time when the ownership of land, and gains from what could be produced on it, meant wealth. It demonstrated superiority and social dominance not only in a physical/spatial sense but also in a sociocultural sense—and it became even more protected. People had only to *look* at the fenced-off property in order to know that the people who owned it were rich and powerful.

Whether from an anthropological or economic point of view, land, and especially the appropriation of land (wrongful appropriation in most instances), has contributed decisively to the emergence of superior-subordinate relationships, with whoever grabbed the land (by whatever means) becoming superior(s) and others becoming their subordinates. For most of human history, the unequal distribution of land and property has been one of the primary sources of social inequality: of unjustified and extravagant privileges on the one hand and undeserved and widespread misery on the other. For example, in his 'The Future Progress of the Human Mind,' Marquis de Condorcet (1795, cited in Kramnick 1995, p. 31) criticised those,

> Who live either on revenue from land, or on the interest on capital, which is almost independent of their own labor. Here then is a necessary cause of inequality, of dependence and even of misery, which ceaselessly threatens the most numerous and most active class in our society.

However, with the Industrial Revolution and the emergence of capitalism, it soon became clear that not land *per se* but the ownership of the *means of production* that was crucial for accumulating wealth, gaining privileges and demonstrating social dominance. For example, Burnham (1941, p. 155) defined 'ruling class' as

> The group of persons which has (as a matter of *fact,* not necessarily of law or words or theory), as against the rest of the population, a special degree of control over access to the instruments of production and preferential treatment in the distribution of the products of those instruments.

As a consequence, the ruling elites' attention turned to technology, machinery, and factories. And, again, most if not all of the ownership of, access to, and use of these 'modern' means of production was allocated unequally— *extremely* unequally. A single owner of a factory commanded and exploited hundreds if not thousands of people—of course, with the help of a few layers of semiprivileged watchdogs in between and with all the means and institutions of control and oppression economically developed societies can provide. Economic activities were institutionalised as certain types of ownership and production; some social groups managed to become in charge of the new economic means and resources (owners, managers, financial investors) whereas others were only allowed to fit into the systems designed by their superiors (tenants, employees, consumers).

But it is not only material resources and economic activities that make a difference. Members of any power elite have another economic tool with which to underline, secure, and increase their status and social position: *money*. As Mills (1956, p. 346) put it so poignantly about American society, 'Whenever the standards of the moneyed life prevail, the man [and woman] with money, no matter how he [or she] got it, will eventually be respected.' Money makes everyone who has got it superior—and it makes everyone who is in need of it subordinate. For those who have plenty of it, it turns society into one big opportunity where everything is possible: 'Money—sheer, naked, vulgar money—has with few exceptions won its possessors entrance anywhere and everywhere into American society' (Mills 1956, p. 50). Whether in terms of living conditions, education, health, the whole range of mundane leisure time activities, or even beauty, intelligence, personality, and character, those who are higher up the hierarchical ladder in financial terms will have more of everything, are able to enjoy more things, and can make use of societal institutions at a scale that changes their lives and life chances *fundamentally for the better*. The 'haves' can exert social influence and enjoy social wealth, the 'have nots' can't—it is as simple as that. In all countries of the world, societal institutions and resources, services and activities are always more accessible and available for the rich than for the poor (Mosca 1971, p. 260). Mills (1956, p. 163), therefore, was absolutely right when he criticised the idea that being rich allegedly does not make one happier:

> The idea that the millionaire finds nothing but a sad, empty place at the top of this society, the idea that the rich do not know what to do with their money, the idea that the successful become filled up with futility, and that those born successful are poor and little as well as rich—the idea, in short, of the disconsolateness of the rich—is, in the main, merely a way by which those who are not rich reconcile themselves to the fact. Wealth in America is directly gratifying and directly leads to many further gratifications.

That 'money can't buy you happiness' is one big lie used as rhetoric equally by the rich who are keen to enjoy their material wealth without interference, by the aspiring middle classes who want to cover their egoistic and primarily material ambitions, and by those who cannot change their poor living conditions to assuage their desperation. Although the positions of the rich and the poor are diametrically opposed, most of them agree at least on this spin to manipulate their own and public opinion about social reality.

Of course, material, economic, and financial assets can also constitute problems for their owners. For example, in his 'Discourse on the Origin of Inequality,' Jean-Jacques Rousseau (1755, referred to in Kramnick 1995, p. 427) rightly criticised most wealth of the rich as 'usurpation' for which there had originally been neither a legal basis nor moral justification. Members of the ruling elites have always been very aware of this problem, and of the danger that others may start to realise that 'something is rotten in the state of Denmark.' Hence, in every culture superiors have been keen to give their institutions, resources, privileges, and prerogatives the appearance of legality, even legal entitlement. And usually they find ways to do so; if an elite has been ruling for a longer time, its members manage to get into place all those constitutional rights, laws, and law enforcements that especially protect the possession of material, economic, and financial assets—*their* assets. In any stratified society, the law provides all means necessary to guarantee and protect the power and wealth of the ruling elites and their supporters.

Over time, in countries with a tradition of private ownership, the basic issues (such as possession of land and property, ownership of material and immaterial means of production, and the right to claim the returns) are so institutionalised and legalised that hardly anyone questions them anymore. But even in transitional economies such as former or current communist countries, elites' gaining ownership of everything of any worth has been wrapped into 'legal' frameworks within an astonishingly short period of time. As soon as such issues are legalised, the rich (private persons as well as large and influential organisations) do not need to justify ownership and (their) private wealth anymore. They can then focus more on twisting, bending, shaping, circumventing, and exploiting existing laws for their direct benefit (Mills 1956, p. 99)—which is even more efficient. And, if this is still not enough, they can formulate additional policies and regulations that are tailor-made for their specific purposes. Needless to say, this, again, is only the prerogative of superiors. The task of subordinates is primarily confined to obeying the law (Beetham 1991, p. 67)—but this is what is expected from them concerning every societal institution and resource, anyway.

3.5.3   Sociocultural Institutions and Resources

Material resources, economic conditions, and legal institutions play a crucial part in establishing social dominance and inequality. Beetham (1991, p. 48) even went so far to say that 'dominance and subordination are constituted in the first place through the possession of, and exclusion from a key material resource, and by the rules that determine these respective conditions.' However, although the material or 'objective' phenomena might constitute and shape large parts of social reality, it matters even more how people perceive, interpret, and make sense of these issues (see Section 3.3.1). Theorem 7 proposed quite explicitly that 'hierarchy is first and foremost in people's *minds*.' In addition to physical and factual aspects and mechanisms, hierarchy and social dominance are 'mind games.'

This is where *sociocultural institutions and resources* come into play; they give everything (additional) meaning and, in doing so, contribute to the forming of people's minds, behaviours, and actions. For example, if someone does not know the meaning of a fence, they see it only as an obstacle and physical challenge to climb over it. But, if someone knows the sociocultural meaning of a fence, they will also worry about the possible consequences of climbing over it. If someone has been made a 'good' (i.e., submissive and functioning) subordinate, they will not climb over the fence but remain in awe and wonder outside the estate—or, even worse, they will protect the fence against others (perhaps even with their own life) and will even take pride in doing so.

The strongest sociocultural institution one can imagine is 'norms' and 'values'.[11] Norms and values are the prevailing social standards of thought and behaviour in a given social system that indicate how and what people ought to think and what people should or should not do under specific circumstances (Dequech 2006, p. 473). Norms and values give sense to everything; in any social system, the most fundamental and general norms and values provide, for all members, explanations and justifications of the natural and social world, the system, its corresponding institutions, and people's behaviour. In so doing, they also create and protect the fundamental ideas and principles a society, organisation, or group is based on as well as the way(s) in which they are explained, justified, maintained, and put into practice every day.

Norms and values shape *all* parts of people's mindsets (Hamilton 1987, p. 38); although individuals have their own views, opinions, beliefs, and convictions, much of their morality and interests—even identities and emotions—are influenced (if not created and maintained by) comprehensive and well-developed sets of collectively held norms and values. The prevailing arrangements of social structures and processes would hardly be stable over a long period of time if they were not based on and supported by deeply held beliefs and worldviews, and by norms and values that members of a given social system have internalised and share to some extent.

If norms and values claim to provide not just 'a' but 'the only possible' view of things and the conduct of social affairs, they might be called 'ideology' (Diefenbach 2007, 2009a; Brookfield 2005; Abercrombie 1980). They prescribe how natural or social reality *ought* to be and they claim that this is 'the best,' if not to say 'the only', way that reality can (even should be) designed and maintained. Conservative ideologies explain and justify 'the way things are,' and why they will not change and must not change. They prescribe how social reality ought to be, prescribe what is appropriate behaviour, and even outline what happens (whether in this or another life) if people do not behave accordingly.

In most social systems there is usually one 'dominant ideology' (Abercrombie et al. 1980) representing 'the beliefs which dominant groups hold and disseminate' (p. 130). In stratified societies, the *ideology of hierarchy* is the dominant ideology. As outlined in Section 2.2, every hierarchical social system comes with elaborated systems of justification and legitimatisation. Ideology explains where hierarchy comes from, how it is structured and functions, and why it is 'the best of all possible worlds.' Hierarchical systems are justified in the name of the stars, destiny, God, morale, natural laws, historical laws, functionality, efficiency, productivity, justice, the markets, or whatever the ruling *few* picked as the leading principles—and *everyone* is expected to live accordingly. The ideology of hierarchy provides reasons for why the social system is as it is, why certain groups and individuals inherit certain positions and functions, and why certain groups and individuals enjoy particular privileges and prerogatives and carry out specific tasks and duties within the system. The ideology is about the goodness and rightness of hierarchical order as a functional and social system, about its superiority to other possible designs, and about why it is good for people. It is primarily about the foundation and justification of the necessity and legitimacy of superiors' dominance, authority, privileges, and prerogatives; the need for subordinates' obedience and control; and how social systems such as groups, tribes, organisations, and whole nation states should be run and organised accordingly (Chiapello and Fairclough 2002, p. 186).

On the one hand, any ideology about a hierarchical social order is *exclusive*—i.e., it tries to justify the separation of superiors from their subordinates (why members of the ruling elite are 'different' and why the ruling elite is a 'members only' club). On the other hand, the ideology is *inclusive*—i.e., it tries to create common interests between superiors and subordinates (e.g., facing a common enemy, sharing the same destiny, or having other things in common). It is therefore accompanied by an ideology of 'the collective,' to give subordinates the *feeling* of belonging to the same entity. This can be anything (team, family, organisation, tribe, nation, or a people or race) but it must help to keep superiors and subordinates apart and together at the same time. Even if superiors and subordinates have their own separate and distinct values and belief systems (e.g., an elite ideology and a working-class ideology), they nonetheless will share the key features of the dominant ideology, which explains why one group dominates and another is dominated, why superiors are higher up and subordinates lower down the hierarchical ladder, and why the former give orders and the latter take orders (Chiapello and Fairclough 2002, p. 187). The ideology of hierarchy provides elaborated explanations and legitimisation for hierarchical social order as social normality. In doing so, it contributes a lot to the stability and continuity of hierarchy (Mast et al. 2010, p. 461).

Although superiors' and subordinates' ideologies are very different, and serve very different group interests, they nonetheless *complement each other* and jointly work towards *one* common goal: to explain and justify unequal social structures and group-based hierarchies (Zaleznik 1989, pp. 149–50; Abercrombie et al. 1980, p. 143). Based on Sidanius et al.'s (2004) social dominance theory, O'Brien and Crandall (2005, pp. 4–5) argued that

Dominant and subordinate groups alike actively participate in and contribute to subordination. Both groups justify the presence of group-based inequality with legitimising myths. The legitimising myths consist of attitudes, values, beliefs, stereotypes, and ideologies that provide moral and intellectual justification for the social practices that distribute social value within the social system.

The dominant belief system is re-established and reconfirmed on a daily basis by people's social actions, which enact their interests and identities—usually without them being fully aware of which values and ideas they actually reproduce in their daily routines (Brookfield 2005, p. 67). Because of dominant ideology, people do the things they do without really knowing *why* they do them and why they are convinced that this is 'the right way' to do them.[12]

This is also due to the fact that within a particular hierarchical social system people's unequal positions, tasks, and functions are justified and protected by a culture-specific ideology of 'merits' and 'virtues.' These (alleged) traits and aspects materialise as 'status.' In a hierarchical social system, higher positions—as well as the persons who inherit those positions!—are ascribed higher status (and greater importance). As Ravlin and Thomas (2005, p. 968) explained:

> Cultures, societies, or smaller aggregates associate certain concepts, objects, and events with high quality or value [. . .], as opposed to lower quality or value, and to the extent that these concepts, objects, or events are associated with an individual, that person takes on a higher status value.

For example, managers do not only have power because of their *actual* roles and positions within an organisation; they also incorporate and represent the very idea of 'the manager' and 'management.' Such ideas are communicated and legitimised by ideological frameworks and a whole range of societal institutions on a daily basis; economic theories, management theories and organisation concepts, business schools, politicians, business associations, consultants, and media all praise the status and importance of managers and management (Diefenbach 2009a; Watson 2006; Akella 2003; Willmott 1987, 1984; Burawoy 1985; Rosen 1984; Burnham 1941). Senior managers, business leaders, and entrepreneurs have attained an image and social status similar to priests, knights, and army officers have had in other epochs and societies. 'Management,' and the alleged competence and necessity of 'managers,' is a high-status societal institution.

Elevated positions like that of 'the manager' (often ranked explicitly or implicitly against other managers) can be found in every stratified society. In every hierarchical social system, the higher a position is located, the greater the power and influence that come with it. Higher-status positions emerge particularly where those special tasks and functions are carried out that are portrayed as the most important ones within a given cultural context. These tasks usually have to do with sense-making and sense-giving—for example, reading the stars, interpreting oracles, conveying divine messages, outlining holy scripts, developing a battle plan, giving the queen's speech, drafting political manifestos, giving movements direction, making sense of the business environment, analysing financial or market data, formulating strategies, or providing leadership. In every stratified society, those who carry out such tasks and functions (often as a calling, not because of fairly mundane reasons—so they say) are provided with higher status, privileges, and prerogatives. Such positive discrimination increases social differences and transforms them into persistent social strata. Individuals' elevated positions become an 'institution' because those individuals do what the society and the people (allegedly) need most.

Furthermore, the higher a position is, the more important are the tasks and responsibilities associated with it. Since these tasks are 'so important,' only members of the ruling elites, or at least highly ranked superiors, are allowed to carry them out (especially when the tasks and functions carry high symbolic meaning, such as rites and rituals). For example, in monarchies it is often a member of the royal family who opens a new national museum and hands it over to the public, only the priest can pass around the chalice in churches, only the president of the International Olympic Committee can declare the Games open, and it is the CEO of a company who presses the 'start' button for a new production line. In a hierarchical system, only the highest superiors are allowed to perform such highly symbolic acts.

In addition, in order to signal and underline the higher status of superiors' positions and functions (and of the actual people carrying out them), countless artefacts and symbols serve as constant reminders: insignia and seals, flags and colours, epaulettes, medals, gowns, job titles, company cars, office size, and personal parking spaces. Very often, rites and rituals come together with artefacts and symbols to define social situations in a way that leaves people with little option other than to perform role-plays. As strange and antiquated as many of these measures may look, they are there for a reason; they symbolically underline superiors' higher position, force people to re-enact leaders' and followers' positions and functions within the system, and, in doing so, re-establish the superior–subordinate relationship in countless little acts on a daily basis. Rites and rituals, and artefacts and symbols are mostly there in order to signal, strengthen and secure vertical social differentiation.

And it works. Most members of hierarchical systems usually take these artefacts and symbols, and rites and rituals quite seriously—and they have good reasons to do so. For example, all the pomp and circumstance of England's monarchy and its Houses of Parliament may look quite silly and ridiculous—but only to the outsider. For the people entrenched in this radical form of superior–subordinate relationship, the minutely prescribed rites and rituals are *very* serious; one wrong step (literally) and one might be out.

As pathetic as such a system and its rituals might be, it produces exactly the results intended; it strengthens superiors' power and status, and it conditions and infantilises subordinates, not only during the actual ceremony but also way beyond, before and after the specific event.

But rites and rituals, signs and symbols of status differentiation are not confined to official ceremonies or special events such as Remembrance Day. They are also deeply embedded in our daily lives and can come in quite unspectacular forms: from talking about the right wine for a meal to wearing clothes of certain brands or being a member of a particular sports club, all sorts and forms of etiquette and a thousand other little signs meaningful and relevant within a certain cultural context (also) carry symbolic messages— whether deliberately or accidentally, consciously or unconsciously. They indicate a person's social status and background and differentiate people along hierarchical lines. Within a stratified society, (almost) everyone has the chance to demonstrate, via symbolic means, his or her superiority to those who are further down the pecking order and (almost) everyone has the duty to show the expected signs of obedience. Hence, the symbolic re-enactment of hierarchical social relationships via regular rites and rituals and always-present artefacts and symbols means that the ideological foundations of hierarchy (superiors' superiority and privileged positions as well as subordinates' inferiority and lower positions) are propagated on a daily basis. Crucially, it is not a single rite or ritual, artefact or symbol that achieves this but the combined and constant presence of a whole range of these means that adds up to a *consistent framework of symbolically institutionalised social dominance and obedience.*

Handling all the artefacts and symbols, and rites and rituals 'in the right way' and carrying out all the special tasks and functions associated with a higher position satisfactorily requires one thing especially: the 'right knowledge'—i.e., the knowledge that differentiates superiors from subordinates, leaders from followers, and members of the ruling elites from other classes.

However, the 'right knowledge' is institutionalised—i.e., access to it is controlled and limited. This may sound paradoxical, since nowadays most of us live in information societies and much knowledge about how to become a (better) superior or even leader is publicly available (e.g., management theories and concepts, theories about leadership and biographies of successful leaders, courses and seminars in personal development, and practical guides teaching 'etiquette,' i.e., the right attitudes, behaviours, tastes, and conversation topics for all sorts of situations). Nevertheless, the more sophisticated and sublime parts of the 'right knowledge,' and how it can be used for certain purposes, are *not* disseminated at the same scale and publicly. Examples of such knowledge include how to represent higher social positions, how to signal that one has got the right background, how to interpret symbols of power and influence, and how to correctly carry out all rites and rituals that are especially important in the so-called higher circles of society. Such knowledge and skills cannot be found in textbooks, in management seminars, or in the curricula of common higher-education institutions. In stratified societies, this more exclusive knowledge is developed, nurtured, kept, and disseminated within *exclusive communities,* for example, religious orders, elite schools, social clubs (members only), certain formal associations, and, most crucially, informal networks. Such social institutions help their members to develop the 'right' attitudes, skills, and competences, they get them in contact with the 'right' persons, and they provide opportunities so that new members of the power elite can make their way up the ranks of society.

In modern societies, most of these institutions are no longer completely closed (or even secret) societies. At least theoretically, they are open to (almost) 'everyone.' Nonetheless, in reality the 'right' social and family background and connections to the 'right' people are still decisive elements for this type of social differentiation and advancement (Mills 1956, p. 69). If this is missing, it is very difficult, though not impossible, for individuals to progress. Such an individual can pursue his/her career and might even become a member of the power elite(s)—but he/she needs to be *much* more talented and ambitious, flexible, and calculating than those who are born to privilege.

Either way, for superiors and members of power elites, it is not so much that they need to *have* the relevant and/or the 'right' knowledge but that they are *able to access* it relatively easily. And, because of their superior position and their social interconnectedness, they have ample opportunities to do so and to use that knowledge (primarily for their own purposes). In contrast, people lower down the social ladder do not have these opportunities. For subordinates, only two types of 'knowledge' are disseminated via institutions to which the public have access: 1) functional knowledge that helps people to fill their lower positions and fulfil their tasks and 2) ideology that helps them to understand and to accept that they have these lower positions and that the fulfillment of their tasks (i.e., their functioning) is good for them as well as the system. In this sense, the famous adage 'knowledge is power!' is not quite true; 'knowledge of, and access to, the *right* knowledge is power!' might be closer to the social reality of hierarchical systems.

All in all, there are quite a few sociocultural institutions and resources that support, at the societal level, any type of hierarchical system and in particular people in higher social positions such as members of power elites and superiors:

- *norms and values,* which create and protect the notion of hierarchy, and corresponding institutions and behaviour;
- *ideology,* which justifies the foundations of the hierarchical system as well as people's unequal positions, tasks, and functions within it;
- *higher status* (and importance), which is ascribed to higher social positions and to those who inherit these positions;
- *rites and rituals,* which are carried out as ceremonial and representative tasks and functions only by members of the elites, thus underlining their higher status;

- *artefacts and symbols,* which carry and convey symbolic meaning indicating higher-status positions, constantly reminding people of the social positions of those who handle them;
- *right knowledge,* i.e., the knowledge that differentiates superiors from subordinates, leaders from followers, and members of the ruling elites from other classes, and is accessible only to the former;
- *exclusive communities* (e.g., elite schools, formal associations, and informal networks), which provide access to the 'right' knowledge and the 'right' people for members of the power elite.

3.5.4   The Systemic Nature of Societal Institutions and Resources

This brief analysis of some material, economic, legal, and sociocultural resources and institutions has shown that they correspond with the idea of hierarchy quite considerably; they strengthen superiors' and ruling elites' social positions above those of others, primarily serve those superiors' and elites' interests, and support the (further) institutionalisation of hierarchical social order as the prevailing mode of organising social affairs and people. Societal institutions and resources have a direct impact on people's power and influence, privileges and prerogatives, opportunities and even life chances; these are either better or worse depending on where people are on the social hierarchical ladder (whether people are superior or subordinate).

According to Willmott (1984, p. 361), 'The power or powerlessness of any particular group or individual is directly related to their structurally limited access to the resources needed to secure compliance with their demands.' With the inclusion of societal dimensions, it becomes clearer that it is not just the direct hierarchical relationship between superiors and subordinates that privileges the former and disadvantages the latter. In addition to superiors' and subordinates' direct power differential, their institutionalised mindsets and social actions (as routine or deviant behaviour), as well as abstract organisational order and societal institutions and resources, represent another layer of *structural* social asymmetries. As Sidanius et al. (2004, p. 847) put it, 'chronic group-based oppression is driven by systematic institutional and individual discrimination.' *Institutional discrimination* contributes considerably to the differences in conditions and consequences people experience in a hierarchical social order. In this sense it can be proposed:

Theorem 22: Any societal institution or resource positively related to the principle of hierarchical social order privileges superiors and disadvantages subordinates systematically.

This means that in any stratified, comprehensively developed society, members of the ruling elite or other dominant groups 'possess a disproportionately large share of positive social value' (Sidanius and Pratto 1999, p. 31) *across the whole range* of societal institutions and resources. They have, for example, 'political authority and power, good and plentiful food, splendid homes, the best available health care, wealth, and high social status' (Sidanius and Pratto 1999, p. 31). Obviously, all these things add up to what most would regard as 'having a very good life' in a particular sociocultural context at a particular point in time. Superiors are simply better off in absolute as well as in relative terms.

> Theorem 23: The higher people are ranked within a hierarchical system, the greater is their possession of and access to institutions and resources that enable them to pursue what is portrayed in that cultural context as a 'good' and/or 'successful' life.

Correspondingly, subordinates 'possess a disproportionately large share of negative social value, including such things as low power and social status, high risk and low-status occupations, relatively poor health care, poor food, modest or miserable homes, and severe negative sanctions' (Sidanius and Pratto 1999, pp. 31–2). They are *systematically* excluded from many of those aspects of societal institutions and resources that enable a good and successful life (Beetham 1991, pp. 48–50)—again, in relative as well as in absolute terms.

> Theorem 24: The lower people are ranked within a hierarchical system, the more they are excluded from institutions and resources that enable a 'good' and/or 'successful' life.

For every hierarchical system that is part of a stratified society, there is a complex institutional context that provides a strong framework and incentives for the hierarchical system's existence and continuation (DiMaggio and Powell 1983; Meyer and Rowan 1977; Zucker 1977). All of the institutions and resources already mentioned (and others) contribute on their own a great deal to the continuation of the social dominance of the few over the many. The ultimate source of superiors' social dominance, though, exists when all these institutions and resources are positively related to each other—i.e., when they support and complement each other. This is particularly the case in developed societies with well-regarded (or at least accepted) institutions and established actors. In this case, sociocultural, material/economic, legal, political, technological, and environmental institutions and resources fit with and complement each other, creating *one comprehensive framework* that is supportive of *any* system—as long as it is hierarchical.

> Theorem 25: In developed stratified societies, societal institutions and resources complement each other towards one comprehensive and systemic framework enabling and supporting any system of hierarchical social order.

3.6   SYSTEMISATION AND ITS MAIN MECHANISMS

In Sections 3.2 to 3.4, we saw how hierarchical social order emerges out of a direct superior-subordinate relationship. In Section 3.5 we then looked at a few of the many societal institutions and resources and how they enable and support hierarchical social relationships. It is now time to link the two—i.e., to analyse how institutions and individuals are related within hierarchical social systems.

This 'individual-system link' will be outlined in this section by describing a process I call 'systemisation.' Systemisation describes sociopsychological processes or mechanisms that link the individual and social institutions and make people able and willing to function within any kind of hierarchical social system. The process of systemisation comprises six main mechanisms, as shown in Figure 3.7.

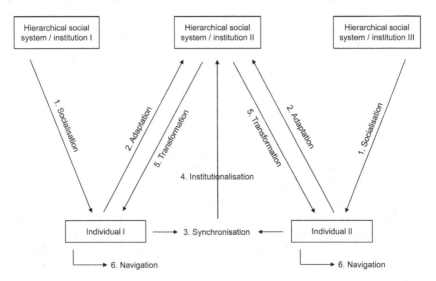

Figure 3.7   Systemisation and its main mechanisms.

The process of systemisation and its main mechanisms can be described as follows:

1. *Socialisation:* Via formal and informal processes, people are *socialised,* or conditioned, by various existing hierarchical institutions and their members—i.e., they are made increasingly able and willing to fit into established hierarchical structures and processes, and to fit into *any* kind of hierarchical social system.

2. *Adaptation:* Appropriately socialised people are keen to *adapt* actively to a hierarchically structured environment and to function smoothly in order to avoid or reduce negative consequences for themselves and

to enjoy (even increase) the advantages the hierarchical system offers in absolute and relative terms.

3. *Synchronisation:* People endeavour to *synchronise* their behaviour, decisions, and actions with others' behaviour, decisions, and actions so that routine work and life within the hierarchical system run smoothly.

4. *Institutionalisation:* People's synchronised routine behaviours and mindsets, and even most of their deviant behaviours, are *institutionalised* as abstract organisational order, which provides policies and procedures to cope with any type of behaviour and make it compatible with the system.

5. *Transformation:* Abstract organisational order feeds back into people's mindsets and social actions, and formal hierarchical organisation is *transformed* into informal hierarchical organisation and even applied in areas outside the existing (formal) hierarchical structures and processes.

6. *Navigation:* People *always* have some scope of individual freedom, which they use for *navigating* their way through institutions and social relationships.

Systemisation and its mechanisms do not only describe the links between individual reasoning and acting on the one hand and longer-lasting hierarchical social systems/societal institutions on the other. The process of systemisation represents a—if not *the*—crucial part of the explanation for why hierarchical social order persists (and even why it increases). In the following sections, the six mechanisms will be described in more detail. For the sake of keeping the argument short, these sections will only occasionally refer to people's various social roles and positions—i.e., how each of the six mechanisms might work differently for superiors and subordinates.

3.6.1   Socialisation

In the Introduction, the hierarchical social order was called the 'one great scaffolding' that has existed throughout time. It exists in various forms and might change its shape and appearance, but it nonetheless is always there; people, groups, and classes come and go but the hierarchical system and its institutions remain. For people, the hierarchical system is omnipresent: people are born into stratified societies, go through several well-established hierarchy-based and hierarchy-oriented institutions (e.g., parental care, nursery, school, college, army, university) and afterwards join hierarchical organisations (or set up their own). Even in their spare time, people are part of hierarchical social systems (e.g., family, sport club, civil society organisations). 'From the cradle to the grave'—most people spend most of their time in a hierarchical system of one form or another. They are *socialised,* if not to say conditioned, throughout their whole lives mainly in and by hierarchical institutions.

All these institutions serve different purposes, have different objectives, and contribute to the development of the individual in different ways. But they have at least one thing in common: through them, people are made to accept, to appreciate, to fit into, and to function within existing institutions. Most socialisation is about individuals not (only) having to learn the meaning of limits and restrictions and how to behave and function well within a *social* context but also about having to learn how to behave and function well within a *hierarchical* context. One might say that it is the *primary* aim of hierarchy-based socialisation to make sure that individuals function smoothly within the boundaries of the relevant institution or hierarchical social relationship as well as of *any* hierarchical social system without ever reflecting on the fundamental principles of the system.

In order to achieve this aim, within every hierarchical institution there is a whole range of formal and official as well as more informal and collegial measures and processes that work on the individual on a daily basis. These might sometimes lead to clashes, even open confrontation, but it is mostly steady, quiet, and undramatic processes that slowly shape the individual and his/her mindset and actions ('Little strokes fell big oaks'). Sooner or later, (most) people will have learned their lesson—if necessary, with the 'help' of special institutions and units that cope with 'difficult'—i.e., deviant—behaviour. And, every time an individual joins another hierarchical institution, he or she will be a little bit more able, and a little bit more willing, to blend in. It is a combination of proactive willingness and silent acceptance of one's 'destiny' that over the years turns people into domesticated pets. People call it 'experience.' In this sense, the first mechanism that enables individuals to fit into hierarchical systems is their (lifelong) *socialisation*.

Theorem 26: Via formal and informal processes, people are *socialised,* or conditioned, by various existing hierarchical institutions and their members—i.e., they are made increasingly able and willing to fit into established hierarchical structures and processes, to fit into *any* kind of hierarchical social system.

3.6.2 Adaptation

Societal institutions, and especially hierarchical systems, are large machines that socialise and condition the individual—and most experiences the individual has will reaffirm this impression; rules and norms, structures and processes, and policies and procedures have already been established and it is up to the individual to comply and to fit in. *People* have to adapt, *not* the system! As soon as an individual joins a hierarchical institution, he/she has no choice other than to (try to) fit in and, if necessary, to change. Hence, a second mechanism that makes people keen to function and to behave within a hierarchical social order is *adaptation*. Socialisation works from the system towards the individual; adaptation is the corresponding mechanism that works from the individual towards the system.

There are two main sets of reasons for individuals to adapt: *fear* and *attraction*. These two psychological motivators on the side of the individual perfectly match the usual approach of hierarchical systems and superiors to managing people by providing positive and negative sanctions, motivating with incentives and threatening with punishment (i.e., the well-known carrot-and-stick approach).

Quite understandably, coming into contact with a hierarchical system can be quite a frightening, if not to say intimidating, experience for an individual. Most hierarchical institutions appear to the individual as large, anonymous, solid, and unchangeable organisational orders. Especially when a person first becomes a member of a pre-existing hierarchical institution, everything is new to him/her: people, structures, processes, and 'how things work.' The individual does not know what is expected from him or her, nor what will happen next. This uncertainty goes together with fear of negative consequences/punishment. Especially in the beginning, people are eager to do everything right, to comply with the rules and regulations, to meet everyone's expectations, and to avoid mistakes—they have been socialised to act in such ways before. Moreover, almost every action of the individual will be followed by reactions from others: from his/her superiors but also from peers and colleagues. And most of it will be feedback that signals to the individual (directly or indirectly) what is 'appropriate' or 'inappropriate' reasoning and behaviour, often followed by some more or less severe consequences. Of course, after a while the individual will have gained some experience about how things work and how to behave within the hierarchical context. Nonetheless, although knowledge and certainty may have increased, fear of the possible negative consequences for unruly or deviant behaviour will remain. People are therefore keen to adapt—and they are immediately reminded if they don't do so.

At the same time, hierarchical systems offer a whole range of *actual advantages*. To many people, hierarchical systems are quite attractive *per se*. This is important to understand. All too often, this aspect has been underestimated, if not neglected, by more critical observers. Hierarchical systems provide, for example:

- *psychological advantages* (self-esteem, feelings of belonging, purpose, order, safety);

- *organisational advantages* (more efficient work because of division of labour, less input required, career perspectives, fewer working hours compared to other types of organisations or opportunities to earn a living, reliability of services provided by others);

- *social advantages* (status and power, privileges and prerogatives, protection against others because of rules and regulations);

- *material advantages* (access to tangible and intangible resources, higher salaries and remuneration, other benefits or incentives);

- *physical advantages* (built environment, decent workplace, health-and-safety policies).

What hierarchical systems offer reads like Maslow's pyramid (if grouped accordingly) and covers the whole 'hierarchy of needs'—even for subordinates. Of course, as discussed in Chapter 2, hierarchy provides advantages *and* disadvantages—and it does so differently for different people. Some of the largest downsides of hierarchy can be traced back to the fact that it institutionalises social inequality, oppression, and exploitation. The disadvantages are very real and can be very severe, especially for people further down the hierarchical order; some of the most common disadvantages subordinates experience on a daily basis are being the weaker link in social relationships based on a power differential; limited access to resources, privileges, and prerogatives; and reduced opportunities and life chances.

However, most people look at particular social systems in quite practical terms; they look at the benefits and advantages the system offers them, at the inconveniences and disadvantages that come with them, and at what the possible alternatives are (e.g., leaving the current social system and joining a different one). By and large, the advantages provided by the system often outweigh the disadvantages, the cost of switching systems might be too high, or people are simply too turbid to change. People's whole lives may depend to quite some extent on their belonging to a particular social system—at least in terms of what they get from it, what they do, and even who they are. Thus, for many people there are enough reasons to remain within hierarchical systems and to function smoothly.

Nonetheless, this way of viewing things might portray the whole mechanism of adaptation, or subordinates' part in it, as too passive. It is not only the actual advantages or disadvantages *as such* that make people behave. Incentives and punishment systems are meant to steer people's behaviour. Moreover, they are meant to signal to people that they can influence the situation they are in to their favour with their own behaviour; *if* people adapt and behave properly, they can reduce (some of) the disadvantages and increase (some of) the advantages. Thus, subordinates' reasoning and acting do not so much concern behaving and functioning well *per se;* rather, they are about constantly maintaining and improving the individual's situation within the hierarchical system, guided by the incentives provided by the system and/or the individual's superiors. From the individual's perspective, adaptation is an active process and makes (a lot of) sense.

Theorem 27: Appropriately socialised people are keen to *adapt* actively to a hierarchically structured environment and to function smoothly, in order to avoid or to reduce the negative consequences for themselves and to enjoy (even increase) the actual advantages the hierarchical system offers in absolute and relative terms.

3.6.3   Synchronisation

Because of their socialisation and willingness to adapt, people are not only keen to demonstrate the 'right' behaviour but also to fit their behaviour to others' ('right') behaviour. People orientate their individual reasoning and acting towards what is expected of them—or what they *think* is expected of them. Within a hierarchical social system, people (or groups of people) take into account the views and possible responses of others—even pre-emptively—mainly depending on which social positions those other people inherit (Magee and Galinsky 2008, p. 17); the higher ranked another person is, the more important and relevant are that person's views and possible responses.

Hence, although (for example) superiors' and subordinates' positions are quite different, even sometimes contradictory, they nonetheless consciously and unconsciously *synchronise* their routine behaviour; the two work together. This view is shared by Sidanius and Pratto (1999, p. 45): 'Systems of group-based social hierarchy are not maintained simply by the oppressive activities of dominants or the passive compliance of subordinates, but rather by the coordinated and collaborative activities of both dominants and subordinates.' Superiors and subordinates do not just synchronise their routine behaviour because of the expectations they have developed of each other and the tasks they have to do. The same is true concerning their specific mindsets—i.e., their interests, identities, emotions, and moral characters; they are also synchronised according to what is expected. Synchronisation is a mechanism that brings people's social actions *and* mindsets in line. It means that people develop a more or less conscious interest in their reasoning, behaviour, decisions, and actions corresponding with other members' reasoning, behaviour, decisions, and actions.

Nonetheless, synchronisation does not mean 'harmonisation' or 'harmony.' People still have their different opinions about how things could or should be done and they may clash quite severely over technical and practical issues—but this is exactly the point: because of synchronisation, *people's attention shifts away from fundamental concerns towards technicalities* of coordinating work, for example from reasoning about how a social system should be designed towards how the system can be run more efficiently. It is no longer about who should make decisions but how decisions can be made and put into practice more efficiently. Synchronisation of people's mindsets and actions prevents people from more fundamentally reflecting on, or even challenging, the principles on which their coordinated work is based. In the face of a whole range of pressing daily problems, the fundamental questions of the social system thus simply disappear, becoming mere problematic issues—at least in people's perceptions.

In this sense, because of synchronisation, superiors' and subordinates' actions do not only complement each other to a very high degree but also contribute considerably to the continuation of the hierarchical system.[13] The scope and strength of this synchronisation have regularly been underestimated by critics of hierarchical systems.

Theorem 28: People are keen to *synchronise* their reasoning, behaviour, decisions, and actions with others' reasoning, behaviour, decisionsand actions so that routine work and life within the hierarchical system run smoothly.

3.6.4 Institutionalisation

From the synchronisation of routine behaviour it is only a small, but decisive, step to its *institutionalisation* (Dillard et al. 2004; Barley and Tolbert 1997; DiMaggio and Powell 1983; Meyer and Rowan 1977; Zucker 1977). Institutionalisation means that (some) people's sense-giving schemata not only become commonly shared values but also are regarded as objectively given, unchangeable metastructures for human agency. In Section 3.4.3 we saw an example of institutionalisation—i.e., when superiors' and subordinates' direct hierarchical social relationship changes into 'abstract organisational order' because of expectations that routine behaviour will continue even when people change.

The moment a direct hierarchical relationship has been institutionalised, the hierarchical system starts to exist on its own; the hierarchical system then provides general rules and repertoires for social roles and positions, related tasks and functions, policies and procedures. It provides rules of engagement, even general and specific rules of thinking. As a consequence, what used to be the behaviour and mindsets of particular individuals is now the interests, identities, emotions, and moral character as well as corresponding actions of 'the' superior and 'the' subordinate. Individual role-holders have become replaceable—and they will be replaced if they do not function properly.

This is the difference between adaptation and institutionalisation: the former is *specific* individuals' attempts to fit into and comply with a system's requirements and to gain individual advantages; the latter is the conversion of individuals' (synchronised) behaviour into general, anonymous social rules.

Usually, institutionalisation is about (synchronised) routine behaviour. People's routines are socially accepted, even socially expected, behaviour and, in that sense, represent an institution. But there can also be deviant behaviour/boundary crossing that can be institutionalised. Of course, initially, deviance means a challenge to the existing hierarchical social order. But it can be handled in a variety of ways: via rules, regulations, policies, and procedures already in place or via new ones developed by proponents of the hierarchical system to deal with it. Either way, deviant behaviour must be managed and manageable—i.e., deviant behaviour and its handling must be, or become, part of the established order. Societal and organisational institutions of jurisdiction and law enforcement, betterment, welfare, help and support, learning, training, and personal development can be seen as measures to pre-emptively prevent (or to institutionalise) deviant behaviour and its handling. In every hierarchical social system there is a tendency to institutionalise *whatever* people do or may do until there is nothing left outside the institutions.

As a consequence of institutionalisation, people's routine behaviour, but even most of their deviating behaviour, is part of the abstract organisational order and takes place *within* the boundaries of the hierarchical system. Even if people try to deviate seriously from common practices or to change the system fundamentally, sooner or later proponents of the hierarchical social order will attempt to institutionalise these deviations. For example, 'hard' measures such as laws about outlaws, rules concerning industrial action, and emergency laws are attempts to bring social phenomena within the boundaries of the hierarchical system, where they can be coped with in 'orderly' ways. But there can also be 'soft' measures that turn deviant behaviour into common and accepted practices. The commercialisation of the 1960s and 1970s 'flower power movement' as 'retro fashion' can be seen as such an example for the institutionalisation of a once-revolutionary movement. Even behaviour that is fundamentally opposed to the existing hierarchical social order may be institutionalised, become part of the abstract organisational order and then simply contribute to a further strengthening and persistence of the hierarchical system—which is exactly the opposite of the deviants' intentions.[14] It can thus be said:

> Theorem 29: People's synchronised routine behaviour and mindsets, and even much of their deviant behaviour, are *institutionalised* as abstract organisational order, which, in return, provides policies and procedures to cope with any type of behaviour and to make it compatible with the system.

3.6.5   Transformation

Abstract organisational order—*any* abstract social order—can exist on its own, as principles, rules, and regulations made explicit and stored (e.g., as symbols painted on stone, in writing, or as stories and narratives communicated orally). But it only becomes alive when its principles and mechanisms are actually applied by people in the social realm. People do this in their daily carrying out of tasks and official conduct of office.

But there is more to it. Initially, principle(s) of *formal* hierarchical ordering provide the dominant logic. But soon people also apply the dominant principle(s) to the *informal* ordering of social structures and processes. One might say that the principles of formal ordering are *transformed* into principles of informal ordering. Transformation means that members of a social system apply its dominant formal logics in the informal organising of their social affairs.

For example, every hierarchical organisation comprises aspects of formal and informal hierarchy—but where they differ is, amongst other things, in how formal and informal hierarchy relate to each other and how the former is transformed into the latter.[15] In many traditional hierarchical organisations (especially bureaucratic/orthodox and professional organisations), the *formal principle of line management or seniority* is transformed into the *principle of informal dominance amongst equals;* people at the *same* hierarchical level do not treat each other as equals (any more) but strive for dominance and develop unequal social relationships. There is a constant and continuous hierarchical positioning going on at the same hierarchical level. Members of the hierarchical system increasingly apply its dominant logic to almost *everything,* to the way they think, act, interact, and establish and maintain their social relationships. Even in networks, which are supposed to be (almost) 'hierarchy free,' members often (unconsciously) develop the traditional roles of (informal) superior-subordinate relationships and the corresponding behaviour of dominance and obedience.

Such transformations of formal principles of hierarchical ordering into informal ones happen largely unnoticed. Many members of an organisation will not be aware of the fact that they apply its formal principles to informal structures and processes (perhaps even in their private lives). Indeed, it often might be the case that people even believe that their thoughts and deeds are in a degree of opposition to the formal order—that they change things and 'make a difference'—when, actually, their behaviour is largely a continuation of the principles of formal hierarchical ordering by other means. While people *think* they pursue their own interests and act according to their own principles, what they actually do is apply the logic of the system and, in doing so, contribute to its continuation. As a consequence, hierarchy is propagated as informal hierarchical order even in those areas that are supposed to be based on other principles. Moreover, in return, the informal hierarchical order helps to keep the formal hierarchical order working and intact. The circle is closed.

This is the fundamental difference between socialisation and transformation: socialisation focuses on getting members of a given social system to function and to demonstrate expected behaviour within its existing *formal* hierarchical structures and processes. In contrast, transformation means that members of a given social system also apply its prevailing principles *outside* the formal structures and processes—i.e., in *informal* settings. Thus, transformation is not only one of the mechanisms and reasons behind why hierarchical systems prevail but also another key component in why they *expand.* Because of the mechanism of transformation, 'expansion' is an elementary feature of any hierarchical social order.

Theorem 30: Abstract organisational order feeds back into people's mindsets and social actions: formal hierarchical organisation is *transformed* into informal hierarchical organisation and even applied in areas outside the existing (formal) hierarchical structures and processes.

3.6.6   Navigation

All the mechanisms discussed above are fairly strong, work constantly on the individual, and have a lasting impact. Moreover, they all push in the same direction: to make individuals function efficiently within the hierarchical social system and contribute to its continuing persistence:

1) *Socialisation* conditions people to the extent that most are not only able but also willing to function smoothly within any hierarchical social system.

2) *Adaptation* is the corresponding mechanism on the side of the individual—i.e., people are keen to function and to behave within a hierarchical social order in order to reduce the negative and increase the positive consequences for themselves.

3) *Synchronisation* means that people develop a more or less conscious interest in their reasoning, behaviour, decisions, and actions corresponding with other members' reasoning, behaviour, decisions, and actions.

4) *Institutionalisation* is the conversion of people's routine behaviour and also most of their deviant behaviour into abstract organisational order—i.e., anonymous and general social rules.

5) *Transformation* means that (most) members of a hierarchical system also apply the dominant principle(s) of formal hierarchical ordering to the informal ordering of social structures and processes outside formal superior-subordinate relationships.

Theoretically, these mechanisms could be all-comprising and all-inclusive. But this would only be the case in a fully totalitarian regime—a perfect Orwellian world. In reality, no hierarchical system will ever be so complete that the mechanisms would leave no room for other aspects. Systemisation and its mechanisms do not mean the (complete) disappearance of people's individuality. There are several reasons for this:

• The same mechanisms of socialisation work on everyone *differently* and people *differ* in how, and the extent to which they internalise or even oppose the values conveyed to them during the socialisation process.

• People adapt to a new hierarchical environment *as far as they have to* while at the same time they are constantly on the lookout for ways around official rules and regulations.

• Although people coordinate and synchronise their activities and behaviour (even their mindsets) with others, they also *clash with others* over their differing views and interests and try to *preserve their individuality*.

- When individuals' routine and even deviant behaviours become institutionalised and abstract organisational order starts to dominate, people remain creative, imaginative, and innovative—i.e., they find other ways of doing things that the hierarchical system and its institutions do not have in their repertoire—yet.

- Although people's informal actions are transformed by adapting formal principles of hierarchical ordering and organisation, people also show subversive tendencies and will act in formal and informal situations in ways that do not conform to the system.

Even in hierarchical systems, there is always room for individuality and, as argued in Section 3.3.2, individual freedom—i.e., room for interpretation and manoeuvre. Usually, people join a particular hierarchical system only partly (e.g., they still have their 'private lives') and/or only for a certain period of time. This means that, although people accommodate the first five mechanisms of systemisation, which make them fit in and function, they still have their own personal agendas that they try to pursue. People, so to speak, *navigate* their way through hierarchical institutions and social relationships, which means that a sixth mechanism *must* be added to the penultimate list above:

6) *Navigation* means that people move within and between hierarchical systems following their individual logics but, in doing so, contribute to the continuation of systems' logics.[16]

In this sense, it can be proposed that:

Theorem 31: People *always* have some scope of individual freedom that they use for *navigating* their way through institutions and social relationships.

All in all, the six main mechanisms of systemisation discussed above not only contribute considerably to how 'the system' and people relate to each other but also contribute to how hierarchical social order persists. The important thing to understand is that socialisation, adaptation, synchronisation, institutionalisation, transformation, and navigation *are all part of the same process*—and mutually reinforce each other: individuals are socialised by one hierarchical social system/institution, join another one, adapt and function there more or less willingly and efficiently, synchronise their behaviour with other people's behaviour, and perhaps make a small impact as some of their actions become institutionalised while at the same time they are socialised and transformed even more. In the face of all these forces working on them, individuals nonetheless try to navigate through the hierarchical structures and processes and keep that little bit of individuality until they finally leave the institution for the next one or for good. People come and go, but the hierarchical system remains.

Systemisation is the fundamental process and the reason why hierarchy has been around for so long as the (almost) eternal beast. Overall, with regard to this process, it can be put forward that:

> Theorem 32: *Systemisation and its mechanisms* make up a multidimensional and interactive process that links hierarchical institutions and individuals, ensures that people function within any kind of hierarchical system, and, in doing so, guarantees the persistence and continuation of hierarchical social order.

3.7   THE FUNCTIONING AND PERSISTENCE OF HIERARCHICAL SOCIAL ORDER

So, in general, why and how does hierarchical social order persist over time? This question has both a short answer and a longer answer. The short one is that people think and act according to the logic of hierarchy. The longer answer is provided by the theory put forward in Sections 3.2–3.6. How hierarchy functions is displayed in Figure 3.8.

Superiors' and subordinates' roles and positions, interests and ideologies, power and social actions, and thoughts and deeds differ considerably and are often in stark contrast to each other. Nonetheless, exactly this strange relationship of diametrically opposed but dialectically intertwined unequal social positions, mindsets, and actions guarantees the continuation and persistence of hierarchical social order. The main argument of the general theory of hierarchical social systems is as follows:

- *The core structure of all hierarchical social relationships (Section 3.2).* Whether as an established social order or in a new encounter, hierarchy develops as an *unequal social relationship* between 'superior(s)' and 'subordinate(s)' whereby both are understood in relational and relative terms. And, whether hierarchy is more formal or more informal, the 'special relationship' is based on a *power differential* that means that superiors can impose their will on subordinates directly or indirectly, even against the latter's opposition.

- *People's mindsets and social actions (Section 3.3).* According to their social roles and positions and based on the power differential, superiors and subordinates have different interests, identities, emotions, and moral characters ('mindsets') that influence their *social actions.* Yet, there is always individual freedom, which means that people are responsible and that their *moral character and moral development* are relevant to their mindsets and social actions. Via their behaviour, superiors and subordinates jointly create and (re-) establish a direct hierarchical relationship: the hierarchical system of superiors' dominance

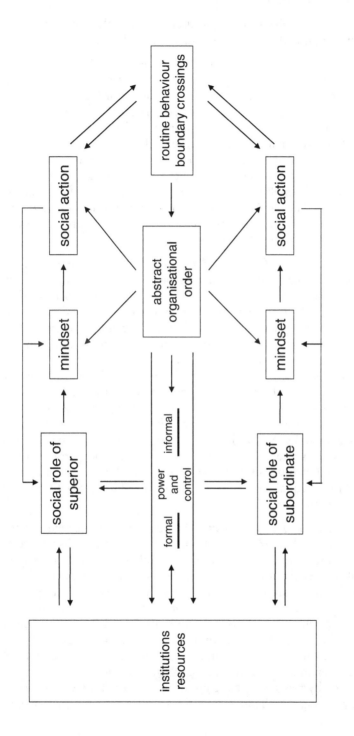

Figure 3.8　The functioning of hierarchical social order.

and subordinates' obedience. In so doing, they both contribute to the very system that makes them superior or subordinate.

- *Basic dynamic processes (Section 3.4).* Superiors' and subordinates' repeated social actions lead to *routine behaviour.* Such behaviour is expected to continue even if the superior or subordinate is replaced. Because of these expectations, the direct hierarchical social relationship develops into an *abstract organisational order;* what used to apply only to particular superiors and subordinates becomes roles, functions, and even behaviours and mindsets of 'the' superior and 'the' subordinate. Moreover, there can be deviating behaviour/*boundary crossings,* which can lead to multiple, increasingly unmanageable, and uncontrollable processes that further increase the need for abstract organisational order—i.e., systems and measures that supervise and control (especially subordinates).

- *Societal dimensions of hierarchical social order (Section 3.5).* Over time, abstract organisational order develops and diversifies into societal *institutions and resources* (material/economic, legal, sociocultural, political, technological, environmental, or organisational) that become increasingly differentiated. This is mainly a result of the constant acting and interacting of the people who run these institutions and use them for pursuing their own interests. In this way, hierarchical social order is reconstituted at several societal levels on a daily basis. At the same time, institutions and resources provide the institutional framework. In stratified societies, they privilege or disadvantage people according to their social status and position, and shape and reiterate superiors' and subordinates' social positions and factual resources, interests and identities, norms and values, and social actions and responses. In this sense, societal institutions and resources mean a further institutionalisation of the unequal and unjust social relationship between superiors and subordinates.

- *Systemisation and its mechanisms (Section 3.6).* All elements of the hierarchical social order (i.e., superiors' and subordinates' social roles and positions, moral character, mindsets and actions; abstract organisational order; institutions and resources) are connected and interrelated via several main mechanisms. These mechanisms are all part of the same overall process—*systemisation;* individuals are *socialised* by existing hierarchical institutions, *adapt* to the one(s) they are currently part of and are keen to *synchronise* their reasoning and actions with others in order to function smoothly. This leads to (further) *institutionalisation* of unequal social relationships. Individuals are then (further) *transformed* by the abstract organisational order and try to *navigate* their way through all the hierarchical institutions they encounter until they leave the system.

It is now possible to explain why hierarchical social order persists. Appendix 5 provides a list of all theorems that have been put forward so far in this chapter. Theorems 1–32 offer descriptions and explanations of all elements of a hierarchical social system, their relationships, and how hierarchy actually works. On this basis the argument can now be concluded and a *general* explanation formulated:[17]

Theorem 33: Hierarchical social order persists because it represents a comprehensive, consistent, multidimensional, and differentiated 'social cosmos' of various elements (superiors and subordinates, social roles and positions, mindsets and social actions, abstract organisational order, institutions and resources) that interact with each other via various mechanisms of systemisation (socialisation, adaptation, synchronisation, institutionalisation, transformation, and navigation).

Hierarchical social order persists at *all* levels—i.e., at the individual, micro, meso and macro levels:

1) *Individual level:* Hierarchical social order persists because of the interests, reasoning, and acting of *people with hierarchy-conforming mindsets and personalities* who at least willingly accept, if not actively promote, structures and processes of social inequality, injustice, and exploitation.

2) *Micro level:* Based on an original power differential, superiors and subordinates (re-) establish their direct hierarchical relationship via their routine behaviour, and even via boundary crossing, as *abstract organisational order*—which in return shapes and institutionalises people's different social roles and positions and further strengthens superiors' dominance and subordinates' obedience.

3) *Meso level:* Interactive processes of *systemisation* (i.e., socialisation, adaptation, synchronisation, institutionalisation, transformation, and navigation) between individuals and hierarchical social systems enable the continuation of hierarchical systems.

4) *Macro level:* Hierarchical social order represents a *comprehensive and structured cosmos of institutionalised inequalities*—i.e., societal institutions and resources that privilege certain individuals and groups systematically.

Figure 3.9 shows this cosmos (for the sake of completeness the aspect of 'ethics', which will be discussed in the next section, has been already included).

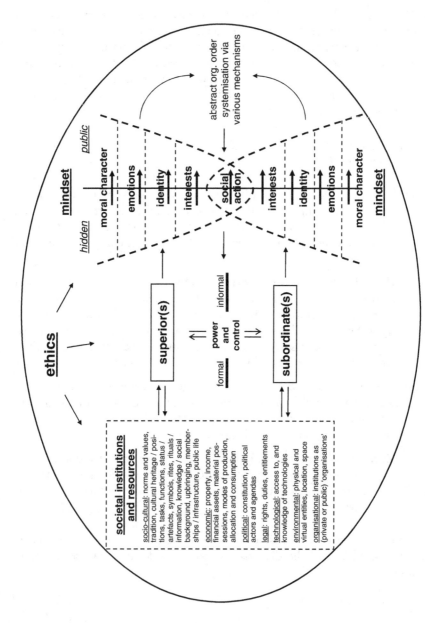

Figure 3.9 The complex cosmos of hierarchical social systems.

3.8   THE RELEVANCE OF ETHICS FOR SOCIAL SCIENCE THEORIES

3.8.1   Why Ethics is an Integral Part of any Social Reality—and the Analysis of that Reality

There is one more, quite crucial, element to be added to the model and theory, one that is very often largely ignored: *ethics*—i.e., the value-oriented reasoning about the morality (or immorality) of people's thoughts, deeds, and being in the world, about the moral aspects of specific social systems and institutions as well as the world in general. Ethics is addressed last here because it is relevant to *all* of the aforementioned elements of the social cosmos of hierarchy and their relationships as shown in Figure 9; it is relevant to the direct relationship between superiors and subordinates, to superiors' and subordinates' ways of reasoning and doing things (mindsets and social actions), to the single and multiple processes that unfold between the two (routine behaviour and boundary crossings), to the abstract organisational order that emerges out of this, to the societal institutions and resources, and to the processes of systemisation and its mechanisms that hold everything together. Ethics is relevant to the whole cosmos of hierarchical social order in two respects: 1) ethics is an integral part of social reality; 2) ethics is an integral part of the (scientific) reasoning about social reality. In the following both aspects will be discussed.

1) Ethics is an integral part of social reality
That ethics is an integral part of social reality can be demonstrated from the perspective of methodological individualism and methodological holism. As argued in Section 3.3.2, individual freedom means, amongst other things, individual responsibility. Whether people do things consciously or unconsciously, deliberately or accidentally, 'rationally' or 'irrationally', people capable of making decisions can be held responsible for what they do or don't do because there are *always* different options they can choose from; they can do so and so—or otherwise. People are responsible for the decisions and social actions they take or do not take; the norms and values they follow or reject; the ways they treat other people; and how they interpret, shape, and develop themselves in particular as well as the world in general. Individuals' freedom and responsibility to act or not to act in certain ways mean that there is *always* a moral dimension concerning everything with which human beings are directly or indirectly involved. Hence, ethics is an integral part of any social reality.

A similar argument can be put forward with regard to the social conditions in which humans exist (which they shape and by which they are shaped). The world of humans is made up of materialised value statements—whether they have occurred deliberately, coincidentally, or as an indefinable mixture of both. Every part of social reality, including reasoning about it, comprises value statements, value-based propositions, and implications for its members. For example, as shown earlier, hierarchical social order provides unequal conditions *by definition;* privileges and prerogatives are *always* more numerous higher up and fewer lower down the hierarchical ladder.[18] The direct social relationship between superiors and subordinates means a pre-existing power differential and it provides both with different types of status and positions, roles and responsibilities, opportunities and access to resources. Moreover, superiors' and subordinates' actions based on their interests, identities, emotions, and moral characters differ and also produce different outcomes. And abstract organisational order and the societal institutions and resources of hierarchy treat people very differently according to their social positions and status; they *systematically* privilege the few while marginalising the many.

Whether one agrees or disagrees with the fact that hierarchical social order creates and shapes social reality for people quite differently, it is also a fact any social reality is open to human design and intervention. Whether one believes in functionalistic theories and agrees or disagrees with the necessity of hierarchical social order, the theoretical and practical possibility that a social system may be designed and maintained in different ways means that there is an inherent moral question about the rights and wrongs of how any particular social reality is designed and unfolds. Any hierarchical social system—whether as stratified society, hierarchical organisation, or horizontally differentiated groups of people—as well as its principles and mechanisms are also up for scrutiny: on what grounds are they justified and/or justifiable?

2) Ethics is an integral part of scientific reasoning about social reality
That ethics is an integral part of any social reality (whether people or systems) is a statement with which most can agree. However, people, and especially scholars, disagree when it comes to the question of whether ethics, or value statements, is also part of the scientific reasoning about social reality. Particularly in modern Western philosophy of science, the prevailing position has been that descriptive and normative statements cannot coexist in the same theoretical framework. Referring to Hume's (1985) well-known adage formulated in 1739 that no 'ought' can be derived from an 'is' (i.e., that normative statements cannot be based on 'facts' or positive statements), proponents of positivistic approaches claim that social science also is, or has to be, value free. Social science must maintain neutrality concerning values; it must describe and explain the world but it must not make value judgements. This position is problematic in several respects.

One is that positivists don't follow their own advice. Within orthodox approaches, such as neoclassic economics or conservative management and organisation studies, models and theories are designed in quite some contrast to the notion of a value-free social science. For example, neoclassical theories such as the model of the perfect market, the theory of the firm and the shareholder-value maximisation concept claim that under market conditions companies *must* strive for profit maximisation and *must* function accordingly since they otherwise would disappear. They also assume that individuals strive for value or utility maximisation—that they *must* strive for it if they are to be regarded as rational human beings ('homo oeconomicus').

Such claims are in direct opposition to Hume's position, they are a classical 'ought' derived from a (theoretically designed ideal) 'is.' True, in a market economy, companies and individuals need to make a profit, need to earn income respectively—and usually they want to do so. And that some, or even many of them, want to make even more profit or want to earn 'as much as possible' is also an aspect of social reality that can often be observed—perhaps even increasingly in our time. But why do they (allegedly) *have* to *maximise* profits or utility functions? Most business owners are happy to earn *enough* money for what they perceive as their needs—and their businesses survive over generations in competitive environments. And most people are either happy or not happy if they do 'OK'—more is simply not possible on a daily basis. In social reality it is impossible to maximise anything. From the social reality of market economies ('is') no maximisation ('ought') can be derived whatsoever. This evidence and logic flies in the face of any neoclassical market theory but has been always neglected. And, that human beings are perfectly rational when they don't (try to) maximise outcomes for themselves is also a fact of life—but again it is ignored by positivistic fanatics.

That individuals and organisations are held to function according to theoretical maximisation principles—whatever the reality—means that these principles are actually *prescriptive* or *value statements* ('If you don't maximise/strive for maximisation of profits or utility you will disappear!'). Positivistic/functionalistic economics and business studies entail many such explicit (or, more often, implicit) value statements, especially as founding and fundamental principles of their theories and models. Ideal concepts of the perfect market, profit maximisation and efficiency; orthodox management; theories of the firm; strategic management concepts; and theories of leadership or leaders—all are founded on normative statements and ethical judgements. What is even more problematic is the fact that these value statements are often hidden and that many proponents of orthodox theories knowingly or unknowingly continue to claim that their theories are 'value free.' In this sense, neoclassical economics and orthodox management and organisation studies are in some of their key aspects *pseudoscience* and pure *ideology.*

However, the inclusion of value statements in scientific reasoning is not a specific characteristic or problem of positivistic approaches (only in the sense that its proponents claim or pretend that it does not exist) but of *all* social science theories; whenever in social science a *limited* proposition about social reality ('Under the conditions x, y, and z *some* people do a') provides the basis for the formulation of a *general* proposition ('Under the conditions x, y. and z people do a—which means *all* people *always* do a'), it turns into a *prescriptive* or *value* statement ('Under the conditions x, y, and z people *must* do a'). In social science, general propositions represent expectations that in a certain situation people *should,* or even *must,* act like the statement suggests—and that otherwise they are not acting 'normally,' at least not as the theory proposed. Thus, whenever a theory is formulated in social science, value statements are a normal part of it. Value-free social science is theoretically and practically *impossible*.

3.8.2   A Moderate Position Concerning the Explicit Inclusion of Value Statements in Theories

The radical position of positivists is not tenable. It is neither possible nor advantageous to exclude value statements from social science theory. Thus, here a more moderate position concerning the explicit inclusion of value statements will be briefly outlined.

In social science, every concept, model, or theory provides a certain approach towards, and interpretation of, social reality that is more favourable concerning some issues and less favourable or even critical concerning other issues. Every social science approach entails explicit or implicit ideas concerning what is important or not important, what to appreciate and what to criticise about a certain social reality as well as what to keep and what to change of it. *Any* social science approach not only interrogates social reality from (a) certain perspective(s) but also comprises descriptive *and* prescriptive statements *with necessity*. And, whenever moral judgements are made, ethics is part of the reasoning. In other words, social science is (directly or indirectly) *applied ethics*.

That social science is applied ethics requires a much more conscious and explicit handling of aspects of scientific research than prevailing orthodox approaches allege and demonstrate. This will be discussed with regard to three areas: 1) focus of investigation and research design; 2) serving and fighting different interests; and 3) interpretation of, and recommendations for, social reality.

1) Focus of investigation and research design
Social reality is complex. Hence, when it comes to any kind of reasoning about this reality, or reconstructing social realities, one can focus only on certain aspects—and must exclude other aspects with necessity. It is the nature especially of theoretical reasoning that it reduces complexity via focusing, simplifying, and generalising. There can be quite different understandings concerning what to focus on, what to include and what not to include, and what to highlight and what to leave on the sidelines. Decisions concerning the inclusion or exclusion of certain issues or aspects mean judgements about their importance and relevance. Hence, these decisions are value statements. The research design of any theory-based reasoning about reality (i.e., the formulation of the research question, the identification of the elements and their relationships that will be looked at, the use of an existing or development of a new theory, and the formulation of propositions) inherently bears ethical relevance. From whatever approach one starts to reason about social phe-

nomena, one automatically takes either an affirmative or negating position towards them simply by deciding what to focus on, what to include in and what to exclude from the investigation, and how to look at, or (re-)construct the phenomena in question. It is not possible to have theory-based reasoning about phenomena within the social realm without having value statements as part of that reasoning (if not explicit then at least implicit). Every social science theory, therefore, can be only strengthened by attempting to include value statements explicitly and to make them visible from the very beginning.

2) Serving and fighting different interests
That every social science approach is in favour of certain issues draws attention to the perhaps even more crucial aspect that every approach is also in favour of certain individuals' or groups of people's *interests* concerning these issues. For example, in Section 3.4.3 it was shown that abstract organisational order is the abstract and anonymous extension of individual superiors' direct social dominance. Abstract organisational order is primarily designed and maintained according to the interests of superiors and ruling elites. Hence, proponents of so-called 'functionalistic' approaches do much more than merely defining and coping with 'functional' or 'technical' problems when they try to improve the functionality and efficiency of markets and organisations. In fact, first and foremost they are serving the interests of certain superiors and power elites—e.g., owners, managers, shareholders, or institutional investors (Diefenbach 2009a; Clegg and Walsh 2004; Fournier and Grey 2000; Jacques 1996, p. 166).

The same, of course, is true for those who oppose the established social order and who see the social dominance of certain individuals or elites in particular, or of any power elite in general, as highly problematic. They, too, not only provide a functional analysis and try to make the case for a technically 'better' social system but also (allegedly) serve the interests of those individuals or groups of people that seem to be disadvantaged, exploited, and oppressed by the existing social order.

Generally speaking, every social science approach supports and serves the interests of certain individuals or group(s) of people (and excludes or even fights others' interests) and tries to shape social reality accordingly. Also researchers do not only try to make sense of but also attempt to create and shape social reality according to (their) ideals, values, and convictions. Value statements *are meant to influence social reality*. Social science is applied ethics serving particular interests.

There is nothing wrong with the fact that people try to shape social reality according to (their) ideals, values, and convictions; on the contrary, it is a characteristic of being human. To put forward value statements is legitimate. What is *not* legitimate is to deny and to cover up this fact and to pretend that social theories do not comprise value statements (as argued in the previous section). This is not only misleading and unscientific but also extremely worrying: such a strategy usually plays into the hands of dominant ideologies and ruling elites and strengthens the inequalities and injustices of a given status quo—though this might well be the interest of positivists and proponents of a certain social order. Thus, it helps a lot if it is made clear from the very beginning whose and which interests a particular social science theory serves, whose interests it does not serve (or even fights or ignores) and the reasons why, and how interests are put into perspective.

3) Interpretation of, and recommendations for, social reality
The previous point indicates that there can be very different opinions concerning how hierarchical social order *can, could,* or even *should* be interpreted and judged—and what should be done about it.

Proponents of orthodox management and organisation concepts regard hierarchical structures and processes as functionally advantageous. Moreover, they believe that the positions people inherit on the hierarchical ladder reflect their merits (e.g., competence, experience, seniority, skills, performance, and the like). In this sense, affirmative approaches portray hierarchy and the inequalities it produces not only as a functional but also as a just social order.

In contrast, opponents argue that, within any hierarchical social order, most people (especially subordinates) do not only receive comparatively less but rather too little in return for their effort and contributions while others (mostly superiors) receive comparatively more, if not to say (way) too much in return for their effort and contributions. In Section 3.5 it was shown that hierarchical social order is *specifically* designed to enable, maintain, and guarantee social dominance. Hierarchical social systems are nothing more but comprehensively institutionalised and systemised forms of oppression and control, discrimination and exploitation of the many by the few. The systematic privileging of some individuals and groups at the expense of others for the sole reason that they are higher up the hierarchical ladder is unjust, unjustified, and unjustifiable.

As a result of the proponents' and opponents' different views and interpretations, their conclusions also differ: proponents of orthodox approaches want the continuation of hierarchical social systems and institutions (and just want to make them more efficient) whereas critics want to discontinue and to replace them with alternative social systems (such as democratic organisations/cooperatives, or egalitarian societies). As argued above, social science is applied ethics—and social theories help to design and maintain social reality one way or the other. In this sense, recommendations stemming from theory-based reasoning about social reality are not 'neutral' suggestions but value-laden moral advice—and people should be honest about this.

All in all, as the argumentation above has shown, there are several reasons why ethics is an integral part of social reality—and of any reasoning about it. The relevance of ethics for social theory is *fundamental and comprehensive*. Ethics is not just an 'add-on' or 'nice-to-have' feature after all 'important' things have been said and done; it is an integral part of any social theory—and of *all* its elements and relationships.

Ethics plays the same role in the social cosmos as gravitational force plays in the universe: as soon as there is matter in space, gravitational force exists; and, as soon as there is 'something' in the social realm (e.g., individuals or phenomena caused by and relevant to humans), ethics is relevant. In this sense, we have to acknowledge that ethics is an integral part of social reality *as well as* of *any* social theory about it—*with necessity.* It is not possible in social science *not* to make value statements. It is theoretically and practically not possible to have a theory within social science without value statements because social reality is interest-laden and open to various designs. Mechanisms and outcomes are not predetermined but are consequences of human decisions and actions—and they have different implications for different people. Thus, the social scientist cannot, and should not try to, be merely a neutral observer of the social world. Social scientists *have to* take a stand and *have to* make value statements. But, and this is crucial, social scientists must make their value statements and ethical judgements explicit and clearly separate them from other parts of their scientific analysis. This is what really distinguishes scientific theory from ideology: value statements are made explicit.

3.9 HOW THE THEORY RELATES TO STRUCTURATION THEORY AND SOCIAL DOMINANCE THEORY

Finally, the theory formulated here should be put into perspective. Of course, it has not been developed in a theoretical vacuum. There are many approaches and theories that contribute to our understanding of how people and institutions relate to, and interact with, each other; how (parts of) social systems function (or don't function); and even how hierarchical systems may persist over time. The general theory of hierarchical social systems refers to quite a few other social theories and approaches, especially critical, political, and moral-philosophical theories as well as anthropological, sociological, sociopsychhological, and psychological concepts (see Appendix 2 for a systematic, but still incomplete, overview).

It is not possible here to discuss comprehensively how this general theory relates to other theories. Also, the main idea of this chapter was to *develop* a theory, *not* to compare theories at a metatheoretical level. Nonetheless, there are two other theories that have particularly attempted to explain the persistence of hierarchical social systems similarly to this general theory—i.e., via referring to a dynamic interplay between individuals or groups of people and institutional contexts/structures. These are Giddens's (1984, 1976) structuration theory and Sidanius et al.'s (2004, 1999) social dominance theory. Thus, in this final section of this chapter it shall be briefly indicated how the theory developed here relates to these two other theories.

3.9.1   Structuration Theory

When the process of 'systemisation and its main mechanisms' was introduced as one of the cornerstones of the theory developed here (see Section 3.6), the reader may have been reminded of Giddens's structuration theory (1984, 1976). Both theories try to explain how social systems are produced and reproduced by dynamic relationships between structures and human actors who are both enabled and constrained by these structures (Dillard et al. 2004, p. 19).[19] For example, in one of his earlier works, Giddens (1976, p. 121) explained that:

> *Structuration,* as the reproduction of practices, refers abstractly to the dynamic process whereby structures come into being. By the *duality of structure* I mean that social structures are both constituted by human agency, and yet at the same time are the very *medium* of this constitution.

However, there are some quite fundamental differences between Giddens's structuration theory and the theory developed here:

Giddens's theory is quite abstract. Actors constitute an element of the model only in the most impersonal (one might say surreal) way, as 'agency' or, at best, 'agents.' They have neither individually nor socially defined interests or identities; they are nameless and faceless robots. It is almost paradoxical that Giddens's theory is called a 'social' or 'sociological' theory in the face of the fact that it neither comprises *individuals* nor *social beings* explicitly. As a consequence, structuration theory remains quiet about individuals as well as social relationships. It does not, and *cannot,* say anything about (unequal) social relationships or about how individuals might act differently within (or are treated differently by) social structures and processes.

In contrast, the theory developed here not only has specified individuals (superiors and subordinates) at its very core but also has their different social statuses and unequal social relationship as an explicit element (as a power differential, the abstract organisational order or societal institutions and resources). Moreover, it explicitly includes people's moral character, interests, emotions, and identities as well as their social actions—and how all of these relate to each other within specified social settings.

In Giddens's theory of structuration, structures are seen as rules and resources representing *regular* social practices. They are, thus, similar to what have been termed 'routine behaviour' in the theory developed here. However, Giddens's theory is limited to such regular social practices; boundary crossings are neither included in the model nor part of the investigation. As a consequence, the theory of structuration does not interrogate deviant behaviour, clashes between people, or any other social dynamics that are caused by differing understandings and actions with regard to social expectations, norms, and values.

Because of the missing elements, Giddens's theory of structuration has very little explanatory power, if any; it remains unclear why actors do or don't do things (if one interprets 'agency' as actors), why structures remain or change, and why the whole social system remains, changes, disappears, or re-emerges. Giddens's theory is primarily descriptive and can be used for some very general reasoning at an abstract level, but it cannot provide explanations. In contrast, the general theory of hierarchical social systems provides explicit and detailed theorems concerning each of its elements and their relationships and core processes, systemisation and its mechanisms, and how hierarchy as a social cosmos persists through time.

Finally, the theory of structuration is extremely orthodox and conservative. It only focuses on the reproduction of social structures without even starting to ask why and how they persist—and whether or not they *should* continue to exist and according to which normative principles. It has no critical potential; it cannot explain why things are how they are, why they are not different, or why they should be different. In contrast, the general theory of hierarchical social systems is explicitly critical with regard to hierarchy and with regard to the status quo of any hierarchical system. It is meant to contribute to attempts in the tradition of the Enlightenment and Critical Theory to overcome systems of social dominance and oppression.

All in all, because of its fundamental theoretical deficits, practical limitations and explicitly conservative character, Giddens's structuration theory is of little use in investigating social reality.

3.9.2   Social Dominance Theory

Sidanius et al.'s (2004, 1999) social dominance theory probably comes the closest to the theory developed here. It analyses how unequal distribution of social power, prestige, and privileges happens in group-based social hierarchies as well as why such hierarchical, oppressive structures are so widespread and persistent. In a foreword, Sidanius and Pratto (1999, p. 1) formulated their goal: 'This volume focuses on two questions: Why do people from one social group oppress and discriminate against people from other groups? Why is this oppression so difficult to eliminate?' O'Brien and Crandall (2005, pp. 4–5) provide quite a good description of the theory:

> Social dominance theory (SDT) starts with the observation that all human societies tend to be structured as systems of group-based social hierarchies [. . .]. SDT posits the existence of a basic human drive toward group-based inequality known as social dominance orientation—people desire and support group-based hierarchy and the domination of 'inferior groups' by 'superior groups.' SDT argues that dominant and subordinate groups alike actively participate in and contribute to subordination. Both groups justify the presence of group-based inequality with legitimising myths. The legitimising myths consist of attitudes, values, beliefs, stereotypes, and ideologies that provide moral and intellectual justification for the social practices that distribute social value within the social system. In SDT, the powerful and powerless are seen as deserving their respective positions. There is a desire to maintain the

power structure in their society, regardless of the group's own position, because the social structure is seen as inherently legitimate and just. Social dominance pressures and legitimising myths promote acceptance of the status quo.

According to social dominance theory, there are the same or similar psychological, social, societal, and institutional forces at work in almost every cultural and historical context; these forces mutually reinforce each other towards the persistence of hierarchical social order (Sidanius and Pratto 1999, p. 304). In its aims and objectives as well as in its multidimensional approach, social dominance theory is very close to the theory developed here. Nonetheless, there are a few differences.

Social dominance theory focuses on *group-based* social hierarchies. The main assumption is that individuals (can) dominate others, or are subordinate to others, because of their membership of a particular group (Sidanius and Pratto 1999, p. 32). Such a focus has its merits; Sidanius and his colleagues have produced comprehensive empirical data at the individual, micro and macro levels in various sociocultural contexts showing how much individuals' identities and actions are shaped by their group status.

The theory developed here also comprises this aspect; for example, it stresses the fact that individuals' interests, identities, emotions, and moral character as well as actions depend on, and differ according to, which group of people to which they belong—for example, superiors or subordinates, managers or employees, rich or poor, and the like. But the general theory of hierarchical social systems does not *only* have group status as a core variable. Instead, it focuses on 1) several aspects of individuals and groups (interests, identity, emotions, moral character, social actions), 2) the organisational/institutional context they are in (such as abstract organisational order or societal resources and institutions), and 3) how the two relate to each other with regard to the persistence of (hierarchical) structures and processes. It therefore covers a much broader range of possible explanatory variables, copes with more phenomena, and offers more explanations for the functioning of hierarchical systems. In this sense, one might say that social dominance theory is more *specific* and focuses on group-based hierarchies, whereas the theory put forward here is the more *general* theory and copes with *any* kind of hierarchical system. The theories thus do not contradict but rather complement each other.

For their analysis, Sidanius et al. reduced their model to a 'trimorphic structure of group-based social hierarchy' that comprises age, gender, and stratification systems (Sidanius and Pratto 1999, pp. 33–7). These three categories are introduced somewhat out of the blue and it is not clear why they are chosen over other possibilities. More problematic, though, is the authors' keenness to portray group-based hierarchy and social oppression largely as a gender-dependent phenomenon. Some of their findings seem to be selected and presented only in order to make the case that social dominance is predominantly male-based. In contrast, group-based hierarchy and social oppression carried out by women is not addressed. Moreover, other, more relevant, factors that cause and maintain social dominance—such as power, access to institutions and resources, and sociocultural factors—are largely ignored or undervalued. In this sense, social dominance theory, at least in its original design and so far, is quite limited and even biased in parts.

Seen in a more general way, it is important to understand that social dominance and hierarchy as such (and all that comes with them—e.g., privileges, oppression, exploitation, and injustice) are not caused by *any* single social category, be it race, gender, religion, education, nationality, social background, and so on. These are all *indicators* or *effects, not* causes! Reasons and, therefore, explanations for hierarchical social order can be found at the individual level (e.g., the moral character, mindsets, and actions of particular people), at the micro level (e.g., mechanisms of abstract organisational order) and/or at the macro level (e.g., societal institutions and resources)—or in the specific links between those levels (as demonstrated by the process of systemisation and its mechanisms). Sidanius et al. address this to some degree via three mechanisms in their model: 'aggregated individual discrimination,' 'institutional discrimination,' and 'behavioural asymmetry' (Sidanius and Pratto 1999, pp. 39–45). But, even then, they again focus too much on the categories of 'age' and 'gender,' limiting their model in quite unnecessary and unfortunate ways.

Another weakness of Sidanius et al.'s theory is the (probably deliberate) omission of sociophilosophical and ethical aspects such as individual responsibility; moral character; and the morality of institutions, organisations, groups, and individuals. With the exclusion of these aspects and dimensions, Sidanius et al.'s analysis and reasoning remain fairly incomplete. During and after going through all the data presented in research based on social dominance theory, one cannot avoid asking the question 'So what?'. Sidanius et al. have analysed group-based hierarchies, social dominance, and oppression at great length (though in rather limited and descriptive ways)—but that's it. What is missing is a *critical* impetus and *critical* analysis.

In contrast, the general theory of hierarchical social systems provides a comprehensive basis from which to critically examine any hierarchical system; individuals' and groups of people's positions and behaviour within such systems; and how social structures and processes either contribute to or challenge social dominance and obedience, privileges, and the exploitation of certain people. It provides not only some technical analysis but also criticism and argumentation in the tradition of the Age of Enlightenment—and we need such foundations if we ever again want to reason seriously about how oppressive regimes such as (group-based) social hierarchies could be changed and true alternatives developed.

Beside the aspects mentioned above, which in my view represent some serious weaknesses and limitations of social dominance theory, it nonetheless should be stressed that social dominance theory is quite developed, provides a wealth of compelling arguments and interesting facts, and is much more specific and applicable than Giddens's structuration theory.

4   Application of the Theory—How Hierarchy Works

'In any stratified society there is a set of limits of what [. . .] dominant and subordinate groups can do. [. . .] What takes place, however, is a kind of continual probing to find out what they can get away with and discover the limits of obedience and disobedience.'

Barrington Moore (1978, p. 18)

4.1   INTRODUCTION

The general theory of hierarchical social systems developed in the previous chapter outlined that hierarchy exists and persists over time because of a complex and dynamic interplay of actors and institutions, structures, and processes. The theory can be applied to any hierarchical social relationship (whether it is a dyad, group, organisation, or society) and within any cultural context. In this chapter it will be shown paradigmatically how the theory can be used in order to explain and to examine some of the key aspects the theory addresses.[1] In particular, it will be analysed how:

1) superiors' and subordinates' *routine behaviours* work towards the institutionalisation of people's mindsets and social actions—and how they work together towards the persistence of hierarchy (Section 4.2);

2) superiors' and subordinates' *deviance* and *boundary crossings* may contribute to the further stabilisation and continuation of hierarchical social order—and when they might seriously threaten it (Sections 4.3–4.5);

3) hierarchy continues as abstract organisational order in *different types of organisations* via an interactive combination of formal and informal hierarchy (Section 4.6).

4.2   ROUTINE BEHAVIOUR AND THE PERSISTENCE OF HIERARCHICAL SOCIAL ORDER

According to orthodox management concepts, hierarchical organisations must function efficiently and smoothly—and so ought their members. Hence, opposition to and deviance from prevailing norms and expectations is regarded as a threat not only to other members of the organisation but also to the survival of the whole, and will trigger more or less appropriate responses (e.g., Bennett and Robinson 2000; Robinson and Bennett 1995, 1997). Usually, both superiors and subordinates know this and therefore try to function accordingly. Their behaviour, as well as the continuing inter-action between them, largely takes place in the form of learned, widely expected and accepted *routine behaviour* (as explained in Section 3.4.1).

This section will be focused on how superiors' and subordinates' routine behaviour unfolds with regard to people's social action as well as the various elements of their mindsets (i.e., interests, identity, emotions, and moral character) and how this contributes to the persistence and continuation of hierarchical social order. The analysis here will be relatively undramatic. It will mainly demonstrate how quiet it is at the Western front of hierarchy—how normal this unnormal normality usually is. But there nonetheless is a good reason for looking at it; by and large, people who are involved in the daily treadmill of hierarchical organisations and stratified societies, as well as researchers who are trying to make sense of them, hardly reflect on it anymore—which is precisely one of the main reasons for its continuing per-sistence. Hence, in order to understand some of the reasons for the longevity of hierarchy, it makes sense to look at its unnormal normality.

4.2.1   The Relevance of Routine Social Action for the Persistence of Hierarchy

As indicated above, members of a social system, whether they are in a superior or subordinate position, function well on a regular basis. Superiors are quite aware of what is expected from them and how they should do their jobs. The set of tasks and responsibilities they (have to) carry out officially reflects a fairly conventional understanding of managers' and leaders' roles and functions. More or less, their main tasks are to define and identify problems; make deci-sions and/or influence decision-making processes; set objectives; plan, assign, and organise work; provide leadership and guidance; coordinate, communi-cate, motivate, and control; evaluate and appraise performance; and promote, reward, and sanction (Braynion 2004, p. 449; Jost and Elsbach 2001, p. 182; Hales 1999; Jacques 1996, p. 120; Mintzberg 1994; Lawler III 1988, pp. 6–8; Taylor 1967; Chandler 1962; Drucker 1954; Fayol 1949).

Thanks to elaborated catalogues of managerial tasks and role repertoires, superiors not only know what is expected from them but they also behave and act accordingly. In their daily work, superiors follow the public tran-script of professional conduct of office—i.e., the 'image of the manager as a functionally necessary facilitator and coordinator of others' actions' (Willmott 1984, p. 353). Even the occasional scandals regarding individual superiors' gross misbehaviour are seen more as exceptions to the rule than evidence of underlying systemic problems. Usually, superiors simply want to get done the jobs they are responsible for and are keen to function accord-ing to the requirements of the system (Grey 1999; Reed 1984; Rosen 1984;

Willmott 1984). Biggart and Hamilton (1984, p. 546) found in their empirical research that:

> The importance of obedience to role obligations as the route to power was described in numerous ways by actors. People often spoke of the importance of 'honesty,' 'integrity,' or 'credibility' meaning the willingness to uphold the standards of the job.

Public obedience with regard to the organisation's rules and norms ensures the personal legitimacy of the superior and the continuation of his or her career (Courpasson and Dany 2003, p. 1233). It is, thus, barely surprising that superiors' routine actions guarantee not only the smooth functioning of the hierarchical system but also its continuation.

Subordinates function and behave probably even more—because this is the very idea of 'the good subordinate'; subordinates are expected to follow orders from their superiors, to obey rules and the existing order, and to function well. And subordinates usually do exactly that—not only because they have to but even because they want to (Milgram 1974). Subordinates conform to the expectations of their superiors and follow 'rituals of subordination' in countless little acts on a daily basis (Scott 1990, pp. 2, 66; Thompson 1961, p. 493). Sidanius and Pratto (1999, p. 260) even went so far to say that 'self-destructive and self-debilitating behaviors are the primary means by which subordinates actively participate in and contribute to their own continued subordination.' Obedience, submissiveness, and functioning well are the public face of the subordinate.

With their routine behaviour, subordinates support and strengthen the very same rules, structures, and processes that infantilise them, but at the same time protect them (Jacques 1996, p. 111). Most of subordinates' routine behaviour, thus, is cooperative and supportive of the hierarchical system, rather than subversive. Sidanius and Pratto (1999, p. 44) suggested that:

> It is subordinates' high level of both passive and active cooperation with their own oppression that provides systems of group-based social hierarchy with their remarkable degrees of resiliency; robustness is not maintained primarily by the oppressive behaviour of dominants, but by the deferential and obsequious behaviour of subordinates.

Altogether, superiors *and* subordinates re-establish the hierarchical social order via their routine behaviour on a daily basis. Moreover, and perhaps more crucially, their routine behaviours complement each other perfectly; with their smooth functioning and obedience, subordinates reinforce their superiors' power. And, with their smooth functioning and dominance, superiors make their subordinates behave even more smoothly.

4.2.2 Superiors' and Subordinates' Interests Towards Hierarchy

As the theory developed in Chapter 3 proposes, behind superiors' and subordinates' behaviour and social actions are *interests* (or self-interest: Darke and Chaiken 2005; O'Brien and Crandall 2005; Rutledge and Karim 1999). Superiors' individual and collective interests stem largely from their elevated roles and positions, their functions, and their areas of responsibility. Officially, superiors' primary interest is serving the whole; their greatest concern is said to be the survival of the whole, the (further) development of the common good and the care of (their) people—whether this is the country, a people, a tribe, an organisation, or a group (Deem and Brehony 2005, p. 230; Pettigrew 2002, p. 97; Burns 1961, p. 260; Mills 1956, p. 17). Rulers of any hierarchical social system (and members of ruling elites in general) are always very keen to portray themselves as working 'very hard' and 'unselfishly' 'for the sake of the whole.' Willmott (1996, p. 326) pointed out that the 'privileged yet dependent positioning of managers within the industrial structure induces them to represent their work—to other employees and owners—as impartial and uncompromised by self-interest or class-interest, motivated only by seemingly universal virtues of efficiency and effectiveness.'

And superiors may indeed have a professional interest in carrying out those tasks that their positions require them to do. However, since their social position is so instrumental for 'doing their duty,' many superiors probably have an even stronger interest in keeping and protecting their roles and positions—and all that comes with them (e.g., status and prestige, power and influence, privileges and prerogatives, material and immaterial resources and benefits, and career opportunities and other life chances) (Clegg and Walsh 2004, pp. 230–1; Willmott 1996, p. 326; Zaleznik 1989, p. 152; Rueschemeyer 1986, p. 47). As a consequence, over time many superiors become more concerned about their own affairs and prospects than those of the social system they belong to (if they weren't so right from the start). Thus, one can argue that superiors' 'real' interests are in quite some contrast to what is portrayed as their 'official' interests for the whole.

But there is another aspect or twist. Members of any ruling elite who primarily pursue their own interests and agendas are keen that their decisions and actions are *not* regarded as driven by their (self-)interest. As explained in Section 3.4.4, with the institutionalisation of hierarchy as an abstract organisational order, members of the ruling elite have managed to institutionalise their individual and group interests;[2] what were once *their* interests are now *the system's* interests. Of course, they still need to pursue *some* of their interests secretly because these might go (too much) against superiors' public claims of serving the prevailing norms and values, or even the laws and regulations of the social system. But superiors can now pursue all of their interests that they have managed to link *routinely* to the conduct of their office, because in doing so they allegedly serve the 'common good.' 'Real' interests and 'official' interests have become one.

To claim that their partial individual and group interests are an integral part of the whole, and good for the whole, has been the cunning and cynical strategy of the privileged in all hierarchical systems at all times—and it works. Rulers and their followers *truly believe* the rhetoric that the personal interests of the members of the ruling elites and the interests of the system are identical, that everything they do is good for the whole, that they represent the whole, that they *are* the whole. Quite understandably, most superiors have a strong interest not only in keeping and nurturing their roles and positions within the hierarchical system but also in defending and maintaining the very system that provides them with the means for pursuing their interests.

But how about subordinates' interests? Since hierarchy has been institutionalised as an abstract organisational order primarily according to *superiors'* interests, and is maintained in order to continue *their* social dominance, the interests of subordinates in fitting into the very societal and organisational conditions that make them subordinates seem to be quite 'irrational.' For example, from a Marxian perspective they have been explained as a 'false consciousness' (Engels 1893). There might be some truth in this. As argued in Section 3.6.1, subordinates' interest in functioning smoothly and behaving well within hierarchical systems is to a great extent the result of lifelong socialisation and conditioning by various societal institutions (e.g., parental care, nursery, school, university, army, religion, media, government, business organisations). These institutions are all themselves hierarchical organisations and they make sure that people are able and willing to function in *any* hierarchical system.

Yet, it would be misleading to portray subordinates' interests within a hierarchical social order solely, or primarily, as 'irrational' or 'false' interests. In Section 3.6.1 it was also argued that hierarchical systems provide a whole range of advantages, such as physical advantages (better health and safety), material advantages (access to valuable resources, higher wages), social advantages (status and power, privileges and prerogatives), organisational advantages (more responsibilities, doing better jobs with less input required) and psychological advantages (self-esteem, and feelings of belongingness, purpose, order, safety). Together, these features constitute not just *some* incentives but *a whole range of tangible advantages* that—*on balance*—make the system, as well as life and work within it, quite attractive even for its less privileged members. Many hierarchical organisations and stratified societies provide subordinates with opportunities they could not easily get somewhere else.

Usually, people are *very* aware of all the advantages the system has to offer (in absolute as well as in relative terms)—and they know that they can benefit from these advantages only as long as they function within the boundaries of the system. Moreover, people know that they can 'steer' their way through a hierarchical system while reducing disadvantages and increasing advantages for themselves. Thus, most subordinates' interests largely orbit around gaining advantages and avoiding punishment or other negative consequences, while otherwise accepting the existing order and structures as they are (Jost and Hunyady 2005, pp. 261–2; Hogg and Terry 2000, p. 124; Beetham 1991, pp. 26–7; Milgram 1974, 1963). It is in the interests of the obedient personality and calculative mind to every day celebrate little victories and count little losses in systematically oppressive structures that it otherwise leaves unquestioned and unchallenged.

Hence, many subordinates not only function within the boundaries of a hierarchical, unjust, and oppressive social system because of a 'false consciousness' but also *because of very understandable reasons and rational interests*. It is much more advantageous for subordinates to pursue their individual goals and interests within, and according to the parameters set by, the system than to challenge it. Although subordinates' interests might seem to be in this sense quite limited, they are nonetheless their 'real' interests; it simply makes (a lot of) sense for subordinates to function within hierarchy. Many critics of hierarchical social systems have regularly underestimated these *positive* reasons for subordinates to function within, even contribute actively to, the continuation of the system.

All in all, although superiors' and subordinates' interests differ quite fundamentally with regard to their different positions and privileges, they complement each other with regard to the social system as a whole. *Both* are mainly interested in performing and functioning well, the former because most of their interests have been institutionalised as abstract organisational order and the latter because they can improve the situation they are in via complying with rules and following orders—or pretending to do so. Superiors and subordinates share a common interest in stabilising and maintaining—even actively contributing to—the continuation of the very hierarchical system that makes them superiors and subordinates. *This* is their 'real' interest. While functioning routinely, superiors *and* subordinates largely follow and realise their own interests.

4.2.3 Hierarchy—Conforming Identities of Superiors and Subordinates

As is the case with routine social actions and interests, people's identities also have to be compatible with the social system they are part of. Within a hierarchical order, a person's social identity, hence, is first and foremost a position- and status-related identity. Superiors' and subordinates' identities are mainly shaped by their roles and positions, privileges and responsibilities, rights and duties, and interests and actions.

Superiors' publicly portrayed identities represent their advanced position. It is the classical identity of '*the*' superior, of powerful rulers who see themselves, and want to be seen, as the ones in charge, as the guarantors of order and control (Scott 1990, p. 70; Zaleznik 1989, pp. 45–58). 'Order' and 'control' are the main rationales and concerns in superiors' and power elites' reasoning about themselves, their subordinates and the social system they are responsible for; superiors like to see themselves as self-disciplined; as deciding and acting in rational and thought-through ways; as having everything (and everyone!) under control; and as managing the organisational issues of the social system as well as social relationships in a way that is unbiased and objective.

At the same time, superiors' public identity also includes the ideas of 'doer' and even 'leader' (Coutu 2005). Such an identity is in quite some contrast to that of a 'rational commander in chief' because it comprises 'entrepreneurial,' 'creative,' 'risk-taking,' and even 'irrational' aspects (e.g., 'natural' skills to lead people or a 'sixth sense' for identifying threats and opportunities). Allegedly, superiors have, and need to have, personality traits and cognitive skills that cannot really be explained. This leadership mystique is a key part of superiors' identity as well as the image they and their followers portray. Hence, the public identity of superiors is a rather inconsistent set of rational *and* irrational elements. Somehow, paradoxically, it is probably exactly this kind of (partly) contradictory (if not to say schizophrenic) public identity of 'the' superior that helps to portray and justify them as the ones responsible for the whole; hierarchical systems *need* superiors who simultaneously set directions as irrational leaders *and* organise and control subordinates as their rational overseers.

Subordinates' identity is also largely shaped by what the logic of hierarchical social order suggests; for people lower down the hierarchical ladder, it ought to be the identity of 'the' subordinate—i.e., of the submissive servant who defines himself or herself via the requirements of functioning well, conforming, obeying, and following orders (Alvesson and Willmott 2002, p. 619; Merton 1961, p. 52). Subordinates should see themselves as function- and performance-oriented automatons that strictly adhere to rules and procedures, willingly accept the authority of their superiors, and reliably carry out superiors' orders (Ashforth 1994, p. 759; Zaleznik 1989, p. 49). Moreover, the psyche of subordinates shall primarily reflect their inferiority with regard to their superiors and the system (Sidanius and Pratto 1999, p. 229). One therefore might say that the public identity of the subordinate is quite simple, one-dimensional, and infantile: it represents a deeply internalised 'learned helplessness' (Bassman and London 1993, p. 22) and submissiveness.

That subordinates' identity represents and reconfirms their lower position and inferiority is a necessary requirement from the perspective of the hierarchical system; subordinates who are reduced to dependants 'are less likely to take the initiative in social situations' (Van Vugt 2006, p. 361). Recall Immanuel Kant's allegorical description of subordinates as 'domestic cattle' (see Section 2.2.3). Subordinates conditioned in such ways have the 'perfect' identity for any hierarchical social system. They 'tend to be somewhat insecure, suspicious, authoritarian, dogmatic, and lower in ability, and tend to place a higher value on conformity and order, and a lower value on treating others with consideration' (Ashforth 1994, p. 759).

Altogether, subordinates' identity as dependent and insecure followers complements superiors' identity as 'leaders' and 'powerful rulers' perfectly.

Members of the lower layers of a social system are always portrayed in ways that explain and justify the functions, even existence, of the higher classes. Superiors' and subordinates' identities are not only congruent with each other but also fit well into the logic and the requirements of the hierarchical system; with fully developed hierarchy-compatible identities, neither superiors nor subordinates are willing nor capable any more of imagining any other social reality than hierarchy. And, even if there were an alternative, they would not be able to fit into it.

4.2.4 Superiors' and Subordinates' 'Appropriate' Emotions

On the one hand, hierarchical social relationships are not entirely defined by conscious reasoning (and consequent actions) as captured in the idea of 'interests.' There are also emotions in play that can arise spontaneously and add an affective dimension to people's thoughts and deeds. On the other hand, within social settings, and especially within hierarchical social systems, emotions are not entirely free and random—at least not the public demonstration of emotions. As Lurie (2004, p. 5) says, 'Emotions are expected to fit the situation. People do not only have feelings, but manage and display them according to what they deem right as well as according to what they think is expected.' This can be seen in two respects:

The superior-subordinate relationship *as such* inherently causes the expectation and creation of particular emotions. People have certain feelings in accordance with their social roles and positions. For example, people feel superior or inferior, dominant or obedient, powerful or powerless— or should feel so. At the same time, people are expected to show feelings that do not relate specifically to their social roles and positions; whether they are superior or subordinate, *all* members of a hierarchical social system should have, and should show, (strong) feelings of belonging, duty, and responsibility.

Or there might be are 'emotional events'—i.e., certain situations in which the experience and demonstration of emotions (at a particular intensity and in a particular manner) are expected. For example, when superiors make a joke, subordinates are expected to laugh; in the face of an (alleged) external enemy, subordinates should feel scared; when subordinates underperform, or show other forms of deviant behaviour, superiors should get angry; and so on.

Hence, it is not (only) emotions as such (or the individual and his/her emotions) but more the 'appropriateness' or 'inappropriateness' of emotions with regard to social expectations and within certain social settings that is important. Showing 'appropriate' emotions does not mean that people have to constantly show 'positive' emotions (e.g., happiness, pleasure, comfort, excitement, calmness)—although it certainly helps in most social relationships when someone comes across more as likeable than off-putting. People can also show 'negative' emotions such as annoyance, fury, embarrassment, depression, shame, bitterness, sadness, anger, fear, nervousness, impatience, or unhappiness without receiving negative reactions—*if* such emotions are expected and regarded as appropriate within a certain situation. Showing routine behaviour in the realm of emotions means demonstrating the 'right' emotions at the 'right' time and in the 'right' ways and intensities.

However, it would be a rare coincidence if a person's true emotions happened to exactly fit what are perceived as 'appropriate' emotions. Therefore, emotion *regulation* has long been at the centre of all social systems, such as families, groups, organisations, and even whole societies. Norbert Elias (1969) provided a comprehensive and thorough analysis of what he called the grand 'civilising process' (from Medieval Europe through to modernity). According to Elias, the notion and practices of 'court etiquette' increasingly disseminated into literally every aspect of social life; in terms of speech, table manners, courting, sexual behaviour, and body functions, all daily activities were gradually channelled and transformed into culturally and stereotypically defined practices by lowering thresholds of shame and repugnance (Scheff 2000, p. 89). People learn from all sorts of institutions which feelings and attitudes are appropriate and when and how to express, talk about, and regulate them in 'civilised' manners (Fitness 2000, p. 148). External social norms are transformed into internal self-constraint with the result that people assess their every move and feeling for appropriateness *before* the move or feeling surfaces and becomes obvious to others—and others respond in a similar fashion. Socialisation, and the whole process of systemisation in the centre of the 'civilising process' (as outlined in Section 3.6), is an endless loop or vicious circle of conditioning oneself and others.

But it is not only a process in which individuals are passively moulded. During their socialisation, individuals learn to cope with their emotions actively (Lazarus 1991); and individuals develop skills to not only shape their emotions (pro)actively according to social expectations but also, and increasingly, to shape them according to *their* interests and how they pursue them. The *management of emotions* has become paramount and a key activity of individuals. Ostell (1996, p. 527) even reasoned about the 'tactics of emotion management,' and gave related advice. The introduction of the concept of 'emotional intelligence' (Salovey and Mayer 1990) can be seen as such a management tool in the tradition of the grand 'civilising process.' Emotional intelligence entails the ability to (Rubin et al. 2005, p. 847; Mayer et al. 2003):

1) perceive emotions correctly (i.e. identify emotions in faces, pictures, and so on);
2) facilitate thought with emotion (i.e., harness information about emotions in one's reasoning);
3) understand emotions (i.e., make sense of and interpret emotions in the way they were meant); and
4) manage emotions (i.e., handle them in line with one's own aims and purposes).

In the spirit of the orthodox concept of emotional intelligence, the experience and demonstration, interpretation and perception, management and use of emotions have become fairly instrumental and calculative.

Nonetheless, although every member of a social system needs to manage his or her emotions to some degree, there are differences related to which roles and social positions people inherit. In our case the significant differences are those related to which emotions are deemed appropriate for superiors and subordinates. Conservative ideologies of 'the superior' and 'the leader' usually portray such people as rational in the sense of unemotional. However, since the 'discovery' of 'soft skills,' 'intangible assets' (Diefenbach 2006), and 'social capital' (Granovetter 1973), it is now increasingly portrayed as 'professional' (or even expected) that superiors will show emotions (though—and this is crucial—*in functional and instrumental terms:* the emotions have to support the achievement of those goals superiors and leaders pursue for the sake of the system).

One aspect of this is managing their own emotions: superiors and leaders should feel powerful and superior (to anyone else). And, the higher their position, the more it will help if a superior has developed (inflated) feelings of superiority, dominance, and even invincibility. A second aspect is that superiors should show their emotions particularly to their subordinates since 'displaying and experiencing emotions can make a manager more humane' (Lurie 2004, p. 8). Showing 'good' emotions—such as empathy, sympathy, humour, and passion for the job one is doing, but also anger or impatience when subordinates don't perform as expected—helps to strengthen superiors' position and to 'motivate' subordinates (Lewis 2000, pp. 222–3). Rubin et al. (2005) even suggested that it is important for leaders to accurately recognise and assess followers' 'authentic feelings' so that they can conduct their transformational leadership behaviour more efficiently.

What has been said about superiors' experience and expression of routine emotions is almost exactly the same with regard to subordinates. Again, for a long period of history, subordinates were expected not to show any signs of emotions—'hands' function without complaining (and, perhaps even more importantly, without anger). But decades of attempts to tap into followers' energy and employees' motivation have finally shown that subordinates' internal management of their emotions is more effective (from their superiors' or a systems' perspective) than external measures. Intangible assets such as 'motivation,' 'happiness,' and 'satisfaction' increase subordinates' performance and produce very tangible outcomes such as higher productivity and higher profit margins (Mast et al. 2010; Johanson et al. 2001; Kaplan and Norton 1992).

Thus, as in the case of superiors, management of subordinates' emotions in functional and instrumental terms makes a lot of sense. With regard to their own emotions, subordinates should develop (inflated) feelings of inferiority and intimidation so that they are even keener to perform and function as required. Moreover, subordinates nowadays are expected to demonstrate motivation, enthusiasm, even joy: subordinates shall be self-motivated and happy not only to perform, but to follow their superiors and to (further) condition themselves into performance-oriented automatons—and most of them are.

All in all, both superiors and subordinates (shall) experience and demonstrate their routine emotions in functional and instrumental terms; the former with regard to leading people, the latter with regard to following leaders.

4.2.5   The 'Right' Moral Character for People in Hierarchies

Notions about the moral characters of people and their (alleged) virtues and merits serve to explain and justify why people are where they are within the social system, why they deserve to be where they are, and why what they do routinely is right. These character traits can be anything that is portrayed as crucial in a given social system: certain virtues, attitudes, or skills; appropriate behaviour; the right social background; knowledge; looks—or something else only 'specialists' know. Whatever these traits are, they are regarded as sufficient explanation and justification for people's positions and statuses, privileges and prerogatives, and opportunities and obligations.

Superiors' public image is one of functioning and performance not so much *within* but *for* the system. Since this means great responsibility, there must be good reasons why superiors are superiors, why they routinely inherit positions higher up the hierarchical social order (and enjoy the privileges that come with them), why they deserve to be there, why they should be there, and why they must be there. Brookfield (2005, p. 47) described this orthodox logic as follows: 'After all, if the fittest really do survive then the ones who are in positions of power must be there by virtue of their innate strength or superior intelligence since this has obviously allowed them to rise to the top.'

In order to justify superiors' positions, the ideology of superiors is mainly based on rhetoric about the awe of the leader, the superiority of superiors, and superiors' competences, (leadership) skills, unrivalled character traits, and exceptional will (Groves and LaRocca 2011; Kark and Van Dijk 2007; Van Vugt 2006; Bass et al. 1987; Burns 1978). Leaders, even mediocre managers, seemingly have (or at least are capable of and willing to develop) all the positive leadership attributes and behaviours textbooks and proponents of orthodox leadership ideology propagate. Leaders and superiors are portrayed as working 'very hard' 'for the sake of the whole', caring about their subordinates and standing for all the norms and values of the social system. Their moral character is a best-practice example of how members of the social system should be.

Superiors, therefore, *deserve* their positions and responsibilities within the hierarchical system, along with their power and authority, and privileges and prerogatives (especially concerning decision-making with regard to the organisation of tasks, management of people, and allocation of resources)

(Baker 2005, p. 699; Chiapello and Fairclough 2002, p. 186; Kezar and Eckel 2002, p. 298; Zammuto et al. 2000, p. 263). Superiors are superiors because of their virtues and moral character, and they deserve to be superiors because of their merits.

Correspondingly, the public image of subordinates presents them as functioning smoothly and behaving within the limits and parameters set by their superiors and the system. In this image is the moral character of the servant and subordinate who functions smoothly within the system, and whose task, duty, and even honour it is to do whatever is expected of him or her 'for the sake of the whole.' These 'virtues' of 'the good subordinate' have been further operationalised by a variety of belief systems, for example traditional ones such as religion and nationalism (the 'true believer' or 'good soldier') and more recently developed ones such as managerialism and neoliberalism (the 'good worker' or 'confident consumer'). Such ideologies hold subordinates accountable and provide them with nagging doubts if they do not fit, behave, function, and perform as the various catechisms suggest. In this sense, most of people's doubts are not that genuine but rather more artificially created and nurtured by the dominant ideology—and, if these doubts do not work as hoped, there is a whole range of promises, threats, rewards, and punishments in place for getting the individual back in line.

Quite cynically, at the same time, subordinates 'ought' to have a strong sense of belonging—i.e., they should feel lucky and be happy to be part of the very hierarchically structured system that makes them subordinates. For this, they are provided with specifically designed moral ideas of obedience and serfdom so that they know not only how but also why they should function well (Stoddart 2007, p. 196; Courpasson and Dany 2003, p. 1232; Scott 1990, p. 58; Burnham 1941, p. 25).

In the following section it shall be looked at in more detail which levels of people's moral development (superiors and subordinates alike) corresponds with the requirements of hierarchical social systems.

4.2.6 Levels of Moral Development and Hierarchy

As indicated in Section 3.3.1, people's morality or immorality of their thoughts and deeds are highly relevant to how they actually fit into a given social system. Here in this section Kohlberg's 'stages of moral development' (Kohlberg and Wasserman 1980; Kohlberg and Hersh 1977; Kohlberg 1973) shall be used in order to interrogate which levels of people's moral development are routinely compatible with hierarchical social order.[3]

4.2.6.1 *Preconventional Level of Moral Development*
Most superiors' and subordinates' moral characters are close to Kohlberg's preconventional and conventional levels of moral development. According to Kohlberg, stage 1 of the 'preconventional level' describes a 'punishment-and-obedience orientation' (Kohlberg and Hersh 1977, pp. 56–7; Kohlberg 1973,

p. 631). At this stage, 'avoidance of punishment and unquestioning deference to power are valued in their own right, not in terms of respect for an underlying moral order supported by punishment and authority (the latter being stage 4)' (Kohlberg 1973, p. 631). Milgram (1974) has brought this 'obedience to authority' to the world's attention with his famous experiments on *ordinary people like you and me* following orders many would have assumed only fascists, sadists, or otherwise mentally ill people would follow.

It is debatable whether or not structural and procedural arrangements and social relationships within hierarchical social systems are equally, less, or even more authoritarian than Milgram's experimental situation. But usually most people (have to) follow some sort of factual or perceived pressure in the conduct of their daily (working) lives. Especially in the specific context of hierarchical social order, the most widespread subordinate moral character is very often that of the *submissive servant*, who defines himself or herself primarily via the requirements to function, to conform, to obey and to follow orders and, in doing so, to avoid negative sanctions (Alvesson and Willmott 2002, p. 619; Merton 1961, p. 52).

This is true for subordinates *and* superiors. It is commonly assumed that subordinates adhere to rules and regulations, that they comply more or less willingly with authority, that they follow the orders given by their superiors (Ashforth 1994, p. 759; Zaleznik 1989, p. 49) and, most importantly, that they have internalised these rationales as normal and accepted behaviour. However, many superiors, too, demonstrate the same low level of moral development—i.e., obeying and using authority, power and control primarily because they work in many ways. They follow the classical image and identity of 'the' superior, of those who rule via power differentials. Functioning in accordance with the order provided by an authoritarian regime and upholding its structures and processes are the main concerns of *both* superiors *and* subordinates who remain at the preconventional level of moral development. The 'obedient personality' of stage 1 fits perfectly with the logic of hierarchy.

At stage 2 of moral development (Kohlberg 1973, p. 631),

> Right action consists of that which instrumentally satisfies one's own needs and occasionally the needs of others. Human relations are viewed in terms like those of the market place. Elements of fairness, of reciprocity, and of equal sharing are present [. . .]. Reciprocity is a matter of 'you scratch my back and I'll scratch yours,' not of loyalty, gratitude, or justice.

Individuals see social relationships, interaction, and exchanging favours primarily as instrumental for the pursuit of their individual advantages (Crain 1985). The basic rationale is a kind of 'calculative selfishness'—i.e., the tendency of an individual to assess the opportunities and threats of a given or possible situation primarily with regard to the possible outcomes for himself/herself. Many people 'do their maths' in that way; they compare the opportunities institutions and other people provide for them with the (possible) downsides and decide on the strategy that seemingly offers the best deal *for them* compared to the time and effort they have to 'invest.' In this sense, 'calculative selfishness' is close to the psychological concept of egoism but also sees individuals as being within a specific social context and acting within it in tactical ways (though not completely rational or with all information provided, unlike the heroic/unrealistic assumptions of the 'homo oeconomicus' concept).

The pursuit of one's own individual interests, often reduced to sheer egoism and egocentrism, meanwhile forms a constituting element of the zeitgeist in most countries—traditionally more in developed Western countries, but increasingly also in developing countries, not only amongst ruling elites but increasingly amongst the aspirational (new) middle classes. With a 'calculative mind,' many people have *very explicit and conscious* interests in functioning smoothly within the parameters set by the system—*any* system, as long as it is advantageous for them. This is important to understand. People do not only function within the boundaries of a hierarchical, unjust, and oppressive social system (such as a hierarchical organisation) because they are not 'conscious' or 'reflective' enough; on the contrary, they are *very* aware of what is on offer (for them) and they are *therefore* very interested in functioning. Functioning makes considerable sense for the individual and is rational from the individual's perspective.

In our time, the calculative mind is seen most prominently in the form of the modern careerist (Musson and Duberley 2007, p. 158)—which is 'the' role model for superiors and subordinates alike. Like people with an obedient personality, people with a calculative mind seem to be equally drawn particularly towards (larger) hierarchical organisations because particularly *here* they can find the sources of power, privileges, and prerogatives they seek to accrue to themselves.

Either way, superiors and subordinates with a predominantly preconventional level of moral development fit 'perfectly' into any system of hierarchical social order since they follow in their behaviour largely what the system provides as incentives and punishment, opportunities and limits.

4.2.6.2 Conventional Level of Moral Development

In contrast to the self-centred perspectives people have at the preconventional level of moral development, at the conventional level (which comprises stages 3 and 4), people demonstrate a social conscience. According to Kohlberg (1973, p. 631), at this level of moral development

> Maintaining the expectations of the individual's family, group, or nation is perceived as valuable in its own right, regardless of immediate and obvious consequences. The attitude is not only one of conformity to personal expectations and social order, but of loyalty to it, of actively maintaining, supporting, and justifying the order, and of identifying with the persons or group involved in it.

At stage 3, it is about the importance of good interpersonal social relation-ships and there is, hence, an intention to demonstrate 'good behaviour' towards others (Kohlberg 1973, p. 631; Kohlberg also called this stage 'interpersonal concordance or "good boy-nice girl" orientation'). In contrast to people with a calculative mind, at stage 3 people not only want to function well for their own advantage but also (if not primarily) because of others' perceptions and expec-tations. One therefore might call this orientation 'social mind.' At this stage, a superior might genuinely try to support his/her staff, accommodate their concerns, and try to ensure that the working conditions and social relation-ships are much more developed than functional considerations would suggest are necessary, because the superior wants to be seen by his/her subordinates as a 'good boss.' Equally, at this stage subordinates might be, for example, concerned about the opinions and emotions of their coworkers (and superiors) because they are eager to be regarded as good team members.

It is a similar story concerning stage 4 of Kohlberg's taxonomy, the 'law and order' orientation. According to Kohlberg (1973, p. 631), at this stage there is 'orientation toward authority, fixed rules, and the maintenance of the social order. Right behavior consists of doing one's duty, showing respect for authority, and maintaining the given social order for its own sake.' The last part is the important bit. People obey rules because they are more broadly concerned with the stability of the social system or the society as a whole. That social order is maintained is regarded as a value in itself since otherwise the social system could not continue and, presumably, chaos would result (Crain 1985, p. 122).

People at this stage of moral development might be called 'good citizens'. They actively contribute to the continuation and stabilisation of the social order not for personal advantages (at least not primarily) but because they genuinely believe in the importance of those institutions—*whatever they are.* This is immediately understandable concerning superiors; as members of the ruling elite, their main values are represented and protected by the institu-tions (Mill 1956). In hierarchical social systems (such as stratified societies or orthodox organisations), institutions, structures, and processes are usually tailormade according to the preferences and interests of superiors. It would be very surprising if superiors found it difficult to appreciate the existing social order, its maintenance, and its protection as values in themselves.

But the same is true for most subordinates. Whether because of the hege-monic power of the dominant ideology (Abercrombie et al. 1980), because of psychological needs for certainty and stability, because of decades of socialisation and conditioning by different institutions, because of apathy, because of inability to imagine change, because of the absence of a positive alternative, or because of a combination of all of these factors, usually, most subordinates also appreciate the existing social order—despite all the struc-tural and systemic disadvantages and injustices with which it might provide them. To be a 'good citizen', hence, has positive but also, at the same time, quite paradoxical connotations. It means that, even for the disadvantaged with the moral character of the good citizen, there are good reasons to uphold hierarchical social order since it represents 'law and order.' The good citizen has many good reasons to contribute quite actively to the continuation of hierarchy.

4.2.6.3 *Postconventional Level of Moral Development*

According to Kohlberg, the highest level of moral development is the *postconventional level* which comprises stage 5 and 6. At this level, 'there is a clear effort to define moral values and principles that have validity and application apart from the authority of the groups or persons holding these principles and apart from the individual's own identification with these groups.' (Kohlberg 1973, pp. 631–2). Kohlberg's stage 5 implies a social-contract orientation— i.e., at this stage people are keen to implement and defend general principles and consensual rules for a good society that everyone with a free will could agree to. As Crain (1985, p. 123) says, 'Stage 5 respondents basically believe that a good society is best conceived as a social contract into which people freely enter to work toward the benefit of all.' In this sense, one could call people with such a moral character 'consensus-oriented citizens.'

However, even if people with free will were to decide in favour of, for example, fully participatory democracy, this, again, would not necessarily produce a hierarchy-free and egalitarian social system. As routine behaviour, conscious as well as unconscious communication and social interaction can lead over time to social relationships of dominance and subordination— i.e., informal hierarchy. Particularly, more active and ambitious members of democratic committees or other representative bodies may develop quite strong interests, tactics, and routine behaviour, using formal democratic structures and procedures in order to influence and to dominate consensus-building processes. In such cases, the paradox is that it is *especially* consensus-oriented members that contribute to the emergence of nonconsensual decision-making processes and informal hierarchy *because* of their efforts to achieve consensus and nonhierarchical/egalitarian forms of community. The outcome is participation of a few but no or little participation of the many; democracy in some respects but no democracy in many other respects; equality on paper but not in reality.

But there might be a solution to this problem. In his original taxonomy, Kohlberg had a sixth stage, representing a 'universal-ethical-principle orientation'. According to Kohlberg (1973, p. 632), at this stage,

> Right is defined by the decision of conscience in accord with self-chosen ethical principles appealing to logical comprehensiveness, universality,, and consistency. These principles are abstract and ethical (the Golden Rule, the categorical imperative); they are not concrete moral rules like the Ten Commandments. At heart, these are universal principles of justice, of the reciprocity and equality of human rights, and of respect for the dignity of human beings as individual persons.

With regard to nonhierarchical social systems, such 'universally true principles' could be liberty, egalitarianism, or tolerance. Such principles can be found in most cultures. In the Western context, many of these ideals were (re-)formulated in the 18th century during the Age of Enlightenment (mainly via reference to Greek philosophers). Accordingly, one might say that people who have reached this stage of moral development have an 'enlightened personality.'

People with enlightened personalities do not obey authority that is not democratic and egalitarian (Passini and Morselli 2010, p. 11; Rothschild-Witt 1979). They do not, and do not want to, contribute to the continuation of social dominance and hierarchical order in any form—whether knowingly or unknowingly, formally or informally. They reject hierarchical structures and processes, superior-subordinate relationships, dominance and obedience, order and control, and privileges and inequalities *per se*. They do not fit into *any* hierarchical system.

4.2.6.4 *Compatibility of Stages of Moral Development with Hierarchical Social Order*

To conclude, within a hierarchical social system, superiors' and subordinates' routinely shown moral characters are very similar and consistent, even mutually reinforcing. These moral characters largely concern obedience and calculative selfishness (preconventional moral character), and orientation towards peers and rules (conventional moral character), but even a social-contract orientation (stage 5 of postconventional moral character). Thus, hierarchy-conforming routine behaviour stretches almost over the entire range of moral development (see Table 1).

Table 1 Kohlberg's stages of moral development and their compatibility with hierarchical social order.

Kohlberg's stages of moral development	Individuals' predominant moral character	Compatibility with hierarchical social order
6) Universal-ethical-principle orientation	'Enlightened personality'	Not compatible with hierarchical social order
5) Social-contract orientation	'Consensus-oriented citizen'	
4) 'Law and order' orientation	'Good citizen'	
3) Interpersonal concordance, 'good boy–nice girl' orientation	'Social mind'	Stages 1)–5) Compatible with hierarchical social order
2) Instrumental-relativist orientation	'Calculative mind'	
1) Punishment-and-obedience orientation	'Obedient personality'	

People with preconventional and conventional levels of moral development (stages 1–4), and even those at the postconventional level (stage 5) are keen to function and to fit into the hierarchical system, either because of fear of negative consequences from authorities (stage 1), because it is to their advantage (stage 2), because they think their peers expect it from them (stage 3), because they appreciate rules and regulations as such (stage 4) or because they appreciate the common will (stage 5). Although the motivation at each stage is quite different, almost all rationales lead to routine behaviour which is compatible with hierarchy. Occasionally, people at these stages of moral development might show some minor forms of misbehaviour, but their prime concern is to pursue their interests and to navigate *within* the boundaries set by the system. Only those who are able, willing, and determined to cross boundaries *seriously*—i.e., with at least moderate if not strong intensity (see Sections 4.4 and 4.5)—might challenge the system and could even initiate system change. People who demonstrate behaviour consistent with stages 2 or 6 of moral development (the 'calculative mind' and the 'enlightened personality') would theoretically and practically be able to do so via their navigation. But there is a big difference between the two.

People with calculative minds (stage 2 behaviour) are interested in gaining, and securing, advantages primarily for themselves (and perhaps for some who are close to them and/or could be useful to them). They try to make the best of their individual situations in very practical terms; their energy and efforts focus on navigating tactically *within* the system. Thus, people who predominantly follow the rationale of 'calculative selfishness' (pretend to) comply with a system's rules and regulations like others *and* they deliberately cross boundaries. But, and this is crucial, they cross boundaries only if it suits *them*. They cross boundaries largely with weak or medium intensity and only for the purpose of gaining personal or group advantages (i.e., for practical reasons)—but not to challenge or change a hierarchical system fundamentally. They want to take advantage of the system, not to destroy it.

In contrast, people showing stage 6 of moral development challenge the system of hierarchical social order fundamentally and might be able to overcome and replace it with an alternative social system (see Sections 6.2.2 and 6.2.3). This is so because only they show personality traits and behaviour that are incompatible with hierarchical social order and that constitute medium- or even strong-intensity (i.e., system-threatening) boundary crossings. People who demonstrate stage 6 of moral development have an antiauthoritarian identity; adhere to ethical, truly democratic, and egalitarian norms and values; have strong interests in overcoming all forms of social dominance, injustice, inequality, and exploitation; and act correspondingly, showing empathy, altruism, and similar philanthropic principles and attitudes via their deeds. In so doing, they represent a fundamental challenge to any hierarchical system.

With regard to people's navigation within hierarchical systems, one can conclude that most people make use of their individual freedom only insofar as to function and to fit better into the system (stages 1–5). Only a very few challenge hierarchical social order on the basis of fundamental ethical concerns (stage 6).

This is remarkable in several respects. One is the sheer number of people who can live and work without protest within hierarchical systems. It is probably fair to assume that in most societies people at stages 1–5 of moral development represent the vast majority—perhaps 95 percent, to provide a rough guess. Most people might not be entirely happy about working for a hierarchical organisation and face the usual problems at their workplace. They might also complain about all the privileges and prerogatives 'the rich and powerful' enjoy in their society. However, they mostly do this at home in front of their televisions and otherwise comply.

To *some* extent, people reflect on their own and others' behaviour as well as the specific conditions of the situation they are in—i.e., what is 'good' or 'bad' about it—but they do not spend much time on considering the morality or immorality of hierarchy *as such*. Why should they? In their daily lives, people have to cope with a whole range of pressing problems with limited time and resources available to them. Hierarchy provides *practical* challenges—and most people usually try to carry out their tasks and to solve the problems they face in fairly pragmatic ways. People have very concrete concerns related to the opportunities and necessities their different social roles and positions bring—but not much beyond. They do not reason about the rightness or wrongness of the whole system; most people's reasoning and reflections happen *within* the framework of the hierarchical system. The system is taken for granted.

There are many possible reasons for the fact that most people see hierarchical systems and superior-subordinate relationships in more pragmatic than fundamental/ethical ways, and routinely comply. Actual and very tangible advantages, lifelong socialisation and conditioning, hegemonic ideology, and fear of change and the unknown might play parts.[4] But, whatever exactly it is that has made a certain person accustomed to hierarchical social order, one of the main consequences is that most people do not have a problem with the morality or immorality of the superior-subordinate relationship *as such* or with the moral aspects of hierarchy. From a moral point of view, most people have little problem with living and working within, and fitting into, a hierarchical system.[5] It is only a few who question, and perhaps even challenge, hierarchy and unequal social relationships in *fundamental* ways.

4.2.7   The Steady Reign and Persistence of Hierarchy

As outlined above, superiors' and subordinates' routine behaviour is highly compatible with the hierarchical system. Most people, superiors and subordinates alike, fit quite well into hierarchical social systems.

Moreover, superiors' and subordinates' social actions, interests, identities, emotions, and moral characters *complement and mutually reinforce each other*. Superiors' and subordinates' routine daily actions fit together perfectly in the sense that one gives orders and the other carries them out. Both have a strong common interest in the continuation of this unequal social relationship since both receive a whole range of advantages from it.

Moreover, superiors and subordinates see their identities in line with system requirements: superiors see themselves as capable leaders working hard for the common good; subordinates see themselves as well-functioning (and perhaps cunningly efficient) servants. With their tactical manoeuvring, both demonstrate emotional intelligence that supports their behaviour and meets others' expectations. Stereotypes of moral character, such as the 'caring leader' and 'loyal follower,' do their bit to synchronise superiors' and subordinates' contributions. And everything is held together by the prevailing ideology of hierarchy, which explains and justifies superiors' and subordinates' social roles, positions, statuses, and tasks, and why both deserve what they get (or don't get) and why this should not be changed. Table 2 summarises the findings of the (official) routine behaviour.

Superiors' and subordinates' mutually complementing routine behaviours are a very prominent example of *synchronisation* as outlined in Section 3.6 with regard to the process of systemisation. In any hierarchical social system, superiors' and subordinates' duties, tasks, attitudes, and behaviour *must* complement each other. But this is a synchronisation of unequal comrades in arms; superiors' power and their oppressive activities are completed by their subordinates' compliance and submissiveness. No social group could ever have dominated if it had not had submissive groups underneath it. Superiors' dominance is their subordinates' obedience; subordinates' obedience is their superiors' dominance. Since both groups take into account the views and possible responses of the other group, their behaviours and actions contribute to the stabilisation of their social relationship—their *hierarchical* social relationship. The unjust hierarchical social order is institutionalised and reconstituted on a daily basis and, at the same time, provides the framework for people's actions. Hierarchy creates a social system in which superiors and subordinates collaborate and coexist—each at their place and according to the powers and possibilities ascribed to their social roles and positions. In return, the system reaffirms and strengthens people's roles and positions. With regard to synchronised routine behaviour, hierarchical social order represents a harmonious cosmos. With their routine behaviour, superiors and subordinates work together in 'perfect' harmony towards the continuation and persistence of the very system that makes them function.

Table 2　Superiors' and subordinates' routine behaviours.

	Superiors	Subordinates
Social action	Professional conduct of office, functioning according to the requirements of the system.	Following orders from superiors, obeying rules and the existing order, functioning and behaving well.
Interests	Prime interest is to gain, keep, and increase their elevated position, and to keep the hierarchy intact, since, with the institutionalisation of hierarchy as an abstract organisational order, members of the ruling elite have managed to institutionalise their individual and group interests.	Prime interest is to function within, even contribute actively to, the continuation of the hierarchical system since it provides a whole range of advantages and because subordinates can improve their situation by behaving.
Identity	Classical identity of 'the' superior, reflecting their higher position, their identity as powerful rulers who guarantee order and control, and their identity as 'doers' and 'leaders' who provide guidance and direction.	Identity represents and reconfirms subordinates' lower position and inferiority. The public identity of 'the good subordinate' is quite simple, one-dimensional and infantile; it represents a deeply internalised 'learned helplessness' – the identity of a dependent and submissive servant.
Emotions	Managing one's own emotions in functional and instrumental terms. Developing inflated feelings of superiority and invincibility.	Confining one's own emotions to required demonstrations of feelings. Developing inflated feelings of inferiority and timidity.
Moral character	Moral character of the leader and superior who works very hard 'for the sake of the whole', who cares about his or her subordinates and stands for all the norms and values of the social system.	Moral character of the servant and subordinate who functions smoothly within the system, and whose task, duty, and even honour it is to do whatever is expected of him/her 'for the sake of the whole'.

4.3　BOUNDARY CROSSINGS AND THEIR OPERATIONALISATION

Although superiors' and subordinates' routine behaviour and hierarchy-compatible moral development dominate the daily affairs of any hierarchical social system, behaviour within organisations is not all routine and people do not always behave as they are expected to. Within any hierarchical system, *deviance* from expectations also happens on a daily basis.

Deviating behaviour can vary enormously in nature. For example, when it concerns organisations and the workplace, by and large the focus is on *negative* deviance—i.e., 'dysfunctional' behaviour or 'workplace deviance' (Biron 2010; Bryant and Higgins 2010; Spector and Fox 2010; Wahrman 2010; Lehman and Ramanujam 2009; Vardi and Weitz 2004; Prasad and Prasad 1998; Boye and Slora 1993). Terms such as 'organisational *misbehaviour*' (Vardi and Weitz 2004), 'workplace *aggression*' (Bryant and Cox 2003), '*hostile* workplace behaviour' (Keashly and Jagatic 2003), or '*bad* behaviour in organizations' (Griffin and Lopez 2005) make it even clearer that most (intentional) deviation is regarded negatively. This is mainly so because deviating behaviour challenges dominating norms and expectations. Robinson and Bennett (1997, p. 6) defined deviant workplace behaviour as 'those behaviors that violate norms that are perceived by organizational members to be pivotal or significant norms to the dominant administrative coalition of the organization'. In this sense, deviant behaviour can be understood as a *boundary crossing* (as outlined in Section 3.4—particularly Section 3.4.2).

Deviance/boundary crossings not only challenge social norms and people's expectations but also might be even seen as a threat to the larger entity, 'the system' (Griffin et al. 1998, p. 67). Nonetheless, there seems to be a paradox: deviance and boundary crossings may not only *threaten* the hierarchical system (and its representatives and proponents) but also often *re-establish* or even *strengthen* the hierarchical order *because* they challenge it!

In itself, this phenomenon is quite self-evident: individuals' (potential) deviance regularly triggers control activities and punitive sanctions by their immediate superiors as well as the wider system. Moreover, individuals' 'misbehaviour' often serves as a justification for precautionary measures and the implementation of more numerous, more comprehensive, and increasingly elaborated surveillance and punishment systems. Hence, the actual or alleged threats of deviance and related reactions strengthen the positions of superiors as well as the existence and continuation of the whole system. Boundary crossings at the same time both challenge and reconfirm the priority of the system and those who represent it. What is not clear, though, is when, why, and how *exactly* subordinates'—and superiors'(!)— deviance or boundary crossing may contribute to the (further) stabilisation, continuation, and persistence of the hierarchical social order—and when they might be, or become, system-threatening. In order to interrogate this question systematically, in this section, a concept of boundary crossings will be developed. In the following two sections, boundary crossings of subordinates, superiors respectively will be investigated based on this concept.

How one exactly operationalises boundaries, and crossings of them, depends on the phenomena one looks at and the aims of the investigation. As Table 3 shows, key aspects of boundaries and crossings of them can be operationalised in various ways.

Table 3 Aspects of boundary crossings and their operationalisation.

Aspect of boundaries and their crossing	Examples of their operationalisation
1. Type of boundary	Clear line or lines, clearly demarcated zone, vague line, vaguely demarcated zone or 'grey area'
2. Scope	Actual event and/or consequences (for the people involved, third parties and/or the system)
3. Identification	In more or less objective or subjective ways, by the people involved and/or third parties
4. Quality	Positive, neutral or negative (for the people involved and/or the system)
5. Intensity	Weak, medium, strong
6. Quantity	Single event or multiple crossings
7. Time horizon	Immediate, short-term, long-term

1) Within the social realm there can be very different *types of boundaries* (and, thus, different types of boundary crossing). For example, Scott's model of public and hidden transcripts (1990), which will be used here for the analysis, assumes one clearly defined boundary between the two transcripts. But boundaries do not necessarily need to represent one or more clearly demarcated line(s). Geddes and Callister (2007) have developed a more psychologically oriented model that comprises two 'thresholds' between zones of feelings or behaviour of the actors involved. The space between the thresholds represents 'grey areas' where social behaviour might become increasingly more deviant. In such cases there is no clear and well-defined 'line in the sand' that indicates what is socially accepted and what is not. Moreover, there could also be changes in the boundaries themselves—for example, a change in type; weakening or strengthening over time; or discursively agreed shifts in boundaries.

2) Boundaries and crossings of them raise a question about the actual *scope* of the phenomenon. For example, they could be analysed independently of the outcomes—i.e., examining only the actual event as well as the perceptions and interpretations of the people involved at the time. However, in most cases boundary crossings not only trigger immediate responses but also have further implications—i.e., *consequences*. There could be consequences for the people who were directly involved in the event, consequences for people who might be affected more indirectly, or consequences with regard to the wider social system. It often makes sense to include such consequences (the intended as well as unintended ones) in the analysis.

3) Acceptance or rejection of certain behaviour indicates that boundaries (and crossings of them) are socially constructed phenomena. Hence, boundaries and crossings of them can be defined and identified in various ways. For example, they can be defined relatively 'objectively,' as is often the case in legal or professional regulations. But, even in cases when a boundary and its crossing are established as a 'fact,' people may have very different understandings and interpretations of this particular phenomenon as well as what actually constitutes a crossing of a boundary in general. The definition (even identification) of boundary crossings is primarily a social and subjective phenomenon and, hence, depends greatly on the (sociocultural) context, the specific situation and the people involved. In addition, observers who are not directly involved in the actual boundary crossing (third parties such as representatives of institutions investigating the phenomenon or researchers) might interpret the event quite differently from the people involved (the well-known anthropological differentiation between 'etic' and 'emic' perspectives).

4) That boundary crossings and their consequences are open to interpretation suggests that their *quality*—i.e., how they are perceived and judged—can vary quite substantially. What is perceived by some as 'negative' deviance from expectations/boundary crossings (especially by the party 'on the other side' of the boundary) might be seen by others very differently, perhaps even as a positive act. Or it could be that 'positive' boundary crossings/deviations from norms and expectations challenge people's understandings in negative ways and might even threaten the whole social order.

5) Whether boundary crossings and/or their consequences are perceived as 'positive' or 'negative,' they can be of various magnitudes and can challenge boundaries with varied *intensities*. Since these are qualitative phenomena, there are several possibilities concerning the operationalisation of their intensity; specifically, along nominal, ordinal, or even cardinal scales. For the analysis of boundary crossings carried out in Sections 4.4 and 4.5, intensity is differentiated into three non-numerical categories: 'weak,' 'medium,' and 'strong':

a) A boundary crossing is *weak* when the actual boundary crossing, perceptions of it, and the immediate consequences following it are all within the range of typical daily life experiences for the parties involved. Besides coping with the boundary crossing itself *within the actual situation,* no further adjustments are needed by the actors. Example: an employee arrives at work late without informing his/her supervisor. The supervisor has a conversation with the employee in which the issue is discussed and solved without further consequences and hard feelings.

b) A boundary crossing is *medium* when the boundary crossing is (perceived as) so severe that further adjustments *beyond the actual situation* are required, along with additional resources to cope with the consequences. Example: A manager is accused of having bullied her employees over a longer period of time. An internal committee is set up with the help of the personnel department. If there is sufficient initial evidence, external agencies (i.e., a law enforcement agency) will be contacted and new policies formulated and implemented organisation-wide.

c) A boundary crossing is *strong* when the boundary crossing and/or its perceived relevance not only have fundamental consequences for (some of) the actors involved but also entail a *severe challenge to the fundamental principles, general order, and core values of the whole social system*—i.e., the system's future existence is at stake. Example: when a group, an organisation, or a whole nation is on the verge of disappearance because core values, principles, or mechanisms are not being accepted anymore and might be superseded by others.

6) Besides quality and intensity, the *quantity* of events is also of some relevance. Boundary crossings can happen once or several times. There can be a singular crossing followed by no reaction (or a confined reaction), after which people simply continue with their accepted routines. Nonetheless, social processes are often more complex and unfold over longer periods of time. In some cases, a boundary crossing by one person or group might trigger reactions with further implications and/ or might be answered by a boundary crossing from another actor or group involved—which may trigger yet another reaction. Thus, there can be multiple crossings with reciprocal, mutually reinforcing behaviours and increasingly severe consequences (so-called 'escalations of conflict,' 'tit-for-tat' strategies or vicious circles).

7) Looking beyond the actual boundary crossing and considering the possibility of multiple crossings draws attention to the *time horizon* of events and their consequences. One might differentiate between immediate/short-term, medium-term, and long-term perspectives. Seeing boundary crossings as a process in time and including consequences add further problems to the analysis. The effects of events may become visible only after a while. Usually, the further apart the actual boundary crossing and its consequences, the more difficult it is to identify, isolate, and analyse the direct links between the two (not to mention that, because of the complexity and multidimensionality of social phenomena, in social sciences it is always difficult to identify cause-and-effect linkages in the same way as in other sciences). Moreover, the intensity of the actual boundary crossing and the severity of its consequences may differ quite considerably. What was originally a weak crossing

may produce the most severe consequences—but such differences in magnitude only become obvious after a period of time and often only with hindsight.

In the following two sections, subordinates' and superiors' weak, medium, and strong boundary crossings will be analysed. The discussions primarily concern single, negative, clearly identified boundary crossings. In Chapter 5 a more complex, empirical case of multiple boundary crossings and escalation of conflict will be investigated. Since in this book the focus is on the persistence of hierarchical social order, the events of boundary crossings and some of their main possible consequences are interrogated primarily with regard to the stability and continuation of the social system. This is not to deny that most boundary crossings usually have more numerous and more important consequences for (some of) the actors and parties involved than for the social system of which they are a part. Particularly for weaker actors, the reactions and consequences that might follow boundary crossings may be quite severe (e.g., physical punishment, material disadvantages, legal consequences, negative sociopsychological effects, social disadvantages, and/or political defeats). Nonetheless, this investigation will concentrate on how boundary crossings may or may not constitute a challenge, or even threat, primarily for the continuation and persistence of the superior-subordinate relationship and the hierarchical social system as such, and not so much for individual actors involved.

4.4 SUBORDINATES' BOUNDARY CROSSINGS

4.4.1 Social Action—When Subordinates Don't Behave

In contrast to their publicly demonstrated ability to function well, subordinates often do not behave and function smoothly. Subordinates' organisational misbehaviour has been interrogated to quite some extent—especially how their dysfunctional behaviour and oppositional practices might impact negatively on organisations and how it can be punished or 'managed' (Courpasson and Dany 2003; Fleming and Spicer 2003; Bennett and Robinson 2000; Prasad and Prasad 1998; Robinson and Bennett 1997, 1995; Collinson 1994; Boye and Slora 1993).

Weak or low-level dysfunctionality in subordinates is recognised mostly in relation to behavioural tasks or responsibilities, for example as absenteeism, lateness, 'work-to-rule,' disengagement, minimal compliance, or 'playing the system.' While investigating workers' 'resistance through distance' at a heavy vehicle manufacturing company in the early 1980s, Collinson (1994) found a whole range of such low-key strategies of resistance. When Anderson (2008) investigated academics' resistance and tactical behaviour in the modern managerial university, she also found that minor deviance from expectations and minimal compliance were used as resistance strategies. Very often, such oppositional practices are accompanied by cynicism, scepticism, irony, or other forms of 'coping strategies' (Courpasson and Dany 2003; Fleming and Spicer 2003) and 'short-term escape attempts' (Collinson 1994, p. 39). Such 'routine resistance' (Prasad and Prasad 1998) is seen by many subordinates as a safer way to show their dislike of organisational arrangements than open acts of protest or refusal. Low-level dysfunctionality is difficult to detect, difficult to identify as deliberate resistance, and, therefore, difficult to punish.

Subordinates' weakly deviating social actions are meant to be small, cunning manoeuvres *within* the system. They largely observe the rules—even if they are intended to undermine them (Scott 1990, p. 93). With their weak social actions, subordinates predominantly seek tactical advantages—but they do not challenge superiors' positions let alone the foundations and principles of the system. As Burawoy (1981, p. 92) put it so poignantly: 'one cannot play a game and question the rules at the same time; consent to rules becomes consent to capitalist production.' At the end of his empirical analysis, Collinson (1994, p. 40) concluded that 'workers' resistance through distance reinforced the legitimacy of hierarchical control, left managerial prerogative unchallenged, and increased their vulnerability to disciplinary practices.' Common or minor organisational misbehaviour actually reiterates the importance of managerial responsibilities, comprehensive systems of surveillance and control and hierarchical order. Thus, subordinates' weak boundary crossing in the realm of social action not only provides the basis for subordinates' consent to and compliance with the hierarchical order but also contributes to the further strengthening and stabilisation of the hierarchical system.

However, there can be more severe forms of deviance by subordinates in the realm of social action. These can be either lawful or unlawful. For example, *unlawful* acts could be property deviance (theft, sabotage, vandalism) or serious personal aggression (bullying, sexual harassment, physical assault). If such unlawful challenges become public, they need to be stopped and sanctions introduced. Elaborated social systems usually have the legal and practical means to do so. Handling unlawful acts of deviance not only punishes the offender (and serves as an example to deter others) but also reconfirms the legitimacy of the hierarchical order. And, even if such unlawful acts are not detected and punished, the damage done is limited; some other individuals and/or assets and resources may be harmed, but not the whole system. The system of hierarchical social order will remain intact.

Nevertheless, there might also be *lawful,* medium-intensity deviance, for example open (organised) workplace resistance or confrontations between workers and management (Prasad and Prasad 1998; Robinson and Bennett 1997). Such acts can be quite powerful and forceful, but they are meant to remain within the legal framework of labour and civil law (Spicer and Böhm 2005, p. 3). Their goals are limited to tactical gains within the system, for example achieving a pay increase, securing jobs, improving working conditions, or the like. In addition, the means used to achieve these goals will conform to the system; examples are (threat of) strike, negotiations, and bargaining. Hence, although lawful resistance can be quite challenging indeed, it remains within the existing structures and processes the system provides. It can therefore be said that, in the realm of social action, any medium-intensity boundary crossing, whether lawful or unlawful, does not threaten the hierarchical order.

It is a different story, however, when it comes to subordinates' *strong* boundary crossings in the realm of social action; these can severely disrupt the order of whole organisations or even societies. There have been a few examples of strong boundary crossings by *individuals*. One of the most prominent is the unknown 'tank man,' who stopped a column of tanks near Tiananmen Square in 1989 simply by stepping (unarmed) into the path of the tanks and remaining in front of them. Other famous examples are Socrates drinking hemlock in ancient Athens and Martin Luther posting his 95 theses against the Catholic Church and its questionable practices on a church door in Wittenberg in 1517. There are many more examples of unsung heroes who have seriously challenged hierarchical social order by mere social action—but we do not know of them because often their stories are not told. However, what these examples, and the aftermath of each, show is that such strong social actions by individuals are rarely successful in the immediate situation. In the particular moment, such actions carried out by a single person (or a few individuals) are mainly of 'symbolic' value—sometimes it is not even clear whether the actors involved are aware of the historical meaning and long-term implications of their actions. But, exactly because of the symbolism of their actions, established order is seriously challenged.

Usually, the challenge gets bigger the more people are involved. Then, social actions and their consequences might seriously challenge the status quo. Such actions may involve *collective* open resistance, general strikes, coordinated output restrictions, collectively organised sabotage of production, revolt, ousting of management, company owners or ruling elites—and lastly revolution. If such widespread collective actions happen either in a very determined manner and/or over a long period of time they, indeed, constitute a very serious threat to the existing order. Comprehensive, intense, and/or longer-lasting social actions of subordinates test to the limit the system's mechanisms and its ability to respond; they may even overcome those mechanisms and abilities, meaning the end of the current social order and its replacement by a new one—i.e., revolutionary change.

To summarise, within the realm of social action, subordinates' *weak* and *medium-intensity* boundary crossings do not really challenge the system of hierarchical order; on the contrary, such deviating social actions simply justify the existence of the control and punishment systems already in place or prompt the introduction of new ones. Moreover, they leave the underlying rationales of hierarchical order intact and, in so doing, reiterate subordinates' consent to and compliance with the hierarchical order. Only subordinates' *strong* boundary crossings (i.e., individual action with strong symbolic meaning or comprehensive and determined collective social action) can constitute a serious threat to the system, since these challenge the existing order and the system's means to respond to their limits—or even beyond.

4.4.2   Interests—Why Subordinates (Sometimes) Do Not Want to Function

Subordinates' interests are relatively straightforward and, therefore, can be discussed quite briefly. Notwithstanding subordinates' very 'rational' interests in functioning well within the hierarchical system (as explained in Section 4.2), there might also be good reasons why they do *not* want to function. For example, within a larger social system one does not need to have an interest in functioning 'perfectly.' In many cases, giving the *impression* can be enough—and even more efficient than the actual deeds. Hence, while having an interest in functioning (or in pretending to function according to the official requirements), at the same time one can have an interest in secretly breaching or bypassing rules and regulations in order to gain personal advantages. If these advantages are relatively small, such an interest constitutes only a weak boundary crossing. Moreover, it does not threaten the hierarchical order since the interest focuses solely on gaining advantages *within* existing power-and-control relationships, not on changing them.

In contrast, medium-intensity boundary crossings in the realm of interests go against or beyond the immediate situation subordinates operate in. For example, subordinates might be interested in changing the direct power-and-control relationships they are part of, changing policies and procedures, changing key indicators of performance-measurement and management systems, or being more involved in the organisation of their work. Such interests go beyond the traditional understanding of what constitutes the 'legitimate' interests of subordinates. Nonetheless, in most organisations (i.e., nontotalitarian ones), even these kinds of expectations or demands do not constitute a serious threat to the system; contemporary discourses of change management, organisational learning, and personal development easily incorporate, if not to say hijack, themes of participation, empowerment, and equal opportunities. Hence, subordinates' possible interest in far-reaching participation can cross boundaries while at the same time disappear in the no-man's-land of managerial rhetoric and functional 'necessities.' It challenges the system without challenging it.

The situation would be different if subordinates were to develop a strong interest in changing the system of hierarchical order *fundamentally*—i.e., if they were to demonstrate a serious interest in overcoming the prevailing social order and replacing it with another system. Of course, in itself, such an interest is not sufficient to achieve its ends. In addition, it needs to be based on a comprehensive and compelling alternative ideology, to be supported by determined people with a non-obedient identity and to lead to corresponding social actions over a longer period of time (e.g., collective open resistance; general strikes; ousting of management, company owners or ruling elites; or, ultimately, revolution—or any other means that could contribute to overthrowing the current system). Nonetheless, subordinates' strong interest in system change represents a very serious threat to the system—because everything starts with people's interests; interests shape how people see and interpret the world, and they form people's ideas, intentions, decisions, attitudes, and actions (Darke and Chaiken 2005; Meglino and Korsgaard 2004; Suttle 1987; Hindess 1986). Interests provide the crucial link between people's reasoning and their decisions and actions. Interests are the link between what is and what could be. If subordinates were to develop an interest in overcoming the hierarchical system, this would constitute a serious threat to the system because then subordinates would look for ways to overcome the system and would attempt to actually do it. And, if they first fail, if the interest is alive, it will eventually happen.

4.4.3 Identity—The 'Good Modern Subordinate'

Although the identity of the subordinate is largely one of a dependent and submissive servant demonstrating 'learned helplessness,' there are other aspects in subordinates' identity that counterbalance, and could even dominate, these features. For example, particularly in Western cultures the notion of 'individualism'—i.e., the idea that the individual should make up his/her own mind and formulate and follow his/her own goals (whether these are egoistic or altruistic) as *he/she* deems appropriate—forms a very strong part of many people's identities. Most Western people are socialised that way in various institutions (e.g., by their parents, at kindergarten, in school, and in further- and higher-education institutions) alongside the notion of 'conformism,' which is the main outcome of systemisation and its mechanisms (see Section 3.6). Trends towards individualism, in addition to other value orientations, can also be seen increasingly in cultures that are predominantly collectivistic (e.g., many Arabic and Asian cultures).

In this sense, on the one hand many subordinates see themselves as 'creative' and 'knowledgeable' members of social systems with their *own* identities, personal aspirations, professional aims, and individual goals. They see themselves as capable of voicing their opinions and of deciding and acting independently—whether they are allowed to do so or not. Such a self-image based on the values of individualism can be understood as a weak boundary crossing in the realm of identity since it goes against the ideal of the dependent, infantile, and submissive servant.

On the other hand, in contemporary management concepts and many modern/postmodern organisations, there is already a fair amount of talk about individualism in the form of 'individual skills development,' 'potential,' 'empowerment,' and even 'intrapreneurship.' Subordinates are encouraged to 'express themselves' and to show their 'personality' and 'creativity' (Prasad and Prasad 1998, p. 251). Although such concepts and appeals are often not really meant as seriously as their labels or the rhetoric about them might suggest, they are nonetheless used for tapping into the capabilities of subordinates that superiors and the system cannot reach with more traditional methods.

As a result, the notions of conformism *and* individualism, dependency *and* independency, and learned helplessness *and* individual mastery form large parts of *the same identity* of the modern subordinate. The identity of the modern subordinate is a paradoxical combination of contradictory features that subordinates have to demonstrate and apply according to situational requirements. The 'good modern subordinate' is a chameleon.

Thus, *some* nonconformism and *minor* deviance from the classical image of the subordinate are not only accepted but even expected and required—of course, within the limits and parameters set by superiors and the system. A kind of 'rule-based nonconformism' is required; nonconformism is the norm both superiors and subordinates have to conform to (though to different intensities). In this sense, demonstrating little signs of individualism shows that the subordinate functions well. But this also means that using the space and opportunities organisations provide to show one's 'personality' and to develop one's (professional) identity in the spirit of 'rule-based nonconformism' does not challenge but rather complies with system requirements. *Some* deviation from the ideal of the solely submissive and infantile subordinate hardly crosses boundaries—and it definitely doesn't challenge the hierarchical order.

There is another paradox related to subordinates' identity—but this time it means a greater challenge for the system. It is of central importance to hierarchical organisations to make sure that only subordinates' 'professional'—i.e., status-related identity—manifests at work (Selznick 1961, p. 21) and that all other parts of their identities are excluded, contained, or at least domesticated into functional channels. Realising individualism by showing 'little signs of an individual identity' is acceptable within a nontotalitarian hierarchical social system. But it would be a very different matter if subordinates were to dare to take the idea of individualism or empowerment (too) *seriously*—i.e., if they, for example, dared to bring their *whole* identity to the workplace. Such a process might be called 'individualisation.' It means that people become fully aware of their own identity and that they live out their whole identity within a given situational context and institutions. Individualisation, thus, means disentanglement from system conformity and from expectations that subordinates will function well.

The problem is that we know little about subordinates' whole identities. In contrast to the public image and identity of 'the good subordinate' (which has been comprehensively developed and disseminated in every epoch), we have very little information about the whole, but hidden, identities of subordinates. A first glimpse of them comes from looking at how subordinates actually see themselves and behave *outside* formal hierarchical settings, for example in areas of their private lives and spare time. People can behave differently compared to their public role-playing when they are on their own, amongst their family and friends, pursuing their hobbies or maintaining everything that makes up their private lives. In their private lives, most people manage their own affairs; they are able to gather information and to analyse and use it; they are capable of making operational *and* strategic decisions; and they are motivated to put those decisions into action and to manage the multidimensional consequences. In many areas of their private lives, people cover the whole range of activities that at work are the prerogatives of their superiors. And people do not only behave differently— they *are* different. In their back yards, subordinates reveal everything that is oppressed at the workplace.

However, one needs to be also cautious not to idealise people's private lives and identities. In alternative approaches one often finds the (implicit) assumption that, if people had more opportunities to develop and to live out their whole identities, they would be 'better' people. This does not necessarily need to be the case. For example, as the description of the mechanism of 'transformation' outlined (see Section 3.6, on systemisation), outside formally established hierarchical social relationships, people can continue (or fall back on) formal or informal superior-subordinate relationships. They may continue to think and act like subordinates (e.g., when they have yet another dominant superior in form of their partner, family members, or friends) or may reverse the order and develop into superiors to others. In such cases, even when they have the opportunity to live and act freely, they do little other than repeat and re-enact their hierarchy-conforming identities and show the same traits as they do within hierarchical organisations. Their whole identity is not much different from their limited, obedient, and functionalistic identity—whether this is the result of more sociopsychological/ external factors of socialisation and conditioning by hierarchical institutions or psychological/internal characteristics of their personality.

In contrast, 'whole identity' in the sense of individualisation would mean that people show the personality traits of a free individual as well as the related antihierarchical reasoning and behaviour. The focus is on seeing oneself and others as individuals and ends in themselves.[6]

One can imagine that in hierarchy-free areas of people's private lives individualisation shapes social reality quite considerably. But it would have even more fundamental and far-reaching consequences if subordinates were to begin to realise their whole identities *within* the hierarchical context. If that were the case, subordinates would start to understand that the hierarchical social order and their thoroughly defined roles within the system are in quite some opposition to their own identities and interests. If subordinates were to become fully aware of how much institutional context on the one hand and their personal interests and whole identities on the other hand actually differ, they would begin to think about ways to change the situation they are in so that it corresponds with their whole identities and needs. The concept of individualisation goes directly against the idea of superiors and subordinates, of hierarchical systems *per se*. Subordinates' medium-intensity boundary crossing in the realm of identity therefore means a serious threat and challenge to the hierarchical order.

Interestingly, 'solidarisation,' which represents the idea of a collective identity, produces similar outcomes to individualisation; solidarisation also makes subordinates aware of how much their interests and hierarchical social order actually differ. Subordinates are the majority, but have little to say. They do the work, but don't participate equally in the outcomes. They are humans, but are treated like machines. If subordinates were to develop (again) a strong collective sense of themselves, it would become much more difficult to handle them; the historical slogan of all oppressed all over the world, 'Together we are strong!', reflects the core principle of solidarisation. For example, in their case study on clashes between the proponents of new managerialistic methods (e.g., 'just in time,' total quality management) and opponents in an engineering company, Ezzamel et al. (2001) provided evidence for how workers' identities (and resistance) became stronger via the growth of a 'them-and-us philosophy' that seriously challenged the company's management. Subordinates' collective identity goes directly against the position of superiors and their interests. And what goes against superiors goes against the very idea of hierarchy. Subordinates' solidarisation in the sense of a collective identity *always* represents a serious threat to the system.

With regard to the idea (or threat) of individualisation, one might say that superiors can only work with *subordinates,* not with *individuals*. And, if we add the idea (or threat) of solidarisation, one might say that superiors can only work with *isolated* subordinates, not with individuals who have also a *collective* identity. In this sense, it is quite a misinterpretation (perhaps deliberate) when individualisation and solidarisation are portrayed as exclusive opposites. *Both* significantly challenge the publicly portrayed image of the 'good'—i.e., domesticated and isolated—subordinate. *Both* make subordinates 'unmanageable'—the former because of its strong sense of a sovereign and autonomous individual, the latter because of its 'together-we-are-strong' notion. And *both* threaten the very established social order that implies the necessity of superiors and subordinates. Hence, any attempt of subordinates to either bring in their whole identity (individualisation) or develop a strong collective identity (solidarisation) constitutes at a medium-intensity level a serious threat to the hierarchical system.[7] And, if subordinates' individualisation and solidarisation were to come together, they would mean the end of any hierarchical system.

Individualisation or solidarisation could lead to even stronger boundary crossing if they not only challenged the prevailing understanding of subordinates' identity *within* the *existing* system of hierarchical order but also provided a convincing *alternative* identity for subordinates as well as an outline of the social order in which they could exist. Subordinates who have developed a truly alternative identity based on the ideas of individualisation and solidarisation would no longer obey hierarchical power; on the contrary, they would begin to 'take things into their own hands.' They would be determined to change the fundamental conditions of their lives and social practices—i.e., to overcome the prevailing social order and replace it with another system. Such an alternative system would entail social relationships in which all people could live out and develop their whole identities, and in which there were no longer superiors or subordinates. An alternative social system based on the ideas of individualisation and solidarisation would comprise organisations and institutions that no longer put people into hierarchical social relationships, instead providing them with equal rights and opportunities.

4.4.4   Emotions—What Subordinates Are (Not) Allowed to Feel

As outlined in Section 4.2.4, subordinates' public experience and expression of routine emotions are largely about showing the expected feelings of inferiority and intimidation, and at the same time showing motivation, enthusiasm, and even joy about fulfilling the tasks subordinates are expected to do and belonging to the very system that makes them subordinates. However, subordinates' hidden emotions are fundamentally different from these publically displayed functional and instrumental emotions; their hidden emotions represent the whole range of human emotions, from love to hate, from calmness to anger, from apathy to passion and from sadness to happiness. Human emotions do not ask whether they are appropriate or not, nor whether they are instrumental for the individual, for others or for the social system, and they may impact on the individual and his/her social relationships in unintended ways, or ways that no one has ever thought about.

Nevertheless, subordinates' weak boundary crossings in the realm of the emotions are largely about *not* showing the 'appropriate' or 'right' emotions—or showing too much or too little of those emotions that are required to function properly within a certain hierarchical social system. For example, employees may show low levels of motivation or job satisfaction, school children may be keen to play instead of do their homework, and soldiers may show too much fear before or during combat. Whatever the reasons—and however reasonable or otherwise these emotions might be for the individual subordinate—with respect to what is expected (by superiors, others or 'the system'), within a hierarchical social order showing too much, too little, or no emotions is regarded as 'emotional malfunction.'

Whether or not such emotional malfunctions are detected and dealt with (individually or systematically) depends on how totalitarian a hierarchical social system is. Such issues might be captured in employees' job-satisfaction surveys, in reports officers forward to their generals, or via control and surveillance measures applied by governmental agencies. Low-intensity boundary crossings in the realm of the emotions may cause some concern because, according to an orthodox understanding, emotions influence the smooth functioning of subordinates, their performance, and overall outcomes negatively (Lewis 2000, p. 231). For example, Reisel et al. (2010) provided evidence that lower job security and/or lower job satisfaction reduce organisational citizenship behaviour (i.e., system-conforming behaviour of employees that goes beyond their contractual obligations) but increase deviant behaviour, anxiety, anger, and burnout. And Ostell (1996, pp. 552–3) was even clearer on this issue: 'Dysfunctional emotional reactions are commonplace and can result in poor work performance and disturbed relations with colleagues which represent a significant cost for both the individuals concerned and the organization.'

In addition, emotional deviance may generate questions or even doubts about the individual subordinate, his/her commitment to the 'common cause' and his/her suitability to fit in. Thus, emotional malfunctions usually raise 'developmental' concerns and trigger some form of action (e.g., direct intervention by superiors, training and skills development seminars, or other measures aiming to 'boost morale').[8] Whatever the actual measures are, they all happen at a fairly 'technical' level. Subordinates' weak boundary crossings in the realm of emotions do not constitute a threat to the system.

This could be different if subordinates began to show emotions that are not part of their role repertoire. As the discussion above about the 'whole range of human emotions' indicated, there could be many such emotions. But perhaps the strongest negative emotion in the social realm is *anger*. One might assume that subordinates are not allowed to show any anger at all— but that is not true. They are allowed, indeed sometimes even encouraged, to show their anger—about very specific matters and in ways their superiors want them to be angry. Subordinates are allowed to be angry about clearly identified peripheral issues, such as problems or threats outside the social system (e.g., a foreign enemy, an unfair market competitor); unlawful or stigmatised issues within the social system (e.g., illegal immigrants, whistle-blowers); or technical issues (e.g., insufficient tools for carrying out assigned tasks). But by no means should subordinates ever show their anger about their superiors or the system because anger means danger: 'Anger is associated with tense, energized feelings and a tendency to attack (or at least, want to attack), the anger target, both verbally and non-verbally' (Fitness 2000, p. 149). In this sense, subordinates' anger about their superiors and/or the system can be seen as a medium-intensity boundary crossing.

Genuine anger is usually triggered when people perceive the way they or others are treated as 'unfair,' 'unjust.' or humiliating (Fitness 2000, p. 147). When subordinates publicly show their anger about superiors or the system, this is always regarded as disobedience, as opposition—and perhaps even taken personally by superiors as an insult. Subordinates' anger, therefore, will usually trigger quite determined reactions and may lead to 'tit-for-tat' strategies and vicious circles of increasingly stronger feelings, opinions, and actions on both sides—including more emotional distress and deviance.

How much of a challenge subordinates' anger actually constitutes for their superiors or the system depends on various factors. The intensity and potential danger of anger depend on the kind of incident it relates to, how many people share this feeling and their level of intensity, and how the system responds. If subordinates' anger is restricted to single incidents and if the angry individuals are isolated and their anger is managed and channelled into structures and processes provided by the system (e.g., complaint procedures, committees, legal processes), then the anger might last only for a short period of time and will not constitute any real threat to the system or its representatives (any more).

But, if the incident is regarded as representative of systemic failures, if there are strong feelings of injustice and if there is collective anger of subordinates targeted not only at individual superiors but also 'the system,' then this constitutes a serious threat to the hierarchical system. In his book *Pedagogy of the Oppressed*, the Brazilian educator and philosopher Paolo Freire gave a vivid description of the kind of situation that provides fertile ground for the anger of subordinates (1996, p. 26): 'thwarted by injustice, exploitation, oppression, and the violence of the oppressors; [humanisation as people's vocation] is affirmed by the yearning of the oppressed for freedom and justice, and by their struggle to recover their lost humanity.' Sooner or later, subordinates will come to the point where they conclude that enough is enough—and their collective anger will turn into collective action. It was probably the intellectual contributions of the philosophers of the Enlightenment that laid the groundwork for the French Revolution—but it was the collective anger of the common Parisian people that led to the storming of the Bastille.

When subordinates become angry they become superiors. Individual anger can be quite intense, but subordinates' collective anger can easily turn into a serious threat. Thus, subordinates' medium-intensity boundary crossings in the realm of emotions are system-threatening because, if unleashed, no one can tell where they will stop.

Moreover, subordinates may show emotions that not only go against the very idea of what subordinates ought to feel but also provide alternatives— *positive* alternatives—and, thus, represent strong boundary crossings in the realm of the emotions. Intuitively, one would assume that positive emotions might not cause much concern. But, as the example of Mahatma Ghandi's successful strategy of nonviolent civil disobedience against the British colonial oppression in India showed, emotions such as calmness, tolerance, and love can have very strong and challenging power. These positive emotions strengthened the Indian demonstrators' strategy of 'nonviolent resistance' and became a powerful weapon in the social struggle for independence and freedom because they were in direct opposition to everything the colonial superiors stood for. This was crucial; the emotions and values Ghandi and his fellow citizens propagated and practised broke with the logic of hierarchy. The main feelings people have within a hierarchical system are of social dominance and obedience. If an alternative to hierarchy is provided, the corresponding emotions *have to* be the opposite.

Such alternative emotions reflect the idea of a 'prosocial motivation' (Grant and Berg 2010) or 'other orientation' (Meglino and Korsgaard 2004)—i.e., 'the desire to have a positive impact on other people or social collectives' (Grant and Berg 2010, p. 1). People who predominantly show such feelings and concerns will demonstrate less dominance-oriented and selfish interest and show more prosocial values, empathy, and altruistic and socially responsible behaviour (Meglino and Korsgaard 2004, pp. 947–8). Such values, personality traits, and emotions do not go together with any form of hierarchy or processes of social domination.

Of course, a 'prosocial motivation' or 'other orientation' (for example) alone is not enough to realise an alternative social system that does not reduce people to superiors and subordinates. But such positive beliefs and emotions indicate that there can be alternatives to hierarchy-conforming emotions, that the urge for social dominance and obedience is not necessarily in people's behavioural repertoires and that prosocial orientations can even overcome oppressive regimes. Nonhierarchical emotions are always *anti*hierarchical emotions. They, thus, represent a serious challenge and threat to any hierarchical social system.

4.4.5   Moral Character—How and Why Subordinates Misbehave

As outlined in Section 4.2.5, the public image of 'the good subordinate' largely concerns functioning smoothly and behaving within the limits and parameters set by superiors and the system. Officially, moral norms and values are taken quite seriously since they explain and justify the different roles, positions, privileges, and duties of individuals and groups within a social system as well as the goodness and rightness of the whole system (Beetham 1991). Challenges to such underlying principles thus make people aware of fundamental aspects of their lives that otherwise usually remain quite unexamined. And, whenever people start to think about fundamental issues, the situation becomes dangerous! Established worldviews as well as the prevailing order are challenged. One could therefore assume that *any* boundary crossing in the realm of moral character, norms, and values—whether weak, medium, or strong—could constitute a serious threat to the system. However, in this section a more differentiated argument will be provided.

Despite the prevailing ideology of obedience and functioning well, most people would portray themselves as independent individuals who have their own minds and who do not buy into 'official rhetoric.' Keeping a cynical distance from the officially prevailing norms and values of a hierarchical system is probably the hidden transcript of most subordinates. For example, very often employees do not believe in the mission and vision statements of the companies they work for (and most superiors probably do not believe in them, either)—but, actually, this is not necessary. It is quite typical of hegemonic nontotalitarian ideologies such as managerialism that people keep a fair distance between themselves and all official 'gobbledygook.' What is important, though, is that they act and behave *as if* they believed in the official principles (Fleming and Spicer 2003, p. 169)—and they can do so enthusiastically or detachedly, cynically or grumblingly. According to Brookfield (2005, p. 140), 'in both hegemony and disciplinary power, the consent of people to these processes is paramount. They take pride in the efficiency with which they learn appropriate boundaries, avoid "inappropriate" critique, and keep themselves in line.' Subordinates' cynical distance *together with* their practical compliance is one of the cornerstones of nontotalitarian value and belief systems.

But subordinates' cynical distance can easily turn into noncompliance with the moral norms and standards of a social system, as discussed in Section 4.4.1 with regard to subordinates' tactical manoeuvring. Minor unethical behaviours or organisational misbehaviours such as dishonesty towards others, petty theft, or noncompliance with minor social or organisational rules (Vardi and Weitz 2004; Griffin et al. 1998; Boye and Slora 1993) might be carried out by subordinates every now and then. Such unethical behaviour and organisational misbehaviour crosses lines of social norms and values and may breach the psychological contract (between, for example, employer and employee), organisational policies, professional standards, or social and/or legal rules. They not only constitute weak boundary crossing in the realm of social actions but also raise questions about subordinates' moral character, especially if they are done deliberately and consciously. Weak boundary crossings in the realm of moral character are typical of people whose moral development remains largely at stage 2 of Kohlberg's taxonomy—i.e., they follow the logic of calculative selfishness. But such boundary crossings are not rare instances; they happen on a more or less regular basis. They are part of the unnormal normality of hierarchical social systems—and these systems are designed for the (assumed or factual) misbehaviour of their members. Moreover, hierarchy is based on the assumption that subordinates are not 'perfect' and that their moral character is low. In this sense, subordinates' weak boundary crossings in the realm of moral character do not threaten the status quo; on the contrary, they strengthen the hierarchical social order.

Nonetheless, subordinates may cross boundaries in the realm of moral character in a more challenging manner. One quite realistic possibility is to take the prevailing rhetoric about moral norms and standards *seriously*. For example, while investigating prisoners' daily struggles to cope with the regime of imprisonment, Scott (1990, p. 94) found surprisingly cunning tactics employed by the inmates not only towards each other but also towards staff, who were, of course, in a much stronger position concerning almost every aspect of prison life:

> Deprived of realistic revolutionary options and having few political resources by definition, inmates nevertheless manage to conduct an effective struggle against the institution's authorities, by using hege-

monic ideology to good advantage. [. . .] This consists in stressing the established norms of the rulers of their small kingdom and claiming that these rulers have violated the norms by which they justify their own authority. [. . .] Their behaviour in this respect is moralistic; it is the staff who are deviating from legitimate norms, not they.

Such tactics can also be found in an organisational context. Companies' visions and strategic change initiatives are often based on a 'people-are-our-greatest-value' rhetoric and concepts of empowerment and participation. Subordinates may explicitly refer to these statements and, in so doing, can hold their superiors and the organisation accountable (Fleming and Spicer 2003, p. 172). This would mean quite a challenge since the realities of social systems usually do not live up to the claims made in official statements. In his empirical study of forms of resistance amongst workers in a car factory in Turkey, Yücesan-Özdemir (2003) found that the ideological discourse of empowerment constituted the regime's Achilles heel. Workers' resistance against the managerialistic work regime and control methods was successful by taking the new discourses and methods seriously and, in doing so, revealing their mendacity.

Taking the prevailing ideology literally challenges the (alleged) consistency between words and deeds and between claims and facts on moral grounds. It questions the integrity of the system as well as the integrity of its proponents. What makes it even more challenging is the fact that taking norms and values literally cannot be downplayed or handled as 'irrelevant' or as 'personal opinions'; on the contrary, it needs to be treated very seriously and sincerely, at least officially. And, whether it is operational norms and values or the basic principles the system is built on that are being tested, any rifts that might occur between public claims and actual practices could be interpreted as a (moral) weakness or even untruthfulness of the system—or, probably even more worryingly, of its proponents. Taking the prevailing norms and values literally is perceived by the proponents of the system as if *their* moral character is under scrutiny (which, indeed, it is) and as if subordinates are claiming to be of higher moral standards (which they might or might not be).

The above notwithstanding, although taking prevailing norms and values literally will likely constitute some temporary difficulties for the representatives of the system, it may not develop into a serious challenge. One reason is that the challenge remains within the logic of the system, its terminology, and its prevailing rhetoric; it does not provide a fundamental critique, nor does it ask for the termination of the current system or the creation of a new one. All it asks is that the reality of the social system is brought closer to what is officially said about it. Another reason is that proponents of the system are usually quite experienced in official rhetoric, political debates, and the use of practical means to handle deviance. And the prevailing norms and values are their home turf. Hence, when it comes to discourses about living up to the norms and moral standards of a social system, subordinates' challenges may trigger *some* changes in rhetoric and technical adjustments but will not alter the foundations on which the system is built.

But there is another medium-intensity boundary crossing in the realm of moral character that is quite the opposite of taking the prevailing moral standards literally. Specifically, this is an open and straightforward challenge to those moral standards, for example when subordinates openly refuse to comply with what is publicly expected of them. Scott (1990, p. 203) described this idea quite fittingly:

> Any public refusal, in the teeth of power, to produce the words, gestures, and other signs of normative compliance is typically construed—and typically intended—as an act of defiance. Here the crucial distinction is between a *practical failure* to comply and a *declared refusal* to comply. The former does not necessarily breach the normative order of domination; the latter almost always does.

How serious this challenge is for the system depends on whether or not *heresy* (in which members of a social system question the leading principles of the social order) is at the same time *deviance* (in which members of a social system deviate either positively or negatively from normatively sanctioned patterns of behaviour). Harshbarger (1973) found that, if deviance and heresy are both present, the proponents of the system can deal with this type of 'problem' comparatively easily; renegades can be accused of 'immoral behaviour,' be punished for their obvious or alleged noncompliance with 'technical' rules of the system, and, in doing so, be isolated, silenced, or forced to leave.

In contrast, in the case of heresy *without* deviance, the system and its proponents face a much more serious problem. Then, heretics air their nonconformist views and fundamental disagreements (or what are perceived or portrayed as such by parts of the ruling elite and their supporters) but otherwise 'technically' comply with the rules and regulations of the system. When subordinates start to challenge the system in such ways *from within*—i.e., to criticise it on ideological and moral grounds without officially opposing it—the situation becomes really dangerous.

Sooner or later, every social system faces such opposition from within. It then depends on the legal foundations of the system as well as the moral character of its proponents how such criticism is handled. In the case of heresy without deviance, direct forms of punishment—as well as other actions that are often used against rebels—are no longer applicable (or can only be applied with quite some difficulty). More cunning, often only partly legal (or even criminal), twists by the ruling elite are then required. For fighting heretics, the representatives of the establishment have a whole range of (questionable) means and measures at hand—for example, sheer physical force or other primitive means; labelling opposing views as political deviation (or even 'treason'); finding, constructing, or making up other 'serious' reasons to punish the heretic; or the use of sophisticated and mendacious rhetoric and slander. Usually, representatives of the system or their henchmen try a combination of different means.

Of course, heretics are aware of this. Hence, an important part of their 'no-deviance strategy' is to avoid being found out for as long as possible—i.e., to play cat and mouse with the system. The longer it takes to punish or even silence the heretics, the higher are the chances that their criticism and deviating ideas will be spread and that followers will emerge and join the heretic. Proponents of the system and/or the authorities will therefore be keen to find, or create, reasons for punishing the heretic sooner rather than later. Often, though not always, they will manage to silence the heretic one way or another. But, even if the system has coped 'successfully' with the heresy (and the heretic!), the intellectual/ideological challenges he or she has formulated will not go away.

This is so for several reasons. One is that the dissidents voiced and disseminated their ideas when they were still members of the system. It is significant that, although people are probably no longer allowed to refer publicly to 'the dissident' (he or she is now a *'persona non grata'*), intellectually (and often emotionally) some still will because the dissident was 'one of us.' Since dissidents/heretics have been part of the system, often even part of the establishment or at least part of an intellectual elite, their criticism is usually accurate and effective. Heretics can often reveal the weaknesses of the system and its representatives in a knowledgeable, thorough, and compelling manner. Especially since in this situation the criticism is being put forward from within the prevailing system and its logics, it is usually difficult to rebut it or portray it as irrelevant. In addition, the more or less questionable ways in which the heretics are likely to have been treated by the establishment will strengthen their arguments even more. Hence, even if the heretics have been discredited personally, their ideas will be still convincing and will contribute to the evaporation of the prevailing order from within. Even if the heretics are gone, their ideas will live on and continue to oppose the system until it is finally terminated and replaced by another system. You can burn houses, books, and even people, but you can't burn ideas.

Proponents of hierarchical orders might possess a whole arsenal of measures against *heretics*, but against *heresy without deviance* they have not found a recipe yet—because there is none. Heresy without deviance is probably one of the sharpest swords available to system critics. Although just a medium-intensity boundary crossing, it constitutes a serious threat to the system.

Yet, the sword of heresy is only sharp on one side. Heresy *as such* 'merely' criticises and challenges an existing order—it does not say what could or should be in its place. Heresy, as important as it is for challenging prevailing norms and values on moral grounds, is a necessary but not sufficient precondition for system change. To be sufficient, it must be accompanied by *alternative* values (very) different from the currently dominating ones. In the case of a hierarchical system, these alternative moral values must be of a nonhierarchical nature, for example egalitarianism, communitarianism, or similar concepts. And if people practice such values they show nonhierarchical moral character traits—which are obviously in fundamental opposition to the idea of being a subordinate and, hence, entail strong boundary crossing.

For example, the ideas of 'liberty, equality, fraternity' provided a powerful, convincing, and morally superior alternative ideology to the ideals and morality of the French monarchy and aristocrats. But they also required morally higher developed people—which didn't materialise, as the usurpation of power by Robespierre and the Jacobins and their 'reign of terror' showed so dramatically (another typical, though rather bloody, example for Michels' 'iron law of oligarchy'—see the Introduction). In contrast, as the aforementioned example of India's successful fight for independence from its British colonial oppressors showed, Ghandi and his followers won because they remained true to the ideals of 'nonviolent resistance.' They kept the moral upper hand because they didn't break the law, remained true to their own political agenda, and did not obey even in the face of brutal physical force. Whenever subordinates develop and practice alternative, nonhierarchical norms and values and show the corresponding moral character traits, this constitutes a serious challenge for any prevailing hierarchical social order.

4.4.6 Subordinates' unproblematic deviance—and exceptions

This section began with the paradox that some of subordinates' deliberate or coincidental challenges of hierarchical order do not threaten but rather stabilise, even strengthen, the system. The question was how and when exactly a boundary crossing might have either such system-stabilising or system-threatening consequences. A closer analysis focusing on the various elements of subordinates' social actions and their mindsets (i.e., interests, identities, emotions, moral characters) and on the three intensities of subordinates' boundary crossings produced some possible answers. Table 4 summarises the analysis carried out in the previous sections.

Cases in which subordinates' deviance and misbehaviour actually contribute to the further continuation of the system of hierarchical order are relatively straightforward. Concerning social actions or interests, weak-intensity and even medium-intensity boundary crossings (e.g., minimal compliance, rule-based nonconformism, active resistance, and changes of existing practices) *never* challenge hierarchical social order; on the contrary, they further strengthen the hierarchical system. This is so because all such boundary crossings happen not just within the system but within the *logic* of the system of hierarchical social order. To some extent, they are even expected by the proponents of the hierarchical system and there are more than enough measures in place that can handle such crossings.

Hierarchical social systems are designed to cope with people's deviance. According to the logic of hierarchy, *any* deviance from prevailing official

Table 4 Subordinates' boundary crossings in the realms of social action, interests, identity, emotions, and moral character.[1]

	Social action	Interests	Identity	Emotions	Moral character
Public transcript	Demonstration of obedience, submissiveness and conformism; functioning well	Functioning, conforming, performing, obeying and following	The 'good' subordinate (i.e. submissive servant), learned helplessness	Demonstration of required emotions (such as motivation, enthusiasm) in the right intensity	Values of functioning and performance, obedience, serfdom; work ethos, nationalism, hedonism
Hidden transcript	Cynicism, scepticism, deviance, resistance, illegal action, sabotage, conspiracy	Personal interests	Non-conformism, breaking out of routines, 'private life identity'	Whole range of human emotions, some perhaps inflated (e.g. confidence)	Cynical distance
a) Weak boundary crossing	'Work-to-rule', minimal compliance	Breaching or bypassing 'technical' rules in order to pursue one's own interests	Individualism	Showing none of, too much of or too little of the emotions required	Minor unethical behaviour
b) Medium boundary crossing	Rejection, active resistance within existing rules and regulations	Changing existing immediate social situation and practices in one's favour	Individualisation; solidarisation	Emotions that are not part of subordinates' role repertoire (e.g. anger towards superiors or the system)	Taking the prevailing norms and values seriously; declared refusal to comply/ heresy
c) Strong boundary crossing	Open (collective) resistance; revolt, revolution	Changing the system fundamentally	Alternative identity to the one superiors want subordinates to have	Alternative, non-hierarchical emotions	Alternative value system, or anti-hierarchical utopia

Consequences for a) weak, b) medium and c) strong boundary crossing				
a) and b) can and will be dealt with within the system and, hence, strengthen the system; c) is system-threatening, especially when it develops into widespread collective action	a) and b) can and will be dealt with within the system and, hence, strengthen the system; c) is system-threatening when subordinates find their common interest	a) has a safety-valve function and is system-stabilising; b) and c) are system-threatening because they go against the very idea of hierarchy and being subordinates	a) can and will be dealt with within the system and, hence, strengthens the system; b) and c) are system-threatening because they go against the very idea of hierarchy and being subordinates	a) can and will be dealt with within the system; b) is system-threatening when it consists of heresy without deviance; c) is a serious challenge since it provides alternative ideas and values

[1] Boxes in light grey indicate serious challenges to the system.

norms and policies *must* be, and *will* be, handled and sanctions introduced. If members' hidden actions or deviating mindsets come to the attention of their superiors or 'the system,' they will usually trigger 'appropriate' responses. And, if the direct intervention through superiors is not enough, special institutions or units of the social system set up for the purpose of coping with members' noncompliance will join in (e.g., law enforcement agencies or social services at a societal level; human resource management or other administrative units within organisations). In any developed hierarchical social order, various layers of elaborated control and punishment systems, policies, procedures, and measures are in place that can, and *will*, cope with all sorts of challenges—either via relatively crude and direct sanctions or, increasingly, by providing 'feedback,' 'support,' 'guidance,' 'help,' 'training,' or 'skills development.' But, whatever the actual label is, these measures are designed to cope with almost all possible forms of boundary crossings and deviant behaviour. And, if new forms take the system by surprise, they will not last long in the no-man's-land of unmanaged deviance. Such incidents will trigger either the further development of existing power-and-control systems or the introduction and implementation of new systems and measures of surveillance, control, punishment, and betterment. Hierarchical social systems are built on the assumption that members do not, perhaps even do not want to, function perfectly and that they try to deviate from rules, regulations, official policies, and procedures. Hierarchical social systems have an 'innate inertia'; as soon as they start to exist, they develop mechanisms that defend them and prevent their termination. It is the system, the hierarchical social order itself, that is against change. In this sense, even people's *non*compliance with the routine functioning of the system—i.e., their weak and medium-intensity boundary crossing—contributes to a further strengthening and continuation of the hierarchical social order.

Also, *strong* crossings are relatively easy to explain. *All* strong boundary crossings *always* constitute a serious threat to a hierarchical system since they represent phenomena that can go beyond institutions' capabilities to cope with them (e.g., subordinates' collective open resistance; strong interest in system change; alternative identity, emotions, and/or value system). Subordinates who show strong boundary crossings challenge the very idea of hierarchical social order.

The seriousness, but also necessity, of such strong crossings is perhaps more obvious with regard to oppressive regimes such as tyrannies, dictatorships, oligarchies, extremist monarchies, or radical communist states. But, in *some* respects, the problem of the persistence of hierarchical social order is even greater in moderate hierarchical social systems such as democratic societies or business organisations because the mechanisms are more complex and less obvious than in totalitarian regimes. Most institutions, structures, and processes of moderate hierarchies, even those for controlling and confining subordinates, are no longer 'iron fists' and instead increasingly 'velvet gloves' (Courpasson and Clegg 2006, p. 324; see also Section 4.6). Moderate hierarchical systems usually offer a whole range of advantages not only for the small minority of power elites but also for the majority of the people. Moreover, they provide subordinates with a mixture of identities, values, and emotions—such as 'rule-based nonconformism,' 'pragmatic individualism,' and 'calculative mind'—so that subordinates perceive moderate hierarchical orders as no longer oppressive but rather even as advantageous. The notion of hierarchy is so embedded and established in social relationships, institutional structures, and processes and so overrun by choice and opportunities that most people take it as part of the package and don't reflect on it anymore—let alone criticise it or seek alternatives. In most parts of the world and most parts of our societies, hierarchy is established and maintained via relatively moderate social systems (cultural institutions, traditions, parenthood, educational institutions, and public and private organisations). In the face of this 'normality' of hierarchy, strong boundary crossings seem to be quite inappropriate—at least at the beginning of social conflict.

Nevertheless, there are a few exceptions in the realm of subordinates' *medium-intensity* boundary crossings that could cause serious problems even for very established hierarchical systems: subordinates' *individualisation* and/or *solidarisation* (in the realm of identity), *anger* (in the realm of emotions), and *heresy without deviance* (in the realm of moral character). As outlined above, these concepts oppose the very idea of hierarchy *per se*:

1) *Individualisation* (i.e., seeing oneself and others as individuals and ends in oneself/themselves) is in fundamental opposition to system imperatives, in particular with regard to the ideas of system conformity and expectations of functioning well.

2) *Solidarisation* (i.e., a strong collective identity of subordinates) goes against the position of superiors and their interests—and what goes against superiors goes against the hierarchical order.

3) *Anger* (i.e., subordinates' collective anger towards their superiors and the system because of a strong feeling of unfair and unjust treatment) makes subordinates superiors.

4) *Heresy without deviance* (i.e., criticism of a system's norms and values from within the system) reveals the ideological mendacity of a hierarchical system and its representatives.

In other words, individualisation challenges the very understanding of 'being subordinate' (because it says: 'I am the master of my own destiny!'), solidarisation challenges the understanding of subordinates as the weaker part (because it says: 'Together we are strong!'), anger puts subordinates on an equal playing field (because it says: 'We are as strong as you!') and heresy without deviance challenges the validity of superiors' value claims (because it says: 'Actually, *you* do *not* stand for our common values; *we* do!').

These boundary crossings represent very powerful challenges for *any* hierarchical social system because they do not exist in the blueprint for hierarchy. For the system they are anomalies and, thus, cannot be tackled by its proponents with the usual measures they have at hand. These challenges represent mindsets and personalities that are *not* hierarchy-conforming—and hierarchy-conforming mindsets and personalities are necessary preconditions for the existence and continuation of any hierarchical social order.[9] Together, these medium-intensity crossings lead automatically to a strong interest and strong actions against the established order and, hence, the possibility of overcome it—and *any* hierarchical social system.

4.5   SUPERIORS' BOUNDARY CROSSINGS

4.5.1   Social Action—Superiors' Misbehaviour and its 'Normalisation'

So far, it is mostly subordinates' organisational misbehaviour that has been interrogated. But how about *superiors'* deviance and misbehaviour? In some contrast to their public or routine behaviour, we know very little about the *hidden* practices and activities of members of the power elites—i.e., their hidden misbehaviour, personal insufficiencies, dysfunctions, deviance and malpractices. This section will particularly focus on managers (as one type of superiors) and their malpractices. It will not focus on those extreme cases of corporate scandals where senior managers enrich themselves at the expenses of shareholders and the wider public and then depart with their golden handshakes, leave their companies in disarray. It is more about the *daily countless little acts of managerial misbehaviour,* particularly towards and against (their) subordinates and the organisation as a whole.

Research into such managerial deviance is rare and limited. Bryant and Cox's (2003) investigation of some 'atrocity tales' about managerial violence during organisational change and Vredenburgh and Bender's (1998) brief investigation of 'hierarchical abuse of power' contributed to a small minority of studies that have tried to shed some light on managers' organisational misbehaviour. However, close to nothing is known about the impact of superiors' misbehaviour on the system of hierarchical order—i.e., when and why their deviance contributes to the stabilisation of the system, and when their misbehaviour, indeed, might constitute a serious threat to it.

Some evidence suggests that organisational misbehaviour of leaders and managers is quite a common phenomenon within organisations. For example, when Vandekerckhove and Commers (2003, p. 42) carried out a metaanalysis of several empirical studies, they found that downward workplace mobbing makes up 81 percent of all workplace mobbing cases in the United States, 63 percent in the United Kingdom, and 57 percent in continental Europe. Hence, it is quite realistic to assume that many superiors show the same whole range of deviating or dysfunctional behaviours within organisations as do their subordinates—possibly even more and to a worse degree, since superiors' position higher up the pecking order provides them with more opportunities to deviate from norms of 'good behaviour.' More elbowroom enables superiors to enact more of the little incivilities and bad attitudes people with poorly developed characters and inferior moral value systems demonstrate in the presence of others, particularly weaker and disadvantaged people. Ashforth (1994, pp. 756–7) gave a good description of some of these minor forms of personal aggression and inappropriate behaviour carried out by people he called 'petty tyrants':

Recurring elements appear to include: close supervision, distrust and suspicion, cold and impersonal interactions, severe and public criticism of others' character and behaviour, condescending and patronizing behaviour, emotional outbursts, coercion, and boastful behaviour; they suggest an individual who emphasizes authority and status differences, is rigid and inflexible, makes arbitrary decisions, takes credit for the efforts of others and blames them for mistakes, fails to consult with others or keep them informed, discourages informal interaction among subordinates, obstructs their development, and deters initiative and dissent. Pervasive themes in these descriptions are a tendency to overcontrol others and to treat them in an arbitrary, uncaring, and punitive manner.

Organisational misbehaviour of petty tyrants can be regarded as superiors' weak boundary crossing in the realm of social action (with regard to the hierarchical system—in contrast, subordinates or colleagues who are at the receiving end of such behaviour may regard it as a *strong* crossing with severe consequences). To a certain degree superiors are even *required* to differ from 'societal ideals of good behaviour' in the conduct of their office. They need to 'get the job done' and to give the impression of being capable of 'moving things.' According to a traditional understanding of 'the' manager, leader, or 'doer,' they must demonstrate attitudes such as determination, toughness, and even ruthlessness; crossing lines, overcoming odds and demonstrating noncompliance every now and then seem to be almost a necessity for superiors. Many managers learn this during their organisational socialisation and career. Indeed, they will have had to, since otherwise they could not have reached their position nor stayed there. There seems to be some logic inherent in hierarchical organisations that superiors cross boundaries quite regularly. Most, if not all, such low-level misbehaviour of superiors is perceived, portrayed, and even accepted as 'normal.' Such deviance, thus, does not constitute a threat to the hierarchical system.

However, it is only a small step from superiors' low-intensity boundary crossing to a more medium-intensity form. *Serious* personal workplace aggression, for example systematic abusive behaviour such as bullying over a long period of time, can constitute such medium-intensity boundary crossings (Zapf and Gross 2001; Bassman and London 1993). Alternatively, there can be criminal actions of managers via which moral *and* legal boundaries are crossed, for example corporate tax evasion, personal enrichment, bribery, or other forms of gross managerial misconduct.

Nonetheless, even such medium-intensity crossings in the form of immoral and/or criminal behaviour of individual managers do *not* constitute a threat to the hierarchical order. One reason for this is that such misbehaviour is played down when it becomes public. It is portrayed as an exception to the rule, as the 'unacceptable' and 'regrettable' misbehaviour of 'a', or 'a few' individual manager(s) (the 'black sheep'). Another reason can be found in the way superiors' organisational misbehaviour is usually handled. More or less serious attempts to reveal and punish such misbehaviour take place on the basis of existing rules and regulations (e.g., a company's codes of conduct, policies, and procedures) and via special institutions (e.g., committees and complaints commissions). These systems are regularly strongly biased towards superiors and towards the protection and strengthening of superiors' positions and prerogatives. Quite often, the incident—or crucial parts of it—is swept under the carpet or dealt with by the system in ways that are particularly sympathetic towards superiors' interests and positions. The majority of cases that attempt to punish superiors' organisational misbehaviour by using the organisational systems and procedures in place end up either in a whitewash, minor punitive actions, or recommendations to install further hierarchical and bureaucratic policies and procedures. Somewhat cynically, this 'orderly' handling of cases actually demonstrates that 'the system' works and lives up to its official norms and values. Thus, medium-intensity forms of superiors' misbehaviour are not system-threatening; on the contrary, they often contribute to a further strengthening of the system.

The case is different when there are collective and widespread malpractices (or even illegal practices) by members of the power elite. Incidents then can no longer be portrayed as 'individual' misbehaviour but are evidence of systemic and underlying problems, such as:

- unjustified group-based privileges and prerogatives, larger social inequalities, and unjust allocation of opportunities and resources (e.g., executives' salaries and bonus schemes, pay schemes for certain professions, senior public servants' privileges and salaries, socioeconomic and cultural advantages of members of the establishment or the middle classes);

- systematic exploitation and poor treatment of subordinates (e.g., regular physical and/or psychological violence against workers, withholding of opportunities and resources for personal development);

- mismanagement or unethical behaviour in many organisations, whole industries, or societal institutions (e.g., politics, media, banking and finance, insurance companies, real estate agencies, the automotive industry, the chemical and pharmaceutical industry, and the like).

Such gross misbehaviours of superiors constitute strong boundary crossings since they go against the leading norms and values which the social systems allegedly are based on (e.g., merit-based appreciation of members, fair and just treatment of everyone, moral and/or legal standards).

What makes matters worse is that such practices happen regularly, and are systemic and institutionalised. Moreover, the examples show that such cases are not confined to so-called 'banana republics' or a few dubious industries in industrialised nations. Unethical behaviour, unjustified group-based privileges, systematic exploitation, and injustices are often widely accepted standards and practices in many parts of the societies of developing *as well as* industrialised countries. Superiors' systematic misbehaviour forms a constitutional part of most, if not all, economically well-developed democracies. It is the norm and (unnormal) normality of society as we know it.

This 'normalisation' of superiors' misbehaviour even in so-called 'developed' and democratic countries is further evidence of the fact that power elites are usually quite successful in *legalising* and *institutionalising* their antisocial behaviour by creating fitting images and customs, norms and values, and laws and regulations; *hierarchical organisations and stratified societies are legalised and institutionalised misbehaviour of superiors.*

Superiors know this. Members of power elites all over the world know very well that they can carry on with their dubious practices and antisocial behaviour only as long as they keep their elevated social positions (and have access to and control over the means that come with them) and as long as the system of hierarchical order continues to exist. The very idea of ruling elites is to take advantage *of* the system, not work *against* it. All they want is to exploit the system, not endanger it.

It could be, though, that their actions weaken the system over time—i.e., that superiors' widespread and systematic misbehaviour contributes to a slow erosion of the system.[10] In such cases the whole ruling elite (or parts of it) appears to be corrupt and/or unfit to govern. Sooner or later, some or even all of them will then be replaced. But, if this 'change' in government, or even 'revolution,' is limited to the realm of social action and does not come with a fundamentally different (value) system (and corresponding institutions, rules, and regulations), all that will have happened is the substitution of one ruling elite with another elite (see also Section 6.1.3). Under the new ruling elite, the exploitation and abuse of the people and the system will simply continue—as the history of social evolutionary and revolutionary change has demonstrated so many times.

To sum up, superiors' weak-intensity and medium-intensity boundary crossings in the realm of social action are largely acceptable for a hierarchical system. Even superiors' widespread, collective, and systematic misbehaviour over a long period of time 'merely' abuses people and the system; it does not challenge the very foundations and principles of the existing order.

4.5.2 Interests—Superiors' Interests in the Continuation of Hierarchy

Superiors' hidden personal and group interests are in stark contrast to their public images. For example, like many other employees, many managers' first allegiance is *not* to the company they work for but to their individual aims and careers, their peer groups and profession, and their private lives and concerns (Willmott 1997, p. 1335; Thompson 1961, p. 491). Many superiors do not care (so much) about the system but more about their positions and opportunities within the system—with good reason: if they had not put their personal and career interests first and everything else second (including the organisation they work for), most managers would not have reached their positions (and will not make future progress).

Such an orientation towards personal and career interests is even expected of managers. Many believe that only superiors who are 'ambitious,' who want to excel and who want to make a career are the type of 'doers,' 'achievers,' and 'leaders' who can get things done (and get other people going). Such an understanding corresponds quite well with the system's requirements. The hierarchical organisation is based on the principle that privileges and prerogatives are allocated according to position on the hierarchical ladder—the higher one is, the more one gets. Superiors' prime interests, thus, *have to be* about gaining, keeping, and increasing their formal position—and all that comes with it (i.e., social status, dominance and supremacy, responsibilities and influence, privileges and prerogatives, material and immaterial resources, and career and other opportunities) (Clegg and Walsh 2004, pp. 230–1; Willmott 1996, p. 326; Zaleznik 1989, p. 152). Hence, although superiors' hidden personal and group interests go against the publicly portrayed interest of 'serving the common good,' they are nonetheless perceived as good for the system. Superiors' interests in gaining personal advantages and pursuing their own goals, in playing the system or in increasing their formal and informal status and position do not challenge the system of hierarchical order but strengthen it. Superiors' weak boundary crossings in the form of pursuing their individual and group interests are a crucial component of the continuation of the hierarchical system.

Moreover, most superiors' main interest is that the hierarchical system works for *them*—not that they work for the system. They are interested in having the 'right' conditions in order to pursue their individual and group interests *systematically* and in *organised* ways. They, therefore, have a profound interest in the hierarchical structures and processes, rules and regulations, policies and procedures, performance-measurement systems and management systems reflecting *their* individual and group interests. Of course, ruling elites are not one homogenous group. They consist of subgroups with their own agendas and interests with regard to political power and influence, access to resources, and supremacy. Thus, there can be very different understandings and intense clashes between different groups—for example between current rulers and their challengers, or between proponents of the status quo and proponents of change. Such diverse interests (e.g., changing the key objectives, structures, and processes of a social system via strategic change and/or replacing current superiors with others) can be regarded as medium-intensity boundary crossings since they challenge the status quo of the system in quite profound ways.

Superiors and members of power elites know very well that all their privileges and prerogatives come from the hierarchical system, and only from the system; *without the system they would be nothing.* And superiors are very aware of the fact that only hierarchical systems can provide and guarantee group-based dominance and privileges. Hence, members of power elites usually have a fundamental interest in the continuation of the hierarchical system (in order to further institutionalise their individual and group interests and privileges and prerogatives) and in protecting the system as much as they can. Even when using rhetoric about 'change,' their actual interest is to leave the main principles of hierarchical ordering and social dominance intact. They are interested in obtaining a position for themselves in which they can take advantage of the system, not damage or destroy it. In this sense, even the most far-reaching change initiatives remain within the logically and technically defined limits of the system of hierarchy and, thus, do not constitute a threat to the hierarchical system.

In contrast, it is *extremely* exceptional for members of a ruling elite to develop a strong interest in overcoming the system of hierarchical social order—but it is possible. Mikhail Gorbachev, once General Secretary of the Communist Party of the Soviet Union and a Nobel Peace Prize holder, is perhaps one of the most famous leaders who achieved system change not only from within but also from the top end of the hierarchical system. In the 1980s he initiated *glasnost* ('transparency') and *perestroika* ('conversion'), and at the end of the 1980s he was one of the key figures who brought down the Iron Curtain and ended the communist regimes in the Soviet Union and Eastern Europe. Such exceptional personalities with fundamentally deviating interests can also be found amongst managers, for example social entrepreneurs such as the founder of Wikipedia, Jimmy Wales.

If members of ruling elites develop a strong interest in changing the system, it is even more worrying and potentially dangerous than when subordinates do so. This is mainly the case because members of ruling elites usually have more insider knowledge—i.e., they know better what is actually wrong with the current system, what its weaknesses are, and where one could or even should start in order to achieve fundamental change. They are often also in a better position to initiate far-reaching change, have more resources (or access to them) and can be more capable of formulating and communicating the alternative concept, mobilising support for it, and ensuring that the process will continue to unfold until the objectives have been reached. Whatever the hierarchical social system, if members of the ruling elite develop a strong interest in changing it fundamentally, the system *is* challenged fundamentally. Superiors' strong boundary crossing in the realm of interests constitutes a very serious threat to the system of hierarchical order.

4.5.3 Identity—Superiors can be whoever they are (or Want to be)

Superiors' hidden identities can, like their interests, be very different from their public ones—particularly regarding superiors' public identity as 'the' superior and 'leader' who is self-confident and has a fully developed personality. The hidden identities especially of many power-oriented superiors can probably be described best as 'insecure careerist.' Such superiors compensate for their insecurity by demonstrating excessive self-confidence, compensate for their low self-esteem by bullying others, and compensate for their shallowness by name-dropping. When people with distorted personalities and identities gain power via hierarchical positions, their insecurities, narcissism, and power-and control-orientation can turn into managerial incompetence, tendencies towards grandiosity (concerning themselves, their actions, and ideas) and distrust (concerning others).

Seen in that way, in the realm of superiors' identities, the 'insecure careerist' or 'egotistic leader' represents a weak boundary crossing. As problematic as these petty tyrants' behaviour might be for the people around them, particularly for those who have to work with and under them, such weak crossings do not threaten the hierarchical order; on the contrary, they contribute to keeping the system going. The hierarchical organisation—*any* hierarchical system—*needs* superiors with underdeveloped personalities because they gain most of their self-esteem from the status and power that is related to their roles and positions. They, thus, will defend the system in every respect. Moreover, people with such personality traits seem to be drawn particularly to (larger) hierarchical organisations because here they can find opportunities to live out and nurture their unbalanced identities as well as opportunities to access the power, privilege, and prerogatives they need to pamper their egos.

A boundary crossing in the realm of identity would become medium-intense if superiors were to begin to live out their hidden identities to the full—as described in Section 4.4.3 with regard to subordinates' identity. There are similarities as well as differences between superiors' and subordinates' individualisation. For both, living out their whole identity can be either a continuation of hierarchy-conforming characteristics (transformation) or the start of a hierarchy-free self-understanding and existence (individualisation). The question is how this relates to the hierarchical social order.

In the case of hierarchy-conforming transformation, superiors are no longer just 'insecure careerists' but become 'dictatorial egomaniacs' who see the organisation or the area they are responsible for as *their* realm in which they can (almost) do whatever pleases their distorted authoritarian identity. Obviously, this is quite challenging, perhaps even unbearable, for everyone around them. For the system, though, even superiors with such identities are tolerable, at least for quite a while. Superiors' authoritarian identity might (temporarily) reduce a hierarchical system's efficiency—but it does not challenge its principles. Even more extreme examples of individual superiors' distorted identities are not system-threatening. And, if an individual superior were indeed to become too extreme, he or she would simply be replaced—i.e., promoted (which is often the case), moved to another part of the organisation (which sometimes happens), or sacked (rarely). Either way, in contrast to *subordinates'* individualisation, *superiors'* individualisation does not challenge the hierarchical social order. If superiors demonstrate their whole identity as independent individuals, this is portrayed *not* as a boundary crossing but rather as their 'personality' or even 'charisma'—which is allegedly needed for carrying out their leadership roles. Hence, *their* individualisation is good for the system—they are even encouraged and empowered in that way.

And there is another difference compared to subordinates' medium-intensity crossings; it would *not* constitute a threat to the hierarchical system if superiors were to develop a strong group identity ('solidarisation'). As the discussion of subordinates' solidarisation showed, *their* solidarisation can mean a threat to the system of hierarchical order because united people are stronger—which is exactly the reason why superiors' solidarisation is *not* a challenge. This needs some explanation. Hierarchy is based on the old Roman principle *'divide et impera'* (divide and rule). As long as subordinates can be kept isolated and managed in ways that keep them so, the rulers will remain in power and the system will prevail. Subordinates' solidarisation, thus, goes against the very idea of hierarchy and threatens its continuation (see Section 4.4.3). It is a different story with superiors, though. The main idea is that superiors rule—by (almost) any means. One of the means that makes groups strong—and stronger than others—is group cohesion. Thus, for ruling elites, who are always a minority within the hierarchical social system they govern and exploit, it is extremely important to develop and maintain a strong group identity and cohesion so that they are able to keep and defend their elevated social positions (Westphal and Khanna 2003; Sidanius and Pratto 1999; Useem 1984; Mills 1956). For example, despite all their individual interests and hierarchical competition, managers share a fundamental understanding of what it means to be a manager, to belong to the 'group of managers' and to identify with it to a certain degree (at least with the same type and subgroup of managers at the same level—e.g., lower, middle, or senior managers). According to Mills (1956, p. 11), there is 'a kind of mutual attraction among those who "sit on the same terrace"'; they 'come to understand what they have in common, and so close their ranks against outsiders.' Amongst managers, intense socialisation 'into the normative expectations and priorities of the corporate elite' (Westphal and Khanna 2003, p. 362) happens on a daily basis. Deviance is hardly accepted and will be subject to sanctions. Managers, thus, develop some group cohesion because of their common status *as managers* (Riantoputra 2010; Jost and Elsbach 2001, p. 183; Hindess 1986, p. 123; Hartley 1983, p. 16).

The concepts of individualisation and solidarisation represent powerful and threatening ideas, probably the most powerful ones against hierarchy— when *subordinates* appreciate and realise those ideas. It is a different story when it comes to superiors. Members of power elites have *always* enjoyed individualisation and solidarisation; because of their elevated social positions, they have the means to pursue their lives according to the idea of individualisation while at the same time they are keen to achieve and maintain strong solidarisation with their peers in order to protect their privileges and the means of their dominance as a minority. Hence, even superiors with individually quite deviating identities and whole groups of superiors with a very strong and exclusive but cohesive group identity will defend the very system they seemingly negate and counteract with their egocentrism. Any hierarchical system *needs* (allegedly) strong superiors and coherent power elites because they are portrayed as the guarantors of the system's stability and continuation. Superiors' individualisation and solidarisation are *not* a threat to hierarchical order; on the contrary, they contribute quite considerably to the further stabilisation of the system.

Nonetheless, there could be a strong boundary crossing within the realm of superiors' identity that could threaten the system of hierarchical order quite seriously. As indicated above, most superiors have hidden identities that are fairly compatible with the idea of hierarchy. But there could also be superiors who have fundamentally alternative identities—i.e., ones that go against the very notion of being a superior. Such identities would comprise self-images that have no room whatsoever for seeing oneself as 'superior' to or 'above' others and, hence, challenge the very idea of hierarchy and hierarchical social relationships. Such identities and self-images (and the corresponding views and behaviour) would obviously clash relatively quickly and severely with the identities and expectations of other superiors—as well as with those of many subordinates. Because of their work-related and organisational socialisation, many subordinates would have quite some difficulty with such a 'superior,' Most importantly and decisively, 'the system'—i.e., its senior management, colleagues, and administrative units—could hardly tolerate such an identity. A nonhierarchical identity in superiors simply does not fit into the system of hierarchical order.

However, the problems this might cause are more of a temporary nature. Other members of the system as well as existing policies and procedures might have difficulties with coping with such a deviating identity, but the superior in question can be isolated and coped with one way or the other. Thus, a nonhierarchical identity probably represents even larger problems for the individual superior with this identity than it does for the system: sooner or later, superiors with such identities will leave, or will be forced to leave, the hierarchical organisation and will work in different work environments.

Overall, superiors' boundary crossings concerning their identities do not cause serious problems for the hierarchical order. Their minor deviance is acceptable; their medium-intensity deviance can either be coped with by the system (in the case of individualisation) or accepted, even welcomed, as an exclusive group identity of a power elite (superiors' solidarisation); and even more extreme cases of deviance by superiors will be dealt with by the system in 'appropriate ways.' In other words, *none* of superiors' boundary crossings in the realm of identity constitute a serious threat to a hierarchical system.

4.5.4 Emotions—How 'Human' Should Superiors be?

In their public experience and expression of their emotions, superiors nowadays try to demonstrate those emotions that are claimed to be part of—and even make—successful (transformational) leaders (Kark and Van Dijk 2007; Van Vugt 2006). These leaders demonstrate feelings of superiority and dominance, are concerned about the whole, and have a strong sense of caring for those for whom they are responsible. But they also have strong feelings of anger, impatience, and determination when things don't go the way they would like or when subordinates don't behave and perform as expected. Superiors are keen to show the whole emotional repertoire of the good and caring, but also strict, father figure (male and female superiors, who believe in this sort of leadership style, alike).

Like subordinates, in their hidden transcripts, superiors show the whole range of human emotion. The problem is that we know much less about superiors' real emotions since hierarchical systems never provide any surveillance and investigation means for gathering systematic, or at least anecdotal, evidence about superiors' true feelings (like they do with regard to subordinates' feelings, thoughts, and actions). One way to gain an idea of superiors' hidden emotions might be to deduce them indirectly from advice given to leaders (or to those who want to become leaders)—although this provides more of a rough approximation than a true and complete picture (partly because it is advice made publicly; advice given behind closed doors is probably very different but, again, hard to trace). For example, Offerman (2005, p. 37, emphasis added) suggested:

> Sometimes, good leaders end up making poor decisions because well-meaning followers are *united* and persuasive about a course of action. This is a particular problem for leaders who attract and empower *strong followers*. These executives *need to become more sceptical* of the majority view and push followers to examine their opinions more closely.

Statements like this hint that most superiors actually *fear* their subordinates, particularly their possible individualisation and/or solidarisation and unification. In stark contrast to their public image and appearance, many superiors experience deeply rooted feelings of insecurity and fear on an almost daily basis, as well as anxious worries about their positions and privileges and misanthropic ideas of oppression and control of their subordinates, the units they are responsible for and the social reality as a whole (Maccoby 2005; Diamond and Allcorn 2004; Bassman and London 1993).

In this sense, most superiors' public and hidden transcripts of their emotions are diametrically opposed. The former is about strong superiors and dependent subordinates united under a universally justified set of higher values for a just and common course. The latter is about anxious superiors depending on (potentially) strong subordinates, the two kept together by comprehensive systems of control and oppression, spin and threats so that weak and fearsome superiors can continue to rule and to enjoy their unjustified privileges and prerogatives. Exactly those values and concerns that are excluded from the *official* agenda are very much at the centre of superiors' *hidden* agenda.

With most of their weak boundary crossings in the realm of emotions, superiors want to compensate for their insecurity. This could mean that they try to avoid showing any emotions at all because they fear that this could make them vulnerable and look weak. Lewis's (2000, pp. 224–5) account is quite representative of this type of reasoning:

> In this study, it is anticipated that expression of emotions in general will be considered to represent poor judgement on the part of the leader. This is due primarily to the fact that expressing anger and sadness will be perceived as outside of leader role norms [. . .], representing a lack of emotional control [. . .], and signifying a lack of self-confidence [. . .]. When participants observe these role-violating emotions, it is anticipated that they will perceive the leader to be less effective.

A weak boundary crossing could also entail superiors showing too much or too little of a required emotion so that their demonstrated emotions turn into, for example, megalomania, overconfidence, anxiety, despair, excessive anger, or an increased desire to punish (Kemper 1978b, pp. 33–6). Much organisational misbehaviour, such as bullying of subordinates, is a result of superiors showing too much or too little emotion. For example, in their large-scale survey of managerial abuse of employees, Bassman and London (1993) found psychopathological aspects to be the primary reasons for individual managers' poor management and leadership attitudes towards others. According to these authors (p. 20), 'underlying emotional disturbance' or 'personality disorder characterized by the inability to control aggressive impulses' showed a disturbing picture of many managers' underdeveloped identities and personalities. Behind organisational careerists' and psychopaths' mask of omnipotence often reside deeply seated insecurities that can cause neurotic struggles (Maccoby 2005, pp. 127–8; Diamond and Allcorn 2004, p. 37; Zaleznik 1989, p. 162). That superiors show no, too much, or too little of the 'right' emotions may be rather unpleasant for some people close to them (e.g., subordinates, peers, third parties), but it does not constitute a threat to the hierarchical social order.

This could be different if superiors showed emotions that were not part of their role repertoire. As in the case of subordinates (see Section 4.4.4), superiors are allowed, or even expected, to show anger in certain situations, for example when their subordinates do not function and perform well or with regard to some external forces. But what if superiors were to begin to show deep-seated and principled anger about the very system they represent?

This seems to be rather unlikely to happen. Only if people's needs, wants, or expectations have been violated and they perceive the way they (or others) have been treated as 'unfair' or 'unjust' (Fitness 2000, pp. 147, 157–8) is there the possibility that strong anger might develop. Subordinates are systematically oppressed and exploited by hierarchical social systems and, thus, have many reasons to develop strong feelings such as anger against the system. In contrast, as argued in Section 3.4, abstract organisational order is tailor-made for superiors' and ruling elites' individual and group interests. Thus, there are *no systemic reasons* why superiors should develop strong negative emotions in opposition to the system.

And *if* superiors developed strong negative emotions, this stems from single incidents and is confined to individual superiors—or a small group of superiors at the most. For example, a superior might not receive a promotion or a power elite might be defeated by another power elite and lose access to most of its privileges and resources. In such cases it would be quite understandable that superiors would develop strong anger. But this is exactly why this anger is not system-threatening: it is not targeted at the whole system but at specific individuals whom they deem responsible for their losses and fate. Angry superiors remain within the logic of the hierarchical system, the logic of social struggle, and the logic of the survival of the fittest, social dominance, and subordination. All that they (probably) want is revenge and to have their privileges back. In this sense, superiors' medium-intensity boundary crossings also do not constitute a serious threat to the hierarchical social system.

Yet, there might be superiors who do not feel comfortable at all being a superior. They may simply not enjoy, and not want to propagate, the image of the powerful and confident leader. Laurent (1978, p. 224) suggested that 'Leadership would lose its substance if followership were to disappear.' In this sense we can also assume that hierarchy would lose its substance if superiors were to disappear. That is, if superiors were to develop and demonstrate emotions that represent true alternatives to the idea of leadership, hierarchical relations would cease to exist. Such alternative emotions demonstrated by superiors would obviously represent strong boundary crossings. These could be emotions like those discussed with regard to subordinates' strong boundary crossings in the realm of emotions (e.g., a 'prosocial motivation,' 'other orientation,' or similar concepts).

Regardless, the situation is different when superiors show such emotions from when subordinates show them. When subordinates show prosocial orientations, there is a fair chance that others will understand and share their emotions and that this will lead to solidarisation and collective behaviour that seriously threatens the notion of hierarchical structures and processes. When it comes to protecting and defending the hierarchical social order, superiors also have prosocial orientations—amongst their peers and within their power elites. But, if individual superiors (or a group of superiors) were to target such emotions at attacking the hierarchical social system, other superiors would not join them but rather (try to) isolate, attack, and expel those superiors. And subordinates would not believe the deviating superiors; since superiors are not treated in unfair or unjust ways by the system (on the contrary, they are privileged) it is incomprehensible why they should have strong feelings against the system. Thus, if some superiors were to show strong emotions such as anger against the hierarchical system, there is a great chance that others would not be convinced to join them and that they would remain fairly isolated (and, sooner or later, would be replaced).

As in the case of superiors' social actions and identity, also in the realm of emotions *none* of superiors' boundary crossings constitute serious threats to the system of hierarchy.

4.5.5   Moral Character—Superiors' Claims and their Real Words and Deeds

In contrast to superiors' and powerful elites' *public* norms and values about leaders who 'unselfishly' serve 'the greater good' (see Section 4.2.4), we know very little about their *hidden* norms and values and moral character. This is mainly due to the fact that their *actual* beliefs and values, as we will see, are in quite some opposition to their public claims— and superiors fear nothing more than scratches on their public image. For example, publicly, leaders are portrayed as having high moral integrity. As stated by Groves and LaRocca (2011, p. 523):

> Transformational leaders' ability to demonstrate idealized attributes and behaviors, inspirational motivation, intellectual stimulation, and individualized consideration behaviors may well rest on a strong deontological ethical foundation. The results suggest that a leader's beliefs in selflessness, treating followers, and teammates as ends rather than means, and viewing leadership practices as having ethical significance regardless of their consequences, facilitates an authentic demonstration of transformational behavior.

Nonetheless, superiors' actual behaviour and moral conduct of office raise quite some doubts about their hidden moral character: Rayburn and Rayburn's (1996) study on superiors' organisational misbehaviour found a close relationship between personality traits and ethical orientation—and called people who show such personality and ethical orientation via their behaviour 'Machiavellians.' Aronson (2001) called them 'egotistic leaders.' Their conscious concerns and deliberate actions are primarily geared towards personal gain (under official rhetoric of serving the greater good and masked by demonstrating the etiquette of collegiality). They 'care about their own personal power and status, often depending on conspiracies and excuses, and resorting to distortion of truth and manipulation of followers to their own ends' (p. 253). Vickers and Kouzmin (2001) found that such 'modern careerists' often have a stage 2 character and show corresponding ethical orientations. They described the modern careerist as 'an essentially calculating animal pursuing the necessities of organizational life' (p. 105). As argued by Knights and O'Leary (2006, p. 126), their conduct of business and managerial responsibilities is 'a failure of ethical leadership that derives from the pre-occupation with the self that drives individuals to seek wealth, fame and success regardless of moral considerations.'

Whether 'Machiavellian,' 'egotistic leader,' or 'modern careerist'—or whatever other terms might be used to describe superiors who demonstrate unethical behaviour—such labels describe actors who are emotionally and morally damaged because of their calculative reasoning and opportunistic tactics (i.e., pursuit of their personal and career interests within social systems and at the expense of others). Yet, within hierarchical social systems such boundary crossings are largely forgiven; as long as superiors do their jobs and deliver the results they are expected to produce, minor frailties in the moral conduct of their office can be neglected since they do not harm the system.

However, there may be an issue with superiors' deviant or unethical behaviour that cannot be dismissed so easily. When one looks at how the *individual* moral behaviour of many superiors compares to their *public* claims, it becomes quite obvious that there is quite a gap between the official rhetoric/public set of values on the one hand and superiors' hidden moral character on the other. Examples include personal greed, enrichment, and lavishness while talking about the need to 'tighten our belts' in the face of limited resources; bullying of subordinates while giving 'people-are-our-greatest-asset' speeches; reducing subordinates' responsibilities and controlling them even more in the context of the introduction of a new initiative based on 'empowerment.'

Inconsistencies between words and deeds reveal superiors' *hypocrisy* and might be seen as medium-intensity boundary crossings. If such hypocrisies become apparent (and can no longer be denied or swept under the carpet), proponents of hierarchy usually try to portray them as 'individual shortcomings,' as 'isolated incidents' or 'individual misconduct.' In this sense, publicly exposed cracks between superiors'/leaders' official images and their moral conduct might cause some irritations and perhaps even some problems for the establishment. It might well be that the proponents of the hierarchical system hope that this will likely be only a temporary 'nuisance' and that they soon can go back to 'business as usual.' And, for subordinates, it might be just yet another proof of what they knew already: that superiors and members of the ruling elite do what they want and that they are no better than 'normal' people. However, portraying superiors' hypocrisy as individual malpractice might work with regard to people's interests or social actions. But when it comes to norms and values it is a different story; here, differences between official rhetoric and personal beliefs and actions question the validity of superiors' public claims and weaken the 'moral' base for those claims. Such differences weaken superiors' assertions of their distinct qualities, their justification of the rightness of their position and the privileges they enjoy, and their claims regarding why they deserve what they have.

Moreover, it is not just superiors' personal integrity that will suffer a severe blow; the exposure of superiors' hypocrisy can have quite severe negative effects on the hierarchical system and its ideological foundations. Usually, people generalise their experiences and perceptions; *one* superior's hypocrisy becomes *superiors'* hypocrisy—and 'their' hypocrisy stands for the mendacity of 'the system.' Thus, any gaps between public claims and actual practices are interpreted as the weakness or even falsehood not just of individual superiors but of the whole system. In this sense, superiors' hypocrisy undermines the whole hierarchical social order. It represents a serious threat to the system because people will no longer accept 'functionalistic' explanations of the prevailing norms and values and, as a consequence, will begin to challenge them and to look for alternatives.

Finally, it could be that superiors have not only stopped believing in the very norms and values of the social system they represent but also begun to believe in fundamentally different, *alternative* norms and values (such as egalitarianism, communitarianism, or similar concepts; see Section 4.4.5). Whatever the exact nonhierarchical moral concept is, such alternative values would also require quite a different moral character compared to the traditional understanding of a superior or 'leader'; instead of dominance orientation there would need to be a belief that all people are equal; instead of megalomania there would need to be humbleness; instead of vigilance there would need to be trust; and, above all, there would need to be personal integrity.

Obviously, such moral character traits are incompatible with hierarchical social systems (which are based on the ideas of inequality, power, and control) and, thus, could mean a serious threat. However, superiors' strong boundary crossings in the realm of moral character have similar outcomes to their strong crossings in the realms of identity or emotions; they cause more technical problems than problems of principle. Superiors who demonstrated nonhierarchical moral character traits would have increasing difficulties with both their colleagues ('breaking ranks') and their superiors, who expect 'leadership.' They would simply no longer fit in and, sooner or later, would leave the hierarchical organisation.

Overall, there is a mixed picture concerning superiors' boundaries crossings in the realm of moral character. Their minor unethical behaviour is not perceived as very unusual and their strong boundary crossings will be dealt with in more pragmatic terms. Weak and strong boundary crossings do not really threaten the hierarchical system. The big exception is superiors' medium-intensity boundary crossings in the form of hypocrisy; if the gaps between superiors' words and deeds are such that they progress in the public perception from hazy assumptions to concrete issues, then at stake is not only superiors' integrity but also everything they stand for—and, thus, the very hierarchical system they represent.

4.5.6   The (almost Entire) Acceptance of Superiors' Boundary Crossings

The discussion of superiors' boundary crossings has generated some results that could have been expected as well as some possibly more surprising insights that might even contradict common-sense assumptions. Table 5 presents and summarises the key findings.

Table 5 Superiors' boundary crossings in the realms of social action, interests, identity, emotions, and moral character.[1]

	Social action	Interest	Identity	Emotions	Moral character
Public transcript	Professional conduct of office, functioning well, responsible behaviour	Serving 'the whole' unselfishly (e.g. team, family, group, organisation, people or nation)	'The' superior and rational 'commander in chief'; irrational 'leader' and 'doer'	Demonstration of required emotions (such as self-confidence, enthusiasm) in the right intensities	Values of serving the greater good unselfishly; ethics of leadership, leaders
Hidden transcript	Insufficiencies, malpractices, illegal practices	Personal interests	Psychopathological traits of Machiavellian character	Whole range of human emotions, some perhaps inflated (e.g. anxieties)	Darwinism, oppression, control
a) Weak boundary crossing	Minor individual insufficiencies and malpractices	Breaching or bypassing 'technical' rules in order to pursue one's own interests	'Insecure careerist' or 'egotistic leader'	Showing, none of or too much of or too little of the emotions required	Minor unethical behaviour
b) Medium boundary crossing	Severe, longer-lasting workplace aggression; bullying; individual criminal actions and scandals	Changing rules, regulations, policies, measurement and management systems in one's favour	Individualisation; solidarisation	Emotions that are not part of superiors' role repertoire (e.g. anger towards the system)	Personal values and beliefs contrast with those publicly upheld (hypocrisy)
c) Strong boundary crossing	Widespread malpractices or illegal practices	Changing the system fundamentally	Alternative identity to the one ascribed to superiors	Alternative, non-hierarchical emotions	Alternative values, non-hierarchical moral character

(Continued)

Table 5 (Continued)

	Social action	Interest	Identity	Emotions	Moral character
Consequences for a) weak, b) medium, c) strong boundary crossing	a) and b) are system-stabilising because they will be either swept under the carpet or dealt with by the system; c) does not challenge the system since superiors' misbehaviour is or will be institutionalised	a) and b) are system-stabilising because they will be either swept under the carpet or dealt with by the system; c) is system-threatening because superiors have the means to realise their interests	a) is not system-threatening because it is confined to individual superiors; b) is system-stabilising because it strengthens power elites and their members; c) is not system-threatening since individual superiors can be replaced	a) can and will be dealt with within the system and, hence, strengthen it; b) is not system-threatening because it remains within the logic of social dominance; c) is not system-threatening since individual superiors can be replaced	a) is not system-threatening since most people expect it; b) is system-threatening because members start to question the basic values on which the system is built; c) is not system-threatening since individual superiors can be replaced

[1] Boxes in light grey indicate serious challenges to the system.

It could have been assumed that most, if not all, of superiors' deviance is quite problematic for a hierarchical system. Superiors represent the system in their words and deeds and any deviance might undermine it. It is therefore quite astounding that superiors can get away with much more misbehaviour than is commonly thought. Superiors and members of power elites (can) do many things that are quite damaging for organisations, for others and/ or for society as a whole. But even severe forms of superiors' boundary crossings and deviance do not seem to constitute too much of a problem for hierarchical social systems; in the realms of social action, identity, and emotions, *none* of superiors' boundary crossings threaten the hierarchical order. Even strong ones—such as superiors' collective, widespread malpractices or illegal activities; their alternative identities; or their nonhierarchical emotions—do *not* develop into a serious threat to the system.

That superiors can cross boundaries in the realms of social action, identity, and emotions without serious consequences for the system can be explained in similar ways for each of the different realms:

- Very often, superiors' misbehaviour is portrayed as 'individual' failures or shortcomings (the 'black sheep' argument). Such incidents are 'regrettable,' and, of course, will be punished—with lukewarm consequences for the individual superior, followed perhaps by some half-hearted suggestions for changes in policies and procedures that are usually watered down as soon as the case has disappeared from the public agenda. The official line of argumentation, or justification, is that individual misconduct in office is not representative of the majority of superiors or of flaws in the system.

- Boundary crossings are simply seen as less of an issue if done by people higher up the hierarchy. Superiors' deviance from norms and their individual 'insufficiencies' or 'malpractices' are excused as the result of too much 'stress' or the 'personal flaws' or 'weirdness' of a person who bears great responsibility and otherwise does a great job.

- Superiors' boundary crossing is regarded as normal, and even as the prerogative of superiors and part of the functions and identity of the superior; 'high status often gives licence to misbehave', as Wahrman (2010, p. 99) said so poignantly. Superiors and members of powerful elites can simply do what others are not allowed to do; this is how things are, how it always has been, and how it always will be.

- Superiors' boundary crossing in the realms of social action, identity, or emotions is even perceived or portrayed *positively*—for example, as 'determination' or 'personality.' Superiors *have to* cross boundaries and be ruthless because the challenges they face and the obstacles they have to overcome require a strong character—and strong leaders and power elites are good for the hierarchical system.

The results of the analysis carried out are consistent with the theory developed in Chapter 3, which argues that 'abstract organisational order is the extension and institutionalisation of superiors' direct power by other means' (Theorem 16). Systems of hierarchical order have been created primarily and especially to serve the interests and support the identities and emotions of superiors and power elites. Hierarchical systems are, so to speak, tailor-made for superiors. This is why superiors can do so much, can get so much—and can get away with it so often.

Hence, superiors have no reason to destroy the very foundations on which they exist. Even those superiors who cross boundaries in more extreme ways are still (very) interested in keeping the system intact because it provides the conditions under which they can pursue their individual and group interests and live out their personalities. All that they want is to take advantage of the system and people as much and for as long as they can. They will not bite the hand that feeds them.

There are only *two* cases when superiors' boundary crossing might constitute a serious threat to the hierarchical system. The case of superiors' *strong-intensity* boundary crossing in the realms of interest is quite comprehensible; as argued above (Theorem 19), abstract organisational order 'means the disguised institutionalisation of superiors' individual and group interests.' If members of the ruling elites develop a strong interest in changing the system, such crossings challenge the very foundations on which the system is built. And, since superiors usually have the capabilities and means to pursue their goals, sooner or later the system will cease to exist.[11]

The big exception is superiors' *medium-intensity* boundary crossings in the realm of moral character. It is *the only* medium-intensity crossing of superiors that is potentially dangerous for the system of hierarchical social order. Superiors' hypocrisy constitutes a serious problem since it not only shows the mendacity of the norms and values on which it is allegedly built and by which superiors allegedly live but also the fundamental injustice and unfairness of the hierarchical order. If it were to become public how much superiors actually deviate from the official claims they make, subordinates would no longer believe the rhetoric and would stop complying with the system's requirements. The hypocrisy of superiors and the mendacity of the whole system is the Achilles heel of any hierarchical system. Hierarchical social order can only continue to exist as long as ideology and rhetoric (supported by very comprehensive and thorough systems of control and punishment) uphold collective fantasies that keep the members of the social system functioning—superiors and subordinates alike. This is where the theory developed here is perhaps most important; it stresses the fact that 'hierarchy is first and foremost in people's *minds*' (Theorem 7).

4.6 HIERARCHY IN DIFFERENT TYPES OF ORGANISATIONS

4.6.1 Organisations and Hierarchy

Of course, hierarchy is not *only* in people's mind and their social actions but also realised via very concrete structures and processes. One of the 'best' (or worst) examples of the realisation and (mal)functioning of hierarchy is the modern organisation. Organisational reality can, and must, be structured and managed only in one way: *hierarchically.* It is the very fundamental idea of organisation that not just functional but especially *social* relationships are institutionalised, legitimised, organised, and managed as *hierarchical* relations between owners and workers, managers and employees, and superiors and subordinates (Spierenburg 2004, p. 627; Zeitlin 1974, p. 1090; Mosca 1971).

This is immediately comprehensible in the context of orthodox and bureaucratic types of organisations. However, new types of organisation have emerged and the spectrum has broadened to include hybrid/postmodern organisations (Clegg et al. 2006; Courpasson and Dany 2003). The proponents of those new kinds of organisations assert that they are quite different from traditional, bureaucratic forms of organisations. The new forms are said to be less hierarchical and formal, and more flexible and competitive. Many promise far-reaching changes, lean organisational structures and processes, crossdepartmental collaboration and knowledge-sharing, team-like relationships between managers and employees, and the empowerment of subordinates, who are now being called 'knowledge workers' or 'intrapreneurs' (Ahuja and Carley 1999). Against this backcloth it seems that in many organisations hierarchy is disappearing.

On the one hand we have claims that hierarchy persists within organisations; on the other we have approaches that make the case for the decline of hierarchy. These positions seemingly contradict each other. But this is so only at first sight. The confusion stems mainly from the fact that, so far, for most parts of management and organisation studies, 'hierarchy' has been understood (and analysed) largely as *formal* hierarchy and has been used almost synonymously with 'organisation.' Yet, every organisation comprises formal *and* informal aspects—i.e., official structures and rules that allocate formal roles and positions on the one hand, and unofficial structures and social processes amongst members of the social system on the other. As outlined in Section 3.2, organisation can mean formal *and* informal hierarchy (see Theorems 5 and 6). Via this mode of thinking, hierarchical organisations are based on an official system of formal roles and positions that put people in unequal relationships of command-and-control (formal hierarchy) *as well as* more person-dependent social relationships of dominance and subordination conveyed by social interaction (informal hierarchy).

Thanks to a long tradition of orthodox management and organisation theories (Chandler 1962; Drucker 1954; Fayol 1949; Taylor 1911/1967), we know a lot about formal hierarchy (especially in bureaucratic/orthodox and hybrid organisations). In contrast, there has been only a small amount of research into the emergence of informal hierarchy, particularly in hybrid and network organisations (Oberg and Walgenbach 2008; Schwarz 2006; Ekbia and Kling 2005; Nelson 2001). And, with the exception of some descriptive analysis of formal and informal (network) organisations (Rank 2008; Allen et al. 2007; Guimerà et al. 2006), thus far we know relatively little about how formal and informal hierarchy relate to and interact with each other. In this section, therefore, *different dynamic relationships between formal and informal hierarchy* will be interrogated, taking into account *different types of organisations*.

In order to investigate organisational hierarchy, the concepts of formal and informal hierarchy will be applied to five different types of organisations: 1) bureaucratic/orthodox organisations, 2) professional organisations, 3) representative democratic organisations, 4) hybrid or postmodern forms of organisation, and 5) network organisations.

The five types represent some of the most common types of organisations and are treated here as *ideal types* in the Weberian tradition (Weber 1980, pp. 4–26; Weber 1949, p. 90). For the purpose of the analysis, the discussion will focus on the typical characteristics of the different organisational forms; neither existing and possible variations on each type nor contextual conditions will be taken into account (Lindbekk 1992; Mcintosh 1977). This allows a more thorough analysis and a better comparison of the types in the sense of comparative sociology (Hayhoe 2007).

4.6.2   Formal and Informal Hierarchy in Different Types of Organisations

4.6.2.1   *Bureaucratic/Orthodox Organisations*

The *bureaucratic or orthodox organisation* is a, if not *the*, synonym for formal hierarchy and for rule-based specialisation and differentiation under a single authority (Weber 1980); *all* positions are placed along official lines of command-and-control—i.e., downward transmission of orders and upward transmission of information (Ahuja and Carley 1999, p. 742). In organisation studies, the blueprint for the modern type of bureaucratic organisation dates back to functionalistic/orthodox approaches (Taylor 1967; Chandler 1962; Drucker 1954; Fayol 1949). In such a system, the distribution of formal authority/institutionalised power is closely if not perfectly correlated with the rank and prestige of positions and independent from the actual holder of the position (Mechanic 1962, p. 350).

Furthermore, it is not only functional aspects, operations, and tasks that are organised hierarchically but also, and probably primarily, *social* relations (Mousnier 1973; Laumann et al. 1971); social relationships within the organisation are institutionalised and legitimised first and foremost as *hierarchical* relationships between managers and employees and between superiors and subordinates (Mast et al. 2010; Lake 2009; Oglensky 1995, p. 1030; Zeitlin 1974, p. 1090; Mousnier 1973; Laumann et al. 1971). *Everyone* must know their position—i.e., their place within that comprehensive system of social positions. Hierarchical social systems like the bureaucratic/ orthodox organisation, hence, come with elaborated systems of symbols indicating status, responsibilities, and, most importantly, differences. These status symbols reach 'an almost pathological intensity' (Thompson 1961, p. 496). And, as if this were not enough, the vertical and unequal social relationships are officially sanctioned, legitimised and made permanent by elaborate rules and regulations, performance-measurement and management systems as well as corresponding social action (largely routines but also even via resistance and deviance).

Although 'bureaucracy' is still used mostly in critical terms (as in its original, early-18th-century meaning implying 'red tape,' 'inefficiency,' and 'unresponsiveness'), its hierarchical principles are still at the core of contemporary orthodox organisations. Even allegedly new management concepts (e.g., lean management, the Balanced Scorecard, learning organisation, knowledge management) are based on the principles of formal hierarchy. Little more than the vocabulary and rhetoric have changed; managers no longer 'command' but 'provide guidance'; employees do not 'obey rules' but 'engage (proactively) with company policies'; staff are not 'told' but 'informed'; and so on. Hales (2002, p. 62) found that 'much of the evidence of variations in organizational forms suggests not alternatives *to* but alternative *versions of* bureaucratic organization.' His comparison of the findings from his research in two UK public-sector organisations and other case studies on change-management and empowerment initiatives revealed that (p. 52):

> Despite their claims, none of the organizations had undergone radical organizational change in that they had retained the defining features of bureaucracy—hierarchical forms of control, centrally imposed rules, and individual managerial responsibility and accountability. It is argued, therefore, that where the *principle* of hierarchical control is retained (regardless of any reduction in the number of hierarchical *levels*), and centrally imposed regulations are retained (regardless of changes in their *focus*) the result is not 'postbureaucratic,' 'network' organizations, but attenuated and more efficient versions of bureaucracy—'bureaucracy-lite,'

Hales' research into, and empirical evidence for, 'bureaucracy-lite' (and, slightly earlier, Courpasson's research into 'soft bureaucracies' in 2000) shows that most managerial principles and concepts largely *reconstitute* the principle of formal hierarchical order—i.e., the *formal principle of line management*. One therefore might say that even 'modern' concepts are developed for supporting, justifying, and legitimising formal top-down relationships (Jaques 1990). In so doing, they contribute to the continuation—even strengthening and deepening—of social stratification and inequalities via functional differentiation within organisations as well as in society.

Bureaucracy always tends to be comprehensive—and people usually comply with formal hierarchy and bureaucratic procedures. In principle, thus, bureaucracy does not provide any room for *informal* hierarchy. However, as Crozier (1964, p. 189) revealed with his research into and analysis of the bureaucratic phenomenon, in practical terms the system 'can never be so tight as it can theoretically. There is always some possibility of play within the framework delimited by the rules' (see also Hales 2002, p. 62). The knowledge and experience people need in order to carry out their tasks within the bureaucracy at the same time enable them to find ways around the official channels. Those who know the rules also know how to bend or bypass them, whom to approach if they want 'to get things done,' and whom and what to avoid if they do not want to do certain things. Such common and understandable behaviours may lead, amongst other things, to the emergence of *informal* hierarchy: those who best know the mysteries of the bureaucratic maze can lead others through it.

It is very difficult, if not impossible, for members of the orthodox organisation to initiate or maintain vertical informal relationships; because of the rigidity of a bureaucracy's hierarchical order, the different levels remain fairly isolated from each other. As Crozier (1964, p. 190) explained,

> A bureaucratic organization [. . .] is composed of a series of superimposed strata that do not communicate very much with each other. Barriers between strata are such that there is very little room for the development of cliques cutting across several categories.

Accordingly, although informal hierarchy cannot *cross* strata, it can emerge *within* them. In orthodox organisations, hence, one can find informal hierarchy *within the same level* of formal hierarchy; people of the same official status and position regularly develop an unofficial ranking amongst their immediate work colleagues or peers; comrades obey other comrades because they are fitter, more experienced nurses tell novices how to carry out tasks, dominance-oriented prison inmates treat weaker ones as their subordinates, and extraverted managers lead and advise their more introverted colleagues (Passini and Morselli 2010, 2009; Schmid Mast et al. 2010). To extend one of these examples: prison inmates develop very comprehensive systems of informal rules, hierarchical order, and control amongst themselves that the formal prison system and the security personnel could not provide or maintain. The informal system of the prison inmates, seemingly in fundamental opposition to the formal prison system, actually works according to the same principles of social dominance and obedience that the formal prison system is based on. In this sense, the *informal* hierarchical order helps to keep the *formal* hierarchical order working and intact. It is its continuation by other means; the informal order further conditions people to dominate and to obey where the formal order cannot reach them.

What is true for prison inmates and their informal system of hierarchical ordering is also true for soldiers, administrators, bureaucrats, and any other people who work in orthodox organisations, from shop-floor assistants and secretaries to members of the Board of Directors: within orthodox organisations, informal hierarchical ordering follows the same logic as formal hierarchy—i.e., *dominance via line management transforms into dominance amongst equals*. This is so because the principle of formal hierarchy is so comprehensive that other rationales struggle to emerge and develop. Within the structures and processes of orthodox organisations, people have become so accustomed to the idea of superiority and subordination that they do not know otherwise but to apply it to everything else—and they know that others view things similarly. It is therefore only logical (for them) that the principle of formal hierarchical ordering is applied to the informal realm with no or only little modifications; formal rules become informal rules, dominance via the formal power of the superior transforms into dominance via informal power amongst equals, and obedience because of lower formal role and status is now obedience because of lower informal role and status.

This system is comprehensive; within any bureaucratic organisation, informal hierarchy based on the principle of dominance amongst equals will occur at every hierarchical level and will support the dominant formal hierarchy as its logical extension. It is as if formal and informal order constitute a Mandelbrot set, in which a principle repeats itself (infinitely). *This* is the actual reason why any system of orthodox organisation is so powerful: formal principles of hierarchical ordering and control extend almost effortlessly into the informal realm.

4.6.2.2 *Professional Organisations*

Public- and private-sector organisations in which people of the same or complementing professions jointly run large parts of the organisational affairs can be subsumed into the idea of the *professional organisation*. Examples are solicitors' offices, health-care organisations, further- and higher-education institutions, and consulting and accounting firms (Ackroyd and Muzio 2007; Deem and Brehony 2005; Kirkpatrick and Ackroyd 2003; Robertson and Swan 2003; Kärreman et al. 2002; Sehested 2002).

Such organisations can differ considerably (Brock 2006). However, one of their most common features is that professional knowledge is structured hierarchically—and so is the profession. It is the very idea of profession to define and demarcate areas of expert knowledge horizontally and vertically *and* to differentiate the bearers of this knowledge (the professionals) both amongst themselves as in relation to others: 'professional knowledge,' *by definition*, is superior to common knowledge, and 'the professional,' *by definition*, is of higher status than anyone else. Amongst professionals, and in their relations to others, the principles of formal hierarchy, superiority, and subordination are paramount and inherent in the idea of the profession and the professional organisation. All work is organised accordingly. In this sense, the professional organisation is purpose-built—designed and built for the purposes of the specific group of professionals. The professional organisation is probably the most explicit, developed, and successful attempt to hierarchically institutionalise group interests (Freidson 2001; Abbott 1991, 1988), and one of the most extreme, thought-through and tailor-made attempts to establish vertical differences between different groups of people and to secure social dominance of a certain group of people over others.

Similarly to the bureaucratic organisation, the professional organisation has elaborate bureaucratic structures and processes and a comprehensive system of formal rules that covers and regulates almost every aspect imaginable (Kärreman et al. 2002). Professional public-sector organisations, particularly, have changed considerably since the early 1980s. With the introduction of so-called 'new public management,' professional organisations became 'managerial' and 'business-like'—i.e., oriented towards performance, cost, efficiency, and audit (Diefenbach 2009a, 2009b; Saunders 2006; Deem and Brehony 2005; Kirkpatrick et al. 2005; Kärreman and Alvesson 2004; McAuley et al. 2000; Pollitt 1990). With the emergence of managerialism as the dominant ideology and managers as the dominant group even in professional organisations (or the conversion of many professionals into semi- or full-blown managers), one might say that professional organisations have changed in many respects into fairly orthodox organisations.

Also in accordance with the idea of formal hierarchical order, professionals are thoroughly stratified and demarcated from each other. In their empirical research into the internal division of labour in law firms, Ackroyd and Muzio (2007, pp. 740–1) found increasing numbers of hierarchical levels that were providing people with disproportionate privileges and opportunities as well as unequal working conditions. Similar things could be said about medical staff in the health sector, academics in higher and further education institutions (Kirkpatrick and Ackroyd 2003; Robertson and Swan 2003; Sehested 2002), consultants, accountants—indeed, *any* profession. In most if not all professions, formal hierarchical order comes first in the form of the *principle of seniority;* more-senior professionals inhabit higher positions, supervise and advise junior colleagues and have the final say. Such vertical (and horizontal) differentiation is achieved through a variety of means typical of the profession—for example, formal degrees, rites of passage, career paths, status, symbols and rhetoric, official codes of conduct and standards, and attitudes and behaviour (Wahrman 2010). Junior professionals can only become fully accepted members of the profession if they obey its written and unwritten rules, if they accept their status as 'apprentice,' and if they behave as expected for the sake of their career. Whereas it is 'only' 'obey or out!' in the bureaucratic organisation, it is also 'up or out!' in the professional organisation.

But there are more (perhaps fundamental) differences between the bureaucratic and professional organisation. In addition to rule-bound tasks, the professional organisation also comprises large areas of genuine professional work. In contrast to administrative tasks and targets set by 'the system', the *content* of professional work is inconclusive and provides room for interpretation. This elbowroom corresponds strongly with professionals' self-image as independent individuals who are knowledgeable and autonomous experts in their field (Brock 2006, pp. 159–60; Robertson and Swan 2003, p. 835). The professional organisation, thus, is also based on the *principle of professional autonomy.*

According to this principle, some formal structures and processes within and outside the professional organisation are especially meant to support professionals' autonomy—for example, self-regulating bodies such as intra-organisational committees, media for publishing and communicating the profession's developments, and associations that represent the profession. The principle of professional autonomy, hence, contributes to an increase in *formal* structuring and hierarchical order (e.g., ranking of professional achievements, journals, and institutions such as universities)—and produces some paradoxical outcomes: it *increases* the autonomy of the profession but in some respects *decreases* the autonomy of the individual professional. This means that (only at the collective level), the principle of professional autonomy corresponds with the principle of seniority (and hierarchical ordering), and even strengthens it.

At the individual level, though, the two principles are in some contrast to each other. It is the very idea of autonomy that it fundamentally *negates* ideas of superiority, subordination, dominance, and obedience. Autonomy means not taking orders from anyone. This ideal represents a problem for the professional within the professional organisation (actually, within *any* type of hierarchical organisation). Professionals, therefore, also use *informal* ways in order to practice the kind of professional autonomy they believe in and to bypass formal hierarchical structures. For example, they may initiate networks and informal collaboration with (like-minded) colleagues within and outside the organisation they work for. Those colleagues may be at the same or different levels (according to their formal degrees or official position). On the one hand, this produces informal structures and processes that stretch across formal hierarchical order and sometimes even contradict it. On the other hand, very often the principle of seniority kicks in and transforms informal professional relationships into informal hierarchical order. In their case study research on the culture within a consultancy firm, Robertson and Swan (2003, p. 841) found that:

> Concerted attempts had been made to sustain a flat organizational structure over time, incorporating only one level of senior management. Below this all consultants were grouped into loosely defined 'divisions' according to their particular expertise. Everyone acknowledged however that an informal hierarchy existed alongside the supposedly flat structure

[. . .]. Positions within it were premised on both marketing and scientific/ technological expertise which, depending on the nature of project work at any given time, could be more or less in demand, thus commanding a higher or lower position within the informal hierarchy. This did lead to a highly combative (a term regularly used by the founder) environment.

And they came to the conclusion (p. 831) that:

> Thus the culture that embraced ambiguity (a consensus that there would be no consensus) engendered a form of normative control whereby consultants operated freely and at the same time willingly participated in the regulation of their own autonomy.

Hence, while trying to pursue their own individual autonomy, professionals also apply the hierarchical logic of their profession in the form of the principle of seniority because they want, or even need, to prove to other professionals (and to themselves) that they are (more) competent and know more. Over time this leads to the emergence of informal hierarchy *even across* organisational levels—and, again, reduces individual autonomy. In other words, the formal principle of seniority, which it was the intention to avoid, has transformed the formal principle of professional autonomy into an informal *principle of domination amongst semiautonomous professionals*.

Such informal hierarchical ordering then feeds back into the formal hierarchical order of the professional organisation. For example, informal networks are used to get people appointed to certain positions in the formal hierarchical order or to raise and address issues in certain ways (e.g., deciding on agendas, official codes of conducts, or allocation of resources). Such cases usually do not constitute a problem; on the contrary, they correspond with the principles and self-image of the profession. The emergence not only of informal networks but also of informal hierarchical structures and processes—even when politically motivated—is perceived as a normal part of the work and activities of professionals. Informal hierarchical structures and processes are regarded as legitimate because they are seen by many as part of the fundamental idea of the profession as a self-organising and self-governing body. And they reflect the self-understanding of professionals as knowledgeable and autonomous actors. Although the principles contradict each other to some extent, professionals have no problem with using a combination of formal hierarchy (the principle of seniority) *and* professionals' idea of autonomy in order to boost their informal hierarchical networks for the pursuit of their individual or group interests—which, in return, will shape the formal hierarchical structures and processes of the organisation, especially via reconfirming the status of the professional within the hierarchical order. As a result, in the professional organisation there is a formal hierarchy of different levels of professional qualifications, skills, and experience *and* an informal, but *equally* legitimate, hierarchy that facilitates interaction between bureaucratic and professional matters.

4.6.2.3   Representative Democratic Organisations

Since the emergence of modern orthodox organisations in the early 19th century, people who are unhappy with the downsides of such organisations have been looking for more fundamental and far-reaching alternatives. One concept, which has been developed comprehensively and has been put in place in many shapes and forms, is the *democratic organisation*. Such organisations take the ideas of empowerment and workplace democracy seriously. They embrace ideas such as genuine worker participation, autonomous work groups, profit-sharing, copartnership, and share-ownership (Gratton 2004; McLagan and Nel 1997; Poole 1996; Cheney 1995; Jones and Svejnar 1982). The democratic organisation gets serious about participation while others remain in the realm of rhetoric only.

At a very general level, one might differentiate between two main types of democratic organisation: the *representative* democratic organisation and the (fully) *participatory* (or egalitarian) organisation. The former represents a combination of employees' direct participation in operational decision-making and indirect participation in strategic decision-making via representatives. The latter stands for more radical forms where people (successfully or unsuccessfully) try to overcome hierarchical structures and processes. In this analysis the focus is primarily on representative democratic organisations. Examples of such organisations are John Lewis, The Co-operative (Co-op), credit unions, and many agricultural and building societies.

In contrast to fully participatory ('egalitarian') organisations, the representative democratic organisation is 'only' meant to make decision-making processes, cooperation, and profit-sharing more democratic, *not* to replace and overcome hierarchical structures *per se;* line responsibilities are kept in place, managers are still appointed and not elected, and most decisions are still made by superiors and carried out by subordinates. In the representative democratic organisation, the formal relationship between superiors and subordinates is perhaps even stronger since it is now justified and institutionalised by 'higher' values in addition to 'mere' business-like (e.g., profit) or technocratic ones (e.g., efficiency). Democratic committees and decision-making procedures are introduced not instead of but *alongside* orthodox organisational structures and processes. Democratic principles are put *on top of* hierarchical principles—formal hierarchy remains the dominant factor. Hence, in the democratic organisation there is still a strong *principle of formal hierarchical representation* at work.

Moreover, whereas in an orthodox organisation an employee is 'only' subordinate to his or her line manager, in the democratic organisation the employee must obey several superiors—i.e., his or her line manager *and* the several collectives he or she belongs to (immediate co-workers, groups, committees, and the organisation as a whole; Stohl and Cheney 2001, p. 371). This probably means an even greater pressure, and necessity, to obey since the values of democracy are not (only) externally imposed by management but represent values (officially) shared by everyone. The additional norms of the democratic organisation (e.g., participation, collaboration, or peer control) *rightly* expect obedience because they represent 'the collective will' of all. Erich Fromm (1956; referred to in Brookfield 2005, pp. 64, 169) talked quite critically about 'the tyranny of the majority' and the oppressive control it might exercise in a democracy. In both the bureaucratic and the democratic organisation, there is little room for deviance—in the former because of regulations, in the latter because of social conformity.

In addition to formal hierarchical structures and processes, *informal* ones can also be quite intense in representative democratic organisations. In the democratic organisation, 'achieving consensus' is crucial. 'Consensus' does not mean that all members must explicitly express their agreement every time. Actually, this is rarely the case. Usually, consensus is achieved by majority votes in official bodies representing the collective, such as committees. Decision-making processes, therefore, are often understood as 'political' (Palgi 2006a, 2006b; Varman and Chakrabarti 2004; Stohl and Cheney 2001; Cheney 1995; Boehm 1993). And, like in political parties, defining agendas, shaping alliances, and getting things through committees becomes an important part of the informal life of the organisation. Most decisions (at least the crucial ones) are often made *before* the actual formal meeting takes place—i.e., they are made during informal decision-making processes of politically active members of the organisation. The importance of informal processes leads to elaborate informal networks and alliances ('political circles') parallel to the formal institutions of organisational governance. In the representative democratic organisation, it is the notion of the 'political' that not only leads to an acceptance of formal hierarchical order (since committees and line management are democratically legitimised) but also to an acceptance of informal networks as a 'normal' part of organisational life.

Individuals who are more active in the informal political processes, who are more present at committees and who voice their concerns more vigorously publicly or behind closed doors will increasingly dominate decision-making processes (Lake 2009). Over time they become informal opinion leaders who are followed mainly by virtue of their widespread and regular presence and the power and influence they have accumulated through their different (informal) political networks and activities. The accumulation of posts, membership of influential circles, and involvement in informal processes form patterns that show how influential individuals are. Members of the organisation are judged accordingly and ranked based on their 'importance.' This process is a formal as well as informal dominance of politically active members over the collective (Sidanius et al. 2004). One, thus, might say that it is not informal political *circles* but informal political *hierarchies* that drive representative democratic organisations—and probably more than the formal hierarchical structures and processes. In their very informative study of the organisational culture and democratic processes within an Indian workers' cooperative called SAMITI, Varman and Chakrabarti (2004, p. 199) found that:

SAMITI has found it difficult to elicit commitment to participatory processes, [. . .] consensual decision-making is a matter of learning and culture, where people care and dare to speak and critique. What actually happens in SAMITI is that a few articulate individuals are able to push through their point and in the process further alienate others. [. . .] The other side of this dialectic has been the persistent tendency toward oligarchization within SAMITI, whether in the beginning it was the MCAs [middle-class associates] and the 'activists' or later when it incorporated some of the workers as well, or at present when all the office-holders are workers. The problem is that the lack of participation and tendency toward oligarchization feed in to each other. Thus at best some kind of a paternalistic system develops, but at times distinctly authoritarian tendencies emerge. Worse, some of the informal members of the oligarchy, such as the MCAs, are very difficult to hold accountable, since they are not part of any formal structure.

The 'oligarchisation' identified by Varman and Chakrabarti is evidence for Robert Michels' 1915 well-known 'iron law of oligarchy' (see Michels 1966); regardless of what form democratic organisations take are at the start, they will eventually (and inevitably!) develop into oligarchies.[12] There seem to be so many cases of this pattern of development that one might say that (the principle of) *formal hierarchical representation* is often dominated by (the principle of) *informal political domination.*

Informal hierarchical domination, then, feeds back into formal structures and processes. For example, people are appointed or elected formally depending on the support they receive from informal networks, or formal structures and processes are modified according to ideas that have been developed in the informal realm. In representative democratic organisations, formal and informal hierarchies form a dialectical relationship: informal hierarchies emerge in addition to the formal hierarchy of line management and official democratic structures and processes. This is mainly because of more active members keen to influence democratic decision-making processes. The democratic organisation becomes a political arena where informal hierarchical networks and informal decision-making processes prevail and determine much of what happens in formal structures and processes. Although such processes may go against the 'true spirit' of democratic decision-making, they are nonetheless often a cornerstone of factual decision-making in systems of representative democracy. In many representative democratic organisations, formal hierarchy is not only provided through elections and representation but also predefined, shaped, used, and perhaps even abused by informal hierarchical networks and by initiatives from politically ambitious members. Informal hierarchical processes might shape formal decision-making and, hence, the direction of democratic organisations to a much greater extent than orthodox research or theories of democratic organisations imply. One, hence, might conclude that, if there is a strong political culture within a representative democratic organisation, formal hierarchy and institutions are only instrumental to informal hierarchy.

4.6.2.4   *Hybrid or Postmodern Forms of Organisation*

Since the early 1990s there have been hopes that *hybrid* or *postmodern* forms of organisations will be able to reform, if not to say replace, bureaucratic/orthodox organisations. New management concepts such as 'lean management,' 'business process re-engineering,' the 'learning organisation,' and 'knowledge management' suggested that even large organisations could function in 'nonbureaucratic' and 'nonhierarchical' ways. According to the proponents of postmodern organisations, concepts such as quasiautonomous teams, self-managing projects, and decentralised work units would supersede outdated bureaucratic work practices and old forms of hierarchical power and control. There were quite some hopes that these postmodern, 'team-oriented' or even 'family-like' ways of organising work would bring new forms of employee participation, commitment, and motivation (Casey 1999, p. 156).

However, there is significant evidence that even those new forms of work organisation leave superiors' rights and responsibilities largely intact and simply reinforce the top-down power relations already in place (Hales 2002, p. 51; Rothschild and Ollilainen 1999, p. 594; Jermier 1998, p. 249). Quite often, with the introduction of these new concepts, employees and lower management are simply given more operational tasks and gain only the *feeling* of being empowered (Courpasson and Dany 2003, p. 1246; Courpasson 2000, p. 155). Rothschild and Ollilainen (1999, p. 610), therefore, called the new forms of work 'pseudo-participation' because they (for example) lack collective ownership, shared control over major decisions, and equality. In this sense, hybrid organisations are very similar to orthodox organisations.

They might be even worse. In addition to these organisations' embeddedness in formal hierarchical structures, in hybrid organisations many employees are involved in teams or projects, temporarily or even permanently. Although located 'outside' or 'across' line management, many of these teams and projects are also organised according to orthodox principles—i.e., in functional and hierarchical ways (e.g., team members and project members are provided with formal authority, responsibilities, and privileges according to their functional roles). Hence, in some contrast to orthodox organisations, where there is 'only' one hierarchy, teams and projects *add a second cosmos of indirect formal hierarchical structuring* to the direct formal hierarchy of line management. In hybrid organisations there is formal hierarchy of line management *plus* fluid and patchy clusters of formal project- and team-based hierarchies. One therefore might say that direct *and* indirect line management is the leading formal principle of the hybrid organisation.

Since one of the original ideas of the hybrid organisation was to reduce formal hierarchy via the introduction of teams and projects, this type of organisation is quite paradoxical; there is a duplication of formal hierarchy *because of* attempts to reduce it. Moreover, there are also paradoxical outcomes with regard to *informal* structures and processes within hybrid organisations. As indicated, via the institutionalisation of teams and projects, more indirect, individualised, and subjectivised forms of power and control are added to direct managerial line control and abstract control and punishment systems (Clegg et al. 2006; Kirkpatrick et al. 2005, p. 96; Kärreman and Alvesson 2004, p. 151). Employees are expected to monitor, control, regulate, and manage each other's contributions and performances, even behaviour and attitudes. Thus, teams, projects, and similar so-called 'collaborative' work arrangements and environments often mean *more* pressure and more 'gentle' ways of *informal* coercive control and punishment for the individual than most of the external methods (e.g., Courpasson and Clegg 2006; Jacques 1996; Barker 1993); they 'retain a need for the iron fist of strong and centralized control mechanisms, wrapped up in the velvet glove of consent' (Courpasson and Clegg 2006, p. 324). With their official rhetoric of teamwork, projects, employee participation, commitment, motivation, and empowerment, (post)modern organisations actually obscure new and more intense forms of formal and informal control (Akella 2003, p. 47; Jermier 1998, p. 249). Hence, although teams and projects could be seen by some as 'escape routes' from formal hierarchy, they actually can be worse for the individual since they represent a very demanding combination of formal and informal pressure held together by the rhetoric of teams and families (Casey 1999) that is difficult to challenge and even harder to escape from.

The 'family' and 'team' metaphors shed additional light onto this situation—but not in the way that their 'romantic' rhetoric suggests. Like in a family, some roles and responsibilities within teams and projects may have been formally defined and organised hierarchically. Nevertheless, ways of organising work, social status, image and prestige, and even access to resources, current prerogatives and future opportunities, need to be clarified and negotiated in social interactions on an almost constant basis (Sillince and Mueller 2008). The combination of formal and informal hierarchical structures and processes within teams and projects creates at the same time certainty and (constant) uncertainty, scarcity and pressure, and chances and opportunities for most of its members (although in different shapes and sizes). There is thus an almost constant need for internal positioning of oneself and for bargaining with, and against, others. In her empirical investigation of 'family-rhetoric' at a large multinational US company, Casey (1999, p. 172) revealed that:

> The flatter organizational structure typical of team family styles of work organization results in fewer opportunities for upward mobility. Although subteams can provide satisfying experiences in self-management and work design, they inhibit individual recognition and advancement. Competition for recognition and reward, therefore, is now more complex and at the same time regressive. Favoritism and political maneuvering were present in the older style bureaucracies, but the more formalized structure in which one expected to progress encouraged impersonality and some protection from advancement by nepotistic practices. But now, the flatter, closer team-family structure covertly revives interpersonal suspicion, sibling-like rivalry and nepotism at the same time as it overtly, officially, promotes egalitarian teammate cooperation, familial warmth, and overriding commitment to the product. Team-family members must compete with each other for the attention and favour of the team's manager-father.

The fluid structures and processes of 'family-like' hybrid organisations contribute to increased competition and peer pressure—which in most cases is probably even intended; in the hybrid organisation, actors *must* strive for informal dominance and participate at least to some extent in the daily struggle for survival because their formal positions no longer automatically provide security. Over time, the internal struggles produce informal leaders and followers (either in line with or in contrast to their formal positions) and lead to informal hierarchy and to further social dynamics around it. One, hence, might say that in hybrid organisations there is a strong *informal principle of continuous hierarchical positioning* at work.

In the hybrid organisation it is particularly the more ambitious members active in the realms of temporary teams and projects who practice the informal principle of continuous hierarchical positioning. As a consequence, informal hierarchy emerges in all areas where formal hierarchy is no longer at work. The informal hierarchy complements formal hierarchy fully; it reaches all those members (and effectively copes with their desires) who wish to escape from direct line management and routine tasks. This is also the reason why the informal principle of continuous hierarchical positioning is so successful; it serves well all those who consciously reject formal authority, collective interests, and responsibilities but who at the same time want to dominate, want to pursue their own interests, and want to have the advantages of larger orthodox organisations without their disadvantages.

This, finally, explains why informal hierarchical positioning feeds back not only into formal team and project structures but also into the formal hierarchy of line management. For example, actors who have successfully managed teams or projects—particularly those teams or projects that are ranked highly and are attractive for whatever reasons—will sooner or later be rewarded by a career step up the formal hierarchical ladder. For some, informal continuous hierarchical positioning pays off and produces dividends in the formal realm of direct and indirect line management. In the hybrid organisation it is the velvet glove that strengthens the iron fist, not the other way around.

All in all, hybrid organisations have a double structure of formal line management *and* informal processes of continuous hierarchical positioning. Thus, they are often not *less* but *more* hierarchical and oppressive than other hierarchies—but in more differentiated, challenging, and sophisticated ways than orthodox, professional, or representative democratic organisations.

4.6.2.5   Network Organisations

Almost simultaneously with the emergence of hybrid forms of organisation, the network organisation was identified as a new type (Palmer et al. 2007; Powell 1990). However, the term 'network' is used for a whole range of organisations. There can be fairly orthodox intra- and inter-organisational 'networks' that are largely based on functionalistic and managerial principles (even research into their structures and processes is functionalistic: Contractor et al. 2006; Podolny and Page 1998). This type of 'network' is structured hierarchically and its members stratified because of 'functional necessities.' For example, there is often still a centre that is responsible for, and keeps control of, most important issues, such as strategic decisions, setting of key performance indicators, and allocation of resources. Other members of the 'network' are fragmented into subgroups—again, for 'functional reasons.' They are located at the 'periphery,' are responsible for more operational and technical issues, are excluded from key decision-making, and have to report to the centre (Clegg et al. 2006, p. 338). In fact, there is not much 'network' in such so-called 'networks.'

In contrast, here it is concentrated on network organisations that are fully decentralised entities comprising (seemingly) autonomous, self-directed and participative units (Ekbia and Kling 2005, p. 163). If they do indeed comprise such units, networks are seen as the collective responsibility of their members, who have equal status and represent a 'community' (Barker 2006; Parker 2002, pp. 12, 70; Casey 1999, p. 162). Quite often, members of such networks try very seriously to establish nonhierarchical and open forms of collaboration built on trust and mutual understanding (Stohl and Cheney 2001, p. 356). Hales (2002, p. 54) gave a good description of the network idea within organisations:

> The internal network organization is conceived as a loose federation of informally constituted, self-managing, often temporary, work units or teams within which there is a fluid division of labour and which are coordinated through an internal market, rather than rules, and horizontal negotiation and collaboration, rather than hierarchy [. . .]. Instead of a hierarchy of vertical reporting relationships there is a 'soft network' [. . .] of informal lateral communications, information sharing and temporary collaboration based on reciprocity and trust.

One might therefore say that networks are based on the *formal principle of autopoietic structures and processes*. With this principle, network organisations are one of the more promising candidates for a truly hierarchy-free type of organisation.

Yet, even when formal hierarchy has been successfully avoided during the organisation's inception and the network reflects egalitarian, participative-democratic and related ideas, even in the best and most well-intended networks things might not be quite like the theory or the founders' initial ideas suggest. When investigating and analysing the internal e-mail communication in an explicitly network-oriented and antihierarchically-run company, Oberg and Walgenbach (2008, p. 183) found

> a split between the symbolic activities for creating a non-hierarchical network organization and the actual intranet communication behaviour of the organization members. In their daily communication on the intranet, they persistently reproduced hierarchical structures and official channels—elements typically associated with bureaucratic organizations. . . . many signals in the content of the intranet messages, reflecting a social hierarchy

that has evolved within the organization. Thus, despite rhetoric to the contrary, our findings regarding this communication behaviour show that, to all intents and purposes, this particular organization displayed characteristics similar to those of a traditional bureaucratic organization.

Obviously, hierarchical structures had emerged over time, particularly with regard to two key aspects. One was *structures* of communication—i.e., official communication channels representing a very clear centre-periphery structure. The other was the *content* of communication—i.e., members developed systematic patterns of addressing certain issues in unequal ways and of using rhetoric in order to signal superiority or inferiority, dominance or submissiveness. That hierarchical patterns had emerged came as a surprise to everyone—to the researchers and even the actors involved when the research findings were presented to them. *Informal* hierarchical structures and processes had developed not only against the best intentions but also against the perceptions and self-images of the actors involved.

The example also shows that network organisations are more vulnerable to the emergence of informal hierarchy than other organisations (Ahuja and Carley 1999). Since (at the beginning) there are fewer formal structures, rules and regulations, and procedures and policies in place for people to comply with, networks are shaped even more by the *actual* activities of their members. One area of concern, hence, is whether or not the actual behaviour is in line with the idea of a network organisation or goes against its fundamental principles. Ekbia and Kling (2005) provide evidence that the often-mentioned positive aspects of work and behaviours in networks can be quite easily accompanied by negative ones. In addition to trust, flexibility, adaptability, deregulation, cooperation, voluntarism, decentralisation, team spirit, empowerment, and transparency, there can also be deception, inflexibility, gaming behaviour, regulation, antagonism, coercion, concentration of power, egocentrism, oppression, and secrecy. Obviously, such behaviours and activities will transform the network very quickly into an informal hierarchy (created and maintained by powerful members) or even formal hierarchy (due to the introduction of formal rules and regulations that will be used and abused by those who are responsible for their introduction and maintenance).

It is perhaps even more revealing to focus on the fact that 'neutral' communication behaviour *as such* can inherently constitute serious problems for the network organisation. People's individual differences in style and intensity of communication (e.g., more active 'doers' and more observant 'contemplators'), not to mention their different worldviews, personality traits, aspirations and attitudes, contribute to the emergence of (informal) patterns of social dominance (Sidanius and Pratto 1999). Consciously or unconsciously, the more active members begin to dominate (virtual) discussions and decentralised communication and coordination processes, whereas the more passive members apply a 'wait-and-see' strategy. Over time, members' individual behaviour manifests itself as social structures and routine processes. Members develop more and more traditional roles and corresponding behaviour of (informal) superiority, subordination, domination, and obedience to such a degree that (unwanted) informal hierarchical structures and structuring emerge. One might say that such processes reflect an *informal principle of communicative dominance.*

As indicated above, it might not be individual or collective conscious attempts, malpractices, or unethical behaviour but simply differences in communication *per se* that lead to communicative dominance and, as a consequence, to informal hierarchical structures and processes. This is the case not only concerning communication but also concerning decision-making processes and resource allocation. Thus, the formal principle of autopoiesis (here: constantly self-organising networks) might speak strongly against *formal* hierarchy—but it is no guarantee against the emergence of *informal* hierarchy; on the contrary, it seems to even lay the ground for the informal principle of communicative dominance to take over.

This represents a serious problem, if not to say dilemma, for the proponents of network organisations: the emergence of informal hierarchical patterns goes against the very ideals of this type of organisation—but its proponents cannot do much against these informal processes since the idea of self-organising processes, and the acceptance of outcomes stemming from such processes, is one of the fundamental principles and values of nonhierarchical systems. And, if the proponents were to begin to intervene systematically in authoritative ways, an element of formal hierarchy would be introduced—which would also go against the idea of a hierarchy-free network organisation. It seems to be a Catch-22 situation—but the problem needs to be tackled since otherwise the informal hierarchical ordering will continue and contribute to a negative feedback loop that takes the network even further away from the ideal of a hierarchy-free type of organisation.

To sum up, it is fair to say that, if the key actors involved in attempts to realise nonhierarchical work relationships such as network organisations lose the ability to reflect critically on their social or communication practices, then informal hierarchy will emerge (unrecognised).

4.6.3 Persistence of Hierarchy in Different Types of Organisations

The analysis of the five types of organisation has revealed that hierarchical structures and processes are present in *all* of them. Table 6 summarises the analysis.

Formal hierarchy is extremely high and comprehensive in bureaucratic/orthodox organisations. This is also the case in the professional organisation, but here the principle of seniority is somewhat counterbalanced by the principle of professional autonomy. Formal hierarchy is reduced in representative democratic organisations and in hybrid organisations, and almost nonexistent (at least in the beginning) in network organisations. In contrast, *informal* hierarchy is very low in bureaucratic organisations, increased in professional organisations and representative democratic organisations, fairly common in hybrid organisations, and dominates in network organisations. Figure 4.1 shows this pattern visually.

Table 6 Formal and informal hierarchy in different types of hierarchical organisation.

	Bureaucratic/orthodox organisations	Professional organisations	Representative democratic organisations	Hybrid/postmodern forms of organisation	Network organisations
Main concept of the system	Bureaucracy, rules, managerialism	Professionalism, managerialism	Managerialism, representative (and participative) decision-making processes	Managerialism, projects and teams	Autopoiesis, decentralised co-ordination and decision-making
Formal principle of hierarchical order	Principle of rule-bound line management	Principle of seniority, principle of professional autonomy	Principle of formal hierarchical representation	Principle of direct and indirect line management	Principle of autopoietic structures and processes
Formal hierarchical order via	Different levels, line of command, line management	Rules and order of the profession, line management	Line management, committees	Line management, formal projects and teams	Emerging formal functions and tasks within the network
Formally higher- and lower-ranked actors	Master and servant, superior and subordinate	Senior and junior, professional and support staff, superior and subordinate	Representatives and represented, superior and subordinate	Superior and subordinate, leaders and members of projects or teams	Network coordinator/ facilitator and members
Informal principle of hierarchical order	Principle of dominance amongst equals	Principle of domination amongst semi-autonomous professionals	Principle of political domination	Principle of continuous hierarchical positioning	Principle of communicative dominance

Informally higher- and lower-ranked actors	Informal leaders and followers at the same hierarchical level	More or less power-oriented professionals at the same or different hierarchical levels	More or less politically active members in and around organisational committees	More or less competitive members in cross-functional teams and projects	More or less communication-oriented members in disperse communication processes
Relationship between formal and informal hierarchy	Informal hierarchy happens within boundaries set by the formal hierarchy as its logical extension and support	Informal hierarchy is facilitative alongside and across formal hierarchy	Formal hierarchy is instrumental to informal hierarchy	Informal hierarchy complements formal hierarchy where the latter cant reach and cope with members sufficiently	Informal hierarchy emerges unrecognised and might become the dominant rationale

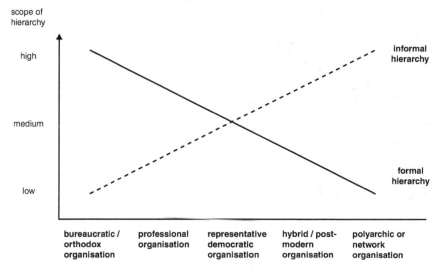

Figure 4.1   Scope of formal and informal hierarchy.

It becomes clear(er) that hierarchy is much more persistent than people might think when one looks at the same time at formal *and* informal hierarchy. When changing from 'older' to more 'modern' or even 'postmodern' types of organisations, formal hierarchy might be reduced—but only in relative terms since at the same time informal modes of establishing and maintaining unequal social relationships emerge. At least concerning the types of organisations investigated here, it seems that *whenever formal hierarchy decreases, informal hierarchy increases.* The overall scope of hierarchy remains fairly stable. One might say that the typology above constitutes a *continuum of dynamic relationships of formal and informal hierarchy.*

Whether these patterns of vertical social relationships have been designed deliberately or have emerged over time, whether they are formal and/or more informal—*none* of these organisations is hierarchy free. This is intuitively understandable for bureaucratic/orthodox, professional, and representative democratic organisations since these types are based explicitly on formal principles of hierarchical ordering. But it has become clear that within hybrid and even network organisations hierarchy is also at work—probably more than would have been expected or hoped. Hierarchical ordering is quite adaptable and flexible enough to continue, even when new forms of work organisation have developed (Kärreman and Alvesson 2004; Jermier 1998). Despite all rhetoric about 'flat,' 'lean,' and 'virtual' organisations and about 'family-based,' 'team-based,' and 'network-based' modes of organising, most organisations still function on the basis of hierarchical principles and mechanisms. Hierarchy is still the backbone and central nervous system of our organisations—even the postmodern ones.

5 Socrates—The Unnormal Normal Person Who Won by Losing

'Throughout history, the truth-seekers and truth-tellers have been aware of the risks of their business; as long as they did not interfere with the course of the world, they were covered with ridicule, but he who forced his fellow-citizens to take him seriously by trying to set them free from falsehood and illusion was in danger of his life.'

Hannah Arendt (1968, p. 299)

5.1 INTRODUCTION

As shown in the previous chapter, analysing the dynamics of social systems via concepts such as boundary crossing can produce important insights into how social systems such as hierarchical orders work. Mostly *single* boundary crossings have thus far been examined in order to demonstrate the relevance and fruitfulness of the concept. Nonetheless, as explained in Section 3.4.2, social processes are often more complex and can comprise *multiple* boundary crossings. During such longer-lasting processes, reciprocal and mutually reinforcing behaviour can lead to an escalation of conflict—i.e., to a spiral of increasingly strong actions with increasingly negative consequences for some or even all parties involved (vicious circles or 'tit-for-tat' strategies, Andersson and Pearson 1999, p. 458; Kim and Smith 1993, p. 38).

The recognition of boundary crossing as multiple processes or dynamic escalation of conflict draws attention to the fact that such crossings have implications beyond their original realm. For example, social action often has a symbolic meaning that challenges the prevailing ideology and even the social identity of others. Challenges in the realms of moral character and of norms and values are often perceived and interpreted as serious threats to one's identity and, as a consequence, trigger certain social actions. Understood in this way, the concept of boundary crossing can contribute to more differentiated and multidimensional investigations of social processes.

This will be done here. This chapter will provide a case study on Socrates and his (lifelong) struggle with the institutions, as well as with many citizens, of Athens.

Why him? Obviously, we do not know much about 'the real Socrates' and we depend solely on secondary sources and differing interpretations (the so-called 'Socratic problem'—e.g., Nails 2009; Colaiaco 2001, p. 2). But what we *do* know is that Socrates' life—and death—is one of the most dramatic stories in human history. It is a story about the uneasy relationship between a (democratic) society and the individual, about common values and dissent, about actual or alleged boundary crossings, and about 'normal' people and an 'unnormal normal' person. Socrates' trial and death, but also his whole life and daily affairs, were *one big challenge* to everyone—to himself, his fellow citizens, and all generations afterwards.

Socrates' life and death still provide several puzzles. On the one hand he is a fascinating figure who devoted his life to philosophy and to the search for virtue, truth, and wisdom. In this, he did not leave one stone unturned. For Socrates, asking questions was valuable in itself; uncompromised inquiry and thorough criticism were the methods he applied to everything—and to everyone. He left no value or belief unchallenged and did not hesitate to draw others' attention to deficits in (their) knowledge and virtue. His inquisitive mind and his critical thinking laid the foundations for the development of the scientific method in particular and for the further development of human society in general. Perhaps most importantly, he himself was an example of his methods; Socrates *lived* his scientific endeavour. He was openhearted and fearless, he was true to himself and his beliefs, and he spoke truth to power. Nails (2009, n.p.), thus, concluded that 'his life is widely considered paradigmatic for the philosophic life and, more generally, for how anyone *ought* to live.' Socrates was an unnormal normal person who won by losing. The story of Socrates has shaped the ways many people think and see the world.

His story is tragic, and at the same time inspiring. On the other hand, Socrates was tried, found guilty, and sentenced to death by an Athenian court. He was accused of 'impiety' (not worshipping the city's gods or introducing new gods) and of 'corrupting the youth' of Athens (Nails 2009; Waterfield 2009b, p. 27; Millett 2005, p. 34; Colaiaco 2001, p. 15).[1]

How did such an outstanding man and citizen as Socrates come to be charged in this way? During most of Socrates' lifetime, Athens was an advanced model of direct democracy that guaranteed freedom of speech, political debate, and criticism (Ober 2006, p. 17; Colaiaco 2001, pp. 5, 11, 99). But how, then, Ober (2006, p. 1) asks, 'did a democratic community, committed to the value of free speech and public debate, come to convict and execute its most famous philosopher-citizen?'[2] Since Socrates' trial, people have been puzzled by the paradox that he was convicted *rightfully* with respect to Athenian law but *wrongfully* with respect to absolute justice (Ober 2006, p. 7). Besides, or behind, the official allegations, there must have been deep-seated and fundamental issues that contributed considerably to how the event unfolded and concluded. But what exactly were these issues—or, we might better ask, *whom* did Socrates offend, for what reasons, and in what ways (Blanchard 2000, p. 421)?

This chapter is not intended to add another theory or interpretation of the 'historically accurate' Socrates to the existing literature. And it will not focus primarily on Socrates' trial and death, his apologia, or the immediate events that may have led to his indictment. Instead, it will provide an analysis of Socrates' *common* views and actions based on the theory developed here (i.e., the general theory of hierarchical social systems). In particular, Socrates' thoughts and deeds are interpreted as boundary crossings (as analysed in Chapter 4). The following sections, hence, will present (or reconstruct) key aspects and consequences of Socrates' life and personality as a pattern of phenomena, events, and processes that represented increasingly stronger challenges to others and the social system. It will be discussed what types of boundary crossings his social actions, interests, identity, emotions, and moral character constituted; how these (probably) were perceived and interpreted by his fellow citizens; and when Socrates' words and deeds became perhaps system-threatening.

5.2 SOCRATES THE ECCENTRIC—WEAK BOUNDARY CROSSINGS

Socrates was what we might call a 'strange guy'—it is likely that most of his fellow citizens found him, his attitudes, and his behaviour somewhat bizarre. For example, in contrast to most well-respected members of Athenian society, he did not spend much of his time participating in official public life (e.g., the Assembly, or the city's many courts). Instead, for the best part of the day he simply walked around and talked to almost anyone (Nails 2009; Colaiaco 2001). In addition, his physiognomy, the way he dressed, and his overall appearance supported people's suspicion that Socrates was quite weird. Colaiaco (2001, p. 40) provides quite a telling picture of him:

> Socrates stood in stark contrast to the Greek ideal of physical beauty. 'It is significant,' declared the acerbic Friedrich Nietzsche, 'that Socrates was the first great Hellene to be ugly.' Short in stature, with bulging eyes, a flat nose, walking barefoot with an idiosyncratic gait, and always wearing the same old cloak, he could be an easy target for ridicule.

Most Athenians certainly knew Socrates' name and some stories about him. They might have seen him occasionally, perhaps even listened to him engaged in conversation with someone else. But they most likely knew him only a little and drew conclusions mainly from his public image and appearance rather than his character—deducing his 'inner nature' from his 'visible nature' without really knowing the latter. And, since outward beauty and inner goodness, appearance and character were linked in the popular imagination (Nails 2009), most people probably did not have a very favourable or flattering opinion about Socrates. However, at the level of the general population there was not much hostility towards him—more irritation and possibly some amusement or annoyance, or even some interest and curiosity.

Socrates probably did not care too much about what people thought about him—perhaps he even *wanted* to irritate or upset people. His 'strange' behaviour may have been no coincidence: he didn't want to fit into traditional roles, he didn't want to provide what people usually expected from a philosopher or Sophist, and in particular he didn't want to give answers. Instead, he was interested in raising questions—or perhaps even more in the unpredictable process of inquiring into phenomena and interrogating problems from different angles via discourse in public. And he didn't want people to remain in their 'comfort zones.' He wanted them to be puzzled, confused, and uncomfortable. He believed that people should begin to reflect critically on their own knowledge—or what they had perceived as such so far. He was interested in people getting rid of their 'pseudoknowledge' so that they would be able to slowly develop true knowledge and wisdom—a process Socrates often compared to giving birth, using metaphors related to midwifery. Colaiaco (2001, pp. 63–4) described this method in some detail:

> The method that Socrates employed against the reputedly wise, pointing out their inconsistent views, was that of cross-examination, the so-called *elenchus,* or refutation. This was how Socrates practiced philosophy. While conversing with an interlocutor, an ethical concept, such as wisdom, justice, courage, or piety, whose meaning was usually assumed, would invariably be introduced. At this point, Socrates would press for a clear definition of the concept, claiming his own ignorance. Once eliciting a definition from his interlocutor, he proceeded to illustrate that it was either too broad, or too narrow, or that the conclusions arrived at directly contradicted some initial assumption. The respondent's definition was usually based upon little reflection, as was readily demonstrated when Socrates attempted to apply it to specific cases. Forced to amend his definition, Socrates' interlocutor was ultimately left in a frustrating position by a new series of questions. Attempting to answer the philosopher's questions, he was caught in further inconsistencies, revealing that he lacked clear knowledge of basic concepts.

Socrates believed in critical inquiry and reason as methods to gain knowledge and wisdom—for himself as well as for everyone else. He was convinced that one of the main tasks, if not 'the' prime duty, of a philosopher is to reveal and to interrogate problems to the very bottom, asking disturbing questions and addressing even the most difficult issues—and increasing the capabilities of people to do the same, to *reason on their own* and to develop inquisitive and critical minds.

At this stage, most likely people didn't have much of a problem with Socrates; he might have been weird, perhaps the weirdest of all the Sophists (most people probably didn't distinguish between Socrates and the Sophists), but people tolerated him. He was just an old, strange guy—an eccentric. Socrates might have crossed boundaries with regard to what are generally taken to be 'decent' behaviour and attitudes, but he did not represent a real threat or serious challenge; on the contrary, people's values, beliefs, and (perhaps even more importantly) identities could remain intact. Moreover, Socrates' strangeness was a confirmation of *their* normalness, a reassurance that their identity (or better: self-image) was 'normal.' Hence, although Socrates had an inquisitive and independent mind and could be quite a nuisance, he occupied the subordinate position of an eccentric philosopher perfectly and helped many people to nurture their superior self-images. People had someone in their midst to look down on and to ridicule. Although Socrates crossed a few boundaries at a low level, he played *his* part in keeping the superior-subordinate relationship of 'normal' citizens and 'unnormal' eccentrics intact.

5.3 SOCRATES THE DEVIANT—MEDIUM-INTENSITY BOUNDARY CROSSINGS

However, Socrates did not only ask people questions for the sake of asking—and the 'weird, eccentric philosopher' was only the perhaps most visible and recognisable part of him. Socrates' home was the halls and public squares in Athens, where all sorts of orators ('rhetors') courted Athens' citizens for their support. Most of them were Sophists—professional teachers of rhetoric, philosophy, and other arts who made a living out of the services they offered. According to Colaiaco (2001, p. 25),

> [Sophists] perfected the art of debate, composing skilful speeches calculated to win arguments, regardless of the truth. [. . .] The Sophists did not claim to teach objective truth, which they denied, or to improve moral character, but to prepare young men for political success. Truth became less important than winning a legal case or persuading the Assembly to adopt one's proposal.

But Socrates was different; he was interested in the search for *true* knowledge and wisdom. He thought that rhetoric should be used in *decent* ways and *not* as an instrument for winning debates *per se* or for dominating others (Colaiaco 2001, pp. 24, 35). Socrates' interest, thus, was in direct opposition to the main interest of most Sophists.

In addition, the Sophists were convinced that they possessed, or at least gave the impression of possessing, the 'right' knowledge. In contrast, Socrates' search for knowledge and wisdom was based on strong notions of 'eternal scepticism' ("I know that I know nothing!") and 'critical thinking.' Socrates was not only sceptical about his own knowledge but also had radical doubts about *any* claim to possess knowledge and even about absolute and eternal truths (Simpson 2006, p. 140; Colaiaco 2001, p. 69).

He questioned and challenged 'technical' knowledge, but also beliefs, practices, and traditions. He questioned and challenged *everything*. Moreover, Socrates challenged *everyone*—especially those who claimed or pretended to possess true knowledge (i.e., the so-called or self-proclaimed 'experts'). He questioned politicians, craftsmen (artisans, physicians, sculptors, and artists), poets, and Sophists (Colaiaco 2001, p. 63; Blanchard 2000, pp. 441–2). He questioned them until they had to admit their lack of knowledge. Sooner or later, all of these 'experts' *had to* confess that they didn't know what they originally had asserted they knew (Simpson 2006, p. 140; Colaiaco 2001, p. 60). In this sense, Socrates not only demonstrated that these experts did not have the knowledge or wisdom they claimed to have but also exposed their shallow thinking and *hypocrisy* (Colaiaco 2001, pp. 62–3).

Socrates' interest and social actions with regard to exposing ignorance and hypocrisy, especially of experts, represented more serious boundary crossings. In Plato's dialogues, Socrates' discussion partners give the impression that they appreciate his determination to find true knowledge and they even seem to be grateful when he finally reveals their ignorance. This was probably a fictional adornment in order to stress the philosophical side of Socrates' dialogues—but it goes against common understanding. Usually, people do not react positively when their ignorance is exposed. It is an unpleasant experience to realise one's own ignorance—especially when one is forced *by someone else* and when one's ignorance is revealed *deliberately* and *in public*. Most people would find this rather embarrassing and insulting, and would probably become quite angry. Thus, it is more reasonable to assume that Socrates' intensive questioning was perceived as quite offensive (Blanchard 2000, p. 441)—especially by the 'experts' whose professional status was at stake (which also was the main source of their income). Socrates' way of interrogating philosophical and ethical problems revealed that their so-called 'expert knowledge' was shallow, and in many respects simply wrong. It undermined their authority and challenged their very identities—their self-images as well as their public images.

On top of that, Socrates probably also had quite an impact on others' opinions and self-images. For one, some of those who believed in the Sophists and their truths began to develop doubts (Blanchard 2000, pp. 441–5)— and, if these were rich Athenian citizens, it meant lost paying customers for the Sophists. In addition, Socrates especially encouraged his listeners and students (the 'youth of Athens') to develop their critical skills and to question established knowledge, wisdom, beliefs, and traditions (Colaiaco 2001, p. 124). He encouraged them to do as he did—i.e., to challenge everything and everyone. It seems that quite a few (younger) Athenians were willing to apply his method of criticism and to use it against experts, and even against their parents. In this sense, the legal allegation that Socrates 'corrupted the youth' had some merit (Colaiaco 2001, pp. 72, 104, 124).

As a consequence of his influence, Socrates was met with growing anger, and even bitter resentment and hostility. And, since Socrates had criticised many of Athens' (self-proclaimed) experts, Sophists, politicians, and prominent people, he had probably made a lot of enemies—who were looking for the right time and opportunity for revenge. There is some evidence that there were also personal motives behind Socrates' prosecution (Colaiaco 2001, p. 73). All three prosecutors (the poet Meletos, the politician Anytos, and the orator Lycon) seem to have also had private reasons for taking Socrates to court, as they represented professions Socrates had challenged very many times (Millett 2005, p. 32; Blanchard 2000, p. 432).

Personal animosity also played an important role during the trial (Colaiaco 2001, pp. 60, 106). Again, Socrates himself contributed much to this development. The courtroom setting actually provided an unfamiliar challenge for Socrates. In Athenian law courts it was quite common for rhetoric, and even more questionable tactics, to primarily be used by prosecutors as well as by defendants in order to convince the jury—and not necessarily to find the truth. However, because of his personality, philosophical interests, and moral convictions, Socrates was neither able nor willing to engage in such practices (Colaiaco 2001, pp. 31, 35). Even his communication skills were not of much use within this unusual setting. Socrates was used to conducting philosophical dialogues but now he was required to give a rhetorical monologue. In Colaiaco's (2001, p. 30) words, 'The master of the dialectical method of question-and-answer, directed to exposing the culpable ignorance of his interlocutors, was now compelled by law to deliver a formal monologue to persuade a large audience of his innocence.'

Because of his philosophical unwillingness or practical incompetence with regard to courtroom tactics, Socrates felt back into his usual method of interrogating problems. Instead of defending himself against the charges made, he actually crossexamined his prosecutors with regard to the meaning of words (Colaiaco 2001, p. 129). Moreover, in his speech Socrates made it very clear that he was *deliberately* at odds with popular views. As in his daily life, Socrates did not want to behave as people expected. His speech was a radical critique of the very foundations of Athenian culture and an explicit provocation (Ober 2003, p. 5; Colaiaco 2001, p. 34). Colaiaco (2001, p. 146) therefore concluded: 'Notwithstanding his loyalty to Athens, the aggressive stance that Socrates adopted throughout the trial, reminding his fellow citizens of their moral and political failings, alienated many jurors.'

But it was not just his interest in exposing everyone's lack of knowledge, his stinging criticism of Athenian culture and his (unintended) challenges of people's identity that created so much hostility against him. It was also his identity that increasingly upset people.

Socrates had a high level of personal integrity. In contrast to the Sophists, he did not charge for his services because he felt that he did not know anything that would be worth selling (Schindler 2009, p. 394). He did not believe in rhetoric as a tool for impressing or defeating others and used language very cautiously and only for the sake for seeking knowledge (Nails 2009; Waterfield 2009a, p. 160; Colaiaco 2001, p. 42). He lived his life as he claimed in his speeches, and he was true to himself and to others. Even in the face of serious allegations and the possibility of the death penalty, he continued to behave as he had acted and behaved before. But some of his ways of demonstrating his personal integrity were too much for his fellow citizens. For example, in his apologia, Socrates told the jurors quite directly that he would not be willing to show the expected signs of subordination (Ober 2003, p. 15):

> Perhaps you think, Athenians, that I have been convicted for lack of words (*aporia logon*) to persuade you, that I thought it right to do and say anything to be acquitted. Not so. It is true I have been convicted for a lack; not a lack of words, but lack of bold shamelessness, unwilling-ness to say the things that you would find it most pleasant (*hedista*) to hear—lamenting and wailing, saying and doing many things I claim to be unworthy of me, but things of the sort you are accustomed to hear from others. I did not then think it necessary to do anything unworthy of a free man (*aneleutheron*) because of danger; I do not now regret so having conducted my defense; and I would far rather die with that defense than live with the other.

Even in the courtroom, Socrates seemed to feel quite comfortable with his deviant identity. He even called on an exceptional witness who (alleg-edly) supported his claim of being special: the Delphic Oracle (Nails 2009; Colaiaco 2001, p. 56). According to the Oracle, no one was wiser than Socrates—and Socrates went still further to interpret the statement in the sense that he was the wisest man of all (Schindler 2009, p. 394).[3] It might well be that Socrates truly believed the Oracle—at least, he seemed to pres-ent the issue during the trial in the usual serious and philosophical manner that was so typical of him. But he produced nothing less than evidence that the gods themselves regarded him as outstanding and superior—which was probably perceived by most spectators and jurors not as humbleness but as pretension and arrogance.

Moreover, Socrates not only argued that he was wiser/better than anyone else but that the higher institutions had appointed him to 'help' his fellow citizens; in Colaico's (2001, p. 148) words, Socrates claimed that 'God [had] assigned him to Athens to play the role of a "gadfly", to interrogate, exhort, reproach, and provoke the Athenians, awakening them from their dogmatic slumber and stimulating them to lives of virtue.' Colaico then let Socrates speak:

> If you kill me you will not easily find a successor to me, who, if I may use such a ludicrous figure of speech, am a sort of gadfly, given to the State by God; and the State is a great and noble steed who is tardy in his motions owing to his very size, and requires to be stirred into life. I am that gadfly which God has attached to the State, and all day long

and in all places am always fastening upon you, arousing and persuading and reproaching you. You will not easily find another like me, and therefore I would advise you to spare me. I dare say that you may feel out of temper (like a person who is suddenly awakened from sleep), and you think that you may easily strike me dead as Anytus advises, and then you would sleep on for the remainder of your lives, unless God in his care of you sent you another gadfly.

And, as if this were not enough, Socrates made it very clear that he would never change. Even if he were to be offered a reduced sentence or acquittal for the alleged crimes he was indicted for, he would reply (Colaiaco 2001, p. 3): 'Men of Athens, I honour and love you; but I shall obey God rather than you, and while I have life and strength I shall never cease from the practice and teaching of philosophy.'

All in all, Socrates' identity deviated quite strongly from what would have been expected of an (eccentric) philosopher: Socrates 1) demonstrated his unwillingness to obey and to show the expected signs of subordination, 2) claimed that even the gods regarded him as an outstanding philosopher, 3) alleged that the gods had given him the role of a gadfly to provoke his fellow citizens, and 4) stressed that he would never change in challenging his fellow citizens and questioning everything, and everyone, and would stay true to himself.

With those claims, Socrates indicated that he saw himself as morally superior to most, if not all, other Athenian citizens, and that he considered himself to talk and act on higher moral ground (N.N. 2010b; Waterfield 2009a, p. 18; Ober 2003, p. 13; Colaiaco 2001, pp. 31, 71)—and all these assertions he made (also) as a defendant facing the death sentence in front of an Athenian jury! To him, his words might have appeared to be a compelling argument and a humble attitude reflecting his self-understanding and identity as a true philosopher. To others, he probably appeared to be merely defiant and arrogant. To them, each of Socrates' statements was a provocation. Together, they were infamy.

Quite understandably, his speech was not perceived very well. He was repeatedly interrupted by angry outbursts from jurors (Millett 2005, p. 25; Colaiaco 2001, p. 56) and his unwillingness to show obedience infuriated many jurors (Colaiaco 2001, p. 56). His reference to the Delphic Oracle was seen by many as a preposterous claim (Nails 2009). His metaphor of Athens as a slow horse and him as a gadfly getting it going 'was most likely regarded by the majority of jurors as an impudent insult' (Colaiaco 2001, p. 148). And his bold statement that he would never change angered many jurors even more (Colaiaco 2001, p. 3).

Some commentators have taken the opinion that Socrates infuriated the jurors *intentionally* because he *wanted* to be sentenced (e.g., Ober 2006, p. 3 referring to Xenophon; Colaiaco 2001, p. 220 referring to Nietzsche). After an initial verdict by the jury in which only a small number found him guilty, Socrates made quite some unreasonable, outrageous demands that obviously upset and alienated many jurors so much that they changed their vote from 'innocent' to the death penalty (Millett 2005, p. 25; Lane 2002, p. 44; Colaiaco 2001, p. 175). Colaiaco (2001, p. 147) neatly summarised this turn of events:

> Socrates seemed to have forgotten that his position before the court was that of a defendant, not a prosecutor. From here on, Socrates' offensive becomes increasingly blatant, and the trial takes an inevitable path, with the philosopher bringing about his own condemnation. In choosing to lecture the Athenians on their moral weaknesses, Socrates reveals his commitment to philosophical rhetoric, speech designed to edify morally his listeners. But the arguments he made and the patronizing tone he adopted merely antagonized many jurors and spectators. Those sympathetic to Socrates must have been dismayed as they witnessed him seal his fate.

We cannot tell whether Socrates upset the jurors deliberately or naïvely. But what we can say is that his behaviour was consistent with his identity. His unusual identity is one of the earliest—and most prominent—examples of *individualisation*—i.e., identity-based independence and deviation from social norms and expectations. Socrates was free from any form of political, religious, ethical, or intellectual authority and from any single value system or dogma, and only listened to his individual conscience, employing the method of critical thinking (Colaiaco 2001, p. 68). He not only had an independent mind—he *was* independent.

Socrates' individuality—his individualistic and, thus, independent approach to piety and social life—challenged traditional understandings in the most serious way. Usually, a strong sense of the *polis* (city) prevailed in Athens. Most Athenians saw Athens as a community in which collective values and shared traditions guided and regulated social affairs. Individual citizens and their rights and freedom were subordinate to the interests of the *polis* and there was considerable coercive power over possible deviants. According to Colaiaco (2001, p. 100), in Athens:

> The individual could not be understood apart from the social matrix of values and relationships. With virtually everything the state's business, the ancient Greeks would not have comprehended the modern liberal view of individual rights. Nor would they have comprehended the liberal view that limits the state's function to the protection of rights.

In this sense, it was not so much what Socrates *actually* said or did that troubled many people.[4] It was his personal identity and self-image as an independent individual, which went against the common understanding of Athens' citizens and were unbearable and acceptable for them. Socrates' independent identity constituted a serious challenge not only for his fellow citizens' norms and values but also for their individual as well as collective identity; with his individual conscience, Socrates challenged those collective and traditional values that were the foundations of Athens.

However, Socrates' individualisation and deviance *as such* did not make him reach the level at which he would have become a serious threat to the whole social system. There are several reasons for this.

One, quite crucial, reason is that Socrates remained largely isolated as a philosopher. True, some of Athens' youth imitated Socrates' method of interrogation (Nails 2009). And, if many (more) had followed his example and had begun to question and to challenge the traditional values, beliefs, behaviours, and attitudes (of their parents), Socrates could have increasingly been seen as a serious threat to the established order (Lane 2002, p. 43; Colaiaco 2001, p. 107). But, although Socrates might have had some students or followers (and a few of them even became philosophers or politicians), he never established a 'school' or initiated a 'movement.' He was not interested in creating a community of like-minded Athenians; on the contrary, he pursued his endeavours on an individual basis—and encouraged others to do likewise. He achieved independence and individualisation *for himself*, but *without* larger solidarisation—and (some of) Athens' youth did the same *for themselves*.

A similar case can be made with regard to Socrates' heresy and deviance. For example, one of the charges Socrates faced was that he was impious— i.e., that he did not worship Athens' traditional gods, that he failed to carry out his ritual obligations and that he even introduced new gods (Waterfield 2009a, p. 39). At first sight, it appears that Socrates was prosecuted for unorthodox and nonconformist religious beliefs and practices (Colaiaco 2001, p. 122). However, it seems that it was not unusual in Athens for people to practise different religious rites or to believe in different gods or introduce new ones (Waterfield 2009a, p. 45; Millett 2005, p. 34). In this sense, many of his fellow citizens could also have been prosecuted for (alleged) impiety or even heresy. A few were, but most were not. Thus, there must have been more reasons why Socrates' way of demonstrating piety was not only deemed inappropriate but also used against him in order to take him to court (Waterfield 2009a, p. 38; Kiblinger 2006, p. 7; Blanchard 2000, p. 430). We will come back to these reasons in Section 5.4. Here, the argument will be stretched just a little further within the context of piety and with regard to Socrates' (alleged) heresy and deviance.

A main aspect of religion in ancient Greece was keeping the gods happy, since they were regarded as crucial for the prosperity and survival of the state, for warfare, and for agriculture (Waterfield 2009a, p. 36). Perhaps even more importantly, religious rites and other means to demonstrate one's piety were primarily *social* events. And, as social activities, one of their prime functions was to create and maintain a sense of community, togetherness, and group cohesion: piety was patriotism and conformity (Waterfield

2009a, p. 43; Waterfield 2009b, p. 27; Colaiaco 2001, p. 121). Only those who showed the right type and amount of conformity with regard to religious activities were regarded as pious persons and good citizens. Socrates, too, *was* a pious person and good citizen—but he showed his piety and citizenship on *his* terms and in ways *he* deemed to be right. And he demonstrated publicly and in very obvious ways his unwillingness to act as socially expected and in ways officially understood to be correct. Thus, Socrates' deviance in religious matters was not *religious* heresy but *social* heresy; he challenged the prevailing social norms of Athens. And it was heresy *with* deviation—*deliberate* deviation.

Overall, what Socrates showed in the realm of moral character was individualisation *without* solidarisation and heresy *with* deviation—which together were both his strengths that the proponents of the system feared as well as his weaknesses that the proponents of the system could use to their advantage.[5]

All in all, Socrates was not only a 'weird' *eccentric* but also an 'unruly' *deviant* who crossed lines *deliberately* and *regularly*. He upset and embarrassed many people with his constant questioning, by exposing the ignorance and hypocrisy of (especially) experts, with his strive for individualisation, and with his heresy concerning many of Athens' religious practices. What made things worse was that he did not show the right signs of obedience and submissiveness—he did not behave as he should have done according to his subordinate status. In doing so, Socrates was not only annoying but also increasingly threatened the social system. His interests and social actions, and especially his identity and deviating interpretation of social norms and values—represented quite serious boundary crossings.

As a consequence, many people, and particular influential people, became increasingly hostile towards Socrates. His eccentricity and individualisation, his heresy together with his demonstrated deviance made him hardly bearable, and for many even unacceptable. However, his individualisation was *without* solidarisation and his heresy came *with* deviation. Hence, because of his eccentricity and open deviance, it was relatively easy for Socrates' opponents to deal with him; they could find (or create) reasons and opportunities to attack him, to isolate him, to turn public opinion against him (though Socrates was responsible for this himself), to prosecute him, to silence him and, in doing so, to limit his influence quite considerably. And they did. But this is not the end of the story.

5.4   SOCRATES THE ENEMY—STRONG BOUNDARY CROSSINGS

Socrates had been free to practice his philosophy for several decades (Ober 2006, p. 19; Millett 2005, p. 30)—but then he was prosecuted in 399 BCE. As indicated above, there were probably more motives than piety or a concern for Athens' youth behind Socrates' prosecution (Blanchard 2000, p. 431). It is commonly thought that Socrates' trial was 'political,' or 'politically' motivated (Waterfield 2009a, p. 32). Quite often, political rivalries of upper-class Athenians spilled over into the courts (Waterfield 2009a, p. 20). According to Waterfield (2009a, p. 27), 'If any intellectual got into trouble, he was likely to be accused of impiety, but that happened only if he had made himself politically undesirable on other grounds.'

But what exactly were, or could have been, these 'political' issues or motives in Socrates' case? After the lost Peloponnesian War against Sparta (431–404 BCE), for a brief period of time Athens was ruled by an oligarchic group, the so-called 'Thirty Tyrants.' However, democracy was restored in 403 BCE. Socrates had been close to at least two of the Thirty Tyrants, Critias and Charmides, as well as to a very controversial general, Alcibiades, who was widely seen as a traitor because he had briefly defected to Sparta during the Peloponnesian War (Lane 2002, p. 43). Although Socrates was not directly prosecuted for these connections because of a general amnesty after the war, he was perhaps seen by some as someone who had been *too* close to the Tyrants (Lane 2002, p. 43; Miller 2002, p. 353). He may even have been regarded as an enemy of Athenian democracy (N.N. 2010b), or at least as someone who had not learned his lessons, as he continued with his practices as if the tyranny of the Thirty had never happened (Ober 2006, p. 23).

It might well be that some Athenians who supported Socrates' prosecution wanted to make an example of the tyranny of the Thirty (and all those who were part of it), the lost war with Sparta (which had been long and catastrophic), intergenerational conflict (an unruly Athenian youth), or a general weakening of the moral foundations of Athenian society (the rhetoric of the Sophists). Perhaps people wanted to draw a line under the recent, quite unpleasant, past; to have the values and beliefs of the newly re-established democracy endorsed, not challenged; and to fight off undesirable trends that might (again) undermine democracy and prosperity (Waterfield 2009a, p. 202; Waterfield 2009b, p. 28; Ober 2006, p. 17; Colaiaco 2001, p. 37). Socrates stood for all of these negative issues (or could be seen or portrayed that way) and, thus, made a perfect scapegoat.

All of the aspects mentioned might have been relevant in some way. Nevertheless, Socrates was prosecuted four years after the fall of the Thirty Tyrants—enough time for 'reasons from the past' not to play much of a role. Also, Socrates was prosecuted when he was sixty-eight years old—a fairly advanced age in ancient times. There was no real need to prosecute a very old man if the motive was fears concerning the future of the recently re-established democracy. Hence, there must have been more than some general concerns about Athens' past, present, or future to explain why Socrates was regarded by some as a serious threat. But what could have been reasons that were perhaps crucial in some people's determination to prosecute Socrates? What exactly does it mean that Socrates' trial was called 'political,' that his prosecutors (either the known ones or the ones behind the scenes) were politically motivated? If we are more specific, we will see that the argument for a 'political trial' becomes stronger.

Although Athens was a democracy, even a direct democracy, it was neither an equal nor a fair nor just society. Only about a fifth of all Athenians were eligible to participate in public affairs (adult male citizens who had completed their military training, had no debts and were descended from Athenian citizens). In contrast, common citizens, slaves, freed slaves, and women had only fairly limited rights and opportunities. The society of Athens was highly stratified and diversified, if not to say polarised; Athenian society 'was clearly divided along class lines' (Ober 1989, p. 192). In particular, the well-off citizens of Athens enjoyed unprecedented privileges and prerogatives that set them apart from all ordinary people. Since aristocrats 'shared a common value system, socialized with one another, and tended to intermarry, they were identified by their fellow citizens as a distinct status group' (Ober 1989, p. 251). There was a clearly identifiable elite in Athens of (very) wealthy citizens.

As such, the possession, even accumulation, of material wealth in private hands was not regarded as a problem in Athens at that time, nor did it constitute a direct threat to the democratic political order. But many members of the upper class ran the political and social affairs of Athens not only with their political and rhetorical skills but also with their economic power and material means (e.g., by bribing administrators or jurors). Athenian aristocrats had accumulated and concentrated in their hands economical *and* political power. They did not only own Athens' biggest villas, they also owned its institutions. Because of this, they could demonstrate antisocial behaviour *and* get away with it—on a regular basis.

Socrates criticised members of the power elite for their focus on gaining power and enriching themselves instead of pursuing wisdom and moral goodness (Colaiaco 2001, pp. 33–4, 61)—we will come back to this later in this section. However, rich and powerful people can live with such criticism; everyone knows that rich and powerful people are interested in wealth and power—they 'have to,' since otherwise they wouldn't be what they are and wouldn't do what they do. And only if they stayed rich and powerful, so they say, can they fulfil all those 'duties' that are 'so important' for the whole.

But Socrates did much more than criticise the wealth and power of the rich and powerful *as such;* he criticised how the powerful and rich conducted public office as well as their private lives. In doing so, he challenged the very foundations of their claims that they care for, and are good for the whole. For example, Socrates scrutinised those public occasions that regularly reiterated power elites' superior status. In every stratified society and hierarchical organisation, there are public social events and activities that happen on a regular basis and carry highly symbolic meaning, for example religious rites and rituals, liturgies, public speeches, ceremonies, donations, and the like. Such symbolic acts fulfil a whole range of important functions. They are primarily meant to 1) convey certain 'messages', meanings, beliefs, and ideologies, 2) shape people's reasoning and worldviews, 3) contribute to the creation of a collective identity, 4) form people's individual identities, 5) underline and strengthen members of the power elite's elevated status and positions, 6) justify and legitimise their privileged positions and privileges, 7) create and maintain a positive public image of the power elite, and 8) create and maintain approval from the masses.

In Athens, such social events or activities were quite common; daily life and public affairs were based on comprehensive and elaborate systems of sacred rites, ceremonies at social gatherings, and communal activities. They were used mainly by priests, politicians, orators, aristocrats, and other wealthy citizens to demonstrate their alleged superiority and goodness, and their care for the whole and for the poor. 'The state,' largely represented by members of those power elites, was highly protective of such events and activities and maintained a high degree of control over their organisation and performance; these events not only secured and strengthened the power elites' positions within the hierarchical system but also helped to weld the whole community together and to stabilise the fragile social order (Waterfield 2009a, p. 46; Ober 1989, p. 208). Crucially, every sacred and secular event and activity established and reconfirmed a direct link between the gods, the privileged who carried out the act, and the masses. In this sense, the event or activity symbolised and enacted this perfect tripartite order— and so did the people who carried them out.

This is where and why Socrates' criticism became so serious and system-threatening. First, Socrates argued that Athens' prevailing beliefs and religious and social practices were not mandated by the gods but *manmade* (Simpson 2006, p. 140). They were not of *divine* but of *social* origin. In ancient Greece, such a position had far-reaching implications; *if* the cults and rituals were not of divine nature then those who carried them out (the priests) and paid for them (the aristocrats) were no closer to the gods than anyone else. Moreover, their privileges and privileged positions were also not of divine but of social origin.

In the face of an absent divine justification, the rich and powerful had to legitimise their privileges and prerogatives otherwise. Usually, Athenian aristocrats' material and immaterial advantages and social positions were justified and sanctioned *by virtue of birthright*. Even their character and goodness were allegedly inherited virtues (Ober 1989, p. 251):

> The Athenian aristocrat was differentiated from, and might be perceived to be better than the non-aristocrat because he was thought to have inherited from his ancestors certain desirable traits—especially the qualities of being noble and good (*agathos*) and physically beautiful (*kalos*)—and because he acted differently from ordinary men.

The problem with these 'inherited virtues' was that the reality showed a rather different picture; many members of Athens' upper classes enjoyed not just wealth and privileges but *excessive* wealth and *offensive* luxuriousness. They demonstrated severe levels of ostentation, decadence, hubris, and arrogance (Ober 1989, p. 208)—quite the opposite of what one would call 'noble' and 'good' behaviour. Hence, what Socrates exposed, and criticised, was not just aristocrats' wealth and power *per se* but their *hypocrisy*. Above it was said that Socrates' deviance or heresy in religious matters was not a criticism of the gods but a criticism of the social norms and practices of Athens. Now this argument can be formulated even more specifically (and more strongly): Socrates' deviance or heresy in religious matters was a criticism of *aristocrats'* social norms and practices, a critique of *their* hypocrisy.

The revelation of their hypocrisy was a very serious threat; members of the Athenian power elite had to produce an image of personal superiority (and of the inferiority of others) and the superiority of aristocracy as an institution while at the same time addressing collective ideas and the importance of democratic institutions (Ober 1989, pp. 286, 291) in order to hold the whole hierarchical social order together. But this delicate balancing act of emphasising at the same time elitist superiority and collective principles could work only as long as people believed, or were made to believe, that members of the power elites truly believed in both values—and behaved accordingly. As soon as the aristocrats' hypocrisy was exposed by Socrates, the legitimacy of the power elite (and its privileges) was at stake; it became quite clear that the real interests and behaviour of (most) members of the power elite were antithetical to those of the common people (Ober 1989, p. 218)—in stark contrast to the public claims about 'common values and interests' aristocrats made at every possible occasion.

As a consequence of Socrates' revelations and criticism, people became much more conscious of the need to look closely at what certain members of the power elite said or claimed—and what they *actually* did. In the face of the power elites' systemic and widespread hypocrisy, it was more than questionable whether the (self-proclaimed) superiors and leaders were good and wise enough in order to carry out their tasks and to assume the responsibility of governing the *polis* (Colaiaco 2001, pp. 63–4). And, since the social norms and practices as well as elites' positions and conduct were not defined and shaped by divine will but the results of social causes, there was no reason why the situation could not be changed.

Rulers and members of the power elites always have two great fears (there are many more, but these two are the most fundamental). One is with regard to the hierarchical system. They fear that the common people will begin to realise that the status quo is not eternal and the best possible state of affairs for them, that everything *can* be otherwise and that change does not necessarily need to be for the worse but can produce *better* conditions and outcomes. Power elites' second fear relates to their own status and position within the system. The rich and powerful are very concerned about their public image—and they become very worried when their public image is unravelled. They know very well that their actual identities and behaviours are less compelling than their public portraits and that, as a consequence, their social positions are quite vulnerable, since these are not only based on a power differential but also, more crucially, on people's perceptions. With the elites' hypocrisy fully exposed and their public image severely damaged, there is a high possibility that the common people will not only be quite upset but also expect consequences and perhaps even take action. For example, with regard to Athens, Ober (1989, p. 197) made the point that 'Class conflict, leading to forced redistribution of wealth, was more than a theoretical issue for the ancient Greeks.'

All in all, with his social actions Socrates challenged the status quo quite seriously, in particular those aspects with which members of the power elites tried to justify and to secure their privileged positions and privileges:

1) Socrates showed that religious practices and aristocrats' privileges and prerogatives were of social, not of divine, origin—and, thus, open to scrutiny and changeable.

2) Socrates exposed the aristocrats' hypocrisy and showed that the power elites' interests were actually antithetical to those of the common people.

3) Because of Socrates' questions and revelations, people could start to wonder whether the current power elites were really the best leaders and whether their reign and social dominance were justified and the best possibility for Athens.

Socrates' social actions constituted relatively strong boundary crossings. He was not against Athens *per se*—but he questioned and challenged members of the power elites' privileges and prerogatives and their social positions, interests, and alleged 'divine rights.' In doing so, he undermined the very foundations on which Athenian society was built. From the perspective of the rich and powerful there were 'good' reasons to regard Socrates as a dangerous thinker (Colaiaco 2001, p. 70), not (only) because he threatened the stability of the social order but because he threatened *their* social order, positions, and interests.

Socrates' criticism was based on a strong dislike and condemnation of many Athenians' obsession with material wealth and power politics (Colaiaco 2001, p. 145), their keenness to gain and to have more than they actually needed and their tendency to see money not as a means but as an end in itself (Schindler 2009, pp. 399–401). In contrast, Socrates was of the opinion that people should not care about the accumulation of material things, wealth, and power but rather care about pursuing virtue and the welfare of their souls, and about a more simplistic way of life, friendships, and a sense of true community (N.N. 2010b; Colaiaco 2001, p. 131; Taylor 2000, p. 23). As he explained (cited in Colaiaco 2001, p. 145):

> For I do nothing but go about persuading you all, old and young alike, not to take thought for your persons and properties, but first and chiefly

to care about the greatest improvement of the soul. I tell you that virtue is not given by money, but that from virtue comes money and every other good of man, public as well as private. This is my teaching, and if this is the doctrine which corrupts the youth, I am a mischievous person.

Obviously, like his social actions, Socrates' interests challenged the fundamental values and beliefs on which Athenian society was built—and especially the interests and beliefs of the rich. Most of them were interested not in the pursuit of virtue but the pursuit of wealth, not in a good life but an expensive lifestyle, not in filling their souls but filling their pockets. Socrates' ideas threatened their key interests—everything that made life worthwhile from their point of view. They, thus, regarded his interests as a direct attack on their way of life.

Moreover, besides his search for knowledge and wisdom, Socrates was interested in helping people to become better persons (Blanchard 2000, p. 445). According to his understanding, this would entail people developing an interest primarily in the welfare of their souls, friendships, and true community instead of material assets. Such a shift of interests would not necessarily mean that subordinates or common people would start to go directly against the rich and powerful. 'Developing one's soul' is often seen more as (individual) reflection looking inwards. And the ideas of 'friendship' and 'true community' also do not directly threaten the establishment. Hence, compared with his social actions, Socrates' ideas concerning and interests in bettering other people's souls and ways of living together harmoniously do not initially seem to be system-threatening. However, they nonetheless represented quite a challenge. For example, people with virtuous souls and deeply internalised communitarian values can be quite incompatible with hierarchical organisations and stratified societies. People with such personalities might comply, but sooner or later their mindsets and social actions will change the hierarchical system.

Either way, those of Socrates' social actions and interests that challenged hierarchy did not come out of the blue; they were based on, and deeply ingrained in, his identity. Socrates was extremely individualistic. He did not just see himself as an individual independent of the guiding principles and spirits Athens had on offer; he also had his own source of guidance. Socrates was guided by an internal voice, a *daimonion* (Nails 2009; Waterfield 2009a, p. 46; Millett 2005, p. 36). Socrates' *daimonion* was a mysterious, independent power. It 'may have struck his fellow citizens as dangerously individualistic in contrast to the public gods of the city' (Lane 2002, p. 43). Such an individualistic view of piety and an exclusive, very personal relationship with a divinity was in stark contrast to the collective understandings and rituals of piety (Colaiaco 2001, p. 124).[6]

There are perhaps two main reasons why Socrates' *daimonion* represented such a strong challenge. One is that Socrates had introduced this new god on *his* terms—*this* is where Socrates really deviated. The introduction of a new divinity *as such* was not really a problem, provided one did it in 'the right way'—i.e., via established procedures and in accordance with the formal rules and regulations put forward by the authorities. However, according to Colaiaco (2001, p. 158), 'To allege that a god has chosen you for private communications, unmediated by priests or cults, violated the Athenian notion of piety and the prerogative of the *polis* to regulate religion.' By introducing a new god by himself and on his own terms, Socrates challenged the authorities' prerogatives. Moreover, in addition to this non-compliance with technical rules, Socrates demonstrated that he saw himself as being on the same level as those members of the power elites who were in charge.

The second reason that Socrates' *daimonion* represented a challenge was that it showed that he did not need authorities to guide him at all; since his private communication with the *daimonion* represented a *direct* contact with the divine, Socrates did not need a mediator; he did not need the services of priests to please the gods nor to interpret their will, and he did not need any 'help' and guidance from politicians or aristocrats to arrange for and finance the right ceremonies. He saw himself as a free and independent individual who did not need the rich and powerful, or their representatives, as intermediaries to the gods in any way.

Socrates' *daimonion* was, so to speak, a double whammy for Athens' authorities; Socrates showed that his identity was not one of a subordinate *and* he showed that he did not need superiors (at all). That Socrates had sidestepped the authorities with his *daimonion* not only demonstrated that he saw himself as truly independent but also implied that the regulators—the whole power elite—were obsolete. Obviously, such implications represent a serious threat to any hierarchical system. In this sense, to listen and to follow primarily one's 'inner voice' is a very strong, perhaps even the strongest, cornerstone of individualisation. It is evidence of a free and independent individual who does not fit, cannot fit, and does not want to fit into a superior-subordinate relationship.

Finally, Socrates' social actions, interests, and identity were the logical consequence of his norms and convictions. For him, the most important thing was the human *soul*, the soul of a (self-)conscious person. Socrates grounded the ideal of intellectual and moral excellence in *individual* morality and the soul, *inner* reflection and self-knowledge, and the ideas of pursuing virtue and living an examined life as an *individual* endeavour (Colaiaco 2001, p. 143; Taylor 2000, p. 24); to 'care for one's soul means pursuing the truth and living justly' (Colaiaco 2001, p. 144). In other words, Socrates lived his *own* life according to these ideals—*his* ideals.

Moreover (and perhaps even more crucially with regard to the whole social system), Socrates 'sought to convince his fellow Athenians that living an examined life, pursuing virtue and the good of the soul, rather than with power and material wealth, would bring a wayward city into harmony with superior ethical standards' (Colaiaco 2001, p. 137). Socrates argued that people should not 'follow blindly the dictates of the state, but [. . .] consult first their conscience' (Colaiaco 2001, p. 104). And he said that this individualistic approach to moral development, piety and living an examined life was possible *for everyone* (Waterfield 2009a, p. 43). The idea of the prevalence of the individual soul and the notions of 'knowing yourself' and inner reflection carried out by people *independently* challenged traditional authority and customary values seriously. 'Socrates [. . .] threatened the established morality of his culture by striving to base ethics upon reason, in which individuals can think for themselves as autonomous agents and are capable of criticizing the rules and values of society' (Colaiaco 2001, p. 142). If many had followed his ideas, the stability of Athens and its establishment would have been seriously challenged. That is where Socrates' message, and he himself, became really system-threatening and dangerous—especially for the authorities and members of the power elites.

5.5   CONCLUSIONS

Some people are larger than life. Socrates was one of them. His life and death not only influenced Athens but shaped Western culture because he raised *fundamental* questions. And it was not only his nagging questioning of everything (and everyone) and his search for true knowledge *per se* that represented quite a few challenges to his fellow citizens (N.N. 2010b). His thoughts and deeds challenged some of the fundamental values and principles of Athenian society, the (hierarchical) social system and the very fabric of the state. And, his critique was particularly aimed at the rich and powerful, at aristocrats and members of other power elites.

Socrates challenged the establishment in multiple ways; he crossed boundaries *in all realms*—and with various intensities. In this sense, we actually have (at least)[7] three different Socrates:

1) the harmless eccentric;
2) the annoying deviant;
3) the dangerous enemy.

In a logical (though perhaps not precisely chronological) sense, the magnitude of Socrates' challenges increased—and so did people's reactions.

1) At first, Socrates simply annoyed and/or amused many people with his weird appearance and his strange behaviour and attitudes. His continuous questioning perhaps triggered some interest and even appreciation because of its intellectual rigour, and maybe caused some annoyance. Either way, most people's values and beliefs, as well as their identities, remained by and large intact. They may not have fully understood Socrates' approach and intentions, but the impressions

Table 7 summarises Socrates' major boundary crossings in the various realms and with the three different intensities.

Realm	Issue	Others reactions and consequences
1. Weak boundary crossings – Socrates the harmless eccentric		
Social action	Strange behaviour and attitudes	Normal behaviour and attitudes
Interest	Attempts to get answers; people should start to reflect critically on their own knowledge or what they perceive as such	People appreciated his interest, or at least found it acceptable, and complied with it; they were trying to help him
Identity	Weird appearance	Interest in Socrates curiosity, but peoples values and beliefs and (more importantly) identities remained intact
Emotions	Indifference	Irritation in most people, with amusement and perhaps some annoyance, but no real challenge
Moral character	Critical inquiry and reason as methods to gain knowledge and wisdom	One of the prime duties of a philosopher is to inquire and to reason about things; thus, people have little problem with the general idea of developing critical skills per se
2. Medium-intensity boundary crossings – Socrates the annoying deviant		
Social action	Questioning of everything, critical thinking; questioning people until they have to admit their lack of knowledge; encouraging the youth to question everything (corrupting them); lectured, challenged and alienated jurors and spectators as a defendant	Socrates did not behave as he should according to his subordinate status, did not show the right amount of obedience and submissiveness; people became increasingly angry, but could still preserve their identities and self-image as knowledgeable experts and good citizens by putting the blame on Socrates, his hair-splitting interrogation technique and outrageous accusations

(Continued)

Table 7 (Continued)

Realm	Issue	Others reactions and consequences
Interest	Rhetoric should be used in decent ways i.e. to search for true knowledge, not for trying to win debates; demonstration that experts do not have the knowledge or wisdom they claim to have/expose shallow thinking and hypocrisy	People began to get really annoyed and realise that Socrates behaviour/intensive questioning did not happen accidently but deliberately
Identity	High level of personal integrity; moral autonomy and the free individual; individualisation, but without larger solidarisation	Socrates personal identity as an independent individual went against the common idea of Athens and community; his individualistic (and, thus, independent) approach to piety and social life challenged traditional understandings of collective values; people came to the conclusion that he did not blend in, that he was not one of us
Emotions	Arrogance	Annoyance, anger
Moral character	Heresy, but with deviation	That Socrates did not participate in traditional rituals was seen as heresy
3. Strong boundary crossings – Socrates the dangerous enemy		
Social action	Criticism of the rich, of aristocrats wealth; challenges of the dominant ideology e.g. challenges of elites claims to be the link to the gods and their claims of inherited virtues; revelation of their hypocrisy	Socrates challenged the very foundations on which Athenian society was built i.e. established beliefs, traditions, traditional values and behaviour; this constitutes serious threats to the system and even more to the positions, interests, greed and selfishness of the rich, aristocrats and other power elites (such as politicians, priests and Sophists)

Interest	People should care about the welfare of their souls, not about the accumulation of material things, wealth and power	Like his social actions, Socrates interests challenged the fundamental values and beliefs on which Athenian society was built and especially the interests and beliefs of the rich
Identity	Daimonion as an individual guiding spirit	Socrates private communication with his daimonion represented direct contact with the divine; thus, that Socrates had sidestepped the authorities not only showed that he saw himself as truly independent but that showed that the regulators and the whole power elite were obsolete
Emotions	Indifference	Hate, outrage
Moral character	Individual morality, the soul, pursuit of virtue and living an examined life	Socrates challenged Athens official ideology of the polis and the collective; the notions of inner reflection and self-knowledge challenged, and provided an alternative to, unquestioned obedience to traditional authority and customary values

they got were sufficient and not that worrying. Most people, including the members of power elites, could simply continue with the pursuit of their daily life as they knew it—and as they appreciated it.

2) Maybe precisely because of this poor response, Socrates intensified his attempts. He continued to question people until they had to admit their lack of knowledge. And he demonstrated that the so-called or self-proclaimed 'experts' and politicians (especially) did not have the knowledge or wisdom they claimed to have. As one can imagine, this was not perceived very well by them or their followers. Moreover, with his intellectual rigour and uncompromising, stinging questioning, Socrates gave people the impression that he regarded himself as 'better' than them. That he also largely avoided participating in commonly accepted practices and ceremonies did not help his cause either. People became increasingly angry about his attitudes, his hairsplitting interrogation techniques, his 'outrageous' accusations, and what they perceived as his ignorance, if not to say arrogance. He was increasingly seen as a true deviant, as one who did not fit in—and did not want to fit in. True, his deviant identity paved the way for strong individualisation, but it remained without larger solidarisation because of his eccentricity. And, although his heresy was extremely sharp and poignant, it came with deviation and, thus, made it easier for his opponents and enemies to isolate him and to develop a case against him.

3) The situation became very serious indeed when Socrates proceeded not just to challenge established norms and traditions and prevailing beliefs and customs *in general* but also to criticise the wealth, immorality, and hypocrisy of *specific* people—i.e., members of the power elites such as politicians, priests, aristocrats, Sophists, or other so-called 'experts.' In particular, he attacked them where their social status, positions, interests, and identities converged: in the right and power to approve, regulate, and conduct social gatherings, religious rites, and the introduction of new gods. By speaking about his *daimonion*, Socrates showed that he saw himself as truly independent—and that the regulators (the whole power elite) were actually obsolete. On top of all that, Socrates provided a valid alternative: people should care about the welfare of their souls, not about the accumulation of material things, wealth, and power, and they should develop a true sense of community. These ideas challenged Athens as a (stratified) social system as well as aristocrats' identities, ways of life, interests, and privileged positions. At this third level, Socrates provided alternatives in *all realms*—that is why he was so dangerous. As soon as their real interests, the foundation of their power and social influence, and their identities began to be called into question, people became really hostile towards Socrates. Especially for members of the establishment,

it became impossible *not* to react. Socrates' challenges had become too serious; they had hit the very core of power elites' self-understanding, and their interests and influence were at stake. A tipping point was reached;[8] As soon as there was an opportunity they *had to* stop him, to get rid of him. So he was prosecuted.

To sum up, at the first level, Socrates was simply keen *not* to comply, *not* to fit in. At the second level, he played the game—and in quite a virtuosic manner. And, at the third level, Socrates provided an alternative. As Sections 5.2–5.4 and Table 7 show, there was no single reason or event that put Socrates in opposition to Athens. He was prosecuted for a whole range of reasons (Ober 2006, p. 17; Millett 2005, p. 26). In this sense, the case of Socrates is a comprehensive (reconstructed) historical example of conflict escalation—i.e., an escalatory process during which reciprocal ('tit-for-tat' strategies) and mutually reinforcing behaviour lead to a downward spiral of increasingly strong actions (revenge and counterrevenge) with increasingly negative consequences for all parties involved (Zapf and Gross 2001, p. 501; Andersson and Pearson 1999, p. 458; Kim and Smith 1993, p. 38). In the case of Socrates, the process of negative reciprocity (Gouldner 1960, p. 172) stretched over many years, if not to say decades. His trial and verdict were just the final part and logical conclusion of a very complex and difficult relationship between him and his fellow Athenian citizens, especially with certain powerful and influential groups of people. With his prosecution, trial and conviction, this escalation of conflict had reached its climax—and then reached its end.

With his conviction (and death), Socrates' opponents had won. From their point of view, order was restored—*their* order. Their privileges, prerogatives, attitudes, and behaviour would no longer be criticised and challenged. The annoying, and dangerous, gadfly was gone, and the members of the establishment could go back to business as usual. Moreover, an example had been made and Socrates' actual and potential followers had been put in their place. Thus, in the short term, Socrates' case contributed to the further strengthening of the system.

In the (very) long term it has been a different story, though. Although the conservative forces had won and Socrates had lost, at the time of his trial and death probably no one could foresee how Socrates would rise to fame across the world and would leave an unprecedented legacy for many generations to come. There have been quite a few long-term consequences that have contributed to turning his defeat into one of the greatest victories in history. The most important ones might be summarised as follows.

1) Intellectual legacy. Although Socrates probably never wrote anything, his ideas have been widely disseminated via secondary sources (such as Aristophanes' satirical plays, Plato's dialogues, and Xenophon's historical works). His thoughts strongly influenced other ancient Greek

philosophers either directly (Plato) or indirectly (Aristotle), and even some ancient schools of thought traced their beginnings at least partly back to him (e.g., Asceticism, Cynicism, Stoicism). Moreover, Greek philosophy, and Socrates as a central part of it, became the bedrock of Western philosophy, especially during the Age of Enlightenment and thereafter. In this sense, Socrates contributed quite crucially to the foundation of philosophy as an academic discipline (Nails 2009).

Besides his influence with regard to the development of academic institutions, it was probably even more his particular way of reasoning that contributed to the advance of philosophy. Crucially, he applied critical thinking to all problems—whether epistemological, ethical, religious, political, or social—in order to get to the core and expose underlying issues in both the subject and the speaker (N.N. 2010b). His critical inquiry was later developed into a 'scientific method' and he became a major reference and shining example for many leading thinkers of the Renaissance and especially the Age of Enlightenment (such as Hobbes, Locke, Voltaire, and Kant). Seen in this way, the main source of Socrates' inspiration of others was perhaps his academic spirit; Socrates challenged everything (and everyone), he spoke truth to power and he accepted only those authorities that passed the test of rigorous logical and moral critique.

2) *Social criticism.* Moreover, Socrates' spirit of critical thinking and academic freedom translated into social criticism—*radical* social criticism (Ober 2003, p. 23). He challenged social customs and social institutions, people's social actions and interests, and even people's identities, emotions, and moral character. Socrates restlessly criticised hypocrisy and narrowmindedness; greed and the accumulation of wealth; established beliefs and traditional values; ideological claims; and common behaviour. And he did not (only) challenge 'Athens,' 'the state,' or 'the society': his actions were a protest against *certain* people or groups of people—against those who claimed to know but didn't, those who had more than enough and abused their positions, and those who provided poor leadership and false guidance. Socrates challenged the social positions and interests, prerogatives and privileges, and moral character and behaviour of key power elites in Athens, such as the (so-called) experts and the Sophists, politicians, priests, aristocrats, and the rich. He criticised them *fundamentally* and *in every respect that was crucial to them.* His whole life was one big protest against power elites' (false) claims and selfish interests, their decadence and hypocrisy, their arrogance and ignorance, their power orientation and their antisocial behaviour. And what he criticised with regard to members of Athens' power elites has been true with regard to members of power elites in all stratified societies and hierarchical organisations ever since.

3) *Democratic spirit.* Socrates' critical thinking and social criticism have been crucial contributions to the functioning of any democracy—although this might not have been the prevailing view of his fellow Athenian citizens. But Socrates *was* a democrat in the true meaning of the word; he strongly believed that 'people should rule.'[9]

Socrates was one of the greatest supporters of democracy and its institutions that there has ever been (Lane 2002, p. 47). He accepted the principle of majority vote—as evidenced by his acceptance of the verdict in his trial. But he had a different opinion with regard to the relationship between the majority or the collective on the one hand and the individual on the other. For him, democracy was based on the fundamental ideas of *diversity* and *tolerance.* He saw democracy and a democratic society *first* from an individualistic perspective and *then* as a collective endeavour. Socrates was of the understanding that democracy only works when *all* people are enabled and empowered to contribute to its functioning—*especially* against the backcloth of their different and differing convictions, interests, and ideas. Democracy needs a variety of voices, including dissent. People are only full democratic citizens if they not only obey the general, democratically agreed-upon rules but also articulate their individual positions and raise their concerns—however deviant these might be. Socrates was against any 'thoughtless acceptance of beliefs, practices and traditions which could prove detrimental to the flourishing of democracy' (Simpson 2006, p. 141) only because such routines were the (actual or alleged) 'will of the majority.' Instead, Socrates showed that civic participation, critical inquiries and discussions, controversies and deviance, and tolerance are *necessary* preconditions for the effective functioning and maintenance of a democratic society (Simpson 2006, p. 141).

4) *Fundamental alternative.* Socrates' critical thinking and practical disobedience did not only represent negativity and rejection. At the same time, and more importantly, they stood for *positive* values. Socrates not only challenged the establishment in all realms but also stood for an alternative set of ethical values and provided a fundamental alternative.

First, he said that people should care about the welfare of their souls—not about the accumulation of material things, wealth, and power—and should live the lives of philosophers, seeking true knowledge and wisdom independently (i.e., they should live the 'examined life'). Second, they should focus on the improvement of their souls *independently of any external authority.* Not only did Socrates focus on the individual but his whole philosophy was rooted in the ideas of individual freedom and individualisation. Third, Socrates was convinced that free and independent individuals would form a better community, create *a society that was truly democratic* and (as seen in his day) would be closer to the gods.

Perhaps most importantly, Socrates showed people what *they* could do in terms of practicing everything that he taught. With his words and deeds, he set an example for others and encouraged them to do as he did: 1) he questioned everything and everyone; 2) he challenged (especially) the claims made by politicians, aristocrats, priests, experts, and other members of the ruling elites and revealed their falsehood and hypocrisy; 3) he argued that democracy needs to be lived by all—i.e., that there need to be differing voices, diversity, and tolerance; and 4) he himself lived the examined life every day and practised what he preached—i.e., he showed high integrity and offered practical ideas and guidance.

Although perhaps not fully developed as a system, Socrates' philosophy provided a very powerful alternative to the established values and beliefs of a collective life largely regulated and controlled by sacrosanct authorities and several (extremely) privileged power elites. In this sense, Socrates was system-threatening, indeed. He was subversive in his words and deeds. With his lasting intellectual legacy, radical social criticism, democratic spirit, and provision of a fundamental alternative, he challenged the very foundations on which the society of Athens was built and threatened to transform it in principle (Colaiaco 2001, p. 142). He did not succeed then—but he inspired many afterwards. This is Socrates' legacy: he won by losing.

6 Why Things (Almost Always) Don't Change

'It is organization which gives birth to the dominion of the elected over the electors, of the mandataries over the mandators, of the delegates over the delegators. Who says organization, says oligarchy.'

Robert Michels, 'Iron law of oligarchy,' 1911

6.1 WHY DO ATTEMPTS TO OVERCOME HIERARCHY FAIL (SO OFTEN)?

6.1.1 Serious Challenges to Hierarchical Social Order

The case of Socrates is exceptional in many respects—mainly because Socrates was an exceptional person. Whatever he did or said, he challenged everything—and everyone—with his mere existence, let alone with his questions, inquiries, and arguments. Of course, 'normal' people as well do not just function according to the imperatives of a given hierarchical social system. As the analysis in Sections 4.4 and 4.5 revealed, superiors and subordinates cross boundaries *regularly* as the following Table 8 shows. Some of these crossings represent serious threats to any hierarchical social order and might even lead to system change:

1) *All* of subordinates' strong crossings threaten a social system considerably. This probably does not come as much of a surprise. When subordinates revolt openly, have an interest in changing the system, and/or show alternative, nonhierarchical identities, emotions or moral characters, then they do not simply seek specific advantages for themselves within the system; they want the system to be replaced—and with it those who represent it.

2) The case is different with *superiors'* strong crossings: almost all of *their* strong crossings are *not* system-threatening (with the exception of those concerning their interests). This is mainly so because hierarchical systems as well as people in such systems are quite tolerant of their superiors. Superiors' strong crossings can be interpreted as their 'personality,'

Table 8 Superiors' and subordinates' boundary crossings in the realms of social action, interests, identity, emotions and moral character.[1]

	Social action	Interests	Identity	Emotions	Moral character
Weak boundary crossings					
Superiors	Individual insufficiencies and malpractices	Breaching or bypassing rules in order to pursue ones own interests	Insecure careerist or egotistic leader	Showing none of, too much of or too little of the emotions required	Personal values and beliefs contrast with the ideology publicly upheld (hypocrisy)
Subordinates	Work-to-rule, minimal compliance	Breaching or bypassing rules in order to pursue ones own interests	Individualism	Showing none of, too much of or too little of the emotions required	Minor unethical behaviour
Medium-intensity boundary crossings					
Superiors	Workplace aggression, bullying, individual criminal actions, scandals	Changing rules and regulations, policies and procedures in ones favour	Individualisation, solidarisation	Emotions that are not part of superiors role repertoire (e.g. anger towards the system)	Personal values and beliefs contrast with the ideology publicly upheld (hypocrisy)
Subordinates	Rejection, active resistance within existing rules and regulations	Changing the existing immediate social situation and practices in ones favour	Individualisation, solidarisation	Emotions that are not part of subordinates role repertoire (e.g. anger towards superiors or the system)	Taking the prevailing ideology seriously, declared refusal to comply/heresy
Strong boundary crossings					
Superiors	Widespread malpractices or illegal practices of the power elite	Changing the system fundamentally	Alternative identity to the one ascribed to superiors	Alternative, non-hierarchical emotions	Alternative values, non-hierarchical moral character
Subordinates	Open (collective) resistance; revolt, revolution	Changing the system fundamentally	Alternative identity to the one superiors want subordinates to have	Alternative, non-hierarchical emotions	Alternative value system: anti-hierarchical utopia

1. Boxes in light grey indicate serious challenges to the system.

as their 'unique' way of filling the role of being a leader. Even if they show strongly deviating identities, emotions, or moral character traits, as long as they otherwise function and perform, they are still acceptable for the organisational structures and processes in place and/or for their peers. In contrast, superiors' strong crossings in the realm of interests constitute a serious challenge for any hierarchical system. If superiors are really interested in system change, they will find ways to make it happen and usually have the capabilities to realise their ideas.

3) Subordinates' medium-intensity crossings in the realm of identity (i.e., *individualisation* and *solidarisation*) also seriously challenge hierarchical social order; both processes provide subordinates with identities that are in fundamental opposition not only to the image of the obedient and manageable subordinate but also to the very idea of a hierarchical organisation of social relationships. If subordinates start to see themselves as individuals whose lives are severely limited by the current systems, and if they begin to realise that others are in the same situation, a really dangerous situation ensues. The concepts of individualisation and solidarisation represent probably the most powerful and threatening ideas against hierarchy—when applied to *subordinates! Superiors'* individualisation and solidarisation, in stark contrast, *strengthen* a hierarchical social system.

4) Subordinates' *collective anger,* if it is targeted at their superiors and/or the whole system, also represents a serious threat to any hierarchical social system. Anger makes subordinates strong and powerful, it gives them the feeling (and the strength) of being at the same level as their superiors and it produces social actions that do not stop at the first obstacle, on the contrary; when people feel that they are being treated in unfair and unjust ways and see this as a systemic problem rather than a set of isolated incidents, sooner or later there will be a period of time or particular moment in which they will collectively try to overcome the current system. The Arab Spring is only the latest of many such examples in which the anger of the common people was the main cause and driving force behind overcoming a dictatorship or oligarchy.[1]

5) Subordinates' *heresy without deviance* represents a medium-intensity boundary crossing that disputes the norms and values of hierarchy fundamentally. Political struggles between the establishment and proponents of new movements are good examples. Heresy *as such* might not be enough to initiate widespread activities aiming at system change; it also provides no ideas about possible alternatives and may produce (very) negative consequences for the heretic. But it is the ideas, the symbolic actions, and the criticism put forward via heresy that (one day) will become a founding part of attempts to overthrow a hierarchical system.

6) Superiors' *hypocrisy* is also system-threatening. If gaps between superiors' public claims and their actual values and actions become too big and, most importantly, *obvious,* their positions as well as the legitimacy of the whole hierarchical system might be questioned. The phenomena of subordinates' heresy and superiors' hypocrisy show that very often the real battle is about the prevailing norms and values of the system—and who represents them morally. This is why boundary crossings in the realm of moral character are so potentially dangerous; as soon as cracks emerge between people's words and deeds, their credibility is seriously undermined—and, if these cracks cannot be portrayed as isolated incidents and are instead perceived as examples of systemic shortcomings, the whole system might also be at stake.

Boundary crossings of the type outlined above could cause hierarchical social systems to change fundamentally. On the other hand, it seems that most change initiatives, especially ambitious and far-reaching ones, have not delivered what they were expected to. Sidanius and Pratto (1999, pp. 35–6) have even gone so far as to say that:

> Every attempt to abolish arbitrary-set, group-based hierarchy within societies of economic surplus have, without exception, failed. These failures have ranged from attempts at massive, revolutionary change (e.g. in France, Russia, Mexico, China, and the U.S. civil rights movement) to transformatory experiments within small and isolated Utopian communities (e.g. New Harmony, Indiana; New Lanark, Scotland; the Oneida Community, New York).

Whether or not this is, indeed, *always* the case might be disputable. Nevertheless, Sidanius and Pratto definitely have a point when they stress how many attempts have failed, sometimes in the most horrific manner. But why is this so? Why do even serious attempts to overcome hierarchy often go so wrong? In the following sections some of the reasons will be discussed in more detail.

6.1.2   Change but No Change

As indicated in the Introduction, we live in a changing world; globalisation and technological innovations have triggered economic, sociocultural, and social changes that in some respects reduce superior-subordinate relationships. For example, emerging economies such as the BRICS countries (Brazil, Russia, India, China, and South Africa) and some Southeast Asian countries have narrowed the gap between so-called developed and developing countries and are changing the balance of power from unilateral dominance towards more multilateral constellations. In quite a few societies, there have been institutional or even constitutional changes, from communist regimes, oligarchies, or monarchies towards (slightly) more democratic systems (e.g., countries in Eastern Europe and the former Soviet Union, some Arab nations, and some countries in Asia). The internet, social networks, and other communication technologies have made social interaction much more diverse and represent new forms of democratic decision-making processes and social action.

Whether at the macro or micro level, such trends towards democracy, as imperfect and incomplete as they might be, represent a whole range of (new) ideas and forms of social development, empowerment, citizenship, civil society, decentralised information-sharing and decision-making, involvement, and participation of individuals, especially of people lower down social stratification patterns.

One can also see dramatic changes at the organisational level. Many organisations have become more hybrid and various organisational change initiatives have altered organisations in many respects; for example, there has been change—sometimes fundamental—in terms of strategic objectives and strategic direction, mission and vision statements, organisational structures and processes, performance management and measurement systems, budgets and allocation of resources, organisational culture, and modes of organising work. Moreover, new organisational forms have emerged (such as polyarchic, network, and even virtual organisations) that are quite different from fairly traditional hierarchical and bureaucratic forms of organisations—at least with regard to formal structures and processes (see Section 4.6). The new forms, as well as most change-management initiatives, are aimed at designing and redesigning organisational structures and processes towards more collaboration, knowledge-sharing, participation, and empowerment of employees (Musson and Duberley 2006, pp. 143–4).

Obviously, such ideas go against traditional understandings of social relationships as hierarchical. For example, it is the central idea of 'empowerment' that people should have the authority and means to make their *own* decisions and to organise their work and lives as *they* deem appropriate. And 'participation' means that people should be involved in all formal and informal decision-making processes that are relevant to them. Understood in such ways, empowerment and participation could mean quite a radical transformation and upset of established social orders; they have the potential to change hierarchical systems and hierarchical social relationships *in principle*.

However, concepts of empowerment and participation are often propagated, introduced, and managed *top-down* by power elites and superiors such as politicians or intellectual elites, senior management, and management consultants. Musson and Duberley (2006, p. 157), therefore, concluded that:

> The leading managerial rhetoric of participation, based on the language of empowerment, is also coupled with a language of authority and this apparent contradiction is summarized neatly in the official mantra of

'change, change or be exchanged' (MD), a discursive marker that reflects and reproduces the power relationships in the organization.

What we often see is *managed* change and *controlled* empowerment (Paul et al. 2000, p. 477).

Concepts such as 'controlled empowerment' seem to be quite paradoxical, but only at first sight. Usually, people are socialised and conditioned to function appropriately. Their mindsets are shaped in ways that make it difficult for them to react to any idea other than what they (have learned to) regard as 'normal.' Most people mainly respond even to innovative ideas with their learned, hierarchy-conforming routine behaviour; superiors or 'change leaders' see the introduction of empowerment largely as an opportunity to 'demonstrate leadership' whereas subordinates or followers adopt a 'wait-and-see' strategy. As a consequence, the change initiative towards empowerment unfolds in ways that are compatible with the hierarchical system and simply become yet another part of the existing abstract organisational order.

Thus, what actually happens in organisational change-management initiatives and social-development projects time and again is rather different from the original ideas of empowerment and participation—if not to say in direct opposition to them. There is a depoliticisation, instrumentalisation, and domestication of the concepts. Once-revolutionary ideas are transformed into *techniques* for making *existing* arrangements more efficient. The concepts are used as means to achieve *other* ends; for example, to increase the productivity, efficiency, flexibility, or competitiveness of organisations; to pursue individual or group interests; or to secure the privileges and prerogatives of (local) power elites. Subordinates' roles are largely reduced to fitting in and contributing as required while they are given the *feeling* of being empowered (Jermier 1998). It therefore might be more appropriate to talk about 'false' or even 'fake empowerment'—which is exactly what might had been intended by proponents of the status quo from the very beginning: via converting potentially power-challenging concepts into managed and controlled techniques, they make those concepts an institutionalised and nonperilous part of the established abstract organisational order. In this sense, empowerment and participation even contribute to the re-establishment of existing relationships of dominance and obedience and of superiority and subordination. For example, after analysing empirical evidence from several social-development projects, Leal (2007, p. 543) described this process quite compellingly:

> In the hands of the development industry, the political ambiguity has been functional to the preservation of the status quo. Preserving the hegemony of the status quo, in the Gramscian sense, entails the reproduction of discourse through various channels in order to create and maintain a social consensus around the interests of the dominant

power structures, which in the twenty-first century are encased in and are functional to the neo-liberal world order. Thus, the manipulations required to neutralise challenges and threats to its dominant rationale and practice cannot afford to lack sophistication. Whatever the method used to co-opt, the dominant order has assimilated an historic lesson, as White (1996) affirms with simple clarity: 'incorporation, rather than exclusion is the best form of control'. Since frontal negation or attacks to those challenges to the dominant order often serve only to strengthen and legitimate the dissent in the eyes of society, co-option becomes the more attractive option for asserting control.

Cooptation and institutionalisation of system-challenging concepts are pretty clever strategies on the part of the ruling elites in terms of watering down change—or entirely preventing it. Most change initiatives leave the fundamental principles and actual social relations of the social system relatively untouched. Change initiatives are not meant to change the foundations on which the social system is built. The principles of hierarchical organisation and the hierarchical maintenance of social relationships must be kept so that current and/or future superiors can supervise the top-down implementation of the changes and guarantee the continuation of the existing system. Most change initiatives reaffirm and strengthen established hierarchical relations between superiors and subordinates and underline the social roles and positions of both within the hierarchical system. They are intended and designed to change and not to change things.

Even when new forms of work organisation are introduced, and even in cases in which there are the 'best intentions' to establish nonhierarchical ways of working and determined efforts to eradicate hierarchy, formal or informal hierarchical structures might emerge and very soon constitute the familiar patterns of social dominance and obedience and of superiority and subordination (Oberg and Walgenbach 2008; Clegg et al. 2006, chapter 12; Schwarz 2006; Ekbia and Kling 2005; Kärreman and Alvesson 2004; Gould 2002; Hales 2002, p. 51; Ahuja and Carley 1999; Rothschild and Ollilainen 1999, p. 594; Sidanius and Pratto 1999, pp. 1–30, 48–9, 61, 95; Jermier 1998, p. 249; Kanter 1972, pp. 225–9; Berger and Luckmann 1966, pp. 92–128; Mills 1956, pp. 9, 11, 296–7). Polyarchic, network and many so-called egalitarian organisations and societies do not necessarily signify the end of hierarchical, oppressive, and exploitative social relationships. Hierarchical social order may even become stronger *because of* attempts to establish alternative forms of social ordering (see also Section 6.1.4).

Hence, even in the face of serious attempts to change things, there actually might not be much change. The official language might change, perhaps along with some aspects of the structures and processes of the system. But the fundamental principles of hierarchical social relationships, the notions of social dominance and obedience, and the idea of privileging the few and exploiting the many do not change. What we often see is more rhetoric than real change—'technical' but not 'fundamental' change. We see change but no change. Despite the 'revolutionary enthusiasm,' the foundations on which hierarchical social systems are built remain stable and are rarely changed—if ever. The continuing presence of hierarchical social order means that only some rules are changed, not the game.

6.1.3 Change in Personnel

That we often see little or no change is not only due to structures and processes but also, and probably primarily, to people. In Section 2.1 it was mentioned that there have been ruling elites in almost every culture and epoch: druids, priests, prophets, royals, wealthy citizens, military, clergy, knights, aristocrats, merchants, industrial capitalists, bourgeoisie, bureaucrats, technocrats, managers, politicians, bankers, and professionals. Power elites can be *any* religious, aristocratic, military, political, administrative, economic, financial, media, or social group of people that occupies a privileged position in a given society by whatever means (Scott 2003; Mills 1956).

There have been very extreme examples of revolutions in which whole power elites have been replaced in rather bloody ways. Famous historical examples include the guillotining of French aristocrats and the French royal family by Robespierre's and the Jacobins' reign of terror in the aftermath of the French Revolution or the killing of the Russian Tsarist family and Russia's aristocrats and intellectuals during the years of the Bolsheviks' and Stalin's social cleansings after the Russian October Revolution.[2] Unfortunately, such terror is not that rare. One can easily find similar examples in South America, Asia, Africa, and the Middle East.

Nonetheless, it is even more common that the ruling elite or other power elites are replaced by the next elite via longer-lasting, epochal, incomplete, and heterogeneous evolutionary processes. Such trends are the result of countless little acts by individuals and smaller groups or networks of people. Usually, power elites are not homogenous groups. Beneath the surface of an all-inclusive ideology and regular demonstrations of the unity of the ruling elite, there are quite different understandings, opposing interests, and even fundamental ideological differences amongst members or groups within powerful elites. Such differences surface especially during fundamental, if not to say epochal, changes organisations or whole societies go through. During such periods, proponents and opponents of alternative sets of values might go to great lengths to get *their* ideology and concepts through.

Yet, despite the various differing cosmologies and clashing ideological interests, most revolutions and evolutionary social processes replace only *some* leaders; the networks of old power elites usually survive. Even more crucially, the principles and societal institutions, structures, and mechanisms of hierarchy and social dominance that produced these elites remain fairly intact and persist. Thus, changes in personnel, whether evolutionary or revolutionary, do not really change much. There are several reasons for this.

Social changes are often initiated and used by members of power elites in order to either secure their current social positions or attain more attractive positions; to gain access to resources, privileges, and prerogatives; to achieve personal goals; or to realise certain ideas (Dent and Barry 2004, p. 17; Skålén 2004, p. 256; Burrell 2002, p. 29; Sehested 2002, pp. 1516–7; Rosenwein and Little 1974, pp. 31–2). Between and within power elites there is a constant struggle for supremacy; there are clashes over spheres of influence and resources—or anything that is perceived as crucial for individuals' interests and social position; and collaboration and shifting and changing coalitions. Although the actors involved in those struggles might use all 'allowed' means and even dirty tricks, they nonetheless will not cross certain lines. They might clash with other members of the ruling elite (via ideological controversies) but they will not challenge the fundamental principles on which the system of hierarchical order exists. Almost all ideological controversies between power groups—even the peaceful or forceful replacement of one power elite and its ideology with another group—happen *within* the existing boundaries of hierarchy. Even the most severe clashes have little impact on the system since none of the participants in such ideological battles want to damage the hierarchical system, since the system itself is the prize to be won. Hence, all power elites and parties involved in the struggle will do their utmost to keep the idea, principles, and systems of hierarchical order intact.

Even those who are not currently members of the establishment are cautious. For example, those with hierarchy-conforming mindsets among both ambitious members of ascending classes and proponents of strategic change initiatives aspire to reach higher social positions *within* the existing structures and institutions. Hence, they are usually quite keen to demonstrate how well they can blend in. Of course, material wealth, power, and influence stemming from new knowledge or new ways of conducting one's life enable members of an ascending class to climb up the social ladder. But it is the 'right' attitudes that will really open doors for them. They are not only willing to let systemisation and its mechanisms do its work on them but are even eager to change and to adapt themselves *proactively* so that they can become part of the establishment. As an example, consider the daily endeavours of members of the middle class and newly rich to learn and demonstrate the 'right' behaviour (etiquette) and 'right' (and best) way of presenting oneself; to get to know the 'right' people; to do the 'right' sports and leisure activities; to eat the 'right' food and drink the 'right' wine; to have the 'right' beliefs and political opinions; to wear the 'right' clothes; to live in the 'right' neighbourhood. To the unsuspecting observer these endeavours only look silly; however, for the people involved this is serious business. These aspects shape their identities and are the key to a social career and to success.

From the viewpoint of members of the establishment, aspirational members of new power elites are initially seen as a nuisance, perhaps even as a danger (depending on how ambitious and powerful the newcomers actually are and how much members of the ruling elite realise the extent of this power). Usually, the first reactions are attempts to hold off newcomers and to ignore or discredit their endeavours and achievements. Nonetheless, as with system-challenging concepts, it might be more efficient for the ruling elite not (only) to fight members of new power elites directly or indirectly but (also) to coopt and assimilate them, i.e., to turn them into 'candidates.' Such tactics of cooption and assimilation can be quite advantageous for the establishment. Giving aspirational newcomers some limited opportunities, a 'taste of what they could have' and the prospect of a promising career will usually do the trick—i.e., will corrupt most of the newcomers and make them even more keen to demonstrate their ability to adapt and to fit in.

Moreover, people who belong to the ascending new class might bring new skills, knowledge, and resources with them that can strengthen the existing ruling elite. For example, in the early days of capitalism, many aristocrats had become quite poor and were in desperate need of money—*any* money— in order to finance their ostentatious lifestyle. On average, aristocrats were neither capable nor willing to be productive members of society and to earn the means for their living via work. But they had titles, were familiar with the prevailing culture of the upper class, and had access to the circles of power. In contrast, all that the new emerging class of industrial capitalists had was money, endless money—but it was 'dirty' money because it stemmed from 'work' (actually, it stemmed from the *exploitation* of those who worked for the capitalists). Most capitalists were not born into the higher circles of society; they lacked the social background, connections and 'right pedigree' that would have qualified them to become a member of high society or even the inner circles of power. Hence, it made a lot of sense to put the two (i.e., old aristocracy and new money) together. It was a marriage made in heaven (though for the sons and daughters of aristocrats and capitalists who ended up in arranged marriages it sometimes turned out to be more of a marriage from hell).

Collaboration and complicity between members of the old ruling elites and the new ascending class can be very advantageous for both. Abercrombie et al. (1980, p. 107) even talked about a 'harmony of interests' and 'symbiotic relationship' between the new, ascending bourgeoisie and the old, dominating class of aristocrats. They said that (p. 106):

> The bourgeoisie became gentrified, aping the lifestyles and social mannerisms of the old landed aristocracy, and buying themselves and their heirs into the ranks of the landed interest, so that the dominant class remained [. . .] the 'sociological' heirs of the pre-industrial aristocracy. Nevertheless, the reciprocal embourgoisement of the aristocracy is important too, since the landed groups seem to have accepted most of the economic thought and some of the political and social beliefs that made up the dominant bourgeois ideology.

Examples of cooption and complicity show that even ascending classes or aspirational groups of superiors do not provide a clear-cut alternative to the present members of the ruling elite; they usually function according to the same rationales. Even in the face of clashes and ideological controversies between members of (different) power elites, these clashes usually will not challenge the fundamental principles of hierarchy *per se* since it is these principles that make the elites powerful. This is what they have in common. The replacement of one power elite and its ideology with another one (whether peaceful or by force) will leave the logic of hierarchical social order intact. A mere change in ruling elites, however worrying and revolutionary it may look at the time it is happening, only threatens the old elite—but not the system. Ideological agendas may change, but the hierarchical structures and processes remain. A 'change in personnel'—i.e., a transition from one power elite to another—does not change much; whoever the actual power elites are, and whatever technical changes the transition might bring, the very fact that there are still power elites and ruling elites means that there is still (group-based) social dominance, stratification, and hierarchical structures (Sidanius and Pratto 1999, p. 261).

6.1.4   Change for the Worse

But there can also be very serious attempts to establish social systems that are fundamentally different from hierarchical social systems. Unfortunately, history is full of examples of such endeavours turning into disasters: systematic state terror on a large scale during, but especially after, successful revolutions (as mentioned above); totalitarian communes or religious orders run by psychopaths who oppress and exploit their members materially, psychologically, and/or sexually, new political parties or social movements that dissolve into chaos. Radical system change can easily lead to anarchism (the deterioration of governance, societal institutions, moral values, and living conditions) and/or to a totalitarian system that causes unimaginable suffering for people. Social dominance continues, though now under new superiors and (much) worse conditions (Harman 2008, p. 60; Gersick 1991, p. 31).

Thus, there are very obvious examples of *changes for the worse*. But in this section it will be argued that there can also be changes for the worse even in cases when people genuinely try to establish nonhierarchical, egalitarian structures and processes in ethical and democratic ways. In Section 4.6.2, it was argued that even the 'best' and 'well-intended' attempts to realise nonhierarchical structures and processes might not deliver the intended outcomes. Instead, as some of the case studies mentioned there indicated, they might produce negative, and quite unexpected, consequences, for example:

- In a study of 'family-rhetoric' at a large multinational US company given the pseudonym Hephaestus, Casey (1999) found that so-called 'new' work practices do not really empower and free employees but provide in some respect even more challenging and oppressive working conditions; 'these new "designer" cultural practices serve as processes of regulation, discipline, and control of employee subject selves' (p. 155). She concluded her analysis as follows (p. 172): 'In addition to those formal and visible disciplinary practices, the Hephaestus team-family culture contains informal, or hidden, disciplinary practices that form part of the everyday network of power relations and systems of control.'

- When studying the Soar group, a virtual organisation, Ahuja and Carley (1999, p. 751) found that 'virtual organizations can exhibit considerable hierarchical tendencies (degree, centralization, and multiple levels). This finding appears to contradict the predictions of non-hierarchical and de-centralized structure in virtual organizations.' They explained more specifically: 'Our results suggest that virtual organizations may well be non-hierarchical and decentralized from an authority standpoint; yet, from a communication standpoint they may still be hierarchical and somewhat centralized.'

- Varman and Chakrabarti (2004), investigating a workers' cooperative called SAMITI that undertakes contract work in areas such as civil maintenance and cleaning, found a lack of democratic consciousness and persistence of social hierarchy amongst workers, for four main reasons (pp. 192–3): 1) social status differences caused by the Indian class and caste system, 2) differences in professional status, 3) differences in economic power caused by societal stratification, and 4) the company's embeddedness in hierarchical networks of powerful stakeholders (principal employer, government, local community). They came to the conclusion that 'various barriers concerning caste, professional expertise, economic power, and the network of contacts made it extremely difficult for the workers to transcend their socially assigned roles' (p. 193).

- When investigating and analysing internal e-mail communication of a network-oriented and antihierarchically run company, Oberg and Walgenbach (2008) found hierarchical relationships between the organisational members. Hierarchical patterns had emerged over time both in communication structures (a clear centre-periphery structure) and in the content of the communication (systematic use of issues and rhetoric signalling superiority and submissiveness).

Empirical evidence and examples like the ones above show that less formalised organisations—*because* of their less hierarchical and flexible design—are vulnerable to hierarchisation. This can mean in particular (Brown et al. 2010; Diefenbach 2009; Parker 2009; Sauser 2009, p. 155; Clegg et al. 2006; Courpasson and Clegg 2006, p. 324; Kärreman and Alvesson 2004, p. 151; Kirkpatrick et al. 2005, p. 96; Akella 2003; Courpasson 2000; Jacques 1996):

- more sublime, individualised, and subjectivised forms of power and control;

- an increase in control and domination since the new forms of power and control do not replace but are rather added to traditional forms of more direct, top-down power mechanisms and control mechanisms;

- the emergence of informal hierarchical structures and processes and informal social dominance and obedience;

- conversion of the organisation into a multidimensional Foucaultian panopticon of 'normalising' authority.

In this sense, even ambitious attempts to seriously overcome (formal) hierarchical structures and processes might not produce the results hoped for and might lead to a change for the worse.

6.2 INFORMAL HIERARCHY, PEOPLE, AND STRUCTURAL ARRANGEMENTS

6.2.1 The Persistence of Hierarchy—Who or What is to Blame?

In Section 6.1 it was argued that in most cases of attempted change there is at least one of the following:

1) *change but no change* (because all that happens is technical change—the fundamental principles of hierarchical ordering are left untouched);

2) *change in personnel* (because there are merely new superiors, or a new ruling elite, that continue to dominate, to oppress, and to exploit people further down the hierarchical social order);

3) *change for the worse* (because even serious attempts to establish egalitarian, democratic, or at least less hierarchical forms of organisations often produce more numerous and more severe and sophisticated forms of formal and informal hierarchical power and control).

The rather disappointing bottom line is that *things don't change – and, even when they do change, they (almost always) do not really change.* Despite more or less well-meant efforts to get rid of hierarchy, or at least to reduce it, hierarchy remains—or even increases. The problem of (unwanted) *hierarchisation* is even more obvious, and crucial, in *less* formalised social systems—i.e., systems that (temporarily) have less formal hierarchical order and where social roles, positions, tasks, and routine behaviour are less predefined. These may be orthodox hierarchical organisations or existing stratified societies that are going through a period of fundamental changes (of either an evolutionary or revolutionary nature) or unorthodox organisations (such as networks or other alternative social systems).

The different and changing conditions within such less formalised social systems amplify existing problems concerning the relationship between individual actors and the social system, as well as creating new problems. As the examples and empirical cases in Section 6.1 have shown, the existence of hierarchy can sometimes be surprising. Often, the fact that hierarchy has developed is realised neither by those involved nor by external observers. And, if they become aware of it, they describe such phenomena as *unintended* processes or *unintended* consequences. There might be some truth in this; things happen. Especially in the social realm, we often face the problem that the aggregate of single phenomena can be quite different from the prevailing principle at the individual level (i.e., 'no one really wanted the outcome'). In other words: individual rationality can lead to collective irrationality. For example, if every member of a social system tries to maximise his or her happiness, the result will be not a happy but a fairly competitive, hostile, and problem-laden society in which most people are quite unhappy.[3]

Yet, an argument along the lines of 'unintended processes'/'unintended consequences' is also problematic since it implies that no one has caused these outcomes—and, hence, that no one is responsible for them. The outcomes might not be the best results that could have been hoped for, but 'they just happened' (and the argument might go further to suggest that these consequences, although unfortunate, are unavoidable and must be accepted). In contrast, here it will be argued that not only *some* crucial aspects of this microlink/macrolink problem but also *some* possible causes, explanations, and solutions can be found at the level of individual actors.[4]

As the general theory of hierarchical social systems argues (see Section 3.3), behind processes in the social realm are *people*. Hierarchical ordering happens primarily via people's social actions and mindsets—i.e., because of their interests and identities, emotions and moral character, behaviours, and attitudes towards dominance and obedience. The ways people think, decide and act is what shapes and influences any social system's structures and processes (and people are influenced by those structures and processes). People seek to position themselves within the system: they actively seek to pursue their own goals and to *navigate* their way through the structures and processes of social systems (see Section 3.6.6). Behind people's actions are *interests* (Darke and Chaiken 2005; O'Brien and Crandall 2005; Rutledge and Karim 1999); most of individuals' actions (or inactions) are done *deliberately and with intent,* and cause intended as well as unintended consequences. In this sense, it can be said that 'unintended' processes and consequences are also the results of individuals' intentional actions—and that people are indeed responsible for them, although their actions perhaps were meant to produce other outcomes than the unintended ones.

To give an example: within a network-like social system, individual differences in levels of activity, in attitudes, and in style and intensity of communication (e.g., 'doer' versus 'contemplator') can create (informal) patterns of social dominance. Individuals who contribute more actively to social processes, who are more often present, or who more vigorously voice their concerns openly or behind closed doors during discussions and decision-making processes will almost automatically begin to dominate. At the same time, individuals who are less present and outspoken or who are perhaps equally active and engaged but do not demonstrate this openly within the social context and community will increasingly become followers—or will be seen as such. Over time, individuals develop more and more traditional roles and corresponding behaviours of superiority, subordination, dominance, and obedience. Although intended by no one, informal hierarchy emerges and is institutionalised over time. It becomes part of an existing or newly developed abstract organisational order that increasingly represents the typical characteristics of a hierarchical system. This is one of the core problems of social systems: although processes and outcomes might not be intended, they nonetheless are caused by people and their (intentional or unintentional) behaviour. Hence, one of the key questions is what—or who!—*exactly* is behind (unintended) social processes. If the causes (and those responsible for them) can be found, there might be a chance of preventing the emergence of such unintended outcomes in the future.

6.2.2 The (Moral) Behaviour of Individual Actors in Nonhierarchical Social Systems

Behind people's decisions and actions there can be very different rationales or principles that guide their behaviour—as Kohlberg's taxonomy of moral development has shown (see Section 4.2.6 and Appendix 4). People at different stages of moral development relate differently to *formal* hierarchical social order—but they also relate differently to the (intended or unintended) emergence of *informal* hierarchy in less formalised or changing social systems.

Obviously, people with a punishment-and-obedience orientation (*stage 1 of moral development*) fit perfectly into hierarchical organisations. They feel quite comfortable there because they appreciate, even need, clear formal rules and guidelines, hierarchical order and control, and authoritarian management. But even within less formalised and more decentralised social systems they can find their way. People with a predominantly obedient personality have little problem with complying with change initiatives if a 'way forward' is outlined. They will then turn into willful followers and, in doing so, will feed unintended processes of hierarchisation 'from below.'

The bigger problem is people with obedient personalities who are also power-oriented. Within more decentralised and democratic structures and processes, they will seek power and social dominance for the sake of power and dominance. Moreover, and crucially, they will do so particularly when things change—i.e., during change initiatives within organisations, within social movements, and even during revolutions in societies. The more radical individuals with stage 1 personalities often become change agents within organisations or leaders of social movements because they are keen and able to compete with others who also try to dominate. After a successful change, they often will progress within the organisation even further or will become members of the new power elite—perhaps even a, if not *'the,'* new leader. But also less ambitious or capable people with stage 1 personalities will show authoritarian behaviour as soon as there is an opportunity—although perhaps on a smaller scale. In this sense, one can say that people with obedient *and* power-oriented personalities try *deliberately* to (re-) establish hierarchical social relationships within change initiatives, democratic organisations, or social movements in order to gain and use power.

In a similar fashion, individuals at *stage 2 of moral development* also see social relationships, interaction, and exchanging favours primarily as instrumental for the pursuit of their individual objectives (Crain 1985; Kohlberg 1973). They are not only focused on power but also seek all sorts of individual advantages. They have a 'calculative mind.' Boddy (2006, p. 1461) provides quite a telling description of people with such a calculative mind:

> A key-defining characteristic of psychopaths is that they have no conscience [. . .] and are incapable of experiencing the feelings of others. Their other characteristics however [. . .] make them appear very hireable and worthy of promotion; they are smooth, adroit at manipulating conversations to subjects they want to talk about, willing to put others down, are accomplished liars, totally ruthless and opportunistic, calculating and without remorse. Their cold-heartedness and manipulativeness are the traits that are least discernable by others.

Such a focus on the pursuit of one's own individual interests—often reduced to sheer egoism and egocentrism and combined with a professional education, practical knowledge, and work and life experience—makes those actors *very* agile, competitive, and powerful. Organisational psychopaths are particularly drawn to hierarchical organisations since there they can pursue a career and can gain access to power, influence, and resources related to social positions within the hierarchical scaffolding—the higher, the better. However, because of their agility and flexibility, they can find equally advantageous conditions within the fluid and multidimensional conditions of unorthodox organisations. Less formalised settings and changing structures and processes provide much room and many opportunities for people with a calculative mind to manoeuvre. Within less formalised social systems, such people cause hierarchical social relationships unintentionally *as well as* intentionally.

With their one-dimensional achievement orientation (i.e., towards increasing rewards and reducing punishment for themselves), stage 2 individuals are not only more willing to engage with informal processes and organisational politics but also on average more successful in pursuing their personal goals. In contrast, people who are less agile and flexible (with more static and nonpragmatic value systems) and who are less keen and focused on gaining personal advantages are less successful within social processes and will lose out. Over time, this creates patterns of social superiority and inferiority *unintentionally*; people with calculative minds start to dominate, and others become more and more disadvantaged simply because the former are more active than the latter. At the same time, for people with calculative minds, dominance and supremacy are instrumental for pursuing their interests. Gaining, keeping, or increasing one's influence, power, and control usually helps in the pursuit of one's personal interests within changing social systems. People with a stage 2 personality, hence, will often try *deliberately* to establish informal hierarchical social relationships because this strengthens their position and their access to resources and people who can be of instrumental use.

In some contrast, people at the *conventional* (stages 3–4) or even at the *postconventional* (stage 5) level of moral development might genuinely want to make less formalised and/or nonhierarchical institutions or organisations work.[5] They care about the social system (stage 3), appreciate and want to comply with the new rules and regulations (stage 4), and/or actively support the new ideas because this is now the consensus (stage 5). By and large, people with such orientations would not try to create hierarchical relationships *deliberately*. But they have good reasons to contribute to decision-making processes, to get and keep projects going, to engage in debates, and to make suggestions and try to realise them. However good their intentions, the more they are engaged in such processes, the more they might try to influence others. Moreover, for the sake of the 'good cause,' they will use a whole range of means to realise what *they* deem to be important and necessary—including the use of tactics and cunning ways to get others to do things that they otherwise perhaps would not do. Over time, they will come to relate to others mainly via the rationales of informal (moral and resource-based) superiority and inferiority—i.e., informal hierarchical relationships. This is done largely unintentionally, even without reflection.

Finally, there are people at stage 6 of moral development. Such people are not compatible with any type of formal hierarchical social order. Because of their pursuit of universally valid ethical principles, it can be assumed that they do not want to contribute in any form to the emergence of formal or informal hierarchy, whether intentionally or unintentionally. But their 'moral superiority' might itself trigger informal hierarchical structures or processes because of people close to them starting to demonstrate (voluntarily) obedient behaviour. Even authority solely based on morality and the better argument does not automatically lead to hierarchy-free social systems. Thus, people with the highest level of moral development can avoid contributing to the unwelcome emergence of hierarchical structures and processes within less formal social systems only if they: 1) are aware of that possibility, 2) are capable of reflecting critically on their as well as others' roles and behaviour, and 3) actively try to empower others without dominating them. We will come back to this in the next section.

Table 9 provides an overview of people's prime moral principles organised according to Kohlberg's stages of moral development (see Appendix 4), as discussed above.

Table 9   Kohlberg's stages of moral development and prime moral principles for people's navigation.

Kohlbergs stages of moral development	Individuals predominant moral character	Prime moral principle for peoples navigation
6) Universal-ethical-principle orientation	Enlightened personality	Course of humanity and creation
5) Social-contract orientation	Consensus-oriented citizen	Consensus of the majority
4) Law and order orientation	Good citizen	Obedience to the law/compliance with rules
3) Interpersonal concordance, good boy/nice girl orientation	Social mind	Pursuit of social acceptance/fear of rejection from peers
2) Instrumental-relativist orientation	Calculative mind	Personal advantage
1) Punishment-and-obedience orientation	Obedient personality	Pursuit of power/fear of being punished by authorities

To sum up, the emergence of hierarchical structures and processes/hierarchical social relationships in less formalised/changing social systems is:

- *largely intended* by power- and obedience-oriented individuals (stage 1 personality of moral development);
- *mainly intended,* or to a lesser degree *unintended* by individuals with a calculative mind (stage 2 personality of moral development);
- *largely unintended* by individuals with a social mind, good citizens, and those with a consensus orientation (stages 3–5 personality of moral development);
- *unintended* by individuals with an enlightened personality (stage 6 personality of moral development).

Of course, such a differentiation is somehow 'mechanical' and simplistic. Identification of cause-and-effect links between people's (assumed) needs, intentions, and emotions; (assumed) level of moral development and moral reasoning; (identifiable) social actions; and (identifiable) direct and indirect outcomes and consequences is one of the most challenging tasks in social sciences—especially when this chain reaction stretches beyond a specific situation and comprises microelements and macroelements, individual actors, organisational context, and societal institutions. Here such a differentiation simply raises the point that behind 'unintended' developments there are also identifiable people—and that people cause and contribute to the emergence of such phenomena as hierarchisation in diverse ways: authoritarian and/or egoistic individuals seek social dominance *deliberately* even in nonhierarchical settings, whereas other, more socially and consensus-oriented, individuals might contribute to hierarchisation more unintentionally. Either way, even 'unintended processes' and 'unintended consequences' are the results of individuals' behaviour and intentional actions—even if these activities were meant to achieve other outcomes. Consequently, people are also responsible for more abstract developments that might not be directly linked to their immediate actions—and they can, and should, be held accountable.

6.2.3 Nonhierarchical Social Systems and the Problems of People and Institutions

Generally speaking, social systems are made of institutions and people. Thus, if we want to achieve (and maintain) *non*hierarchical social systems, the question is: what kind of people and what kind of institutions do we need? The problem is not so much the theoretical concepts concerning the formal principles, structures, and processes of democratic and/or nonhierarchical organisations or even whole societies. The general ideas exist and are known (e.g., participatory-democratic organisations, nonhierarchical networks, egalitarian or communitarian societies). The key problem is how nonhierarchical, democratic social systems can be maintained without people intentionally or unintentionally causing the emergence of hierarchical structures or processes via their behaviour ('hierarchisation'). It is about having the 'right' people and the 'right' institutions in order to achieve and maintain nonhierarchical social systems.

6.2.3.1 Can the 'Right' People Achieve Nonhierarchical Social Systems?

Researchers who have investigated 'utopian' communities and 'collectivist' or 'egalitarian' organisations have looked very closely at how people in such organisations behave (Rothschild and Ollilainen 1999; Rothschild-Whitt 1979, 1976; Kanter 1972). Kanter (1972, p. viii) described such enterprises as 'major social experiments in which new or radical theories of human behaviour, motivation, and interpersonal relations are put to the test.' Whether these enterprises were 'experiments' at the societal level (e.g., the establishment of communist societies), at the organisational level (e.g., collectivist or participatory-democratic organisations, or cooperatives) or at the group level (e.g., communes), very often they were based on the idea (or hope) that their realisation depended on 'better' people.

Putting aside cynical or even terroristic attempts to create 'better' people with whom a 'better' social system could be established (e.g., via 'reeducation' of those who are able and willing while getting rid of those who aren't), there is a serious aspect to people's morality and actions; nonhierarchical structures and processes with egalitarian, fair and just decision-making processes and allocation mechanisms do indeed require that people have different attitudes and behaviour compared to, say, in hierarchical power-and-control arrangements. Such ideas resonate with Kohlberg's 'postconventional' level of moral development. For example, one of the key features of stage 5 of moral development is a 'social contract-orientation.' The question is whether such an orientation would be sufficient to realise and maintain nonhierarchical relationships.

Logically, a social contract-orientation is a criterion of distinction between hierarchical and nonhierarchical systems. Hierarchically organised groups and societies have general principles, norms, and values that are considered as fundamentally right and no longer in need of negotiation or agreement (e.g., religious revelations; natural laws; sociocultural, political, or organisational ideologies). People accept these principles without having consented to them with a truly free will. In contrast, principles which are compatible with *non*hierarchical systems require the consent of people with a free will, can be contested and need to be interpreted time and again. Their realisation depends on the specific understandings of the particular people involved. This is where things become problematic. For example, the proponents of ethical value systems might interpret the relevant principles in the best way possible—and assume that everyone else will do the same. A consensus orientation and the free will of people at the postconventional level of moral development are usually understood as those people's consensual desire for basic (individual) rights, freedom, and democracy (Crain 1985). In short: a consensus orientation is equated with a democratic orientation. Yet, consensus-oriented citizens could agree that 'the best people' should lead based on the general principle that everyone should do what they can do best and the assumption that this will produce a better society. Obviously, such a principle can lead to democratic solutions, but it may also lead to market-like solutions—or even autocratic or dictatorial systems of governance. Similar outcomes can occur when 'merits'—whatever these actually are—serve as leading principles for selecting the form of governance and those who should govern. Such examples highlight the well-known paradox that democratic decision-making can produce undemocratic outcomes; consensus-oriented people with free will can agree on many, very different principles and procedures that do not necessarily lead to nonhierarchical solutions.

All in all, people with a social-contract orientation collaborate with others in much more advanced ways compared to people at the preconventional or conventional level. Nevertheless, consensus-based principles and concepts can have very different meanings and implications—positive and/or negative. In the context of the aspects discussed here, this means that consensus orientation does not guarantee anything; it can produce more democratic and less hierarchical processes and outcomes, but not necessarily. *As such,* consensus achieved by people with free will does not guarantee decisions that are necessarily compatible with the ideas of democracy, equality, fairness, justice, or a hierarchy-free social system. A consensus orientation is (also) very compatible with hierarchy (see Sections 4.2.6.3 and 4.2.6.4) and often simply (re)produces forms of stratification and social dominance, superiority and subordination, and privileges and discrimination. A consensus-orientation is a necessary but not sufficient precondition; even people who have reached stage 5 of moral development and show quite strong social-contract and consensus orientations are not necessarily guarantors for achieving (truly) democratic, hierarchy-free, egalitarian, and just social systems.

Hence, in order to realise nonhierarchical systems and protect them from hierarchisation, it is necessary to think about people with even more, or higher, moral orientations. Such people would show the necessary behaviour to keep nonhierarchical systems going in formally *as well as* informally nonhierarchical ways. They would demonstrate personality traits and behaviour of stage 6 of Kohlberg's moral development. Such people are in favour of democratic institutions and of democratic governance in groups, organisations, and even the whole of society in principle. They are keen to create alternative, egalitarian/democratic and hierarchy-free communities, organisations, and societies in which there are no superiors or subordinates (Rothschild and Ollilainen 1999, p. 596; Whitley 1989, p. 210). In the words of Rothschild-Whitt (1979, p. 512), 'Like the anarchists, their aim is not the transference of power from one official to another, but the abolition of the pyramid in toto: organization without hierarchy.' Moreover, with their 'egalitarian-democratic perspective' (Passini and Morselli 2010, p. 8; Rothschild and Ollilainen 1999, p. 598), these people are able to achieve this aim. The behaviour of stage 6 people acting on the grounds of 'universally true principles' would not include much, if anything, that could trigger or contribute to hierarchisation, for example a 'prosocial motivation, the desire to have a positive impact on other people or social collectives' (Grant and Berg 2010, p. 1)—one might even say a 'prosocial or altruistic personality [. . .] that is highly correlated with measures of empathy, social responsibility, prosocial values, and concern for the welfare of others' (Meglino and Korsgaard 2004, p. 948). People of stage 6 of moral development believe in the principles, and live up to the ideas of altruism, equality, and solidarity (Nienhaus and Brauksiepe 1997, pp. 1422–3).

It seems that most researchers, including Kohlberg himself, regard stage 6 as largely 'theoretical,' as a level of moral development that not many can reach and maintain (e.g., Crain 1985, p. 124). And, indeed, one may think of the scarcity of such great moral leaders as Mahatma Gandhi, Martin Luther King, Nelson Mandela, or Aung San Suu Kyi, who have consistently shown behaviour that equals stage 6 of moral development (at least in their public image and appearances).

Although one cannot deny that people like the ones mentioned are quite exceptional, such examples have probably also caused some misunderstandings. Many people may have come to the conclusion that stage 6 requires a 'larger-than-life' personality. But this is not (necessarily) the case. From a logical point of view, the idea of 'universal' principles does not only mean that they are, or should be, valid *everywhere* but also that *everyone* is capable of understanding them and potentially capable of practicing them. It was one of the fundamental ideas of the Enlightenment that not only the 'privileged' but (especially) the 'ordinary' people should be able, and be enabled, to live their lives as free people in nonoppressive societies. For example, in his famous essay 'What is Enlightenment?', Immanuel Kant (1784) described the main idea of enlightenment as people's emergence from their self-imposed immaturity and the freedom to use their *own* intelligence ('*Sapere aude!*')—*and he meant everyone.*

Of course, grasping the idea of universal ethical principles requires *some* cognitive abilities. But stage 6 of moral development does not need a sharp intellect. Years or even decades of scholarly studies and/or professional work can help to develop a familiarity with universal principles—but they are no guarantee that an individual will actually reach stages 5 or 6 of moral development. *Other* skills or personality traits are equally, or even more, important than mere intellect, such as empathy, altruism, or similar philanthropic convictions and attitudes—and it seems that some people have or demonstrate such values in quite a 'natural' or 'common-sense' way; they care about other individuals as well as humanity and the Earth in general (and act accordingly), seemingly naturally, and without much effort. Thus, stage 6 of moral development can be demonstrated by 'ordinary' people. Stage 6 is not as exceptional as most might think.

Indeed, there are many people who consistently show the same high level of moral development as those outstanding examples of humanity given above—but they do so on a daily basis without receiving much attention (or even appreciation). These people might be 'average' in many respects, with average jobs, an average single or family life, with an average education and average intellectual capabilities. They may or may not have heard about the 'categorical imperative'; they may or may not have a sound knowledge of the key philosophical, political, academic, and religious texts of their culture; and they may or may not be publicly known and acknowledged for their deeds. But, crucially, such people live up to the ideas of the enlightened personality in their own lives and daily routines. Their thoughts as well as their deeds—their whole lives—predominantly exemplify stage 6 behaviour. So, it is possible and quite realistic, indeed, to imagine people who show all the traits and behaviour necessary to keep nonhierarchical systems going while avoiding hierarchisation. And such people are not necessarily 'larger-than-life' personalities but can be people like you and me.

6.2.3.2   On the Search for the 'Right' Institutions for Nonhierarchical Social Systems

There is definitely a possibility that there can be the 'right' people who are able and willing to initiate and maintain nonhierarchical social systems. However, after her very comprehensive and in-depth research into collectivist and egalitarian organisations, Rothschild-Whitt (1979, p. 521) concluded that 'many people are not very well-suited for participatory-democracy.' She traced this back primarily to individual differences and found that 'all organizations, democratic ones notwithstanding, contain persons with very different talents, skills, knowledge, and personality attributes' (p. 524). In that sense it is not very realistic to suppose (or to hope) that in any given nonhierarchical system *only* people with an enlightened personality will come together and jointly run that system. It might happen, but it would be a very rare coincidence—at least in the societies and cultures we know so far. It is therefore more reasonable to assume that nonhierarchical systems also comprise *all sorts of people*—i.e., people who show *the whole range* of Kohlberg's six stages of moral development (though perhaps relatively more people with higher stages of moral development compared to bureaucratic/ hierarchical organisations and traditional societies, which usually attract and/or socialise relatively higher numbers of people with preconventional levels of moral development).

This means that nonhierarchical systems with a range of diverse people acting at different stages of moral development face problems that cannot be solved (solely) at an individual level but require *institutional* arrangements. For example, as indicated above, despite best intentions, daily communication and routines can have effects leading towards hierarchisation. Over a shorter or longer period of time, individual attitudes and behaviour can establish informal hierarchy and can create patterns of dominance and subordination that go against the spirit of power- and hierarchy-free discourses and decision-making. As a consequence, there is not only a *silent* majority but a *silenced* majority. Oligarchy—i.e., the empowerment of the few and the disempowerment of the many—might be even more difficult to prevent in (initially) nonhierarchical social systems due to the reduced number of formal institutions and bureaucratic means (Leach 2005, p. 314).

Moreover, people at preconventional and conventional levels of moral development might show different types of rivalry and competition, and more sublime and indirect, individualised, and subjectivised forms of power and control (Courpasson 2000) in the face of less formalised and regulated structures and processes. As a consequence, the pressure on individuals (largely through their peers) may be even higher than in orthodox organisations. Oppression and exploitation might not be reduced—it may simply be that structures and processes have changed from formal to informal hierarchy; to some extent, social dominance might be only different—or even more severe. The perhaps biggest challenge for less formalised social systems (for *any* social system) is the calculative and mendacious mindsets of those more aspirational and active members who largely act at preconventional levels of moral development. The immoral behaviour of careerists and organisational psychopaths is quite a common problem and a deeply embedded part of the unnormal normality of orthodox and bureaucratic organisations—but it is also a serious problem in decentralised and democratic organisations since these provide quite favourable conditions for people with calculative minds (e.g., less formalised decision-making processes and more informal communications, providing endless opportunities for tactical manoeuvres). The problem is even bigger because very often such members, although acting at low, preconventional levels of moral development (stages 1 and 2), are very good at 'impression management' and, therefore, may even be widely hailed and appreciated as 'doers,' 'change agents,' 'movers,' or even 'leaders.'

Thus, whether it is 'the steady force of the factual', more 'sublime forms of social dominance' or the 'mendacious manoeuvring of careerists and psychopaths' that is responsible, it might be said that nonhierarchical social systems probably face the same whole range of human behaviour (and misbehaviour) as orthodox organisations and conservative societies.

Nonetheless, there are two differences. One is that people, especially those who set up and try to run nonhierarchical social systems, often underestimate the range and types of problems that these social systems encounter or create. The prevailing picture of nonhierarchical systems is often too positive, if not to say naïve and idealised. The other difference—and problem—is that nonhierarchical social systems are neither equipped with the traditional means to cope with all sorts of deviating behaviour nor are they meant to, or designed for, using such means. Very often, the culture of nonhierarchical social systems is explicitly or implicitly against, for example, bureaucratic rules and regulations, anonymous performance-measurement systems, or managerial power-and-control tools.

The typical features of such systems—such as empowered individuals, decentralised and democratic decision-making, egalitarian participation and allocation of resources, flexible structures and processes, and employee ownership—may represent quite some progress compared to orthodox and hybrid organisations. But these arrangements and aspects do not automatically prevent (informal) hierarchy and stratification, social dominance, oppression, and exploitation as such (Leach 2005, p. 312). Most institutions and settings of most nonhierarchical social systems we have come to know of so far are only *necessary but not sufficient* preconditions for truly democratic, egalitarian, fair, and just organisations and societies.

Those who had hopes that with different types of organisations and societies many things would get (much) better might be disappointed in the face of processes such as hierarchisation. But this disappointment may be largely due to a too idealistic opinion. A more realistic understanding would be that it is quite normal for nonhierarchical social systems, as well as hierarchical ones, to face problems that cannot be solved for good but are an integral part of the functioning of the system.

Therefore, the concern is not so much to try to find 'perfect' systems with 'perfect' people but to seek constellations and mechanisms that are fundamentally different from those in hierarchical systems but can cope with similar problems that orthodox organisations and conservative societies have to cope with. If we want to overcome the deficits or vulnerabilities of nonhierarchical democratic organisations and societies, more—and different—institutions, mechanisms, and arrangements are needed that can prevent the emergence of formal and informal hierarchy, inequalities, and social dominance as well as help to avoid the downsides of radical nonhierarchical social systems. And there need to be arrangements in place that can cope better particularly with people's low levels of moral development as well as arrangements that can empower those who, for whatever reasons, do not actively seek empowerment or participation. Such mechanisms could be: 1) arrangements that allow individual and collective reflexivity without patronising the individual or encouraging public soul-searching; 2) collective decision-making procedures without the tyranny of the majority; and 3) close collaboration without radical forms of communitarianism or group-coherence.

Much of this is uncontested terrain. Hence, we need to further develop our understanding of *all* necessary preconditions for truly hierarchy-free types of organisation and societies—i.e., the right values that guide individual attitudes, behaviour, and social actions *and* the right and necessary institutions to put into place; which types of institution can guarantee the achievement and maintenance of truly democratic and nonhierarchical social systems and the containment of power and control without becoming themselves a bedrock of uncontrolled and oppressive power and control? This is the core question of any attempt to free the individual as well as to create free organisations and free societies. The current forms of organisations and societies are simply not sufficient to achieve what they promise or what people think they can or should achieve.

6.3 CONCLUSIONS

It is time to draw some conclusions. There have (almost) always been superiors and subordinates. However, hierarchy is not a natural law but a social construct—based on highly questionable ideas about humans and their relationships. In the face of an increasingly diversified social reality of organisational forms and social systems, Leach (2005, p. 316) complained about the absence of an adequate theory that could cope with hierarchical structures and processes adequately:

> Since scholars have begun examining a broader range of organizational forms, [. . .] existing conceptual tools have proved inadequate. Measures that have been employed in bureaucratic settings are not directly transferable to nonbureaucratic settings, and measures employed (implicitly or explicitly) in nonbureaucratic settings have offered no way to distinguish between a minority that is merely persuasive and one that is oligarchic. In the end, we are left with a collection of findings that cannot be integrated into a more general theory because they are too often looking for different things and using different yardsticks. In short, the organizational landscape has diversified over the last several decades, and this diversity calls for a conceptualization of oligarchy that can be operationalized in a comparable way across organizational settings.

This book has been an attempt to close this gap—i.e., to develop a general, comprehensive, multidimensional, interdisciplinary, and critical theory regarding why and how hierarchical social order persists at individual, interpersonal (micro), organisational (meso), and societal (macro) levels. In the previous chapters it has been shown that hierarchy is so widespread and persistent not (only) because of a plain top-down power-and-control constellation. The general theory of hierarchical social systems is built on a model that describes and analyses hierarchy as a comprehensive, multidimensional system that comprises several elements related to, and interacting with, each other. Persistent hierarchical social order is a complex 'social cosmos' of dominance and obedience, factual privileges and prerogatives, unequal and unjust allocation of resources, and rights and opportunities (see Figure 9). Moreover, the theory developed here attempts to explain why and how hierarchical social order functions and why it has been so persistent. Nevertheless, the theory has only laid the foundations; future work can contribute to previous and ongoing attempts to further develop three areas in particular: 1) functional analysis, 2) being (much more) critical, and 3) providing alternatives.

6.3.1   Functional Analysis

How hierarchy works in orthodox organisations and totalitarian regimes is fairly well known. In contrast, we still know little about how it works in modern organisations and societies that are diversified and multidimensional and that constantly change and don't change.

Hierarchy is context-dependent. Hierarchical systems vary enormously, in terms of their size (e.g., dyads, groups, organisations, societies), types (e.g., different organisational forms), their specific circumstances (e.g., particular problems the social system faces) and the wider context (e.g., culture, societal institutions, epoch, and megatrends) (Brown et al. 2010; Clegg et al. 2006; Stohl and Cheney 2001; Cheney 1995; Barker 1993; Jones and Svejnar 1982). The exact types and mechanisms of power and control, dominance and obedience, and oppression and exploitation as well as superiors' and subordinates' interests, identities, ideologies, and actions vary with the epochal, cultural, institutional, and organisational context. As Mills (1956, p. 23) put it: 'For every epoch and for every social structure, we must work out an answer to the question of the power of the elite.' Individual and comparative analysis could increase our understanding of the general principles and mechanisms of hierarchy as well as its specific variations in different epochal and local situations and circumstances.

But, whatever the actual hierarchical system looks like, it always comprises formal and informal aspects. Formal *and* informal structures and processes shape social systems to a much greater extent than, for example, orthodox theories of organisation imply. Even in cases in which there are the 'best intentions' to establish nonhierarchical ways of working, informal hierarchical structures can emerge and are more persistent than might be expected

(Oberg and Walgenbach 2008; Ekbia and Kling 2005; Ahuja and Carley 1999). More analysis would help to counterbalance naïve understandings (or hopes) of an automatic emergence and continuation of nonhierarchical structures and processes only because of an 'alternative' impetus or 'unorthodox' approaches. In contrast to formal hierarchy, it is still the case that very little is known about social phenomena leading to informal hierarchy (Nelson 2001, p. 797) and the interactions between formal and informal institutions (Zenger et al. 2001, p. 3).

Moreover, hierarchical systems are not only based on routine behaviour. Boundary crossings happen regularly and are a normal part of social systems. The analysis in Chapter 4 revealed how superiors' and subordinates' different types of boundary crossings might challenge or strengthen hierarchical social order. But only the nucleus of the concept of boundary crossings was applied. Only single crossings of clearly demarcated boundaries and their more direct consequences for the system were interrogated. Social dynamics are often more complex and unfold over longer periods of time. The concept of boundary crossing can also be used for more differentiated, multidimensional, multimethodological, and interdisciplinary investigations of all sorts of social phenomena.

We especially still know too little about what happens when boundaries are crossed in specific social systems and the consequences they trigger. It would be worth investigating in more detail how different social systems cope with boundary crossings and when exactly boundary crossings contribute to a (further) stabilisation or destabilisation of various social systems—and how boundary crossings might contribute to system change. Such research would further our understanding of social relationships and social struggles between individuals and groups; of the mechanisms of hierarchical social systems—i.e., how they conserve and reproduce inequalities, how they continue to exist, and under which circumstances they are being terminated. Seeing boundary crossing as central parts of multiple processes of social struggle could also improve our understanding of escalation of conflict and might produce new insights into how to solve or even end social conflict.

Such crossings are done by people. In this book, for the sake of simplicity, superiors and subordinates have mostly been treated in a fairly general sense and as homogenous groups. The possible divisions among superiors (e.g., struggles between power elites) and among subordinates (differentiation into subgroups) were not an explicit focus of the analysis carried out here. Complex social systems are usually divided into many different groups and subgroups. And, although groups might be coherent, they are not homogenous. For example, the Roman adage *divide et impera* (divide and rule) and struggles between power elites indicate that the social dynamics within hierarchical systems do not just happen between two neatly identifiable groups. Particularly, micropolitics within hierarchical systems often depend on rifts within groups and changing alliances. As indicated in Chapter 3, the superior-subordinate relationship is understood as a *relational* construct—

i.e., whether someone is superior or subordinate depends on the situational context. In this sense, it would help to analyse the dynamics of social dominance and obedience that unfold not only between but also within groups.

The social groups we know the least about are power elites—or, to put it differently, we know everything about their *public* images and *official* rhetoric and we know everything that members of power elites *want us* to know about them, but, beyond that, we have only anecdotal evidence stemming from scandals, media coverage, and leaked inquiries conducted by law enforcement agencies. These provide some hints about the inner lives of the privileged castes and classes, but we do not have a systematic, comprehensive, and detailed picture. There is a great need for more research in order to gain a better understanding of superiors' and power elites' 'hidden world'—i.e., their secret worldviews and real interests, their actual thoughts and deeds behind the cover of official rhetoric and public images.

So far, there have been too few attempts (and opportunities) to disclose power elites' hidden value systems. This is partly the result of technical difficulties: members of power elites may be happy to provide official/politically correct statements and to polish their public images but they are not very keen to reveal their real thoughts or to expose their situation and actions to public scrutiny. Interviews, observations, and other research methods—even investigative journalism and police inquiries—may occasionally uncover some hidden social actions of some individual members of the power elite. But these methods are limited in their ability to reveal superiors' hidden values and beliefs.

Moreover, a more sociopsychological difficulty arises from the fact that many have internalised the ideology of the superiority and legitimacy of the power elites and therefore deem it 'inappropriate' to critically interrogate monarchs, heads of state, bishops, managers, or any other members of power elites. Since these people enjoy above-average privileges and advantages provided by the social system, their actual behaviour also needs to be scrutinised further.

In addition, social groups are not 'faceless'—they consist of individual members. In Section 6.2.2 it was argued that it is actual people and their decisions and actions that produce intended as well as unintended consequences. People navigate their way through hierarchical systems, make decisions, and act in certain ways. The individual freedom to navigate raises the question of how much people are actually responsible for the situations they are in, for their individual actions, and for the consequences of their actions within certain settings—i.e., which stages of moral development people demonstrate. It is very important that social analysis does not only remain at an abstract level. We need to become very specific about which actors do what for what reasons and with what consequences—and we need to name and shame them if their actions or mindsets go against the common good. Within complex and differentiated social systems, it might not always be easy or possible to track down those who are responsible for certain phenomena, but we must try—too many people get away with too many things that are anything but good for others and the social system. In far too many social science studies, the moral dimension is officially excluded because of a misguided understanding of what constitutes 'scientific research.' If a decisive factor is ignored in a research design it does not mean that it is not present in reality. If we ever want to truly understand social reality, we need to include the moral dimension *explicitly* in the core of our social theories and models.

This, finally, is also true with regard to *institutions;* what is really lacking in social sciences is comprehensive and thorough analysis of the morality of social systems and societal institutions. It needs to be interrogated very carefully why there are privileges and prerogatives for the few; why there is inequality, oppression, and exploitation for the many; in what ways exactly a hierarchical system is unfair and unjust; and how all this (im)morality of a specific social system or institution is justified, maintained, and used for what purposes. Such research is desperately needed because institutions shape social systems (and their members) massively. Whether people are privileged or disadvantaged, their thoughts and deeds are shaped to a great extent by their social background. For example, the societal socialisation of individuals—i.e., how institutions such as parenthood, kindergarten, school, college, and university prepare, if not to say condition, individuals for other hierarchical organisations—has a major impact on people's way of seeing and doing things. Moreover, the situation is different for different people within a particular society and people in different societies. Thus, there is a need to investigate how systemisation and its mechanisms actually work on individuals as well as how institutions and individuals relate to each other.

All in all, far too little functional analysis of hierarchical social systems has been carried out that goes beyond a limited focus on the efficiency of existing structures and processes. We must know more about phenomena such as the ones just mentioned since otherwise we will never really comprehend why and how social systems work or don't work—because we are surrounded and shaped by them from the cradle to the grave.

6.3.2   Being (Much More) Critical

However, functional analysis is never enough. In order to examine social systems not only in technical terms but also in fundamental ways (and to really understand how and why they work in what ways and how to maintain them), we need to approach them in *critical* terms.

On the one hand, in social science there is no shortage of critical approaches (see Appendix 1). Critical approaches, theories, and research in the realms of political science, economics, sociology, psychology, anthropology, management, and organisation studies help 'to illuminate the ways in which people accept as normal a world characterized by massive inequities and the systemic exploitation of the many by the few' (Brookfield 2005,

242 *Hierarchy and Organisation*

p. 2). Critical thinking particularly focuses on the shortcomings of the status quo of a given society as well as the rhetoric and ideology used by power elites and proponents of the existing social order in order to justify and legitimise it. As Gorton (2010, n.p.) put it: 'The aim of critical theory is human emancipation, and this is accomplished in part by laying bare structural impediments to genuine freedom, contradictions and incoherencies in people's beliefs and values, and hidden ideologies that mask domination.'

On the other hand, most criticism about political, legal, economical, material, ethical, social, sociopsychological, organisational, and environmental issues concerns specific problems and technical solutions. Of course, this is needed. But what has been missing over the years is *fundamental criticism*—i.e., criticism of the very foundations, main principles, and core values society and organisations are built upon. Too many things, especially elemental issues, are taken for granted and no longer challenged; for example, the assumption that most institutions are not democratic and enabling but antidemocratic and oppressive; that organisations are structured hierarchically; that some people own companies and others work for them; that there are large differences between individual wealth and ownership of land, resources, and tangible and intangible assets; or that there are even superiors and subordinates at all. Why are such fundamental issues only addressed by a few so-called 'radicals' in online forums or during glimpses of public anger and popular protest, and not within the established systems and communities of discourse? Criticism has lost large parts of its system-challenging impetus and become quite a domesticated and tamed version of the whole critical endeavour. What used to be revolutionary potential is now a disgruntled nagging about technicalities. We need to return to a criticism of the *fundamental* issues of our contemporary societies and organisations since they are still anything else but democratic, fair, and just.

Having said that, it is not just the status quo and dominant forces within societies that must be criticised technically and fundamentally; possible and real (existing) alternatives are also problematic and must be looked at critically. Again, contemporary criticism is fairly quiet in this respect. Moreover, there is often a good deal of idealism and naivety surrounding alternative concepts. But, without criticism, reflection, and openness, such alternative concepts might be, or might develop relatively quickly into, fairly orthodox systems (or even worse). A better understanding particularly of the (possible) insufficiencies, weaknesses, and dangers of alternative concepts is needed. This would help to achieve a more differentiated and balanced understanding of such organisations, to raise the awareness of their weaknesses, and to develop them further towards truly democratic and egalitarian organisations and societies. In this sense, critical research must focus more particularly on all sorts of 'alternative' social systems—theoretical concepts and empirical cases alike—and investigate them with the same critical impetus with which orthodox social systems are interrogated.

6.3.3 Providing Alternatives

As important as analysis and criticism are, they are not enough. There is something *seriously* wrong with the state of our interpersonal relationships and with the way our organisations and societies are designed and function. So far, hierarchical systems of all sorts have been made primarily, if not solely, for superiors. The values and objectives, structures and processes, and privileges and prerogatives reflect mostly *their* interests and worldviews, *their* identities and ways of life. Over time, this has led to highly inefficient, unfair, and unjust allocation of resources, privileges, and prerogatives, even opportunities and life chances. *As long as we have stratified societies, hierarchical organisations, and unequal social relationships, we will inherently be encouraged to act at lower levels of moral development and our existence will be a far cry from its potential.*

It is time to change this. We need to think about, and put into place, alternatives—i.e., *fundamentally* different social systems that are truly democratic, nonhierarchical, fair, just, and free from any form of social dominance, oppression, and exploitation.

But is this realistic? The Introduction referred to Nietzsche's pessimistic conclusion regarding 'the eternal return of the always same.' Despite all technological progress, massive gains in productivity and efficiency, buzzwords, window-dressing exercises, and lip-service paid to concepts of 'empowerment,' and 'participation,' our societies, organisations, and social relationships are still based on very orthodox and traditional command-and-control-oriented concepts that enable and guarantee the continuation of hierarchical social order, top-down management of social and organisational affairs, and the exploitation of the many by the few. Orthodox change initiatives and the unreflected introduction of new organisational forms and even megatrends at the societal level have not changed this. With the epochal changes that have occurred since the 1980s (the collapse of the Soviet Union and other so-called socialist countries, the strengthening of conservative forces in many Western countries, and global trends towards market economies, neoliberalism, egoism, and consumerism), in some respects the situation has even gotten worse.

There is no natural law guaranteeing that history or the development of social systems is a linear process of continuous improvements. Social dominance and hierarchy are much more persistent than people claim or think. Thinking and acting in hierarchical terms is the cultural heritage and the primary sociocultural institution in most of our societies, organisations, and even personal relationships. The persistence of hierarchy is a real problem, perhaps 'the' problem, of society. Findings like those discussed in Section 6.1 do indeed support Robert Michels' 1915 'iron law of oligarchy' (see Michels 1966), which was also chosen as the opening quote to this chapter.

Michels definitely has a point. Nonetheless, not all evidence supports the 'degeneration thesis'—i.e., the assumption that nonhierarchical and/or democratic organisations sooner or later *inevitably* transform into fairly orthodox organisations (with a dominating power elite taking over the organisation). In human history there have always been attempts to create democratic, hierarchy-free, and egalitarian social groups, organisations, and even whole societies. In market economies as well as socialist economies and in developed as well as developing countries, one can find many examples of social systems that are at least in some respects quite different from hierarchical social system; for example, grassroots movements, nongovernmental organisations, cooperatives, heterarchic organisations, (Fairtlough 2005), participative-democratic organisations (de Jong and van Witteloostuijin 2004; Rothschild and Ollilainen 1999; Rosen 1984), collectivist organisations (Rothschild-Whitt 1979), utopian communities (Kanter 1972), network organisations, and some not-for-profit organisations.

In social systems like these, people try to realise and practice less hierarchical, or even hierarchy-free, forms of work organisation, collaborations, and social relationships. Nevertheless, most of these attempts are still based on principles of formal or informal hierarchy (as the analysis of different types of organisations in Section 4.6 revealed); some have failed (with sometimes rather disastrous consequences) but others have been quite successful over many years. Very successful examples—Rothschild-Whitt (1979, p. 525) called them 'anomalies'—are empirical evidence of the fact that, even within market economies, alternative social systems can be designed and maintained in quite some contrast to orthodox organisations (Fleming 2012; Parker 2012). There *can* be organisational designs, measures, mechanisms, and institutions that can prevent unwelcome developments such as social dominance or the oligarchisation of nonhierarchical, democratic, and egalitarian social systems (Sauser 2009, p. 153; Varman and Chakrabarti 2004, pp. 185–6). In the same way that one black swan falsifies the statement that 'all swans are white' (Karl Popper's famous example of his falsification criterion), the existence of these anomalies (these long-running democratic and egalitarian organisations) puts into perspective Michels' 'iron law of oligarchy': it is very often, perhaps in most cases, true—but it is not *always* true.[6] His proposition is *not* a (natural or scientific) law that is always true with necessity. That social systems such as groups, organisations, and whole societies are structured hierarchically and run by leader(s) and power elite(s) does not *necessarily* have to be the case; it *can* be the case but it can also be *otherwise*. There is always the theoretical *and* practical possibility of establishing and maintaining hierarchy-free social systems (Rothschild and Ollilainen 1999, p. 585; Whitley 1989, p. 210; Rosen 1984, p. 312; Rothschild-Whitt 1979, pp. 512, 525).

The problem is that the theories and institutions that support such alternative ideas are by no means as strong and as developed as the theories and institutions that support, protect, develop, and disseminate the ideas of hierarchical organisations and stratified societies—they rarely have been, they are not at present and it is not clear whether they could be in the future. At the moment there is no comprehensively developed ideology around which could be built a strong and convincing alternative to neoliberalism, consumerism, and managerialism. And, besides the well-established ideas and theoretical concepts of cooperatives/employee-owned companies, representative democratic organisations, and network organisations, we also lack a very strong and compelling theory and concept (or theories and concepts) that could really provide an attractive alternative to the orthodox organisation.

All in all, as indicated above, we should investigate (the possibilities of) alternative social systems in much more detail in order to find out more about the necessary preconditions; how such systems actually function; what the reasons for their success or failure are; and, most importantly, whether they are truly free of any form of hierarchy, social dominance, oppression, and exploitation, whether this is at all possible and, if so, what we need to do in order to achieve and guarantee it. There are quite a few crucial issues to focus on, for example:

- Hierarchy, hierarchy-based authority, power and control, management, and performance measurement fulfil some important regulatory tasks that support the functioning of (hierarchical) social systems. What institutions and procedures can replace them in order to support the functioning of *non*hierarchical social systems?

- *Formal* democracy and equality are not enough to achieve, and maintain, nonhierarchical and egalitarian social systems. How do formal *and* informal structures and processes of ownership and governance, of decision-making and participation and of collaboration and communication actually happen and relate to each other?

- Democratic/collectivist social systems require people with mindsets different from the 'obedient personality,' and their members may show all sorts of personality traits and all levels of moral development. What are the values, beliefs, attitudes, and behaviours of people that enable nonhierarchical processes—and what are those that may threaten them? How can nonhierarchical structures and processes be maintained by all sorts of people without falling prey to Michels' iron law?

There is a real necessity to further develop our understanding of the whole range of necessary preconditions for the realisation of truly hierarchy-free and egalitarian types of social systems—i.e., the relevant structural arrangements as well as the sets of values that guide individual attitudes, behaviour, and social actions (Rhodes and Bloom 2012). And we need to better understand the theoretical and practical obstacles to the realisation and maintenance of such social systems—and how these can be overcome.

6.3.4 'Freedom' is the Task

As the discussion in the previous sections has shown, overall we need more:

1) *Analysis*—Why and how do hierarchical social systems emerge, function, and persist over time?

2) *Criticism*—What is wrong with contemporary social systems and why should we change them?

3) *Alternatives*—How can we change contemporary practices and realise truly free and nonhierarchical, fair, and just social systems?

Human society, along with any other social system, is not the result of 'natural' forces or the inevitable outcome of functional necessities. It is a social construct—i.e., the result of people's beliefs, interests, actions, and social conflict (Diefenbach 2009a; Braverman 1974; Crozier 1964). And we are able to design and shape social reality as *we* deem appropriate and necessary. Like any other social system, hierarchy can be modified, overcome, and replaced. Hierarchy is not a necessity like the air we breathe, social dominance is not in our genes, and hierarchical social order is not a natural law we have to follow like the planets follow gravity in their course.

Within almost all societies, organisations, and groups, people enjoy certain degrees of individual freedom—but most, almost all, people use it merely for functioning smoothly within the parameters set by hierarchical systems and their peers. *Who says that our lives and affairs should be organised via hierarchical relationships?* We have the choice—and we can strive for more than mere social dominance, oppression, and exploitation. The general theory of hierarchical social systems is part of a much greater endeavour: the aim of the Enlightenment to free humans from any kind of oppression and to achieve free, egalitarian, and just societies. As Paolo Freire (1996, p. 31) stated: 'no longer oppressor nor longer oppressed, but human in the process of achieving freedom.' The theory is about ending oppressive, unfair and unjust structures and practices; overcoming the exploitation of the many by a few; and convincing people that hierarchical social order is not the normal state of affairs but an anomaly within free and democratic societies (Brookfield 2005, p. viii; Fournier and Grey 2000, p. 16). The ruling of elected politicians is *always* preferable to the ruling of dictators, royals, or oligarchs; employee-owned companies are more democratic, fair, and just than orthodox organisations; and social relationships between free and equal individuals are superior to any hierarchical social order.

The development and realisation of truly nonhierarchical social systems is still pending. This would mean the end of hierarchical order and unequal social relationships, of oppression and exploitation and of unjustified privileges for the few and unfair disadvantages for the many—and their replacement by different principles, structures, and processes. 'Freedom' is the task. We can, and need to, develop (again) a 'utopian spirit' concerning the (theoretical and practical) search for 'better' social systems since even with the currently most developed forms we are still far away from the ideal of truly hierarchy-free, democratic and egalitarian, and fair and just organisations and societies. The search for such social systems continues the endeavour and unfinished business of the Enlightenment. And we have to do it because we can.

Appendix 1

Justification and Criticism of Hierarchical Social Order

Aspect	Justification	System-justifying concepts	Criticism	Critical concepts
a) Origins of hierarchy	Natural law, natural order	Sociobiology (Wilson 1975)	Human creation, social conflict	Labour Process Theory, Industrial Relations (Friedman 1977, Braverman 1974)
			Division of labour, social differentiation, stratification	Social differentiation, stratification, discrimination (Bourdieu 1979, Mousnier 1973, Laumann et al. 1971, Moore 1971, Mills 1956, Davis / Moore 1945, Mosca 1971/1939)
	Legitimacy	Functionalism / orthodox management and organisation theories	Ideology	Ideological justification, dominant ideology (Beetham 1991, Abercrombie 1980)
b) Functional aspects of hierarchy as a system	Rational design, functional reasons, efficiency, isomorphism	Functionalism / orthodox management and organisation theories (Donaldson 2003, Zaleznik 1989, Child 1972, Blau 1970, Lawrence / Lorsch 1967, Chandler 1962, Gouldner 1960, Drucker 1954, Friedman 1953, Fayol 1949, Taylor 1911/1967)	Social conflict inequality, injustice, discrimination, exploitation	Labour Process Theory, Industrial Relations (Friedman 1977, Braverman 1974)
	Order, protection, conservation, positive aspects of power and rules		Power and control	Power and control (Clegg et al. 2006, Clegg 1979, Lukes 1974)
			Anti-democratic system and order	Critical Management Studies (Clegg et al. 2006, Alvesson / Willmott 1992a, b)

(Continued)

Aspect	Justification	System-justifying concepts	Criticism	Critical concepts
	Equilibrium, balance of power, reciprocity, common interest	New institutional economics, principal-agent / agency theory (North 1991, Williamson 1975, Alchian / Demsetz 1972, Coase 1937)		Organisational politics (Cohen et al. 1999, Mintzberg 1985, Burns 1961, Thompson 1961)
c) The people	Tasks and responsibilities of superiors	Transformational and transactional leadership theories (Van Vugt 2006, Zaleznik 1989, Bass et al. 1987, Bass 1985, Burns 1978)	Moral violence, organisational misbehaviour Weaknesses of superiors and leadersEmotions	Machiavellianism (Rayburn / Rayburn 1996), petty tyrant (Ashforth 1994), moral violence (Diamond / Allcorn 2004, Bate 1984) Sociological theory of emotions (Lazarus 1991, Hochschild 1983, Kemper 1978a)
	Superiority of superiors, awe of the leader Tasks and responsibilities of subordinates Inferiority and needs of the subordinates Dangers of followers	Conservative ideologies of and for subordinates (Coutu 2005, Offerman 2005, Blau 1964, Prentice 1961)	Well-functioning, obedience of subordinates, conditioning, identity-regulation, infantilisation, learned helplessness, deformation	Social Dominance Theory (Sidanius et al. 2004, Sidanius / Pratto 1999), system justification theory (Jost / Hunyady 2005), social identity theory (Ashforth / Mael 1989) Concept of obedience (Milgram 1963, 1974)
d) Moral justification	Merit-based system	Transformational and transactional leadership theories (Van Vugt 2006, Zaleznik 1989, Bass et al. 1987, Bass 1985, Burns 1978) Conservative ideologies of and for subordinates (Coutu 2005, Offerman 2005, Blau 1964, Prentice 1961)	Unfair and unjust system	Social differentiation, stratification, discrimination (Bourdieu 1979, Mousnier 1973, Laumann et al. 1971, Moore 1971, Mills 1956, Davis / Moore 1945, Mosca 1971/1939)

Appendix 2
Approaches and Theories Relevant for Hierarchical Social Systems

Approach / theory	Main contributors	Main focus and strengths of the approach	Main limits and weaknesses of the approach
a) Conservative / system-justifying concepts:			
Sociobiology	*Wilson 1975*	Theories in the tradition of *sociobiologism* provide good explanations for unreflective behaviour of living organisms, animals and humans. Such theories can contribute to explain individual and group behaviour which is driven by genes / biological programmes, instincts, strong emotions, extreme or irrational forces (for example totalitarian leaders and followers, mass hysteria, immoral behaviour in unusual or extreme situations).	The socio-biological approach cannot cope with issues and situations which are not pre-determined, i.e. where people have choice, are able to reflect on their actions, are able to make up their mind and to make decisions based on a (more or less conscious) assessment of the situation and possible consequences. It also fails where societal values and institutions are involved (e.g. ethics, morale, law, rules). If such factors play a role, but are not specified and ignored, the socio-biological approach descends into *social Darwinism*, i.e. becomes ideological.

(Continued)

Approach / theory	Main contributors	Main focus and strengths of the approach	Main limits and weaknesses of the approach
Leadership theories on transformational and transactional leadership style	*Van Vugt 2006, Masi / Cooke 2000, Jaques 1990, Bass et al. 1987, Burns 1978*	*Transactional leadership style theories* focus more on the actual interaction of and between leaders and followers and, hence, can provide quite some analysis of such relationships and the views of both parties involved. In contrast, *transformational leadership style theory* focuses more on attributes and behaviour leaders allegedly have (e.g. charisma) or demonstrate (e.g. vision, leadership, motivation).	There is *some* informative analysis of leadership styles. However, leadership research is dominated by normative and judgemental transformational leadership style concepts. They provide largely naive and unreal images of leaders (e.g. the awe of the leader) and equally biased images of followers. Most leadership theories are of little scientific value and pure ideology.
Functionalism / orthodox management and organisation theories	*Chandler 1962, Drucker 1954, Fayol 1949, Taylor 1911/1967*	Functionalistic approaches describe and analyse the technical aspects of hierarchical relationships comprehensively and in great detail. For example, they dominate the area of management and organisation studies. They provide a range of ideas under which conditions unequal social relationships like organisations work in what ways, how to keep them functioning, how to manage them and how to make them more efficient.	Functional approaches take hierarchy as a given and do not question social and socio-productive relationships. More problematically, they (try to) justify leadership as well as managers and leaders prerogatives and privileged positions on ideological grounds. Orthodox management theory concentrates largely on (the importance of) superiors and involves subordinates only in their (mal-) functioning.

New institutional economics (NIE), principal-agent theory (agency theory)	*North 1991, Williamson 1975, Alchian / Demsetz 1972, Coase 1937*	NIE focuses on the efficiency of different mechanisms of coordination of human actions (e.g. market, hierarchy, or networks). It raises the awareness of (lower) transaction-costs and other advantages organisations can provide. It also draws attention to the problems of trust, collaboration, and control between principals and agents.	The theory is based on very strict (game-theoretical), unrealistic assumptions (e.g. rational behaviour, Pareto-optimum). In this sense it is of very limited use. Moreover, negative images of humans, such as opportunism, are assumed to be only on the side of agent(s). All recommendations are seen from, and meant to be for the principal, i.e. NIE is partisan and socially biased.

b) Critical, political, moral-philosophical concepts:

Social conflict, Labour Process Theory (LPT), Industrial Relations (IR)	*Friedman 1977, Braverman 1974*	In the tradition of Marxist theory, LPT and IR draw attention to fundamental inconsistencies and problems of capitalist production and other forms of unequal (and exploitative) social order and organisations.	The concepts of class, societal stratification, and struggles between large groups (e.g. capitalists and workers, managers and employees) can address only a few specific aspects of modern, differentiated, individualism- and hedonism-oriented societies. Its psychological foundations are extremely limited, if not to say misleading (e.g. the dominant assumption of a false consciousness of subordinates).
Organisational politics	*Coben et al. 1999, Mintzberg 1985, Burns 1961, Thompson 1961*	Seeing organisations as political arena and contested terrain created a whole range of opportunities to identify struggles not only between classes but between individuals and groups (also) at the same level (e.g. clashes of cosmologies in the boardroom, concerning strategic decision-making and/or change initiatives). Although with a critical impetus, this view (can) contribute(s) also to a better understanding and management of organisations.	Analysed by this approach, almost all decisions and actions (within organisations) are seen and interpreted as political or at least politically motivated. As a consequence, real technical problems, factual necessities of the organisation of work, peoples whole range of different motivations and problem-oriented reasoning are either not seen or mis-interpreted. Social actions and behaviour are reduced to calculated games, only a few (possible) motives behind human actions are recognised.

(Continued)

Approach / theory	Main contributors	Main focus and strengths of the approach	Main limits and weaknesses of the approach
Critical Management Studies (CMS)	*Diefenbach 2009, Clegg et al. 2006, Brookfield 2005, Courpasson 2000, Willmott 1997, Alvesson / Willmott 1992a, b*	This approach concentrates explicitly on the identification, criticism, and change of (dominant) ideologies, (managerial) power and oppressive social structures. It reveals unequal and unjust social phenomena which otherwise are either being covered-up by ideology or ignored because of lack of reflection.	In its strive for critical rigour CMS can be quite one-sighted and biased (e.g. portraying all institutions as only oppressive and all authority as bad). Moreover, in most parts CMS does not provide (convincing) positive alternatives for what it (rightly or wrongly) criticises. It is therefore largely negative and, hence, does not appeal to many academics and practitioners.
Power and control	*Clegg et al. 2006, Clegg 1979, Lukes 1974*	Power is a much needed concept to interrogate social realities. It is multi-dimensional and can therefore be used for analysing both the direct power and control between superior and subordinate as well as institutionalised power, i.e. the institutions which empower and weaken individuals and groups differently (e.g. via hierarchical positions, access to resources, prerogatives and responsibilities, within discourses and so on).	Quite often, power and control are only seen in their constraining and oppressive functions, implications and consequences. Positive aspects of social power and control systems (e.g. provision of certainty and security, stabilisation of behaviour, enabling people, increased accountability, possibility of a more just appreciation of individual contributions, performance and allocation of resources) are often less scrutinised. In some approaches, power becomes such a dominant explanatory variable that other reasons for human action and societal phenomena are quite neglected.

Ideology	*Beetham 1991, Abercrombie 1980*	Ideology is an important factor in shaping peoples worldviews and, hence, actions, social structures and processes. With the focus on ideology it becomes clear(er) that most social structures and functions (such as values, power, tasks and actions) are legitimated and justified by much more good reasons than it might be initially obvious.	Very often, ideology is seen fairly one-way as superiors rhetoric (dominant ideology), subordinates are largely recognised only by their compliance (and false consciousness). Ideology is somehow there and works somehow through institutions, but the precise mechanisms are not clear. Approaches focusing too much on ideology fall short to capture and to explain the whole complexity of what makes the relationship between superior(s) and subordinate(s) and what keeps it going.

c) Linguistic and constructivist concepts:

Linguistic, discourse, perceptions, sense-making	*Weick 2001, Daft / Weick 1984*	Analysis of perceptions, sense-making, discourses and communication reveal many interesting insights into how social realities (such as hierarchical order) are established and maintained.	Discursive and interpretative approaches often abstract (deliberately) from the reasons behind peoples communicative interaction, the factual conditions and material circumstances of the situation. They can overestimate the discursive and communicative aspects of social phenomena and underestimate the more material, factual or real aspects which can be more relevant for people.
Social constructivism	*Berger / Luckmann 1966*	The insight that (social) reality is socially constructed, perceived and experienced differently enabled new understandings of social reality (realities).	Social constructivism can easily end up in relativism and rejection of facts / factual aspects of reality.

(Continued)

Approach / theory	Main contributors	Main focus and strengths of the approach	Main limits and weaknesses of the approach
d) Anthropological, sociological, socio-psychological and psychological concepts:			
Social stratification, differentiation and discrimination (class, elites, ethnics, race, gender, culture, education)	*Bourdieu 1979, Mousnier 1973, Bourdieu / Passeron 1972, Laumann et al. 1971, Moore 1971, Wrong 1971, Mills 1956, Davis / Moore 1945, Mosca 1971/1939*	Critical sociological approaches of the 1970ies explain phenomena such as social inequality, injustice, oppression and exploitation via concepts of stratification, social differentiation and division of labour quite convincingly.	Such approaches work more at a macro-level in the sense that societal structures and processes as well as social action is largely analysed on the basis of class-concepts. Although they also incorporate *some* psychological aspects they nonetheless comprise little about the relationships and processes between actors and institutions.
New institutional-ism / sociological institutionalism	*Dillard et al. 2004, Ingram / Clay 2000, Barley / Tolbert 1997, Granovetter 1985, DiMaggio / Powell 1983, Meyer / Rowan 1977, Zucker 1977*	Sociological institutionalism explains convincingly how much institutions shape society, societal phenomena and how much they influence individuals and human action. It explains their advantages (e.g. they reduce uncertainty, are resources for human action) and at the same time provides a differentiated picture (e.g. institutions both enable and impede human action, provide choice and constraints).	Sociological institutionalism, talks about institutions in a fairly general sense without explaining how institutions are established, continued, re-invented or changed. Moreover, at least in its early forms, it has played down, if not to say largely neglected the importance of agency and individual choice. Because of this, considerations concerning responsibilities and accountability of actors are largely absent.

Structuration theory	Giddens 1979, 1984	General theory to interrogate how social systems are produced and reproduced by dynamic relationships between structures and human action which is both enabled and constrained by these structures.	Giddens structuration theory is a very general sociological theory and difficult to apply to specific situations or to use for empirical research. It only talks about agency but does not have individuals as explicit elements in its theoretical core. Moreover, it only copes with routine behaviour and therefore cannot explain how humans act and behave, how social systems actually work (or dont work), how and why they might change. It is fundamentally conservative and uncritical.
Social Dominance Theory	Sidanius et al. 2004, Sidanius / Pratto 1999	Social Dominance Theory describes, analyses, and explains quite convincingly how group-based social dominance and oppression works and why and how group-based hierarchies are so widespread and so persistent. It successfully links individual and institutional levels of analysis and is very useful for analysing oppression and (institutional) discrimination.	Social Dominance Theory explains individuals behaviour primarily via their membership of certain social groups and doesnt take other variables into account (e.g. individual identities, interests, values). It is therefore quite limited in its explanatory range. Moreover, it is gender-biased since it sees social oppression primarily as male-dependent phenomenon. Finally, it does not have any ethical or morale dimensions as explicit elements of its theory and therefore cannot say anything about individual responsibility or values.
Organisational identity, social identity theory	Musson / Duberley 2007, Elstak / Van Riel 2005, Alvesson / Willmott 2002, Turner 1999, Ashforth / Mael 1989, Tajfel / Turner 1979	Concepts concerning social identity, self and others categorisations cope with important parts of social phenomena where individuals are involved.	Social identity theory sees individuals and their identities large shaped by psychological aspects and / or social groups. Located at a micro-level, it abstracts largely from macro-phenomena such as societal values or economical conditions. As a primarily psychological / socio-psychological concept it has got problems to include material or factual conditions which shape peoples identities.

(Continued)

Approach / theory	Main contributors	Main focus and strengths of the approach	Main limits and weaknesses of the approach
Open and hidden transcripts	Scott 1990	The concept of open and hidden transcripts allows not only a differentiated analysis of the public relationship between superiors and subordinates, but it particularly reveals many interesting and fruitful insights into the hidden actions and ideologies (mainly of subordinates).	It copes only little with superiors hidden transcripts (e.g. their real agendas, values and beliefs, interests and in-official, secret actions).
Sociological theory of emotions	Lazarus 1991, Hochschild 1983, Kemper 1978a	Emotions are often seen (solely) from psychological or physiological perspectives. A sociological perspective contributes much to our understanding of how emotions emerge and work between individuals and shape their relationships and behaviour.	Emotions are only partly comprehensible via general concepts since they emerge (unintentionally) within individuals, are highly subjective and arbitrarily.
Psychological and psychoanalytical concepts of dominance and obedience, deviance, misbehaviour	Boddy 2006, Vardi / Weitz 2004, Bryant / Cox 2003, Vredenburgh / Brender 1998, Robinson / Bennett 1997, Rayburn / Rayburn 1996, Ashforth 1994, Milgram 1963, 1974	Socio-psychological concepts of (organisational) misbehaviour and deviance provide good insights not only into these phenomena and mechanisms, but also into possible reasons behind such behaviour (e.g. personality traits, social attitudes or ideologies of professionalism).	When it is about deviance or organisational misbehaviour, mostly subordinates are being investigated. Research into superiors misconduct is quite rare. In addition, it is mostly psychological issues and dimensions which are taken into account whereas possible organisational, societal or ethical aspects are considered and interrogated less.

Appendix 3
Definition of 'Interest'

In Chapter 3 'interest' was defined as 'a real person's or group of people's conscious attraction towards a certain object or objective. This can either mean a (noninstrumental) curiosity in something or an (instrumental) desire to achieve something whereby the understanding of the object or the realization of the objective is deemed by the person or group of people as useful or advantageous after due consideration.' This definition and understanding of interest is based on the following assumptions:

1. Only living beings with a consciousness can have interests (in something), i.e., human beings and some higher developed animals.[1] In the context of manmade organisations this means that 'interest' is understood solely as a *people-oriented concept*. In this sense, it is *not* possible to say that an organisation 'has got the interest x,' that an organisation 'has got the interest,' that something is or is not, should or should not be the case. Systems and institutions, structures and processes—whether they are natural like an ecological system or manmade like a business organisation—can neither have nor express any interest. It is always and only particular people who claim that something was 'in the interest' of a particular system.

2. 'After due consideration' means that a person's interest is not an immediate urge or need which occurs in a particular moment (Bresser-Pereira, 2001, p. 365). 'Interest-driven' decision-making means that people think consciously about possible alternatives, their implications, and assumed consequences (Moore / Loewenstein, 2004, p. 190). As Stubbart (1989, p. 330) explained: 'Managers take strategic actions mainly for reasons, neither as a habit nor as a mindless repertoire'. To have an interest in something is a *conscious, thoughtful and reflected decision* for a particular objective, its implications and consequences, and against other alternatives and their implications and consequences.

3. 'Due consideration' relates to the aspect of *rationality*—which probably is one of the most contested issues of Western reasoning and society. The concept supported here is *not* meant in the neoclassical

economics' sense and its model of homo oeconomicus which portray an 'image of human beings as 'rational maximisers' of their own 'self-interest" (du Gay, 2005, p. 391). In contrast to such heroic assumptions, human reasoning and decision-making are meant here differently, in particular:

a) People neither have got all information, are able to cope with all information available, nor is this information consistent and certain. Information is usually incomplete, insufficient, and overwhelming, representing uncertainties and perhaps even contradictions (Hendry, 2005, p. 58). People's judgment of (their) interests happens on the basis of *bounded rationality* (Simon, 1979, p. 502).

b) Rational decision-making cannot be reduced to a mathematical problem. Human reasoning and consideration, though 'calculating,' do not happen only in quantitative or quantifiable terms. Like the concept of value, one's interests can be everything that is deemed from a subjective point of view as to one's benefit— whether it is quantifiable or not; 'to say that a policy, practice, or state of affairs is in the interests of an individual or group is to suggest that the individual or group would somehow benefit from it.' (Hindess, 1986, p. 112). It is an assessment and comparison of quantitative and qualitative aspects whereby final decisions are always a qualitative judgment.

c) In this sense, rationality or rational decision-making should also not be understood as 'optimising.' 'Rational' means 'only' that 'a person's consideration of values and risks adheres to the basic rules of logic' (Meglino / Korsgaard, 2004, p. 946). It is understood as calculative in that sense that human beings try to make rough sense whether a certain decision bears more positive or negative possible outcomes and consequences (Meglino / Korsgaard 2004, p. 948). It is about to find out what is assumingly one's 'best' interest, not to find a mathematical optimum.

4. 'Interest' is meant here in a broad sense including not only self-interest but also interest in others, i.e., egoism and altruism, interests only concerned about one's own advantages and interests based on ethics which refer to higher values, the sake of the whole group or system, epochal or even universal ideas (Darke / Chaiken, 2005, p. 864).

5. It is not differentiated between 'true' and 'false' interests. 'Interest' is understood as a subjective phenomenon, i.e., seen from the person's view, not what theoretical models of society or researchers suggest should be 'real' interests of people.

6. The concept is used here solely as a methodological tool. As Miller (1999, p. 1053) has stated, at least in Western cultures 'the assumption of self-interest is not simply an abstract theoretical concept but

a collectively shared cultural ideology'. It is an *ideology of self-interest* which claims that egoism and greed are now 'one of the highest callings of human existence' (Moore / Loewenstein, 2004, p. 195). It may even function 'as a powerful self-fulfilling force.' (Miller, 1999, p. 1059). In contrast to the ideology of self-interest the concept of interest developed here does neither claim to describe man's nature nor proclaim how humans should reason and act in a certain way. It is meant as a methodological tool, not as a normative agenda.

Appendix 4
Kohlberg's Stages of Moral Development

Stage	Interpretation	Example of individual behaviour
III. Postconventional, autonomous, or principled level		
Stage 6 – The universal-ethical-principle orientation	Right is defined by the decision of conscience in accord with self-chosen ethical principles appealing to logical comprehensiveness, universality, and consistency (e.g., the Golden Rule, the categorical imperative).	Trying to live up to the requests of universal ethical principles (enlightened altruism)
Stage 5 – The social-contract legalistic orientation	Right action is defined in terms of general individual rights and standards which have been critically examined and agreed upon by the whole society. Clear awareness of the relativism of personal values, corresponding emphasis upon procedural rules for reaching consensus.	Trying to see how ones own actions and the organisation relate to society and nature (enlightened utilitarianism)
II. Conventional level		
Stage 4 – The law and order orientation	There is orientation toward authority, fixed rules, and the maintenance of the social order. Right behaviour consists of doing one's duty, showing respect for authority, maintaining the given social order for its own sake.	Trying to become a good citizen in the organisation one works for (social concerns)
Stage 3 – The interpersonal concordance or good boy-nice girl orientation	There is much conformity to stereotypical images of what is majority or natural behaviour.	Trying to behave and function well in every respect (developed social behaviour)

(Continued)

Stage	Interpretation	Example of individual behaviour
I. Preconventional level		
Stage 2 – The instrumental-relativist orientation	Right action consists of that which instrumentally satisfies one's own needs and occasionally the needs of others. Human relations are viewed in terms like those of the marketplace.	Trying to make a career by (almost) every means (calculative selfishness)
Stage 1 – The punishment-and-obedience orientation	Avoidance of punishment and unquestioning deference to power are valued in their own right, not in terms of respect for an underlying moral order supported by punishment and authority.	Mere functioning at the workplace because of fear (power-and-control orientation)

Appendix 5
Main Theorems of the General Theory of Hierarchical Social Systems

A) THE CORE STRUCTURE OF HIERARCHICAL SOCIAL RELATIONSHIPS

1. In the social realm, hierarchy represents *social* relationships based on the principle of *inequality*—i.e., rights and duties are allocated deliberately unequally.
2. At its core, any hierarchical social order is defined by *dynamic hierarchical relationships between at least two specific or constructed actors*—'superior(s)' and 'subordinate(s)'—who inherit different social positions of superiority and inferiority.
3. The superior-subordinate relationship is a *relational* construct—i.e., within complex hierarchical systems all actors are either superior or subordinate to at least one other actor, depending on the actual situation.
4. The superior-subordinate relationship is defined primarily by a *power differential* through which the former can impose his/her will on the latter directly or indirectly, even against opposition.
5. Hierarchy can be a *formal order* of unequal person-independent roles and positions which are related to each other via direct lines of top-down command and control within an explicitly defined organisational structure.
6. Hierarchy can be an *informal order* of unequal person-dependent social relationships of dominance and subordination that emerge from social interaction and may become persistent over time through repeated social processes (e.g., communication and routine behaviour).

B) PEOPLE'S MINDSETS AND SOCIAL ACTIONS

7. Hierarchy is first and foremost in people's *minds*.
8. Superiors and subordinates have *specific mindsets* that can be differentiated analytically into identities, interests, emotions, and moral character.

9. Superiors' and subordinates' identities, interests, emotions, and moral character are shaped by their different roles and positions within the hierarchical social order.

10. Superiors' and subordinates' mindsets shape their social actions.

11. Within any social system, individuals always enjoy a certain degree of *individual freedom,* (are able to) reflect on their actions and the situation they are in (*reflexivity*) and, thus, carry *individual responsibility* for how they think and act.

C) BASIC DYNAMIC PROCESSES

12. Most of superiors' and subordinates' *routine behaviour* is about applying the prevailing principle of hierarchical systems—i.e., about carrying out their primary and related tasks to dominate and to obey, respectively.

13. Superiors' and subordinates' *deviating* mindsets and social actions (*boundary crossings* between hidden to public transcripts) are a normal part of any hierarchical social order.

14. Negative boundary crossings can lead to *dynamic multiple processes* and an *escalation of conflict* that increasingly threatens the stability and continuation of the system of hierarchical social order and, more crucially, the role and position of the superior(s).

15. Because of expectations that routine behaviour will continue even when people are replaced, the direct hierarchical social relationship between superiors and subordinates changes into *abstract organisational order* and their ways of thinking and acting come to represent general and anonymous characteristics of 'the' superior and 'the' subordinate.

16. Abstract organisational order is the extension and institutionalisation of superiors' direct power by other means.

17. Via abstract organisational order existing forms of deviant behaviour and multiple processes of boundary crossings are defined, organised, and managed—and new ones created.

18. Any system of hierarchical social order *will expand over time—i.e.,* will become more comprehensive and thorough because of the introduction of abstract organisational order and the processes it triggers.

19. The institutionalisation of the direct hierarchical, unequal, and unjust relationship between superiors and subordinates as abstract organisational order means the disguised institutionalisation of superiors' individual and group interests.

20. With the introduction of abstract organisational order, subordinates' individual freedom and responsibility *decrease* but their individual accountability *increases*.

21. With the introduction of abstract organisational order, superiors' individual freedom and responsibility *increase* whereas their individual accountability *decreases*.

D) SOCIETAL DIMENSIONS OF HIERARCHICAL SOCIAL ORDER

22. Any societal institution or resource positively related to the principle of hierarchical social order privileges superiors and disadvantages subordinates systematically.
23. The higher ranked people are within a hierarchical system, the greater is their possession of and access to institutions and resources that enable them to pursue what is portrayed in that cultural context as a 'good' and/or 'successful' life.
24. The lower ranked people are within a hierarchical system, the more they are excluded from institutions and resources that enable a 'good' and/or 'successful' life.
25. In developed stratified societies, societal institutions and resources complement each other towards one comprehensive and systemic framework enabling and supporting any system of hierarchical social order.

E) SYSTEMISATION AND ITS MAIN MECHANISMS

26. Via formal and informal processes, people are *socialised,* or conditioned, by various existing hierarchical institutions and their members—i.e., they are made increasingly able and willing to fit into established hierarchical structures and processes, to fit into *any* kind of hierarchical social system.
27. Appropriately socialised people are keen to *adapt* actively to a hierarchically structured environment and to function smoothly, in order to avoid or to reduce the negative consequences for themselves and to enjoy (even increase) the factual advantages the hierarchical system offers in absolute and relative terms.
28. People are keen to *synchronise* their reasoning, behaviour, decisions, and actions with others' reasoning, behaviour, decisions, and actions so that routine work and life within the hierarchical system run smoothly.
29. People's synchronised routine behaviour and mindsets, and even much of their deviant behaviour, are *institutionalised* as abstract organisational order, which, in return, provides policies and procedures to cope with any type of behaviour and to make it compatible with the system.
30. Abstract organisational order feeds back into people's mindsets and social actions: formal hierarchical organisation is *transformed* into

informal hierarchical organisation and even applied in areas outside the existing (formal) hierarchical structures and processes.

31. People *always* have some scope of individual freedom that they use for *navigating* their way through institutions and social relationships.

32. *Systemisation and its mechanisms* make up a multidimensional and interactive process that links hierarchical institutions and individuals, ensures that people function within any kind of hierarchical system and, in doing so, guarantees the persistence and continuation of hierarchical social order.

F) PERSISTENCE OF HIERARCHICAL SOCIAL ORDER

33. Hierarchical social order persists because it represents a comprehensive, consistent, multidimensional, and differentiated 'social cosmos' of various elements (superiors and subordinates, social roles and positions, mindsets and social actions, abstract organisational order, institutions and resources) that interact with each other via various mechanisms of systemisation (socialisation, adaptation, synchronisation, institutionalisation, transformation, and navigation).

Notes

NOTES TO CHAPTER 1

1. As indicated, hierarchy is described here as an almost eternal beast, which means that there can be (and indeed have been) alternatives—i.e. non-hierarchical social systems. My next book will focus on such positive alternatives, especially on the fundamental theoretical principles of non-hierarchical forms of organisations as well as the theoretical and practical problems those forms of organisation face.

2. This paraphrase represents the gist of one of Nietzsche's most powerful thoughts, his idea of the eternal recurrence of things. This idea can be found at several places in his works, in particular in §§285, 341 of his 'Die fröhliche Wissenschaft' (1990, pp. 511, 555–556).

3. Since the aim of this book is to develop a general theory, historical examples and specific findings will only be provided in order to support the argument. Otherwise, the argument will be largely abstracted from (possible differences in), for example, race, culture, age, or gender. These factors may become relevant when it is about a specific application of the theory developed here or for comparative analysis.

4. This may suggest Giddens' (1984, 1976) structuration theory. However, in Chapter 3 it should become clear that the theory developed here is more general and differentiated. Moreover, the shortcomings of Giddens' theory will be discussed specifically in Section 3.9.

5. See also Appendix 2.

NOTES TO CHAPTER 2

1. Throughout the book, there are several terms used relating to hierarchy; mainly, 'hierarchical social relationship', 'hierarchical social order' and 'hierarchical social system'. The terms may differ slightly in focus (e.g. on the relationships between people, the overarching order, or the structures and processes of hierarchy). Nonetheless, they are largely synonymous and compatible with the general term 'hierarchy' as it is understood here—i.e. as a long-standing constellation of people in which social positions are differentiated vertically and people are put into superior–subordinate relationships.

2. When analysing these societies, it therefore might be more appropriate to use Weber's concept of social order (1980, pp. 177, 531), which utilises the concept of 'clusters' (instead of 'class' in a Marxian sense). Weber groups people whose life chances share the same specific causal components (particularly

with regard to socio-economic conditions) and whose positions in society are similar because of their occupations and their possession of similar resources to advance their ends (Diefenbach 2009a, p. 183).

3. This argument follows Karl Popper's 'principle of falsification'—i.e. that the sighting of only one black swan is enough to prove wrong the proposition that all swans are white.

4. For example, in countries that are strongly influenced by a religious system (such as Buddhism, Christianity, Hinduism, Islam, Judaism or Sikhism), one can see that the legal system, the laws, the economy and even businesses are quite permeated with religious doctrines (e.g. 'Islamic banking' or 'Christian management'). Hierarchy and hierarchical social relationships are then also justified and maintained mainly based on religious doctrines. But it would go beyond the focus of this book to discuss how theories, institutions and daily life are influenced by religious beliefs and motives.

5. This argument can be expanded further in reference to attempts to change the hierarchical organisation of a given social order and/or to try to establish new forms of organising; they may be said to be doomed to fail from the outset because they go against 'the natural order of things'.

6. According to the theory of isomorphism, an organisation blends in with its external environment in more efficient ways if it adheres to those institutions that appreciate hierarchical structures and processes. In such cases, these stakeholders provide the organisation with additional legitimacy and, often, important resources the organisation (Suddaby and Greenwood 2005; Coopey and Burgoyne 2000; Ingram and Clay 2000; Staw and Epstein 2000; DiMaggio and Powell 1983; Meyer and Rowan 1977). And, since in most societies hierarchy is one of the prime values, it makes sense to structure social systems such as organisations or groups accordingly—i.e. hierarchically.

7. Courpasson and Clegg (2006, p. 329) summarised this fundamental inconsistency: 'Democracy encourages pervasive feelings of equality shared by every member of the society. In the political sphere, these are institutionalized in periodic elections, where we get to choose which members of the political elite will rule over us. In organizations in general, however, we have no such choice. We are, in law, masters or servants—the very categories that democracy was supposed to abolish.'

8. And if it cannot do so any more it will be replaced by other structures and mechanisms. For example, where their wealth, property and money are concerned, the rich and powerful do not want efficient hierarchical order and control or transparent rules and regulations but rather 'chaos'—i.e. insufficient order and control, and unclear rules and regulations with as many loopholes as possible.

9. Some further examples: Erich Fromm (1965, p. 233): 'Why is it that a society succeeds in gaining the allegiance of most of its members, even when they suffer under the system and even if their reason tells them that their allegiance is harmful to them?' De Schweinitz (1979, p. 838): 'Why [. . .] do people not rebel more often against the injustices of life which are so manifest in the way societies establish state authority, organize the division of labor, and distribute goods and services?' Scott (1990, p. 71): 'Why [. . .] does a subordinate class seem to accept or at least to consent to an economic system that is manifestly against its interests when it is not obliged to by the direct application of coercion or the fear of its application? [. . .] Why, in other words, do people seem to knuckle under when they appear to have other options?' Protherough and Pick (2002, p. 41): 'Why do so many people lower down the pecking order, and in so many different realms, choose to behave as if there is no plausible alternative to being a state-managed

zombie?' Stoddart (2007, p. 191): 'For over a century, social theorists have attempted to explain why those who lack economic power consent to hierarchies of social and political power.'

10. Such socio-psychological explanations come particularly from approaches such as social dominance theory (Sidanius et al. 2004; Sidanius and Pratto 1999), system justification theory (Jost and Hunyady 2005) and social identity theory (Musson and Duberley 2007; Elstak and Van Riel 2005; Ashforth and Mael 1989; Tajfel and Turner 1979).

11. 'In German: 'Ruhe ist die erste Bürgerpflicht'. This is the title of a book written in 1852 by Willibald Alexis, a German Romantic writer. In using this title, Alexis was referring to a slogan promoted by the Prussian government in 1806 after the lost battle against Napoleon near Jena-Auerstedt.

12. This privileging of individuals and groups for the sole reason that they are higher up the hierarchical ladder cannot be called 'just' and 'fair'—unless fairness and justice are understood as 'those who are able to get more shall get more'.

13. Appendix 1 provides an overview of the approaches and main arguments put forward.

NOTES TO CHAPTER 3

1. In this book the focus is largely on individual actors (e.g., 'the' manager and 'the' employee) or groups of people (e.g., power elites and the masses), and not so much on hierarchical relationships between larger aggregates such as whole countries (e.g., 'developed' and 'developing' countries).

2. For example, Rosen (1984, p. 305) stressed that 'the very concepts of "manager" and "management" are social artifacts reflecting the social relations, or power order, in our society, based on hierarchical segmentation and value appropriation.'

3. This proposition leaves open the possibility that within complex hierarchical systems some actors might not be superior or subordinate to some others— i.e., they might see and treat others as equals.

4. Of course, a whole range of situational and institutional factors also influence human decision-making and behaviour—and we will include the most important and relevant ones step by step into the model and theory.

5. Interest might also be called 'urge,' 'desire,' 'appetite,' 'craving,' 'lust,' and so on. Appendix 3 provides a comprehensive and detailed definition of the term 'interest.'

6. I avoid here the terminology of 'rational' and 'irrational' that is usually employed to differentiate between interests and emotions since this might imply value judgements (i.e., 'rational' is good, 'irrational' is bad) that are not justified and are quite misleading.

7. For an overview of Kohlberg's six stages, see Appendix 4. Kohlberg's theory and taxonomy of moral development has not been without criticism. There are three main criticisms that have been put forward against his theory. 1) 'Rational actor' paradigm: the (implicit) assumption that individuals make ethical decisions in accordance with their intentions (or interests) and act accordingly under full knowledge of the implications and consequences of their actions has been criticised as unrealistic (e.g., Barraquier 2011; De Cremer et al. 2011; Marnburg 2001). 2) Consistency: situationists (e.g., Barraquier 2011; De Cremer et al. 2011) have also argued that people are not consistent in their moral values and convictions—i.e., that they do not demonstrate a consistent moral character over a range of different situations. 3)

Exclusion of emotions: it is a weakness or incompleteness of Kohlberg's model that it does entail intuition or emotions, which influence people's behaviour to quite some extent, as explicit elements (Barraquier 2011, p. S31).

One can agree with the criticism. Kohlberg's theory could be interpreted and used as a fully fledged rationalist approach towards moral reasoning and acting similar to the 'homo oeconomicus' model about human reasoning and acting in general. In that case, it would be, indeed, a rather poor and misleading approach. But this is not the way it is employed here. One can simply use Kohlberg's taxonomy as a heuristic device in order to understand and to analyse differences in people's moral behaviour that occur in a particular situation or with regard to a specific issue—without assuming that people make their decisions rationally and always act accordingly. In addition, with the explicit inclusion of 'emotions' in the theory put forward here, Kohlberg's taxonomy is completed in that respect.

8. At an individual level, exceptions are insanity, other mental disorders, and situation-specific factors that fully or considerably reduce people's ability to make free and conscious decisions—e.g., strong influence of drugs, physical or psychological pressure, or other reasons that are regularly acknowledged in a developed legal system as seriously limiting a person's free will.

9. These boundary crossings will be investigated comprehensively and in much more detail in Chapter 4. It will be analysed what consequences subordinates' and superiors' weak, medium, or strong boundary crossings within the areas of social action, interests, emotions, identity, and moral character can have for the system of hierarchical social order. The analysis will reveal the specific conditions and mechanisms under which subordinates' or superiors' deviance either strengthens or threatens the system of hierarchical order and its future existence. Further, in Chapter 5 a historical example will be reconstructed and used to show that phenomena of boundary crossing often have implications beyond their original area.

10. 'Institution' means every longlasting social phenomenon that carries shared meanings for members of a social system and, in so doing, influences their reasoning and behaviour. 'Resource' is meant more as a tangible or intangible asset which can be of further usage. In the following, mostly the term 'institution' will be used in order to stress the social dimension more than the practical usefulness of the particular issue in question. However, both meanings overlap and any possible difference or differentiation between 'institution' and 'resource' (as stressed by approaches such as institutionalism or resource-based view) is not important for the argument put forward here.

11. For the issues addressed here it is not really necessary to discuss all relevant definitions of norms and values, nor what they have in common and where they differ. However, in summary, norms might be seen as more specific social expectations members of a social system face, such as rules, customs, conventions, or legal regulations. Usually, norms are directly enforced upon individuals by external pressure. In contrast, values are more general moral standards and are enforced indirectly. Although values can also be enforced externally, they depend even more than norms on being internalised by individuals.

12. Or, as Lukes (1974, p. 23) asked rhetorically when he reasoned about the second dimension of power: 'Indeed, is it not the supreme exercise of power to get another or others to have the desires you want them to have—i.e., to secure their compliance by controlling their thoughts and desires?'

13. This will be shown in more detail in Section 4.2.

14. Having said that, some boundary crossings, which also fight processes of their institutionalisation, might challenge an established hierarchical social

order in such ways that they threaten the existence and continuation of the system. Sections 4.4 and 4.5 will systematically investigate when exactly superiors' or subordinates' boundary crossings might threaten hierarchical social order.

15. Section 4.6 provides a systematic analysis of formal and informal hierarchy in various types of organisations.

16. People may achieve changes in the hierarchical system that over time may lead to system change; alternatively, they might leave hierarchical systems altogether and attempt to establish nonhierarchical forms of organisation.

17. In other words, together, the theorems provide the basis (explanans) for explaining why hierarchical social order persists (explanandum) (Hempel and Oppenheim 1948, p.152).

18. As Theorem 22 stated, 'Any societal institution or resource positively related to the principle of hierarchical social order privileges superiors and disadvantages subordinates systematically.'

19. Giddens' well-known figure 'Dimensions of the duality of structure' (first in Giddens 1976, p. 122, then in Giddens 1984, p. 29) shows how system and actors are linked via modalities.

NOTES TO CHAPTER 4

1. It should be reiterated that the analysis carried out here in this chapter remains at a very general level, i.e. usually no specific context or cultural differences are taken into account, at least not systematically. This somewhat weakens the analysis. For example, when subordinates' and superiors' boundary crossings are discussed in Sections 4.4 and 4.5, one would very soon realise that cultural differences play an important role. American or Japanese managers, for example, have very different understandings of why and how they serve, or don't serve, the organisations they work for. Their interests, identities, emotions, and norms and values differ quite considerably. Such, more detailed analysis of routine behaviour and boundary crossings goes beyond the scope of this book and needs to be left for further research.

2. Theorem 19 stated: 'The institutionalisation of the direct hierarchical, unequal and unjust relationship between superiors and subordinates as abstract organisational order means the disguised institutionalisation of superiors' individual and group interests.'

3. In contrast, in Section 6.2.2 the moral behaviour of individual actors in non-hierarchical social systems will be analysed. And Section 6.2.3 will be about some moral aspects of how people and institutions (could) relate to each other in non-hierarchical social systems.

4. For example, as discussed in Section 3.6, systemisation and its mechanisms triggered and provided by hierarchical institutions condition most people quite severely. Throughout their lives, people are socialised to function properly and appropriately within a hierarchical social order; their mindsets are shaped and conditioned in ways that make them function largely according to learned behaviours. Even if they were to have the opportunity to work and collaborate in non-hierarchical and egalitarian ways, most would remain in the loop of roles that confirm to the hierarchical system.

5. And, if it becomes too problematic to work for a particular organisation, most people change jobs—only to work for yet another hierarchical organisation (or set up one on their own). Only a very few attempt to leave hierarchical systems for good.

6. Such an understanding is close to Immanuel Kant's (1993, p. 30) second formulation of his categorical imperative: 'Act in such a way that you treat humanity, whether in your own person or in the person of any other, never merely as a means to an end, but always at the same time as an end.'

7. It is a different story, though, when superiors show tendencies of individualisation or solidarisation, as will be discussed in Section 4.5.3 with regard to superiors' boundary crossing in the realm of identity.

8. For such paternalistic handling of employees' (so-called) dysfunctional emotions, and a lot of practical advice on managing dysfunctional emotions in conservative ways, see, for example, Ostell (1996).

9. With regard to the individual level, it was argued in Section 3.7 that 'Hierarchical social order persists because of the interests, reasoning and acting of people with hierarchy-conforming mindsets and personalities who at least willingly accept, if not actively promote, structures and processes of social inequality, injustice and exploitation.'

10. There are, of course, well-known examples of dictators or ruling elites (e.g. monarchies, oligarchies, communist countries) who have exploited their people to such an extent (often over decades) that there came a moment when the people said 'Enough is enough!' and overthrew the regime. But, and this is crucial, it was subordinates' social action that put an end to these appalling systems, not superiors' social actions in form of exploitation, oppression or decadent lifestyles.

11. Although this does not necessarily mean that a 'better' or 'non-hierarchical' system will replace the old one, as will be explained in more detail in Chapter 6.

12. Whether Michels's quite pessimistic, but nonetheless realistic, conclusion stemming from his very comprehensive and detailed empirical research is indeed a 'law' that is always true will be discussed in Chapter 6.

NOTES TO CHAPTER 5

1. The precise, official allegations read as follows (Colaiaco 2001, p. 15, referring to the biography of Socrates by Diogenes Laertius; similarly Waterfield 2009b, p. 27): 'This indictment and affidavit is sworn by Meletus [. . .] against Socrates: Socrates is guilty of refusing to recognize the gods recognized by the state, and of introducing other new deities. He is also guilty of corrupting the youth. The penalty demanded is death.'

2. Colaiaco (2001, p. 27) described this puzzle in more detail: 'For years [Socrates] had fulfilled what he regarded as a God-given mission to stimulate his fellow Athenians to abandon their lives of unawareness and pursue wisdom and virtue. Now he was under indictment, charged with undermining the city's fundamental values. But the identity of Socrates was not the only issue. Indeed, his speech would raise the question of the identity of Athens, represented by the prosecution, the jury, and the multitude of spectators.'

3. Colaiaco (2001, p. 58) has explained in some detail the sublime nuances of the story: 'According to Socrates, the Pythian priestess responded to Chaerephon: "No one is wiser" than Socrates! Upon first hearing the oracle's reply, Socrates relates, he was utterly baffled: "What can the god mean? And what is the interpretation of this riddle? For I know that I have no wisdom, small or great." But he proceeds to rephrase the oracle's claim in superlative terms: "What then can he mean when he says that I am the wisest of men?" Socrates extends the oracle's relatively modest characterization of him from "no one is wiser" to "I am the wisest." The oracle may have merely meant that other people were equally as wise as Socrates, but that "no one is wiser."

Yet Socrates applies the most honorific interpretation to the oracle's words, apparently attributing to himself a wisdom superior to all.'

4. Nonetheless, in Section 5.4 it will be argued that some aspects of what he said or questioned constituted, indeed, a very serious challenge to the whole social system of Athens.

5. The relationship between individualisation and solidarisation, and heresy and deviance was discussed in Section 4.4.5 with regard to subordinates' boundary crossing in the realm of moral character.

6. Colaiaco (2001, p. 159) explained this in detail: 'Every society necessarily depends for its survival upon adherence to fundamental values—religious, moral, and political—inculcated through the family, education, and various institutions. While, in many instances, those who threaten the established system are in fact guilty of wanton disregard for order, history provides numerous examples of individuals who were ahead of their times morally and intellectually, who perceived truths that were beyond the comprehension of the average person. These exceptional, individual trailblazers often act in response to some intuitive "voice" in direct violation of the "conscience" of society. As Erich Neumann [1990, pp. 39, 67] explains: "The revolutionary (whatever his type) always takes his stand on the side of the inner voice and against the conscience of his time, which is always an expression of the old dominant values; and the execution of these revolutionaries is always carried out for good and 'ethical' reasons. . . . The revelation of the Voice to a single person presupposes an individual whose individuality is so strong that he can make himself independent of the collective and its values. All founders of ethics are heretics, since they oppose the revelation of the Voice to the deliverances of conscience as the representative of the old ethic."'

7. Colaiaco (2001, p. 172) portrayed Socrates as an even more complex personality and historical figure: 'There is Socrates the bad citizen, the unpolitical man who, by shunning partisan public politics, accentuates his difference from his fellow citizens, setting himself apart from the community; Socrates the critic of conventional rhetoric, who flouts accepted law court discourse; Socrates the provocative iconoclast, the threat to established beliefs and values; Socrates the arrogant self-righteous accuser of Athens, a man without the traditional sense of shame; Socrates, who wears the mask of ignorance, who ridicules the pretence of those who profess wisdom; Socrates the reformer, who claims a personal relation to God, bestowing a divine mission upon himself to sting the conscience of the Athenians; Socrates the obedient servant of Apollo; Socrates the hero, the new Achilles and Heracles; Socrates the gadfly, the moral interrogator and intellectual midwife; Socrates the man of conscience and the advocate of a new rhetoric of truth; Socrates the husband and father, the impoverished elderly citizen, the patriotic defender of Athens in time of war, at once the defender of the constitution and the defiant civil disobedient. From these various images, the jury had to construct the identity of the defendant as they reflected on how to cast their ballots.'

8. Andersson and Pearson (1999, p. 462) explained the idea of a 'tipping point' quite compellingly: 'When at least one of the parties involved in an exchange of incivilities perceives an identity threat, the tipping point is reached, prompting a more intense behavioural response by the threatened party [. . .] so that it escapes the confines of incivility (in which the goal of inflicting harm on the target remains ambiguous) and crosses into the realm of coercive action (in which the goal of inflicting harm to the target becomes obvious). This is the point at which an incivility spiral becomes a deviation-amplifying spiral—an exchange of increasingly counterproductive behaviours—each with the obvious intent to harm the other party.'

9. As indicated by the terms demos, which means 'people', and kratia, which means 'to rule'.

NOTES TO CHAPTER 6

1. From 2010 to 2011 I lived and worked in Cairo, Egypt, and thus experienced the Egyptian revolution at first hand. In crucial moments it was the physical, very heroic actions in Tahrir Square of thousands of simple men and women like you and me that brought about an end to the old Mubarak regime. But the driving forces behind these actions, behind the whole revolution were feelings: strong anger at a regime that did not give people a chance to live a dignified life.
2. In his book The Gulag Archipelago, Alexandr Solzhenitsyn provided a shocking personal account of his years of imprisonment in the system of concentration camps that was set up mainly in Siberia to 'cope' with all sorts of 'enemies of the state'.
3. Obviously, this example refers to parts of the ideological foundations of the United States ('pursuit of happiness' as a key aspect in the US Declaration of Independence) as well as the ideological model of the perfect market (utility maximisation of rational actors lead to an optimal overall outcome).
4. To be clear: this is not to say that causes and explanations for micro/macro-link problems can be found only at the individual level. In Section 6.2.3, an argument will be made for causes and possible solutions at the institutional or macro level.
5. Although there are some significant differences between stages 3, 4 and 5, in the interests of keeping the argument simple the three stages will be treated together.
6. That is why in this book hierarchical social order has been called 'the (almost) eternal beast'.

NOTE TO THE APPENDIX

1. It would be a further leading philosophical question whether or where to draw a line within the human race (e.g. if and when an unborn or newborn, a coma patient or a heavily disabled person has got interests) or between humans and other living beings, i.e. where the class of interest-orientedliving being starts and ends (e.g. most higher developed mammals seem to be able to have interests and to develop some form of tactical behaviour to reach their objectives)—or whether it is possible at all to draw a precise line in such grey areas.

References

Abbott, A. (1988): The system of professions—a study of the division of expert labour, London: University of Chicago Press.

———. (1991): The order of professionalization: An empirical analysis, Work and Occupations, 18 (4): 355–84.

Abercrombie, N. / Hill, S. / Turner, B. S. (1980): The dominant ideology thesis. London: Allen and Unwin.

Abrahamson, E. (1996): Management fashion, Academy of Management Review, 21 (1): 254–85.

Abrahamsson, B. (1985): On form and function in organization theory, Organization Studies, 6: 39–53.

Ackroyd, S. / Munzio, D. (2007): The reconstructed professional firm: Explaining change in English legal practices, Organization Studies, 28 (5): 729–47.

Ahuja, M.K. / Carley, K.M. (1999): Network structure in virtual organizations, Organization Science, 10 (6): 741–57.

Akella, D. (2003): A question of power: How does management retain it?, Vikalpa, 28 (3): 45–56.

Alexis. W. (1852): Ruhe ist die erste Bürgerpflicht oder Vor 50 Jahren. Vaterländischer Roman aus der Zeit der Erniedrigung Preußens. Berlin: Barthol.

Allen, J. / James, A.D. / Gamlen, P. (2007): Formal versus informal knowledge networks in R&D: a case study using social network analysis, R&D Management, 37 (3): 179–96.

Alvesson, M. / Kärreman, D. (2001): Odd couple: Making sense of the curious concept of knowledge management, Journal of Management Studies, 38 (7): 995–1018.

Alvesson, M. / Willmott, H. (1992a): Critical theory and management studies: An introduction, in: Alvesson, M. / Willmott, H. (1992): Critical management studies, Sage Publications, London, 1–20.

———. (1992b): On the idea of emancipation in management and organization studies, Academy of Management Review, 17 (3): 432–64.

———. (2002): Identity regulation as organizational control: producing the appropriate individual, Journal of Management Studies, 39 (5): 619–44.

Anderson, G. (2008): Mapping academic resistance in the managerial university, Organization, 15 (2): 251–70.

Andersson, L.M. / Pearson, CM. (1999): Tit for tat? The spiralling effect of incivility in the workplace, Academy of Management Review, 24 (3): 452–71.

Arendt, H. (1968): Between past and future, Harmondsworth, England: Penguin.

Argyris, C. / Schön, D. (1978): Organization learning: A theory of action perspective, Reading, MA: Addison Wesley.

Aronson, E. (2001): Integrating leadership styles and ethical perspectives, Canadian Journal of Administrative Sciences, 18 (4): 244–56.

Ashforth, B. E. (1994): Petty tyranny in organizations. Human Relations, 47: 755–78.

Ashforth, B.E. / Mael, F. (1989): Social identity theory and the organization, The Academy of Management Review, 14 (1): 20–39.

Bachrach, P. / Baratz, M.S. (1970): Power and poverty. Theory and practice, New York: Oxford University Press.

Baker, C. R. (2005): What is the meaning of "the public interest"?: Examining the ideology of the American public accounting profession, Accounting, Auditing & Accountability Journal, 18 (5): 690–703.

Barraquier, A. (2011): Ethical behaviour in practice: Decision outcomes and strategic implications, British Journal of Management, 22: S28-46.

Barker, C. (2006): Ideology, discourse, and moral economy: Consulting the people of North Manchester, Atlantic Journal of Communication, 14 (1–2): 7–27.

Barker, J.R. (1993): Tightening the iron cage: Concertive control in self-managing teams, Administrative Science Quarterly, 38: 408–37.

Barley, S.R. / Tolbert, P.S. (1997): Institutionalization and structuration: Studying the links between action and institution, Organization Studies, 18 (1): 93–117.

Barney, J.B. (1991): Firm resources and sustained competitive advantage, Journal of Management, 17 (1): 99—120.

Barraquier, A. (2011): Ethical behaviour in practice: Decision outcomes and strategic implications, British Journal of Management, 22: S28-S46.

Bass, B.M. / Waldman, D.A. / Avolio, B.J. (1987): Transformational leadership and the falling domino effect, Group and Organization Studies 12: 73–87.

Bassman, E. / London, M. (1993): Abusive managerial behaviour, Leadership & Organization Development Journal, 14 (2): 18–24.

Beetham, D. (1991): The legitimation of power, MacMillan Education Ltd., Houndmills, Basingstoke.

Bennett, R. J. / Robinson, S. L. (2000): Development of a measure of workplace deviance, Journal of Applied Psychology, 85: 349–60.

Berger, J. / Rosenholtz, S. J. / Zelditch, M., Jr. (1980): Status organizing processes, Annual Review of Sociology, 6: 479–508.

Berger, P. / Luckmann, T. (1966): The social construction of reality: A treatise in the sociology of knowledge, New York: Anchor Books.

Biggart, N.W. / Hamilton, G.G. (1984): The power of obedience, Administrative Science Quarterly, 29: 540–9.

Biron, M. (2010): Negative reciprocity and the association between perceived organizational ethical values and organizational deviance, Human Relations, 63 (6): 875–97.

Blanchard, K.C. Jr. (2000): The enemies of Socrates: Piety and sophism in the Socratic drama, The Review of Politics, June: 421–49.

Blau, P.M. (1964): Exchange and power in social life, New York: John Wiley & Sons, Inc.

Boddy, C.R. (2006): The dark side of management decisions: Organisational psychopaths, Management Decision, 44 (10): 1461–75.

Boehm, C. (1993): Egalitarian behavior and reverse dominance hierarchy [and comments and reply], Current Anthropology, 34 (3): 227–54.

Bolchover, D. (2005): The living dead—switched off, zoned out. The shocking truth about office life, Chichester: Capstone.

Bowler, S. / Donovan, T. / Karp, J. A. (2006): Why politicians like electoral institutions: Self-interest, values, or ideology?, Journal of Politics, 68 (2): 434–46.

Boye, M. / Slora, K. (1993): The severity and prevalence of deviant employee activity within supermarkets, Journal of Business and Psychology, 8: 245–53.

Boyer, R. (2005): From shareholder value to CEO power: The paradox of the 1990s, Competition and Change, 9 (1): 7–48.

Braverman, H. (1974): Labor and monopoly capital. The degradation of work in the twentieth century, New York: Monthly Review Press.

Braynion, P. (2004): Power and leadership, Journal of Health Organization and Management, 18 (6): 447–63.

Bresser-Pereira, L.C. (2001): Self-interest and incompetence, Journal of Post Keynesian Economics, 23 (3): 363–73.

Brock, D.M. (2006): The changing professional organization: A review of competing archetypes, International Journal of Management Reviews, 8 (3): 157–74.

Brookfield, S.D. (2005): The power of critical theory for adult learning and teaching, Maidenhead: Open University Press.

Brown, A.D. / Kornberger, M. / Clegg, S.R. / Carter, C. (2010): Invisible walls and silent hierarchies: A case study of power relations in an architecture firm, Human Relations, 63: 525–49.

Brown, J.S. / Duguid, P. (2002): Organizing knowledge, in: Little, S. / Quintas, P. / Ray, T. (2002): Managing knowledge—An essential reader, The Open University / Sage Publications, London 2002: 19–40.

Bryant, M. / Cox, J.W. (2003): The telling of violence: Organizational change and atrocity tales, Journal of Organizational Change Management, 16 (5): 567–83.

Bryant, M. / Higgins, V. (2010): Self-confessed troublemakers: An interactionist view of deviance during organizational change, Human Relations, 63 (2): 249–78.

Burawoy, M. (1981): Terrains of Contest: Factory and state under capitalism and socialism, Socialist Review 11: 83–124.

———. (1985): The politics of production, London: Verso Press.

Burnham, J. (1941): The managerial revolution, New York: The John Day Company.

Burns, J.M. (1978): Leadership. New York: Harper & Row.

Burns, T. (1961): Micropolitics: Mechanisms of institutional change, Administrative Science Quarterly, 6 (3): 257–281.

Burrell, G. (2002) Twentieth-century quadrilles—aristocracy, owners, managers, and professionals, International Studies of Management & Organisations, 32 (2): 25–50.

Byrkjeflot, H. / du Gay, P. (2012): Bureaucracy: an idea whose time has come (again)?, in: Diefenbach, T. / By, R.T. (2012): Reinventing bureaucracy and hierarchy: from the bureau to network organisations, Research in the Sociology of Organizations, Volume 35, pp. 85–109.

Carson, P. P. et al. (1999): A historical perspective on fad adoption and abandonment, Journal of Management History, 5 (6): 320–33.

Cartledge, P. (2011): Socrates on trial—yet again: 1–5, downloaded 12/03/2012 from http://ancientgreeksmodernlives.org/resources/info-for-venues/.

Casey, C. (1999): "Come, join our family": Discipline and integration in corporate organizational culture, Human Relations, 52 (1): 155–76.

Chandler, A.D. (1962): Strategy and structure: Chapters in the history of the industrial enterprise, Cambridge, MA: MIT Press.

Cheney, G. (1995): Democracy in the workplace: Theory and practice from the perspective of communication, Journal of Applied Communication Research, 23: 167–200.

Chiapello, E. / Fairclough, N. (2002): Understanding the new management ideology: a transdisciplinary contribution from critical discourse analysis and new sociology of capitalism, Discourse & Society, 13 (2): 185–208.

Child, J. (1972): Organizational structure, environment and performance: The role of strategic choice, Sociology, 6 (1): 1–22.

CICOPA (2004): World declaration on worker cooperatives, 'International Organisation of Industrial, Artisanal and Service Producers' Cooperatives', Brussels.

Clarke, T. / Clegg, S. R. (2000): Management paradigms for the new millennium, International Journal of Management Reviews, 2 (1): 45–64.

Clegg, C. / Walsh, S. (2004): Change management: Time for a change!, European Journal of Work and Organizational Psychology, 13 (2): 217–39.

Clegg, S.R. (1979): The theory of power and organization, London and Boston: Routledge and Kegan Paul.

Clegg, S.R. (1994): Power relations and the constitution of the resistant subject, in: Jermier, J. / Knights, D. / Nord, W.R. (eds.). (1994). Resistance and power in organizations: agency, subjectivity and the labor process. London: Routledge: 274–325.

Clegg, S.R. (2012): The end of bureaucracy?, in: Diefenbach, T. / By, R.T. (2012): Reinventing bureaucracy and hierarchy: from the bureau to network organisations, Research in the Sociology of Organizations, Volume 35, pp. 59–84.

Clegg, S.R. / Courpasson, D. / Phillips, N. (2006): Power and organizations, London: Sage Publications.

Cohen, L. / Duberley, J. / McAuley, J. (1999): Fuelling discovery of monitoring productivity: Research scientists' changing perceptions of management, Organization, 6 (3): 473–98.

Colaiaco, J.A. (2001): Socrates against Athens, London: Routledge.

Collins, D. (1997): The ethical superiority and inevitability of participatory management as an organizational system, Organization Science, 8 (5): 489–507.

Collinson, D. (1994): Strategies of resistance. Power, knowledge and subjectivity in the workplace, in: Jermier, J., & Knights, D., & Nord, W.R. (eds.). (1994). Resistance and power in organizations: agency, subjectivity and the labor process. London: Routledge: 25–68.

Collinson, D.L. (2003): Identities and insecurities: Selves at work, Organization, 10 (3): 527–47.

Contractor, N.S. / Wasserman, S. / Faust, K. (2006): Testing multitheoretical, multilevel hypotheses about organizational networks: An analytic framework and empirical example, Academy of Management Review, 31 (3): 681–703.

Coopey, J. / Burgoyne, J. (2000): Politics and organisational learning, Journal of Management Studies, 37 (6): 869–85.

Cotton / Vollrath, D.A. / Froggatt, K. L. / Lengnick-Hali, M, L. / Jennings, K. R, (1988): Employee participation: Diverse forms and different outcomes, Academy of Management Review, 13: 8–22.

Courpasson, D. (2000): Managerial strategies of domination: Power in soft bureaucracies, Organization Studies, 21 (1): 141–61.

Courpasson, D. / Clegg, S.R. (2006): Dissolving the iron cages? Tocqueville, Michels, bureaucracy and the perpetuation of elite power, Organization, 13 (3): 319–43.

Courpasson, D. / Dany, F. (2003): Indifference or obedience? Business firms as democratic hybrids, Organization Studies, 24 (8): 1231–60.

Coutu, D.L. (2005): Putting leaders on the couch: A conversation with Manfred F.R. Kets de Vries, in: Harvard Business Review on the mind of the leader, Boston, MA: Harvard Business School Publishing Corporation, 53–71.

Crain, W.C. (1985): Theories of development, Englewood Cliffs, NJ: Prentice-Hall.

Crozier, M. (1964): The bureaucratic phenomenon, Chicago: The University of Chicago Press.

Currie, G. / Procter, S.J. (2005): The antecedents of middle managers' strategic contribution: The case of a professional bureaucracy, Journal of Management Studies, 42 (7): 1325–56.

Cyert, R.M. / March, J.G. (1963): A behavioral theory of the firm, Englewood Cliffs, NJ: Prentice-Hall.

Dahrendorf, R. (1971): On the origin of inequality among men, first published 1968, in: Laumann, E.O. / Siegel, P.M. / Hodge, R.W. (eds.) (1971): The logic of social hierarchies, Chicago: Markham Publishing Company, 3–30.

Daloz, J.P. (2007): Elite distinction: Grand theory and comparative perspectives, Comparative Sociology, 6 (1/2): 27–74.

Darke, P.R. / Chaiken, S. (2005): The pursuit of self-interest: Self-interest bias in attitude judgment and persuasion, Journal of Personality and Social Psychology, 89 (6): 864–83.

Davis, K. / Moore, W.E. (1971): Some principles of stratification, first published 1945, in: Laumann, E.O. / Siegel, P.M. / Hodge, R.W. (eds.) (1971): The logic of social hierarchies, Chicago: Markham Publishing Company, 124–31.

De Cremer, D. / van Dick, R. / Tenbrunsel, A. / Pillutla, M. / Murnighan, J.K. (2011): Understanding ethical behavior and decision making in management: A behavioural business ethics approach, British Journal of Management, 22: S1-S4.

de Jong, G. / van Witteloostuijin, A. (2004): Successful corporate democracy: Sustainable cooperation of capital and labor in the Dutch Breman Group, Academy of Management Executive, 18 (3): 54–66.

de Schweinitz, K. (1979): Injustice: The social bases of obedience and revolt, by Barrington Moore, Jr., book review in: Journal of Economic Issues, 13 (3): 837–41.

Deem, R. / Brehony, K. J. (2005): Management as ideology: The case of new managerialism in higher education, Oxford Review of Education, 31 (2): 217–35.

Dent, M. / Chandler, J. / Barry, J. (ed.) (2004): Questioning the new public management, Ashgate, Aldershot 2004.

Dequech, D. (2006): Institutions and norms in institutional economics and sociology, Journal of Economic Issues, 40 (2): 473–81.

Diamond, M.A. / Allcorn, S. (2004): Moral violence in organizations: Hierarchic dominance and the absence of potential space, Organisational & Social Dynamics, 4 (1): 22–45.

Diefenbach, T. (2005): Competing strategic perspectives and sense-making of senior managers in academia, International Journal of Knowledge, Culture and Change Management, 5 (6): 126–37.

———. (2006): Intangible resources: a categorial system of knowledge and other intangible assets, Journal of Intellectual Capital, 7 (3): 406–20.

———. (2007): The managerialistic ideology of organisational change management, Journal of Organisational Change Management, 20 (1): 126–44.

———. (2009a): Management and the dominance of managers, London: Routledge.

———. (2009b): New public management in public sector organisations—the dark sides of managerialistic 'enlightenment', Public Administration, 87 (4): 892–909.

———. (2009c): Are case studies more than sophisticated story telling? Methodological problems of case studies mainly based on semi-structured interviews, Quality & Quantity, 43 (6): 875–94.

———. (2011): When does superiors' deviance threaten organisational hierarchy? Working Paper No. 27, March 2011, Faculty of Management Technology, German University in Cairo, Egypt.

Diefenbach, T. / By, R.T. (2012): Bureaucracy and hierarchy—what else!?, in: Diefenbach, T. / By, R.T. (2012): Reinventing bureaucracy and hierarchy: From the bureau to network organisations, Research in the Sociology of Organizations, Volume 35, pp. 1–27.

Diefenbach, T. / By, R.T. / Klarner, P. (2009): A multi-dimensional analysis of managers' power—functional, socio-political, interpretive-discursive, and socio-cultural approaches, Management Revue, special issue on 'Power in organizations—power of organizations', 20 (4): 413–31.

Diefenbach, T. / Sillince, J.A.A. (2011): Formal and informal hierarchy in different types of organisations, Organization Studies, 32 (11): 1515–37.

———. (2012): Crossing of boundaries—subordinates' challenges to organisational hierarchy, in: Diefenbach, T. / By, R.T. (2012): Reinventing bureaucracy and hierarchy: From the bureau to network organisations, Research in the Sociology of Organizations, Volume 35, pp. 171–201.

Dillard, J.F. / Rigsby, J.T. / Goodman, C. (2004): The making and remaking of organization context: Duality and the institutionalization process, Accounting, Auditing & Accountability Journal, 17 (4): 506–42.

DiMaggio, P. (1998): The new institutionalisms: Avenues of collaboration, Journal of Institutional and Theoretical Economics, 154 (4): 696–705.

DiMaggio, P.J. / Powell, W.W. (1983): The iron cage revisited: Institutional isomorphism and collective rationality in organization fields, American Sociological Review, 48 (2): 147–60.

Donaldson, L. (2003): Organization theory as a positive science, in: Tsoukas, H. / Knudsen, C. (eds.) (2003): The Oxford handbook of organization theory. Metatheoretical perspectives, Oxford: Oxford University Press: 39–62.

Drucker, P.F. (1954): The practice of management, New York: Harper and Row.

du Gay, P. (2005): Which is the 'self' in 'self-interest'?, The Sociological Review, 53 (3): 391–411.

Dunbar, R. / Dutton, J.M. / Torbert, W.R. (1982): Crossing mother: Ideological constraints on organizational improvements, Journal of Management Studies, 19 (1): 91–108.

Ekbia, H. / Kling, R. (2005): Network organizations: Symmetric cooperation or multivalent negotiation?, Information Society, 21 (3): 155–68.

Elias, N. (1969): The Civilizing Process, Vol. I: The History of Manners, Oxford: Blackwell.

Ellis, S. (1998): A new role for the post office: An investigation into issues behind strategic change at Royal Mail, Total Quality Management, 9 (2/3) 223–34.

Elstak, M.N. / Van Riel, C.B.M. (2005): Organizational identity change: An alliance between organizational identity and identification, Academy of Management Best Conference Paper 2005 MOC: E1-E6.

Engels, F. (1893): Letter to Franz Mehring, Retrieved 07/12/2012 from http://www.marxists.org/archive/marx/works/1893/letters/93_07_14.htm

Etzioni, A. (2000): Social norms: Internalization, persuasion, and history, Law & Society, 34 (1): 157–78.

Ezzamel, M. / Willmott, H. / Worthington, F. (2001): Power, control and resistance in "The factory that time forgot", Journal of Management Studies, 38 (8): 1053–79.

Fairtlough, G. (2005): The three ways of getting things done: Hierarchy, heterarchy and responsible autonomy in organizations, Greenways, Dorset: Triarchy.

Fayol, H. (1949): General and industrial management, London: Pitman.

Finkelstein, S. (1992): Power in top management teams: Dimensions, measurement, and validation, Academy of Management Journal, 35: 505–38.

Fitness, J. (2000): Anger in the workplace: An emotion script approach to anger episodes between workers and their superiors, co-workers and subordinates, Journal of Organizational Behavior, 21 (2): 147–62.

Fleming, P. (2012): The birth of biocracy and its discontents at work, in: Diefenbach, T. / By, R.T. (2012): Reinventing bureaucracy and hierarchy: From the bureau to network organisations, Research in the Sociology of Organizations, Volume 35, pp. 205–27.

Fleming, P. / Spicer, A. (2003): Working at a cynical distance: Implications for power, subjectivity and resistance, Organization, 10 (1): 157–79.

Floyd, S.W. / Wooldridge, B. (1992): Middle management involvement in strategy and its association with strategic type: A research note, Strategic Management Journal, 13: 153–67.

———. (1994): Dinosaurs or dynamos? Recognizing middle managements strategic role, Academy of Management Executive, 8 (4): 47–57.

Force, P. (2006): First principles in translation: The axiom of self-interest from Adam Smith to Jean-Baptiste Say, History of Political Economy, 38 (2): 319–38.

Fournier, V. (1998): Stories of development and exploitation: Militant voices in an enterprise culture, Organization, 5 (1): 55–80.

———. (2002): Utopianism and the cultivation of possibilities: grassroots movements of hope, in: Parker, M. (ed.) (2002): Utopia and organization, Oxford: Blackwell Publishing: 189–216.

Fournier, V. / Grey, C. (2000): At the critical moment: Conditions and prospects for critical management studies, Human Relations, 53 (1): 7–32.

Frank, L.R. (ed.) (2001): Random House Websters quotationary, New York: Random House Websters.

Freidson, E. (2001): Professionalism: The third logic, Cambridge: Polity Press.

Freire, P. (1996): Pedagogy of the oppressed, first published 1970, London: Penguin Books.

Friedman, A. L. (1977): Industry and labour: Class struggle at work and monopoly capitalism. London: Macmillan.

Friedman, M. (1953): The methodology of positive economics, in: Friedman, M. (1953): Essays in positive economics, Chicago: Chicago University Press.

Friedman, V.J. / Lipshitz, R. / Popper, M. (2005): The mystification of organizational learning, Journal of Management Inquiry, 14 (1): 19–30.

Froese, K. (2008): The art of becoming human: Morality in Kant and Confucius, Dao: A Journal of Comparative Philosophy, 7 (3): 257–68.

Fromm, E. (1965): The application of humanist psychoanalysis to Marx's theory, in: Fromm, E. (1965) (ed.): Socialist humanism: An international symposium, Garden City, NY: Doubleday.

Gabriel, Y. (1999): Beyond happy families: A critical revaluation of the control-resistance-identity triangle, Human Relations, 52 (2): 179–99.

Geddes, D. / Callister, R.R. (2007): Crossing the line(s): A dual threshold model of anger in organizations, Academy of Management Review, 32 (3): 721–46.

Gersick, C.J.G. (1991): Revolutionary change theories: A multilevel exploration of the punctuated equilibrium paradigm, Academy of Management Review, 16 (1): 10–36.

Giddens, A. (1976): New rules of sociological method, London: Hutchinson University Library.

———. (1984): The constitution of society. Outline of the theory of structuration, Cambridge: Polity Press.

Gill, R. (2003): Change management—or change leadership?, Journal of Change Management, 3 (4): 307–18.

Given, J.B. (1997): Inquisition and Medieval society: Power, discipline, & resistance in Languedoc, Ithaca, NY: Cornell University Press.

Gorton, W.A. (2010): The philosophy of social science, in: Internet Encyclopedia of Philosophy (IEP), retrieved 06/02/2012 from http://www.iep.utm.edu/soc-sci/.

Gould, R. V. (2002): The origins of status hierarchies: A formal theory and empirical test, American Journal of Sociology, 107 (5): 1143–78.

Gouldner, A. W. (1960): The norm of reciprocity: A preliminary statement, American Sociological Review, 25 (1): 161–78.

———. (1961): Metaphysical pathos and the theory of bureaucracy, in: Etzioni, A. (eds.) (1961): Complex organizations: A sociological reader, Glenview, IL: Scott, Foresman: 71–82.

Granovetter, M.S. (1973): The strength of weak ties, American Journal of Sociology, 78 (6): 1360–80.

Grant, A.M. / Berg, J. M. (2010): Prosocial motivation at work: How making a difference makes a difference, in: Cameron, K. / Spreitzer, G. (eds.) (2010): Handbook of positive organizational scholarship, Oxford University Press.

Grant, R.M. (1991): The resourced-based theory of competitive advantage: Implications for strategy formulation, California Management Review, 33 (3): 114–35.

Gratton, L. (2004): The democratic enterprise, Financial Times, London: Prentice-Hall.

Grey, C. (1999): 'We are all managers now'; 'We always were'; On the development and demise of management, Journal of Management Studies, 36 (5): 561–85.

Griffin, R, W. / O'Leary-Kelly, A. / Collins J. (1998): Dysfunctional work behaviors in organizations, Journal of Organizational Behavior, 5: 65–82.

Griffin, R.W. / Lopez, Y.P. (2005): "Bad behavior" in organizations: A review and typology for future research, Journal of Management, 31 (6): 988–1005.

Groves, K. / LaRocca, M. (2011): An empirical study of leader ethical values, transformational and transactional leadership, and follower attitudes toward corporate social responsibility, Journal of Business Ethics, 103 (4): 511–28.

Guimerà, R. / Danon, L. / Díaz-Guilera, A. / Giralt, F. / Arenas, A. (2006): The real communication network behind the formal chart: Community structure in organizations, Journal of Economic Behavior & Organization, 61 (4): 653–67.

Hales, C. (2002): Bureaucracy-lite and continuities in managerial work, British Journal of Management, 13 (1): 51–66.

Hambrick, D.C. (2007): Upper echelons theory: An update, Academy of Management Review, 32 (2): 334–43.

Hambrick, D.C. / Mason, P. (1984): Upper echelons: the organization as a reflection of its top managers, Academy of Management Review, 9: 193–206.

Hamilton, M. (1987): The elements of the concept of ideology, Political Studies, 35 (1): 18–38.

Harman, C. (2008): A peoples history of the world, first published by Bookmarks 1999, London: Verso.

Harris, L.C. (2002): Sabotaging market-oriented culture change: An exploration of resistance, justifications and approaches, Journal of Marketing, Summer 2002: 58–74.

Harshbarger, D. (1973): The individual and the social order: Notes on the management of heresy and deviance in complex organizations, Human Relations, 26 (2): 251–69.

Hartley, J.F. (1983): Ideology and organizational behaviour, International Studies of Management & Organization, 13 (3): 7–34.

Hayhoe, R. (2007): The use of ideal types in comparative education: A personal reflection, Comparative Education, 43 (2): 189–205.

Hellawell, D. / Hancock, N. (2001): A case study of the changing role of the academic middle manager in higher education: between hierarchical control and collegiality?, Research Papers in Education, 16 (2): 183–97.

Hempel, C.G. / Oppenheim, P. (1948): Studies in the logic of explanation, Philosophy of Science, 15: 135–75.

Hendry, J. (2005): Beyond self-interest: Agency theory and the board in a satisfying world, British Journal of Management, 16: S55-S63.

Hindess, B. (1986): Interests in political analysis, in: Law, J. (ed.) (1986): Power, action and belief. A new sociology of knowledge?, Sociological Review Monograph 32, London: Routledge & Kegan Paul: 112–31.

Hochschild, A.R. (1983): The managed heart: The commercialization of human feeling, Berkeley: University of California Press.

Hogg, M. A. / Terry, D. J. (2000): Social identity and self-categorization processes in organizational contexts, Academy of Management Review, 25 (1): 121–40.

Howard-Grenville, J.A. (2005): The persistence of flexible organizational routines: The role of agency and organizational context, Organization Science, 16 (6): 618–36.

Huddy, L. (2004): Contrasting theoretical approaches to intergroup relations, Political Psychology, 25 (6): 947–67.

Hume, D. (1985): A treatise of human nature, first published 1739, London: Penguin Classics.

Hussain, W. (2007): The ethical dimension of class society, Social Theory and Practice, 33 (2): 335–44.

Ilies, R. / Judge, T. / Wagner, D. (2006): Making sense of motivational leadership: The trail from transformational leaders to motivated followers, Journal of Leadership and Organizational Studies, 13 (1): 1–22.

Ingram, P. / Clay, K. (2000): The choice-within-constraints new institutionalism and implications for sociology, Annual Review of Sociology, 26: 525–46.

Jacques, R. (1996): Manufacturing the employee—Management knowledge from the 19th to 21st centuries, London: Sage Publications.

Jaques, E. (1990): In praise of hierarchy, Harvard Business Review, 68 (1): 127–33.

Jary, D. / Jary, J. (eds.) (2005): Collins dictionary of sociology, Glasgow: HarperCollins.

Jermier, J.M (1998): Introduction: Critical perspectives on organizational control, Administration Science Quarterly, 43 (2): 235–56.

Johanson, U. / Martensson, M. / Skoog, M. (2001): Measuring to understand intangible performance drivers, The European Accounting Review, 10 (3): 407–37.

Jones, D.C. / Svejnar, J. (eds.) (1982): Participatory and self-managed firms, Toronto: Lexington.

Jost, J.T. / Elsbach, K.D. (2001): How status and power differences erode personal and social identities at work: A system justification critique of organizational applications of social identity theory, in: Hogg, M. / Terry, D. (eds.) (2001): Social identity processes in organizational contexts, Philadelphia, PA: Psychology Press: 181–96.

Jost, J. T. / Hunyady, O. (2005): Antecedents and consequences of system-justifying ideologies, Current Directions in Psychological Science, 14 (5): 260–5.

Jost, J. T. / Nosek, B. A. / Gosling, S. D. (2008): Ideology: Its resurgence in social, personality, and political psychology, Perspectives on Psychological Science, 3 (2): 126–36.

Kant, I. (1993): Grounding for the Metaphysics of Morals, translated by James W. Ellington, 3rd edition, first edition 1785 (in German: 'Grundlegung zur Metaphysik der Sitten'), Hackett.

Kanter, R.M. (1972): Commitment and community, Cambridge, MA: Harvard University Press.

Kaplan, R.S. / Norton, D.P. (1992): The Balanced Scorecard—Measures that drive performance, Harvard Business Review, January - February 1992: 71–9.

Kark, R. / Van Dijk, D. (2007): Motivation to lead, motivation to follow: The role of the self-regulatory focus in leadership processes, Academy of Management Review, 32 (2): 500–28.

Kärreman, D. / Alvesson, M. (2004): Cages in tandem: Management control, social identity, and identification in a knowledge-intensive firm, Organization, 11 (1): 149–75.

Kärreman, D. / Sveningsson, S. / Alvesson, M. (2002): The return of the machine bureaucracy?—Management control in the work settings of professionals, International Studies of Management and Organization, 32 (2): 70–92.

Keashly, L. / Jagatic, K. (2003): By any other name: American perspectives on workplace bullying, in: Einarsen, S. et al. (eds.) (2003): Bullying and emotional abuse in the workplace: International perspectives on research and practice, London, Taylor Francis: 31–62.

Kellerman, B. (2005): Warts and all, in: Harvard Business Review on The mind of the leader, Harvard Business School Publishing Corporation: 1–13.

Kelly, J. / Kelly, C. (1991): Them and us: Social psychology and the new industrial relations, British Journal of Industrial Relations, 29 (1): 25–48.

Kemper, T.D. (1978a): A social interactional theory of emotion, New York: Wiley.

———. (1978b): Toward a sociology of emotions: Some problems and some solutions, American Sociologist, 13 (1): 30–41.

———. (1991): Predicting emotions from social relations, Social Psychology Quarterly, 54 (4): 330–42.

Kerr, S. / Jermier, J.M. (1978): Substitutes for leadership: Their meaning and measurement, Organizational Behavior and Human Performance, 22 (3): 375–403.

Kezar, A. / Eckel, P. (2002): Examining the institutional transformation process: The importance of sensemaking, interrelated strategies, and balance, Research in Higher Education, 43 (3): 295–328.

Kiblinger, W.P. (2006): Understanding the Athenian fear of Socrates: A reading of Plato's Apology of Socrates, Richmond Journal of Philosophy 12: 1–8.

Kieser, A. (1997): Rhetoric and myth in management fashion, Organization, 4 (1): 49–74.

Kim, S.H. / Smith, R.H. (1993): Revenge and conflict escalation, Negotiation Journal, 9: 37–43.

Kirkpatrick, I. / Ackroyd, S. (2003): Transforming the professional archetype? The new managerialism in social services, Public Management Review, 5 (4): 511–31.

Kirkpatrick, I. / Ackroyd, S. / Walker, R. (2005): The new managerialism and public service professions, New York: Palgrave Macmillan.

Kittrie, N.N. (1995): The war against authority, Baltimore: Johns Hopkins University Press.

Knights, D. / Willmott, H. (1985): Power and identity in theory and practice, Sociological Review, 33 (1): 22–46.

Kohlberg, L. (1973): The claim to moral adequacy of a highest stage of moral judgment, The Journal of Philosophy, 70 (18): 630–46.

Kohlberg, L. / Hersh, R.H. (1977): Moral development: A review of the theory, Theory Into Practice, XVI (2): 53–9.

Kohlberg, L. / Wasserman, E.R. (1980): The cognitive-developmental approach and the practicing counselor: An opportunity for counselors to rethink their roles, The Personnel and Guidance Journal, May: 559–67.

Kotter, J. P. (1982): The general managers, New York: The Free Press.

Kramnick, I. (ed.) (1995): The portable Enlightenment reader, New York: Penguin Books.

Lacey, R. (2007): Introduction, special volume on 'Complex organizations', International Public Management Journal, 10 (2): 131–35.

Lake, D.A. (2009): Hobbesian hierarchy: The political economy of political organization, The Annual Review of Political Science, 12: 263–83.

Lane, M. (2002): Was Socrates a democrat?, History Today 52 (1): 42–7.

Laumann, E.O. / Siegel, P.M. / Hodge, R.W. (eds.) (1971): The logic of social hierarchies, 2nd printing, Chicago: Markham Publishing Company.

Laurent, A. (1978): Managerial subordinacy: A neglected aspect of organizational hierarchies, Academy of Management Review, 3 (2): 220–30.

Lawler III, E.E. (1988): Substitutes for hierarchy, Organizational Dynamics, 17 (1): 5–15.

Lawrence, P.R. / Lorsch, J.W. (1967): Organization and environment: Managing differentiation and integration, Boston: Division of Research, Graduate School of Business Administration, Harvard University.

Lazarus, R.S. (1991): Emotion and adaptation, New York: Oxford University Press.

Leach, D.K. (2005): The iron law of what again? Conceptualizing oligarchy across organizational forms, Sociological Theory, 23 (3): 312–37.

Leal, P.A. (2007): Participation: The ascendancy of a buzzword in the neo-liberal era, Development in Practice, 17 (4–5): 539–48.

Lehman, D.W. / Ramanujam, R. (2009): Selectivity in organizational rule violations, Academy of Management Review, 34 (4): 643–57.

Levy, D.L. / Alvesson, M. / Willmott, H. (2001): Critical approaches to strategic management, paper presented at the Critical Management Studies Conference 2001, conference stream: Strategy, 2001.

Lewis, K.M. (2000): When leaders display emotion: How followers respond to negative emotional expression of male and female leaders, Journal of Organizational Behavior, 21 (2): 221–34.

Lindbekk, T. (1992): The Weberian ideal-type: Development and continuities, Acta Sociologica, 35 (4): 285–97.

Lukes, S. (1974): Power: A radical view. London: Macmillan Press.

Lundholm, S. / Rennstam, J. / Alvesson, M. (2012): Understanding hierarchy in contemporary work, in: Diefenbach, T. / By, R.T. (2012): Reinventing bureaucracy and hierarchy: From the bureau to network organisations, Research in the Sociology of Organizations, Volume 35, pp. 113–140.

Lurie, Y. (2004): Humanizing business through emotions: On the role of emotions in ethics, Journal of Business Ethics, 49 (1): 1–11.

Maccoby, M. (2005): Narcissistic leaders: The incredible pros, the inevitable cons, in: Harvard Business Review on The mind of the leader, Harvard Business School Publishing Corporation: 123–48.

Maclagan, P. (1996): The organizational context for moral development: Questions of power and access, Journal of Business Ethics, 15: 645–54.

Magee, J.C. / Galinsky, A.D. (2008): The self-reinforcing nature of social hierarchy: Origins and consequences of power and status (November 9, 2008), IACM 21st Annual Conference Paper.

March, J.M. / Simon, H. (1958): Organizations, New York: John Wiley & Sons.

Marnburg, E. (2001): The questionable use of moral development theory in studies of business ethics: Discussion and empirical findings, Journal of Business Ethics, 32: 275–83.

Mars, G. (2008): From the enclave to hierarchy—and on to tyranny: the micro-political organisation of a consultants group, Culture & Organization, 14 (4): 365–78.

Martin, R.R. et al. (2001): The self-study as a chariot for strategic change, New Directions for Teaching and Learning, 113: 95–115.

Masi, R.J. / Cooke, R.A. (2000): Effects of transformational leadership on subordinate motivation, empowering norms, and organizational productivity, International Journal of Organizational Analysis, 8 (1): 16–47.

Mast, M.S. / Hall, J.A. / Schmid, P.C. (2010): Wanting to be boss and wanting to be subordinate: Effects on performance motivation, Journal of Applied Social Psychology, 40 (2): 458–72.

Mayer, J.D. / Salovey, P. / Caruso, D.R. / Sitarenios, G. (2003): Measuring emotional intelligence with the MSCEIT V2.0, Emotion, 3: 97–105.

McAuley, J. / Duberley, J. / Cohen, L. (2000): The meaning professionals give to management . . . and strategy, Human Relations, 53 (1): 87–116.

Mcintosh, D. (1977): The objective bases of Max Weber's ideal types, History & Theory, 16 (2): 265–79.

McKinlay, A. (2012): 'Little cogs': Bureaucracy and the career in British banking, c. 1900–1950, in: Diefenbach, T. / By, R.T. (2012): Reinventing bureaucracy and hierarchy: From the bureau to network organisations, Research in the Sociology of Organizations, Volume 35, pp. 31–57.

McKinlay, A. / Wilson, R.G. (2006): 'Small acts of cunning': Bureaucracy, inspection and the career, c. 1890–1914, Critical Perspective on Accounting, 17: 657–78.

McLagan, P.A. / Nel, C. (1997): The age of participation: new governance for the workplace and the world, San Francisco: Berrett-Koehler.

Mechanic, D. (1962): Sources of power of lower participants in complex organizations, Administrative Science Quarterly, 7 (3): 349–64.

Meglino, B. M. / Korsgaard, M. A. (2004): Considering rational self-interest as a disposition: Organisational implications of other orientation, Journal of Applied Psychology, 89 (6): 946–59.

Merton, R.K. (1961): Bureaucratic structure and personality, in: Etzioni, A. (ed.) (1961): Complex organizations: A sociological reader, Glenview, IL: Scott, Foresman: 48–61.

Meyer, J.W. / Rowan, B. (1977): Institutionalized organizations: Formal structure as myth and ceremony, American Journal of Sociology, 83: 340–63.

Michels, R. (1966): Political parties: A sociological study of the oligarchical tendencies of modern democracy, first published 1915, New York: Free Press.

Mignonac, K. / Herrbach, O. (2004): Linking work events, affective states, and attitudes: An empirical study of managers' emotions, Journal of Business & Psychology, 19 (2): 221–40.

Milgram, S. (1974): Obedience to authority. New York: Harper-Row.

Miller, D.T. (1999): The norm of self-snterest, American Psychologist, 54 (2): 1053–60.

Miller, J. (2002): Democratic virtue in the trial and death of Socrates, The Review of Politics, 64 (2): 353–5.

Millett. P. (2005): The trial of Socrates revisited, European Review of History, 12 (1): 23–62.

Mills, C.W. (1956): The power elite, New York: Oxford University Press.

Mintzberg, H. (1979): The structuring of organizations: A synthesis of the research, Englewood Cliffs, NJ: Prentice-Hall.

Mintzberg, H. (1985): The organization as political arena, Journal of Management Studies, 22 (2): 133–54.

———. (1994): Rounding out the managerial job, Sloan Management Review, 36 (1): 11–26.

Mitchell, N.J. (2005): Calculating and believing: Ideological norms in the cradle of utility maximization, Social Justice Research, 18 (3): 243–56.

Moore, B. Jr. (1978): Injustice: The social bases of obedience and revolt, White Plains, NY: M.E. Sharpe.

Moore, D.A. / Loewenstein, G. (2004): Self-interest, automaticity, and the psychology of conflict of interest, Social Justice Research, 17 (2): 189–202.

Moore, W.E. (1971): But some are more equal than others, in: Laumann, E.O. / Siegel, P.M. / Hodge, R.W. (eds.) (1971): The logic of social hierarchies, Chicago: Markham Publishing Company, 143–8.

Morand, D.A. (1996): Dominance, deference, and egalitarianism in organizational interaction: A sociolinguistic analysis of power and politeness, Organization Science, 7 (5): 544–56.

Morus, T. (1987): Utopia. Von der besten Verfassung des Staates, 1st edition, German translation of the original edition of 1516, Augsburg.

Mosca, G. (1971): The ruling class, first published 1939, in: Laumann, E.O. / Siegel, P.M. / Hodge, R.W. (eds.) (1971): The logic of social hierarchies, Chicago: Markham Publishing Company, (first published 1939): 252–71.

Mousnier, R. (1973): Social hierarchies, New York: Schocken Books.

Musson, G. / Duberley, J. (2007): Change, change or be exchanged: The discourse of participation and the manufacture of identity, Journal of Management Studies, 44 (1): 143–64.

N.N. (2010a): 'Prehistory', entry in Wikipedia, retrieved 30/12/2010 from http://en.wikipedia.org/wiki/Prehistory.

———. (2010b): 'Socrates', entry in Wikipedia, retrieved 27/03/2010 from http://en.wikipedia.org/wiki/Socrates.

Nails, D. (2009): Socrates, entry in online Stanford Encyclopedia of Philosophy, retrieved 27/03/2010 from http://plato.stanford.edu/entries/socrates/.

Nelson, R.E. (2001): On the shape of verbal networks in organizations, Organization Studies, 22 (5): 797–823.

Nesbit, T. (2006): What's the matter with social class?, Adult Education Quarterly, 56 (3): 171–87.

Neumann, E. (1990): Depth psychology and a new ethic, Boston: Shambhala Publications.

Newton, J. (2003): Implementing an institution-wide learning and teaching strategy: Lessons in managing change, Studies in Higher Education, 28 (4): 427–41.

Nienhaus, V. / Brauksiepe, R. (1997): Explaining the success of community and informal economies, International Journal of Social Economics, 24 (12): 1422–38.

Nietzsche, F. (1990): Das Hauptwerk II: Morgenröte, Die fröhliche Wissenschaft, Munich: Nymphenburger.

Nisbet, R. (1971): The decline and fall of social class, first published 1959, in: Laumann, E.O. / Siegel, P.M. / Hodge, R.W. (eds.) (1971): The logic of social hierarchies, Chicago: Markham Publishing Company, (first published 1959): 570–74.

O'Brien, L.T. / Crandall, C.S. (2005): Perceiving self-interest: Power, ideology, and maintenance of the status quo, Social Justice Research, 18 (1): 1–24.

O'Fallon, M.J. / Butterfield, K.D. (2005): A review of the empirical ethical decision-making literature: 1996–2003. Journal of Business Ethics, 59 (4): 375–413.

Ober, J. (1989): Mass and elite in democratic Athens, Princeton, NJ: Princeton University Press.

———. (2003): Gadfly on trial: Socrates as citizen and social critic, series: Demos: Classical Athenian Democracy, a publication of The Stoa: a consortium for electronic publication in the humanities, downloaded 12/03/2012 from http://www.stoa.org/projects/demos/home.

———. (2006): Socrates and democratic Athens: The story of the trial in its historical and legal contexts, Version 1.0, Princeton / Stanford Working Paper in Classics: 1–30.

Oberg, A. / Walgenbach, P. (2008): Hierarchical structures of communication in a network organization, Scandinavian Journal of Management, 24 (3): 183–98.

Offerman, L.R. (2005): When followers become toxic, in: Harvard Business Review on The mind of the leader, Harvard Business School Publishing Corporation: 37–52.

Oglensky, B.D. (1995): Socio-psychoanalytic perspectives on the subordinate, Human Relations, 48 (9): 1029–54.

Ostell, A. (1996): Managing dysfunctional emotions in organizations, Journal of Management Studies, 33 (4): 525–57.

Palgi, M. (2006a): Experiences of self-management and employee participation, International Review of Sociology, 16 (1): 49–53.

———. (2006b): Pitfalls of self-management in the Kibbutz, International Review of Sociology, 16 (1): 63–77.

Palmer, I. /Benveniste, J. / Dunford, R. (2007): New organizational forms: Towards a generative dialogue, Organization Studies, 28 (12): 1829–47.

Papineau, D. (1976): Ideal types and empirical theories, The British Journal for the Philosophy of Science, 27 (2): 137–46.

Parker, M. (2002): Against management: Organisation in the age of managerialism, Cambridge, MA: Polity Press.

———. (2009): Angelic organization: Hierarchy and the tyranny of heaven, Organization Studies, 30 (11): 1281–99.

———. (2012): Super flat: Hierarchy, culture and dimensions of organizing, in: Diefenbach, T. / By, R.T. (2012): Reinventing bureaucracy and hierarchy: From the bureau to network organisations, Research in the Sociology of Organizations, Volume 35, pp. 229–47.

Passini, S. / Morselli, D. (2009): Authority relationships between obedience and disobedience, New Ideas in Psychology, 27 (1): 96–106.

———. (2010): The obedience-disobedience dynamic and the role of responsibility, Journal of Community and Applied Social Psychology, 20 (1): 1–14.

Pervin, L. (1994): A critical analysis of current trait theory, Psychological Inquiry, 5: 103–13.

Pettigrew, A.M. (1992): On studying managerial elites, Strategic Management Journal, 13, Winter Special Issue: 163–82.

———. (2002): Decision-making as a political process, first published 1973, reprint in: Salaman, G. (ed.) (2002): Decision making for business, Milton Keynes: Sage Publications, The Open University: 97–107.

Podolny, J.M. / Page, K.L. (1998): Network forms of organizations, Annual Review of Sociology, 24 (1): 57–76.

Pollitt, C. (1990): Managerialism and the public services—the Anglo-Saxon experience, Oxford: Basil Blackwell.

Poole, M. (1996); Towards a new industrial democracy, London: Routledge.

Powell, W.W. (1990): Neither market nor hierarchy: Network forms of organization, Research in Organizational Behavior, 12: 295–336.

Prahalad, C.K. / Hamel, G. (1990): The core competence of the corporation, Harvard Business Review, May-June 1990: 79–91.

Prasad, A. / Prasad (1998): Everyday struggles at the workplace: The nature and implications of routine resistance in contemporary organizations, Research in the Sociology of Organizations, 15: 225–57.

Prentice, W.C.H. (2005): Understanding leadership, first published 1961, in: Harvard Business Review on The mind of the leader, Harvard Business School Publishing Corporation: 149–67.

Protherough, R. / Pick, J. (2002): Managing Britannia—culture and management in modern Britain, Denton: Edgeways, Brynmill Press.

Rahim, M.A. / Buntzman, G.F. / White, D. (1999): An empirical study of the stages of moral development and conflict management styles, The International Journal of Conflict Management, 10 (2): 154–71.

Rank, O.N. (2008): Formal structures and informal networks: Structural analysis in organizations, Scandinavian Journal of Management, 24 (2): 145–61.

Ravlin, E.C. / Thomas, D.C. (2005): Status and stratification processes in organizational life, Journal of Management, 30 (6): 966–87.

Rayburn, J. M. / Rayburn, L.G. (1996): Relationship between Machiavellianism and type A personality and ethical-orientation, Journal of Business Ethics, 15 (11): 1209–19.

Reedy, P. (2002): Keeping the black flag flying: Anarchy, utopia and the politics of nostalgia, in: Parker, M. (ed.) (2002): Utopia and organization, Oxford: Blackwell Publishing: 169–88.

Reisel, W.D. / Probst, T.M. / Swee-Lim, C. / Maloles, C.M. / König, C.J. (2010): The effects of job insecurity on job satisfaction, organizational citizenship behavior, deviant behavior, and negative emotions of employees, International Studies of Management & Organization, 40 (1): 74–91.

Rhodes, C. / Bloom, P. (2012): The cultural fantasy of hierarchy: Sovereignty and the desire for spiritual purity, in: Diefenbach, T. / By, R.T. (2012): Reinventing bureaucracy and hierarchy: From the bureau to network organisations, Research in the Sociology of Organizations, Volume 35, pp. 141–69.

Riantoputra, C.D. (2010): Know thyself: Examining factors that influence the activation of organizational identity concepts in top managers minds, Group & Organization Management, 35 (1): 8–38.

Robertson, M. / Swan, J. (2003): Control—what control? Culture and ambiguity within a knowledge intensive firm, Journal of Management Studies, 40 (4): 831–58.

Robinson, S. L. / Bennett, R. J. (1995): A typology of deviant workplace behaviors: A multidimensional scaling study, Academy of Management Journal, 38: 555–72.

———. (1997): Workplace deviance: Its definition, its manifestations, and its causes, Research on Negotiations in Organizations, 6: 3–27.

Rosen, M. (1984): Myth and reproduction: The contextualization of management theory, method and practice, Journal of Management Studies, 21 (3): 304–22.

Rothschild, J. (2009): Workers' cooperatives and social enterprise: A forgotten route to social equity and democracy, American Behavioral Scientist, 52: 1023–41.

Rothschild, J. / Ollilainen, M. (1999): Obscuring but not reducing managerial control: Does TQM measure up to democracy standards?, Economic and Industrial Democracy, 20: 583–623.

Rothschild-Whitt, J. (1976): Conditions facilitating participatory-democratic organizations, Sociological Inquiry 46 (2): 75–86.

———. (1979): The collectivist organization: An alternative to rational-bureaucratic models. American Sociological Review, 44 (4): 509–27.

Rowlinson, M. / Toms, S. / Wilson, J. (2006): Legitimacy and the capitalist corporation: Cross-cutting perspectives on ownership and control, Critical Perspectives on Accounting, 17 (5): 681–702.

Rubin, R.S. / Munz, D.C. / Bommer, W.H. (2005): Leading from within: The effects of emotion recognition and personality on transformational leadership behaviour, Academy of Management Journal, 48 (5): 845–58.

Rueschemeyer, D. (1986): Power and the division of labour, Oxford: Polity Press.

Rutledge, R.W. / Karim, E.K. (1999): The influence of self-interest and ethical considerations on managers' evaluation judgments, Accounting, Organizations and Society, 24: 173–84.

Salovey, P. / Mayer, J.D. (1990): Emotional intelligence, Imagination, Cognition, and Personality, 9: 185–211.

Samra-Fredericks, D. (2000): Doing 'board-in-action' research—An ethnographic approach for the capture and analysis of directors' and senior managers' interactive routines, Corporate Governance—Empirical Research-Based and Theory Building Papers, 8 (3): 244–57.

Saunders, M. (2006): The madness and malady of managerialism, Quadrant, 50 (3): 9–17.

Sauser, W.I. Jr. (2009): Sustaining employee owned companies: Seven recommendations, Journal of Business Ethics, 84: 151–64.

Scheff, T.J. (2000): Shame and the social bond: A sociological theory, Sociological Theory, 18 (1): 84–99.

Schindler, D.C. (2009): Why Socrates didn't charge: Plato and the metaphysics of money, Communio 36: 394–426.

Schmid Mast, M. / Hall, J.A. / Schmid, P.C. (2010): Wanting to be boss and wanting to be subordinate: Effects on performance motivation, Journal of Applied Social Psychology, 40 (2): 458–72.

Schön, D. (1983): The reflective practitioner—How professionals think in action, New York: Basic Books.

Schwarz, G.M. (2006): Positioning hierarchy in enterprise system change, New Technology, Work and Employment, 21 (3): 252–65.

Scott, J.C. (1990): Domination and the arts of resistance: Hidden transcripts, New Haven, CT: Yale University Press.

Scott, J. (2003): Transformations in the British economic elite, in: Dogan, M. (ed.) (2003): Elite configurations at the apex of power, Leiden: Brill: 155–74.

Sehested, K. (2002): How new public management reforms challenge the roles of professionals, International Journal of Public Administration, 25 (12): 1513–37.

Selznick, P. (1961): Foundations of the theory of organization, in: Etzioni, A. (ed.) (1961): Complex organizations: A sociological reader, Glenview, IL: Scott, Foresman: 18–32.

Selznick, P. (1996): Institutionalism "old" and "new", Administrative Science Quarterly, 41 (2): 270–77.

Senge, P.M. (1990): The fifth discipline. The art & practice of the learning organization, New York: Doubleday.

Shapiro, B. / Matson, D. (2007), Strategies of resistance to internal control regulation, Accounting, Organizations and Society, 33: 199–228.

Shenhav, Y. (2003): The historical and epistemological foundations of organization theory: Fusing sociological theory with engineering discourse, in: Tsoukas,

H. / Knudsen, C. (eds.) (2003): The Oxford handbook of organization theory. Meta-theoretical perspectives, Oxford: Oxford University Press: 183–209.

Shrivastava, P. (1986): Is strategic management ideological?, Journal of Management, 12 (3): 363–77.

Sidanius, J. / Pratto, F. (1999): Social dominance: An intergroup theory of social hierarchy and oppression. Cambridge, MA: Cambridge University Press.

Sidanius, J. / Pratto, F. / van Laar, C. / Levin, S. (2004): Social dominance theory: Its agenda and method, Political Psychology, 25 (6): 845–80.

Siebens, H. (2005): Facilitating leadership, EBS Review, 20: 9–29.

Sillince, J.A.A. / Mueller, F. (2007): Switching strategic perspective: the reframing of accounts of responsibility, Organization Studies, 28 (2): 155–76.

Simon, H.A. (1979): Rational decision making in business organizations, American Economic Review, 69: 493–513.

Simpson, T.L (2006): Is Socrates the ideal democratic citizen?, Journal of Thought, 41 (4): 137–56.

Skålén, P. (2004): New public management reform and the construction of organizational identities, International Journal of Public Sector Management, 17 (3): 251–63.

Sluss, D. M. / Ashforth, B. E. (2007): Relational identity and identification: Defining ourselves through work relationships, Academy of Management Review, 32 (1): 9–32.

Spector, P. E. / Fox, S. (2010): Theorizing about the deviant citizen: An attributional explanation of the interplay of organizational citizenship and counterproductive work behaviour, Human Resource Management Review, 20 (2): 132–43.

Spicer, A. / Böhm, S. (2005): The organization of resistance, paper presented at the Collective for Alternative Organization Studies workshop at the University of Leicester in May 2004.

Spierenburg, P. (2004): Punishment, power, and history: Foucault and Elias, Social Science History, 28 (4): 607–36.

Stanford (2010): Socrates, entry in Stanford Encyclopaedia of Philosophy, retrieved 20/10/2010 at http://plato.stanford.edu/entries/socrates/

Starbuck, W.H. (2003): The origins of organization theory, in: Tsoukas, H. / Knudsen, C. (eds.) (2003): The Oxford handbook of organization theory. Meta-theoretical perspectives, Oxford: Oxford University Press: 143–82.

Staw, B. M. / Epstein, L. D. (2000): What bandwagons bring: Effects of popular management techniques on corporate performance, reputation, and CEO pay, Administrative Science Quarterly, 45 (3): 523–56.

Stets, J.E. / Asencio, E.K. (2008): Consistency and enhancement processes in understanding emotions, Social Forces, 86 (3): 1055–78.

Stoddart, M.C.J. (2007): Ideology, hegemony, discourse: A critical review of theories of knowledge and power, Social Thought and Research, 28: 191–226.

Stohl, C. / Cheney, G. (2001): Participatory processes / paradoxical practices— Communication and the dilemmas of organizational democracy, Management Communication Quarterly, 14 (3): 349–407.

Stubbart, C.I. (1989): Managerial cognition: A missing link in strategic management research, Journal of Management Studies, 26: 325–45.

Suddaby, R. / Greenwood, R. (2005): Rhetorical strategies of legitimacy, Administrative Science Quarterly, 50 (1): 35–67.

Suttle, B.B. (1987): The passion of self-interest: The development of the idea and its changing status, American Journal of Economics and Sociology, 46 (4): 459–72.

Tajfel, H. (1978a): Interindividual behaviour and intergroup behaviour, in: Tajfel, H. (ed.) (1978): Differentiation between social groups: Studies in the social psychology of intergroup relations. London: Academic Press, 27–60.

————. (1978b): Social categorization, social identity, and social comparison, in: Tajfel, H. (ed.) (1978): Differentiation between social groups: Studies in the social psychology of intergroup relations. London: Academic Press: 61–76.

Tajfel, H. / Turner, J. C. (1979): An integrative theory of intergroup conflict, in: Austin, W.G. / Worchel, S. (eds.) (1979): The social psychology of intergroup relations. Monterey, CA: Brooks-Cole: 33–47.

Tanner, J. / Cockerill, R. (1986): In search of working-class ideology: A test of two perspectives, The Sociological Quarterly, 27(3): 389–402.

Taylor, F.W. (1967): The principles of scientific management, first published 1911, New York: Norton&Comp.

Taylor, Q.P. (2000): The last day of Socrates: An invitation to philosophy, The Midwest Quarterly, 42 (1): 20–32.

Therborn, G. (1980): The ideology of power and the power of ideology, London:Versons Edidtion and NLB.

Thomas, P. (1998): Ideology and the discourse of strategic management: A critical research framework, Electronic Journal of Radical Organization Theory, 4 (1).

Thompson, V.A. (1961): Hierarchy, specialization, and organizational conflict, Administrative Science Quarterly, 5 (4): 485–521.

Tittle, C. / Welch, M. / Grasmick, H. (2008): Self-control, political ideology, and misbehavior: Unpacking the effects of conservative identity, Sociological Spectrum, 28 (1): 4–35.

Townley, B. (1993): Performance appraisal and the emergence of management, Journal of Management Studies, 30 (2): 221–38.

Useem, M. (1984): The inner circle: Large corporations and the rise of business political activity in the U.S. and U.K., New York: Oxford University Press.

Van Vugt, M. (2006): Evolutionary origins of leadership and followership, Personality and Social Psychology Review, 10 (4): 354–71.

Vandekerckhove, W. / Commers, R.M.S. (2003): Downward workplace mobbing: A sign of the times?, Journal of Business Ethics, 45: 41–50.

Vardi, Y. / Weitz, E. (2004): Misbehavior in organizations, Theory, Research, and Management, London: Lawrence Erlbaum Associates Publishers.

Varman, R. / Chakrabarti, M. (2004): Contradictions of democracy in a workers cooperative, Organization Studies, 25 (2): 183–208.

Vickers, M.H. / Kouzmin, A. (2001): Resilience in organizational actors and rearticulating voice, Public Management Review, 3 (1): 95–119.

Vredenburgh, D. / Brender, Y. (1998): The hierarchical abuse of power in work organizations, Journal of Business Ethics, 17: 1337–47.

Wagner, K.-R. (2002) (eds.): Mitarbeiterbeteiligung. Visionen für eine Gesellschaft von Teilhabern, Gabler Verlag, Wiesbaden 2002.

Wahrman, R. (2010): Status, deviance, and sanctions: A critical review, first published 1972, Small Group Research, 41 (1): 91–105.

Wall, J.A. / Callister, R.R. (1995): Conflict and its management, Journal of Management, 21 (3): 515–58.

Walsh, J.P. / Weber, K. (2002): The prospects for critical management studies in the American Academy of Management, Organization, 9 (3): 402–10.

Waterfield, R. (2009a): Why Socrates died. Dispelling the myth, London: Faber and Faber.

————. (2009b): The historical Socrates, History Today 59 (1): 24–9.

Watson, T. (2006): Organising and managing work, 2nd edition, Pearson Education Limited, Harlow 2006.

Weber, M. (1980): Wirtschaft und Gesellschaft. 5., revised edition, first published 1921, Tübingen: J.C.B. Mohr (Paul Siebeck).

————. (1949): The methodology of the social sciences, New York: Free Press.

Wernerfelt, B. (1984): A resource-based view of the firm, Strategic Management Journal, 5 (1): 171–180.

Westphal, J.D. / Khanna, P. (2003): Keeping directors in line: Social distancing as a control mechanism in the corporate elite, Administrative Science Quarterly, 48 (3): 361–98.

White, S.C. (1996): Depoliticising development: the uses and abuses of participation', Development in Practice, 6 (1): 6–15.

Whitley, R. (1989): On the nature of managerial tasks: their distinguishing characteristics and organisation, Journal of Management Studies, 26 (3): 209–24.

Whittington, R. (1992): Putting Giddens into action: Social systems and managerial agency, Journal of Management Studies, 29 (6): 693–712.

Williams, J. / Swartz, M. (1998): Treatment boundaries in the case management relationship: A clinical case and discussion, Community Mental Health Journal, 34 (3): 299–311.

Willmott, H.C. (1984): Images and ideals of managerial work: A critical examination of conceptual and empirical accounts, Journal of Management Studies, 21 (3): 349–68.

———. (1987): Studying managerial work: A critique and a proposal, Journal of Management Studies, 24 (3): 249–70.

———. (1996): A metatheory of management: omniscience or obfuscation?, British Journal of Management, 7 (4): 323–28.

———. (1997): Rethinking management and managerial work: Capitalism, control and subjectivity, Human Relations, 50 (11): 1329–59.

Wilson, E. O. (1975): Sociobiology: The new synthesis. Harvard, MA: Harvard University Press.

Wilson, F.M. (1999): Alternative organizational ownership forms: Their effect on organizational behaviour, Organizational Behaviour, 171–81.

Wrong, D.H. (1971): The functional theory of stratification: Some neglected considerations, in: Laumann, E.O. / Siegel, P.M. / Hodge, R.W. (eds.) (1971): The logic of social hierarchies, Markham Publishing Company, Chicago: 132–42.

Wunderer, R. (Hrsg.) (1999): Mitarbeiter als Mitunternehmer, Luchterhand, Neuwied 1999.

Yücesan-Özdemir, G. (2003): Hidden forms of resistance among Turkish workers: Hegemonic incorporation or building blocks for working class struggle?, Capital & Class, 81: 31–59.

Zaleznik, A. (1989): The managerial mystique—Restoring leadership in business, New York: Harper & Row.

Zammuto, R.F. / Gifford, B. / Goodman, E.A. (2000): Managerial ideologies, organization culture, and the outcomes of innovation, in: Ashkanasy, N.M. / Wilderom, C.P.M. / Peterson, M.F. (2000): Handbook of organizational culture & climate, Thousand Oaks, CA: Sage Publications: 261–78.

Zapf, D. / Gross, C. (2001): Conflict escalation and coping with workplace bullying: A replication and extension, European Journal of Work and Organizational Psychology, 10 (4): 497–522.

Zeitlin, M. (1974): Corporate ownership and control: The large corporation and the capitalist class, American Journal of Sociology, 79 (5): 1073–119.

Zenger, T.R. / Lazzarini, S.G. / Poppo, L. (2001): Informal and formal organization in new institutional economics, unpublished manuscript.

Zucker, L.G. (1977): The role of institutionalization in cultural persistence, American Sociological Review, 42 (5): 726–743.

Index

Note: page numbers in italic type refer to Figures; those in bold refer to Tables. Page numbers followed by 'n' and another number refer to the Notes.